Global Business

This book is designed to help students understand the key issues of global business by connecting reality with theory. Divided into three parts, it covers critical issues of international business, introducing readers to topics they will connect with before discussing core concepts.

With a user-friendly pedagogy and a host of helpful visuals, the authors offer a practitioner's perspective on global business knowledge, examining familiar theory on trade, direct investment, and political environment alongside fresh topics, like geopolitical conflicts, emerging markets, and sustainability. Over 60 case studies are included to illustrate the magnitude and complexity of global business involving different stakeholders.

Undergraduate students looking for an introduction to international business and graduate students looking to apply their knowledge will find *Global Business* stimulating, since it demonstrates how theories and concepts work in real-world business settings.

Yongsun Paik is Director of the Center for Asian Business and a Professor of International Business and Management at Loyola Marymount University, CA, U.S. He is the co-author, with Charles M. Vance, of *Managing a Global Workforce, third edition*, published by Routledge in 2014.

Jong-Wook Kwon is Professor and Director of the Cross-Cultural Management Research Center at Kangwon National University, South Korea.

Dong Chen is an Associate Professor of International Business and Strategy at Loyola Marymount University, U.S., and Guest Researcher at the Institute for Global Industry of Tsinghua University, China.

"Paik, Kwon, and Chen provide an impressive exploration of the main drivers of global business and their implications for international business practice. This book offers practical, actionable and relevant discussions of the most important aspects of international business, presented in an easy-to-use and understandable fashion."

Jonathan Doh, Villanova University, USA, and co-author, *International Management: Culture, Strategy and Behavior*

"Through the use of case studies, Paik, Kwon, and Chen's book provides an important bridge between theory and practice, thus making it a useful resource to students and practitioners who are interested in understanding and managing in a global context. The book covers a comprehensive range of topics, including the institutional environment of international business as well as the management of different aspects of the value chain."

Rosalie L. Tung, *Simon Fraser University, Canada*

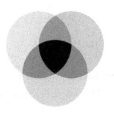

Global Business

Connecting Theory to Reality

YONGSUN PAIK, JONG-WOOK KWON, AND DONG CHEN

Routledge
Taylor & Francis Group

NEW YORK AND LONDON

First published 2017
by Routledge
711 Third Avenue, New York, NY 10017

and by Routledge
2 Park Square, Milton Park, Abingdon, Oxon OX14 4RN

Routledge is an imprint of the Taylor & Francis Group, an informa business

Library of Congress Cataloging-in-Publication Data
Names: Paik, Yongsun, 1956- author. | Chen, Dong, 1974- author. | Kwon, Jong-Wook, author.
Title: Global business : connecting theory to reality / Yongsun Paik, Dong Chen, & Jong-Wook Kwon.
Description: New York, NY : Routledge, 2016.
Identifiers: LCCN 2016028581 | ISBN 9781138222564 (hbk) | ISBN 9781138223639 (pbk) | ISBN 9781315404349 (ebk) | ISBN 9781315404318 (mobi/kindle)
Subjects: LCSH: International trade. | International business enterprises. | International economic relations. | International finance.
Classification: LCC HF1379 .P345 2016 | DDC 338.8/83—dc23
LC record available at https://lccn.loc.gov/2016028581

ISBN: 978-1-138-22256-4 (hbk)
ISBN: 978-1-138-22363-9 (pbk)
ISBN: 978-1-3154-0434-9 (ebk)

Typeset in Minion
by RefineCatch Limited, Bungay, Suffolk

www.routledge.com/cw/paik

For Angie, Michelle, Brian, Hanna Paik, and Joshua Song, my family
—Yongsun Paik

For Eunyoung Park, Jaemin, and Haemin Kwon, my family
—Jong-Wook Kwon

For Rong, Erin, and Adeline, my family
—Dong Chen

Contents

Foreword

The complexity of the global business environment has steadily increased in recent years. More companies than ever are operating at an international level, more countries are participating in the global marketplace, and more people are living and working outside of their country of birth. This has brought about substantive growth in wealth and opportunities but also ever-changing tensions in the economic, social, and political realm. How can a newcomer to the subject navigate the complexity in the global business environment? This book is an insightful guide to understanding the intricacies of the reality we live in today.

Over 13 chapters, the authors survey a myriad of global business topics, ranging from taking stock of the current status to reviewing key economic, social, and political facets to discussing business sustainability and ethics. Three important aspects set this book apart from the larger number of international business textbooks that exist today. First, it complements each chapter with a selection of mini case studies to delve deeper into important topics. These cases often present interesting and unique angles, such as the question of whether U.S. Olympic uniforms should be manufactured in China or a discussion of the recent trend of reshoring manufacturing jobs to North America. Second, the authors match the historical and theoretical foundations of the field with recent developments that impact the global business environment today, including the effects of the financial crisis of 2007–2008 and the pendulum swing towards protectionism in some countries. Third, the book offers a well-grounded point of view by basing arguments on best practices as well as decades of academic literature, recent newspaper articles, and data available. It is this aspect which offers most value to the readers, since it helps parse out the more important from the less important.

The authors are not only highly knowledgeable about the field of global business but also masters in the art of introducing order to a complex subject. Their book offers distinct benefits: a straightforward way of teaching, an easier comprehension of intricate relationships in the realm of global business, and a more in-depth understanding of key issues, which fosters critical thinking. The book will thus be invaluable to readers seeking a deeper understanding of the current global business environment.

Professor Paul W. Beamish
Canada Research Chair in International Business
Ivey Business School
July 2016

Preface

As this book is being published, the global economy is moving toward uncharted territory in which the seemingly endless march of globalization has been halted. The global economy, once driven by expanded trade and foreign direct investment, has not fully recovered from the aftermath of the 2008 global credit crisis. While the U.S. economy has steadily shown signs of improvement, the rest of the world is still struggling to survive the sluggish economy. The EU economy, severely affected by the euro debt crisis, has yet to fully recover from its economic doldrums. China, the world's second largest economy, has substantially slowed down as exports decline and household and corporate debt rise. Similarly, the economic growth of Japan, the world's third largest economy, is expected to decelerate further in 2017 as Abenomics runs out of steam. It is noteworthy that at the time this book went into production, G7 leaders met in Japan and agreed to beef up policies to stimulate their sluggish economies.

Many people predict that emerging economies—rather than developed economies—are going to lead the global economy in the coming decades. However, the short-term prospect of emerging economies like Brazil and Russia does not appear to be a major contributor to the global economy. As globalization has stalled, the prospect of regionalization, which has been regarded as a stepping stone to globalization, is equally uncertain and fragile. On one hand, the conclusion of the Trans-Pacific Partnership may be considered as compelling evidence to support such optimistic views about regionalization as it expands trade and investment opportunities across the Pacific Ocean by integrating the markets of 12 countries representing two-fifths of the global economy: from Canada, the U.S., and Chile to Japan, Vietnam, and Australia. On the other hand, the current debate on the potential impact of Brexit on the EU membership raises concerns about the feasibility of the world's oldest and most comprehensive regional economic integration, making us skeptical about the continued evolution of regionalization as a means to advance globalization.

In this time of growing uncertainty, it has become increasingly critical for companies as well as individuals to keep abreast of these new developments in the global market. We are confident that this book will help readers better understand not only the overall trends of the global economy but also key opportunities and challenges facing companies in conducting business across borders. At the same time, we are well aware that one of the main challenges authors face when writing an international business textbook is how to keep the content fresh and relevant. The very moment this book is published, time-sensitive information will have immediately become outdated. To overcome such pitfalls, this book focuses on discussing fundamental global business issues that are still pertinent and influential regardless of the time frame.

As the title of this book indicates, our extensive teaching experiences have convinced us that readers should first be alerted to interesting real-world topics before discussing theories and concepts. Though there are numerous international business textbooks available on the market, readers will find this book not only readable but also stimulating as it demonstrates how real-world practices reflect textbook knowledge through a wealth of case materials. Divided into three main parts and 13 chapters, this book features more than 60 case studies that cover critical issues in international business such as international trade, foreign direct investment, foreign market choice, political environment, sociocultural environment, internationalization, global marketing, and international human resource management. Readers will learn about the theories and concepts of international business through the eyes of practitioners. Each case is carefully prepared to illustrate a specific theory or concept introduced later in the chapter. Thus, readers will gain invaluable insights and apply their learning to real issues and practices of international business. The cases not only feature developed economies but also emerging markets such as China and India, as well as newly industrialized countries like South Korea and Singapore. These countries play an increasingly significant role in the world economy as multinational corporations (MNCs) such as Samsung, Hyundai, and Haier have emerged as global market leaders. Because the cases in this book feature exciting stories and best practices of multinational corporations from all over the world, we believe this book has international appeal. This book also covers several important topics that are either marginally covered or not covered at all in most international business textbooks, including service trade, exit strategy, sustainable development and corporate sustainability, MNCs from emerging markets, finance, accounting, and tax issues involving overseas operations.

We'd like to thank the many people who have contributed to the development of this book. First, we are grateful to our Routledge editor Sharon Golan and her editorial assistant Erin Arata who provided us with useful guidance and encouragement until we successfully completed the full manuscript. Second, we express gratitude to Professor Paul Beamish of the Ivey Business School at Western University who has endorsed our work by writing a foreword for this book. The publication of this book would have been impossible without the support and dedication of our student research assistants, Peter Jean-François, Christine Gonzalez, Jordan Justus, Lawrence Lim, Zhao Hongyan, and Chui Long. They helped us find and develop interesting cases and draft tables and figures. We also would like to thank our talented colleagues, Kathe Segall and Natalie Drdek, who helped us with proofreading of the first draft. Finally, we thank our families for their understanding and support while we worked on this book.

Yongsun Paik,
Jong-Wook Kwon
and Dong Chen

The Content of Global Business

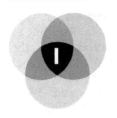

Globalization
Current Status and Future Prospects

Learning Objectives

1. Understand the key dimensions of globalization.
2. Identify the future trends of globalization.
3. Recognize the key drivers behind globalization.
4. Explain the benefits and costs of globalization.
5. Understand the business opportunities and challenges that globalization presents for companies.

Cases

Case 1.1 Uniqlo: Uniquely Positioned in the Global Apparel Industry
Case 1.2 Mexico Emerges as a New Attraction of Outsourcing

Case 1.1 Uniqlo: Uniquely Positioned in the Global Apparel Industry

Uniqlo, a successful Japanese apparel retailer often compared to the American brand Gap, has transformed itself into an extremely profitable enterprise. After dominating the Japanese market, it is now turning its attention to the global market. Fast Retailing, Uniqlo's parent company, is Japan's biggest clothing company. Fast Retailing operates more than 1,400 Uniqlo stores worldwide, including more than 850 in Japan and over 300 in China. The name Uniqlo, is an abbreviation of "unique clothing," as the Japanese often do when they transform English words for their own convenience. The company has opened a vast number of flagship stores in Paris, New York, Los Angeles, Moscow, and Shanghai, which have been met with crowds of customers. The company projects $50 billion USD in sales and $10 billion USD in profit by 2020.

As CEO of Fast Retailing, Tadashi Yanai is the wealthiest man in Japan. Uniqlo, unlike other apparel companies that are trying to find and follow the latest fashion trends, thrives on technology and invests in the company's long-term vision. Zara and H&M bring consumers the latest fashions quickly, ordering new lines multiple times a year. Conversely, Uniqlo sells approximately 1,000 items, far fewer than its competitors, and allow these items to have a longer shelf life. Mr. Yanai said, "In general, the apparel industry isn't about continual process improvement or making the perfect piece of denim, it's about chasing trends." However, "We don't want to chase after 'fast-fashion' trends," explains Mr. Yanai.[a] This approach allows Fast Retailing to secure lower-priced, higher-volume deals with suppliers and makes the inventory management process simpler and less expensive. While Mr. Yanai believes in the power of being innovative or cutting edge, he places more emphasis on longevity, stating, "At Uniqlo we're thinking ahead. We're thinking about how to create new, innovative products . . . and sell them to everyone."

Uniqlo offers basic items such as fleece, slim-down jackets, synthetic thermal underwear, and denim. The company is convinced that their customers are more concerned with quality and value than quick responsiveness to changes in fashion styles. Rather than rushing to market, Uniqlo uses long development cycles, which require testing new materials and designs. Furthermore, instead of jumping from one vendor to another, Uniqlo develops long-lasting partnerships with material manufacturers. The firm believes these basic practices confer a greater benefit to the company. Uniqlo has been able to appeal to a much broader audience and demographic, unlike Gap, Zara, and H&M who are mainly targeting specific groups of consumers, such as the preppy Americana or faddish fashionista.

In a sense, Uniqlo's strategy seems to be comparable to that of automakers. The product development cycle for car manufacturers lasts months or years. The product development process is time consuming as it attempts to create cars that will appeal to a wide range of consumers. Although some manufacturers produce cars according to certain trends, ultimately, in the long term, quality surpasses trendiness. The fashion industry may well be following a similar path as the auto industry. Between 1896 and 1930, more than 1,800 auto manufacturers existed in America because automakers wanted to develop customized cars that suited individual preference and taste. By the early 1940s, a large percentage of these companies had gone out of business and today we have a few major players in the U.S. automaker industry. Mr. Yanai operates Uniqlo comparably to a twenty-first-century automaker. He identifies long-term styles within product categories, differentiates these styles, and then establishes a supply chain to deliver these styles to the end consumer. Uniqlo has also applied a strategy used within the technology industry, known as "planned obsolescence." The company drives consumers to update their wardrobes based on technological changes—changes that Uniqlo discovered and implemented—instead of updating their wardrobes in response to ever-shifting style preferences.

While Uniqlo is performing well at home in Japan; thriving in China, South Korea, and Taiwan; and developing in Europe; the U.S. is a different story. Uniqlo has been in the U.S. for ten years. But its presence with about 50 stores is not only smaller than that of its main global rivals, Zara and H&M, but also smaller than local casual-clothing chains, Gap and Forever 21, and even "off-price" sellers of designer labels, Ross and T.J. Maxx. Success in the U.S. is crucial for Fast Retailing if it wants to attain Mr. Yanai's goal of overtaking Zara, H&M, and Gap Inc. to become the world's number one clothing retailer by 2020. Unfortunately, the company has already scaled back on its American ambitions. Masafumi Shoda at one of the largest Japanese investment banks, states Uniqlo's weakest branches are in suburban American shopping centers.[b]

Uniqlo, Asia's biggest clothing retailer, is struggling to offer a better fit for U.S. consumers. Yet, this presents Uniqlo with a unique opportunity that would allow the company to expand its customer base, in the world's biggest market, and add more stores in its suburban areas. Mr. Yoshihiro Kunii, Group Executive Vice President, who oversees production at Fast Retailing, told Reuters in an interview:

> This is going to be our next challenge in the United States: how to adjust our clothes for a more '3-D' fit, particularly for women. There are many different ethnic groups in the United States, and this makes it tough to come up with the optimal range to match the fit.

Uniqlo has long marketed the "Made for All" concept, offering a universal standardized product rather than differentiated or customized products for individual markets. Uniqlo aims to sell high-quality clothes at medium prices, which is not an easy task. One consumer comments:

> Uniqlo needs a more accurately targeted customer segment. If you compare it with Zara and H&M, there is no design and thus it is too boring. If you consider it to be one of the cozy, casual, athletic styles like Gap or Columbia, it should lower price more.

However, according to Kunii, in the future, Fast Retailing will develop and design roughly 10 percent of Uniqlo's products with local needs in mind. It will adopt and implement a localized strategy focusing on market need with the possibility of selling those products to other markets if demand arises.[c]

Takahiro Kazahaya, an analyst at Deutsche Bank, argues that Uniqlo should remain in the U.S. because brand recognition and winning consumer loyalty is a long and tough process. According to him, since the company is very profitable in Asia, it can afford to bear losses in America for a while.[d] Additionally, if Uniqlo aspires to rise to the world's top fashion brand, it cannot abandon the world's largest clothing market. On the other hand, Toby Williams of Macquarie, another bank, believes that contrary to Mr. Yanai's rhetoric, he may ultimately be satisfied with establishing a stable foothold in America rather than attempting to control the market at all costs. By positioning the company brand in American cities most visited by Asian shoppers, Uniqlo will improve its image as a global fashion success among this consumer base. Mr. Williams states that the overall outcome would be worth bearing modest losses associated with maintaining a few showcase stores in America. These stores will entice Asian consumers, creating major growth opportunities for the company.[e]

Notes

a.   *Economist*. (2010, June 24). Uniqlo: Uniquely positioned. Retrieved from www.economist.com/node/16436304

b.   *Economist.* (2015, November 28). Chicago hope: Uniqlo is struggling in the world's biggest clothing market. Retrieved from www.economist.com/news/business/21679223-uniqlo-struggling-worlds-biggest-clothing-market-chicago-hope
c.   Ibid.
d.   Ibid.
e.   *Economist.* (2010, June 24). Uniqlo: Uniquely positioned. Retrieved from www.economist.com/node/16436304

Sources

1.   Petro, G. (2015, July 17). The future of fashion retailing, revisited: Part 1—Uniqlo. *Forbes.* Retrieved from www.forbes.com/sites/gregpetro/2015/07/17/the-future-of-fashion-retailing-revisited-part-1-uniqlo/#76025bc564ec
2.   *Economist.* (2010, June 24). Uniqlo: Uniquely positioned. Retrieved from www.economist.com/node/16436304
3.   Kim, C. and Shimiz, R. (2014, February 25). Uniqlo tweaks "Made for All" to give U.S. shoppers a "3-D" fit. *Reuters.* Retrieved from www.reuters.com/article/us-fastretailing-strategy-idUSBREA1O0CZ20140225
4.   *Economist.* (2015, November 28). Chicago hope: Uniqlo is struggling in the world's biggest clothing market. Retrieved from www.economist.com/news/business/21679223-uniqlo-struggling-worlds-biggest-clothing-market-chicago-hope

Questions for Case Discussion

1.   How is Uniqlo's strategy different from that of its main competitors such as Zara and H&M in the global apparel industry?
2.   How does Uniqlo develop and sustain its competitive advantage?
3.   Why is Uniqlo struggling in expanding its business in the U.S. market? Do you have any suggestions to improve its performance?

Case 1.2 Mexico Emerges as a New Attraction of Outsourcing

American companies have become hesitant about engaging in business with traditional hubs like India and China, especially in relation to Information Technology (IT). These companies are primarily concerned with the consequences or effects of outsourcing jobs and the risks inherent in sub-par quality. "When working with companies overseas, responsiveness and availability are crucial for creating an efficient work method," said Michael Queralt, president of Queralt, Inc. "If you need something done in a timely fashion and are working on projects that require a lot of communication, your team, if they were in Mexico, is only a couple of hours behind you, rather than days. That's one of the challenges when outsourcing processes to India, you don't always have fast access to the people running your business processes there." As a result, many companies have begun to leverage foreign supplier relationships, specifically in Latin America, for business support and to build new markets.

Latin America is changing the traditional mindset around outsourcing as it plans to return partnerships and superior quality back to U.S. soil. The continent possesses thriving IT industries in Chile, Mexico, and Brazil and is climbing the ranks as a major global player. American firms are also interested in establishing partnerships with Latin American countries due to cultural similarities, time-zone compatibility, and a tech-savvy demographic. Latin America's emergence as a global player in IT and business has redefined how we view outsourcing. It's no longer about having cost-efficient suppliers abroad support a certain IT function or service but it's about the globalization of resources. Companies who figure out how to take advantage of this new trend, i.e. the integration of national economies into international economies, will reap unprecedented benefits. The idiom, "two heads are better than one" will hold true as countries realize the limitless possibilities of a fully integrated global marketplace.

The IT industry in Chile is making a concerted effort not to take jobs away, but instead bring its resources to the U.S. and allow trade among technology companies and businesses, building long-lasting, strategic partnerships. Technology companies in the U.S. and Chile must provide value to one another and goals must align so that a strategic partnership is solidified. The government has invested heavily in building its IT workforce and helping its more than 500 IT companies find opportunities to serve and find partnerships in America through initiatives like Chile-IT and StartUp Chile.

> Outsourcing is about more than just sending certain work processes overseas to get the job done for cheap. For Telsource, it's about forming a long-lasting partnership, one that involves trust and communication for our company. We have had a great experience thus far working with Chile. Rather than feeling a disconnect from not being in the same office or city, they have really embraced themselves with the Telsource business and have become a strategic partner for us.

said Jennifer Whelan, VP Marketing, Telsource.

Mexico is also quickly becoming a major player in the 'nearshoring' sector for tech and business process exporting. The country is emerging as the capital of Latin America's growing IT outsourcing industry. More than 600,000 people already work in IT, with another 65,000 new professionals graduating each year from the dozens of technical and engineering schools clustered throughout Mexico. The industry includes more than 2,000 IT companies, ranging in size from start-ups to veterans like Hildebrando, Softtek, HP, IBM, and Intel. Guadalajara is the capital of the state of Jalisco, located six hours north of Mexico City.[a]

While IBM and HP, global MNCs that reported $104.5 billion and $120.4 billion USD in revenues, respectively, in 2012, have a presence in Mexico, there is also a growing space for smaller companies.

Tech entrepreneurs from across Mexico come to Guadalajara's Centro del Software project, an incubator for small-scale tech start-ups. Established in 2006, there are now 34 companies and 700 people working in the Centro del Software. The government subsidizes rent for the tech companies as well as provides technical and business advisory services. Each company works with the *Instituto Jalisciense de Tecnologías de la Información* (IJALTI), whose mission is to promote the city's expanding IT and business process exporting (BPO) sectors. The start-ups also pool resources and collaborate to handle projects for large, global clients. Jesus Michel, an executive at IBM de Mexico, stated, "Due to a triple play of collaboration between the government, private businesses and universities, Guadalajara is becoming the Silicon Valley of Mexico."[b]

For instance, Infolink, a company which handles customer service and product support for U.S. software companies tripled its work force between 2011 and 2012. The company now employs more than 100 English-speaking engineers and customer support specialists in its Juarez office. "Affiliated Computer Services Inc. (ACS), a business process outsourcing company, now employs 3,000 people in Juarez." ACS senior executive Miguel Hidalgo explained that the company processes and transports 16,000 pounds of documents back and forth across the U.S. border in vans every day, helping to contribute to the $22.4 billion USD in revenues that Xerox earned in 2012. In addition to established IT and BPO hubs such as Guadalajara, Monterrey, and Juarez, Mexico has a number of other cities that are pushing into the sector. "While lesser known for outsourcing than cities such as Guadalajara, Monterrey, and Mexico City, Puebla has a strong industrial base that a number of entrepreneurs are using as a launching pad for business process exporting companies."

Edgar Moreno, a public policy analyst and Latin America-focused political risk specialist, said:

> The state has huge strengths in high skilled workers. Five of the top hundred universities in Latin America are based in Puebla, and all of them offer several options to pursue careers in engineering, communications, and technology. Plus, the incumbent governor is promoting pro-business regulations and working to attract more long-term, capital-intensive, and high-tech investment projects to Puebla.

Puebla's capital city, with 1.5 million residents, is the fourth largest metropolis in Mexico. Situated on the trade route between Mexico City and the port of Veracruz, Puebla was designed and built up by the Spanish during the colonial era. Many of the city's historic buildings still stand, but today trucks carry automobiles and auto parts along the trade route between the coast and Mexico City. Overall, the industry serves as the major engine of Puebla's economy, the sector accounts for about 80 percent of the state's total economic output.

Ulises Mejia, the CEO of Evolucione, a human resource and payroll outsourcing company that directly employs 100 people and pays 2,000 contract workers in Puebla, claimed the automotive sector can provide opportunities for IT and BPO support services. "We have Volkswagen and Audi here," he said.

According to Fernando Macias, CEO of Validata, "As a location for BPO businesses, Puebla stacks up well." His company, with a sales office in Austin, Texas, runs an operation in Puebla and in Mexico City, providing document processing services to U.S. financial sector clients. In Puebla's nearshoring sector, "what we see is consulting more than business process outsourcing." Perhaps what Puebla needs is an incubator to help small start-ups grow.

Notes

a. *Americas Quarterly.* (2012, March 7). Mexico's Silicon Valley. Retrieved from www.americasquarterly.org/mexicos-silicon-valley
b. Ibid.

Sources

1. Tanaka, W. (2011, January 7). Outsourcing redefined. *Forbes.* Retrieved from www.forbes.com/sites/ciocentral/2011/01/07/outsourcing-redefined/#20534f3e307c
2. Flannery, N. P. (2013, October 28). Investor insight: Mexico takes on new roles in outsourcing. *Forbes.* Retrieved from www.forbes.com/sites/nathanielparish flannery/2013/10/28/investor-insight-mexico-takes-on-new-roles-in-outsourcing/#20532f975aa7
3. Cohen, R. (2013, March 20). Outsourcing the outsourced: New Ziptask platform looks to disrupt outsourcing industry. *Forbes.* Retrieved from www.forbes.com/sites/reuvencohen/2013/03/20/outsourcing-the-outsourced-new-ziptask-platform-looks-to-disrupt-outsourcing-industry/#16f048b975f5

Questions for Case Discussion

1. Why are American companies moving offshore outsourcing destinations from Asia such as China and India to Latin America such as Mexico and Chile?
2. How have MNCs' views about offshore outsourcing changed?
3. What roles do Mexican and Chilean governments play in encouraging MNCs to bring businesses to their countries? How do they help develop location advantages?

Globalization

Current Status and Future Prospects

I. What is Globalization?

This introductory chapter provides a brief overview of globalization, its key dimensions, drivers and the effects of globalization, and future trends. Globalization is a buzzword that everyone is talking about and firms are now increasingly conducting business across borders. What do you mean by *globalization*? It means that the world is increasingly becoming a single unified village or community where we see the expansion and intensification of social relations and consciousness across time and space. Globalization has influenced the world in terms of economic, political, and sociocultural dimensions. Yet, the impact of globalization is probably most profound in the economic and business activities that connect consumers as well as producers across the globe. The global market has become the target not only for large multinational corporations (MNCs) but also for small and medium-sized enterprises (SMEs). What makes it possible for these firms to market and sell their products and services all over the world whether on-line or off-line?

First, from a demand perspective, markets across countries have become increasingly integrated and interdependent. For example, fast food chains such as McDonald's and Burger King can be easily found in almost any country where we are traveling. Young people around the world are wearing Zara, H&M, and Uniqlo shirts and jeans, drinking Coca-Cola or Pepsi, and using Apple iPhones or Samsung Galaxy smart phones. Consumers are driving more or less the same types of automobiles, whether they are Toyota Camrys or Honda Accords or Volkswagen Passats. Even the banking and financial service industries are taking advantage of integrated markets by providing rather standardized services for individuals as well as businesses. These phenomena are occurring because consumers' tastes and preferences are converging across countries.

Second, from a supply perspective, companies are producing different parts and components in various countries where they can exploit a favorable mix of cost reduction and differentiation, while performing diverse services in different countries based on the theory of comparative advantage. As a result, the so-called global supply chain has become not only deeper but also wider as an increasing number of companies are sourcing from different suppliers around the world who are most capable of producing high-quality parts and components most efficiently. The benefits of offshore outsourcing include lower labor costs, additional management time—companies can focus on core competencies, and increased speed and delivery of outsourced activities. Companies with labor-intensive operations have enjoyed cost savings while setting up factories in developing countries. However, a new trend has recently emerged among innovative companies to keep production, design, and management at home as a long global supply chain is a disadvantage to offshoring for many companies. Zara, a Spanish retailer in the clothing industry, is a prime example. Unlike their competitors such as Gap and Forever 21, Zara vertically integrates its value creation process. The company uses a very tight supply chain, from initial design to final production, to extract two major benefits, i.e., agility and flexibility. Zara not only keeps lead times shorter but also manufactures items during the season eliminating the need to stock in advance of each season and, actually, is still manufacturing during the season.[1] Figure 1.1 shows the world's top 20 offshore destination countries.

In fact, a growing number of companies are realizing strategic problems that arise from offshore outsourcing. "While the short-term advantage of outsourcing manufacturing processes may allow for a satisfactory quarterly financial performance, this strategy lacks long-term vision and can be an inefficient means of overseas operation."[2] This is why many American companies are moving their offshore outsourcing from China and India in Asia to Mexico and Chile in Latin America as Case 1.2 illustrates. Dispersed operations around the globe make them vulnerable to unexpected events such as political turmoil or natural disaster in the host country. They have also seen poor quality, sluggish response time, and loss of intellectual property while seeking cost savings offshore, only to incur increased costs and end up with lower than expected performance.

The new trend called "reshoring" may continue but will be limited to a few industries. Products that are made with little labor are more likely to reshore.[3] The driving change for bringing operations back to the home country is to have a closer relationship, oversight, management, and access to the entire value chain. To remain competitive in fast-paced industries, companies need to continuously innovate to stay on top and expedite the process of introducing new products or services to the market. Given the competitive landscape revolving more around speed and quality of product in some industries, these companies prefer to keep the value chain within arm's reach and find outsourcing overseas increasingly outdated. Furthermore, robotic process automation, and the growth of business process as a platform sector, will either adversely impact or disrupt the traditional outsource and offshore model. The low-cost arbitrage that has allowed countries such as India and China to become the world's outsourcers cannot compete with higher-level automation and robotic processes. Companies also believe that business processes delivered by software as a service model are growing rapidly and can easily replace the processes that service centers in India and China currently perform. Additionally, U.S. labor is becoming less expensive due to more companies and organizations implementing the taskification or Uber model. Large corporations or small start-ups can now "taskify" everything by posting their needs on the Internet instead of hiring help: from scheduling meetings and debugging websites to generating sales leads and managing employee HR files.[4]

With this general understanding of globalization, we will first look at the major economies that account for the largest share of global GDP production. Figure 1.2 shows who the top ten largest economies are. The U.S. is still leading the world in terms of the size of GDP followed by China, Japan, and Germany. It is noteworthy that the share of developing countries has expanded with the growing contribution of emerging economies. Brazil,

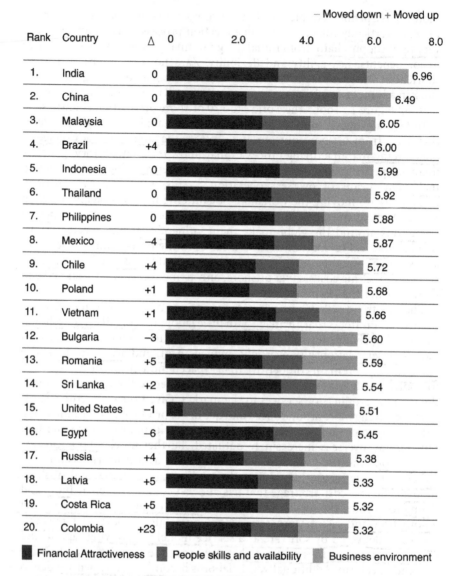

Figure 1.1 2016 A.T. Kearney Global Services Location Index ™ Top 20

Source: Sethi R. & Gott, J. (2016). On the Eve of Disruption, A. T. Kearney 2016 Global Services Location Index. Retrieved from www.atkearney.com/strategic-it/global-services-location-index

Russia, India, and China, the so-called BRICs are now all ranked among the top ten largest economies. By the year 2050, China will take over the U.S. as the largest economy in the world and India will move up to third place after the U.S.

The countries that the World Bank classified as high-income countries in 2012 accounted for 77 percent of world GDP in 1980. Their share was already

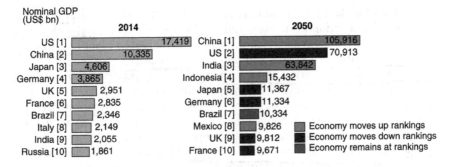

Figure 1.2 Top Ten Economies in 2050 at Market Exchange Rates

Source: Long-term Macroeconomic Forecasts: Key Trends to 2050, A Special Report from the Economist Intelligence Unit, 2015.

reduced to 67 percent in 2012, and is projected to fall to just about half by 2030. Seventy-two percent of GDP growth around the world from 2008 to 2011 took place in emerging market countries, and according to International Monetary Fund (IMF) projections, emerging markets will deliver about 60 percent of growth from 2012 to 2017.[5]

II. Key Drivers of Globalization

What are the key factors that have facilitated globalization? Globalization is mainly driven not by governments but by free-market forces. Both positive and negative drivers behind globalization are identified. First, positive drivers of globalization are discussed. It goes without saying that globalization has become possible through the advance in disruptive technology and its speedy dissemination, mass communications, and sharing information through the Internet. Second, the continued fall of trade barriers, both tariffs and non-tariff barriers (NTBs), has facilitated globalization as goods and services move more freely across borders. Although multilateral trade negotiations (MTNs) such as the Doha Round have achieved very little success, the expansion of regional free trade agreements such as the Trans-Pacific Partnership (TPP) and the Korea U.S. Free Trade Agreement (KORUS FTA) continue to open markets, providing increased business opportunities for companies in the global market. Third, despite the sporadic armed conflict in certain regions such as the Middle East and Africa, overall the world has maintained peace since the end of the Cold War in the late twentieth century. This peace has contributed to the global economy through increased trade as well as capital flows among countries. Finally, company strategies are also attributable to the acceleration of globalization. MNCs preserved dimensions of globalization even as governments closed down flows of trade and capital across borders. Many companies are now targeting the global market whenever they launch a new product to take advantage of the growing convergence of consumers' tastes and preferences. Individual entrepreneurs and managers create new products and shaped consumer demand in the global market. Firms invented and disseminated technologies and products, along with the values in which they were embedded.[6]

On the other hand, we need to recognize the factors that might impede or slow the globalization of markets and production. First, cultural differences will continue to remain as one of the obstacles to globalization. Localization and customization of goods and services are required to the extent that different values and norms prevail among different countries. For example, hamburgers need to be replaced by veggie burgers or lamb burgers in Islamic countries due to their religious tenets. It is also true that countries still rely on protectionism for various political and economic reasons such as retaliation and national security as we will see in more detail in Chapter 2. Protectionism in the form of tariffs and non-tariff barriers will hinder the free flow of trade and capital across borders and thus impede globalization. In addition, national barriers and border controls constitute obstacles to globalization, constraining the cross-border exchange of people as well as goods and services. Armed conflicts among countries arising from geopolitical uncertainty and instability will also make it difficult to pursue globalization efforts since nations are more likely to retreat to isolation and nationalism rather than integration and internationalism. National security, as well as cyber security risk and terrorism, is another factor that will have a significantly adverse impact on globalization.

III. Key Trends in Globalization

Globalization has slowed down in the aftermath of the 2008 global credit crisis. Will globalization soon regain its momentum and fully recover its pace or continue to stay in the doldrums? In predicting the future prospects of globalization, a recent study conducted by McKinsey Global Institute identified four fundamental forces that are likely to have an enormous impact on the global economy.[7]

First, the center of global economic activity has shifted from developed economies such as the U.S. and Japan to emerging economies such as China and India.

> These emerging markets are experiencing both industrial and urban revolutions. 95 percent of the world's largest MNCs listed in the Fortune Global 500 were based in developed economies by 2000. Moreover, nearly half of the world's large companies—defined as those with revenue of $1 billion USD or more—are expected to have headquarters in emerging economies by 2025. Furthermore, the center of economic activity is shifting to the cities within these markets. The global urban population has been growing by an average of 65 million people annually during the past three decades. 440 cities in emerging markets will account for nearly half of global GDP growth between 2010 and 2025.[8]

Second, technological evolution continues to move forward at incredible speed, scale, and scope. "Six million users joined Facebook in its first year, a number that increased 100 times over the next five years. In 2009, two years after the iPhone's launch, developers had created around 150,000 applications. That number had increased to 1.2 million by 2014, when users had together downloaded more than 75 billion total apps, more than ten for every person on the planet."[9] Thanks to data revolution, consumers as well as businesses can get easy access to unprecedented amounts of information and we have seen the rapid increase in technology-enabled business models, from online retail platforms like Alibaba to car-hailing apps like Uber. Billions of people in emerging economies benefit from the economic progress that technological advances have brought about.[10]

③ Third, the world's population is quickly aging. While aging has been evident in developed economies for some time, the phenomenon is now spreading to developing countries such as China. Aging could mean that, for the first time in human history, the population count will level off in most of the world. In 2013, about 60 percent of the world's population lived in countries with fertility rates below the replacement rate.[11] A reduced global workforce will become an obstacle for productivity and economic growth. The need to support the growing population of elderly will put serious pressure on government treasuries.

④ Finally, we expect a continued expansion in the flow of trade, capital, people, and information. A significant change has emerged in the pattern of trade and finance.

> Instead of a series of lines connecting major trading hubs in Europe and North America, the global trading system has expanded into a complex, intricate, and sprawling web. Asia is becoming the world's largest trading region and trade flows between emerging markets in the Southern hemisphere have doubled their share of global trade over the past decade. Global capital flows expanded 25 times between 1980 and 2007. More than one billion people crossed borders in 2009, more than five times the number in 1980.[12]

The global recession of 2008 halted all these movements of trade, capital, and people and they are yet to fully recover. But the connections created by technology have rapidly evolved without interruption, creating unequalled opportunities and triggering unexpected volatility at the same time.

IV. Four Key Dimensions of Globalization

Globalization involves four key dimensions, i.e., the flow of trade, investment, people, and information. As we will see in Chapter 4, DHL—the world's largest logistics company, specializing in shipping, courier, and packaging services—has developed a global connectedness index consisting of these four pillars that capture the dynamics of a country's participation in the global economy. The trade pillar includes the flow of goods and services. The capital pillar covers equity capital, including flows and stocks of foreign direct investment and portfolio equity. The information pillar consists of data on international Internet bandwidth, international telephone calls, and trade in printed material. And the people pillar focuses on the movement of people across three time-horizons: migration (long-term), university students pursuing degrees abroad (medium-term) and tourism (short-term).[13]

Some seven years after the 2008 global financial crisis, the key metrics of global connectedness have not returned to the levels prior to the crisis. This can no longer be attributed to the financial crisis and its immediate aftermath. Rather, the global economy has entered a new phase. We will examine the recent trend within each of the four key dimensions of globalization.

I. Trade

Since the global financial crisis, trade has grown only slightly faster than GDP. World trade actually shrank in both the first and second quarter of 2015—the worst performance since the height of the financial crisis.[14] However, recent research by HSBC and Oxford Economics predicts that global exports will quadruple 2015 levels reaching a total of $68.5 trillion USD by 2050.

> The study predicts a third wave of globalization despite recent falls in trade volume. The report foresees a world in which service-led industries are dominant and where businesses with explicit sustainability goals will succeed. Specifically, the report identifies five key developments that will benefit global trade in the future.[15]
>
> (1) *Digital innovation and the drive to sustainability*—Business opportunities will continue to increase as digital innovation drives development of new environmentally friendly products and business models that can be modified for different markets, without being limited to specific locations. "Increasingly interconnected economies will facilitate rapid change and transmission of ideas around the world. The Internet and the free movement of data across borders reinforces growth in international trade and investment. The global supply chain will need to innovate to respond to increasing expectation and demand for greater sustainability."[16]
>
> (2) *Reverse innovation and mass customization*—Reverse innovation refers to a phenomenon in which companies first develop products and services for markets of emerging economies rather than those of developed economies. This indicates a shift from traditional mass production to mass customization as products can be customized to the conditions of different markets. Companies will seek an optimal balance between globalization and localization to effectively meet the challenge of so-called "*glocalization.*" "As they build intelligent systems that track information and consumer demand, companies will better understand the influence of customer expectations. Along with growing demand, the development of 3D printing will create innovative supply chains and allow local factories to produce goods on demand through additive manufacturing."[17]
>
> (3) *The growth of micro multinationals*—Small and medium-sized enterprises (SMEs) will be able to take advantage of digital evolution and tightly connected global networks to compete against larger firms.

"Digital platforms level the playing field, allowing these SMEs to overcome cost disadvantages that previously kept them from participating in international trade. New technologies such as 3D printing will enable smaller companies to deliver products globally just like large MNCs. Ninety-five percent of SMEs on the eBay network engage in exporting, reaching 30-40 international markets."[18]

(4) *The falling cost and rising speed of trade*—Logistical improvements will also contribute to the continued growth in trade. Shipping costs will fall thanks to the relentless advances in transport technology and improved infrastructure, leading to increased global trade capacity, opening new trade routes.

(5) *Ongoing trade liberalization*—Trade liberalization will continue with the expansion of free trade and continuing harmonization of regulations and standards to lower barriers to trade.

A more stable political and financial environment is expected to make trade easier for MNCs. New rules and terms of organization for trade and investment should allow countries to return to a multilateral system by 2020. China, the U.S., and Germany will keep leading the world's trading patterns with South Korea rising rapidly behind them.[19]

2. Foreign Direct Investment

The growth of Foreign Direct Investment (FDI) has outpaced that of both trade and GDP in the past three decades. While global trade is expected to continue to grow as explained above, the growth of FDI has not fully recovered since the 2008 global financial crisis. "According to the *The Economist*'s report as illustrated in Figure 1.3, net inflows of FDI dropped by 16 percent globally in 2014, to $1.2 trillion USD, as a result of economic fragility, greater geopolitical risks and policy uncertainty. FDI flows to developed countries dropped by 28 percent, to $499 billion USD, their lowest level in a decade. Inflows to the U.S. fell by 60 percent, to $92 billion USD, mainly due to Vodafone's divestment of Verizon, while flows to Europe fell by 11 percent, to $289 billion USD. Asia is largely responsible for the growing share of FDI inflows held by developing economies: they accounted for 55 percent of the global total. Services continue to represent the bulk of investment, occupying 63 percent of the global FDI stock, more than twice the share of manufacturing."[20]

More recently, however, global FDI flows increased during the first half of 2015, up by 13 percent from the second half of 2014. Not counting the decrease in the first half of 2014, global trends have been rising since the first half of 2013. The record levels of inward FDI flows to the U.S. during the first quarter of 2015 largely accounted for the increase in global flows. These flows were driven not only by the improved performance of the U.S. economy, but also by cross-border mergers and acquisitions (M&As) aimed at reducing companies' U.S. tax obligations.[21] The U.S. continues to lead the world as the largest source of FDI, followed by Ireland, Japan, China, Canada, and Germany.

Inflows, $trn

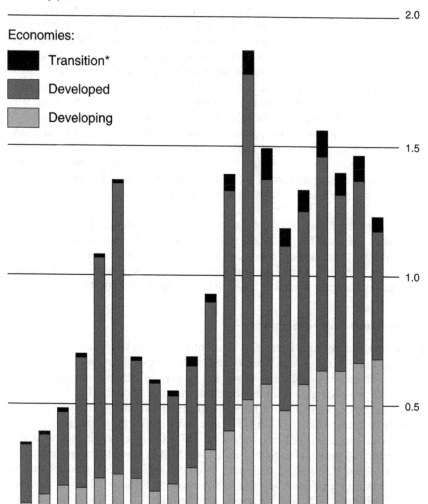

Figure 1.3 Foreign Direct Investment

Source: Foreign Direct Investment, Economist, (2015, June 25).
Retrieved from www.economist.com/news/economic-and-financial-indicators/21656180-foreign-direct-investment

3. People

Increased global connectivity means that workers can move around more frequently and choose to migrate for both permanent and temporary jobs. Approximately one in seven people today are migrants: 232 million are international migrants while 740 million are internal migrants. Communities are adjusting to growing complexity and diversity in their populations.[22] Growth of international migration continued from the implosion of the former Soviet Union in the 1990s and through the subsequent period of globalization, reaching an all-time high between 2005 and 2010. However, international migration has subsided since 2010, and the U.N. Population Division forecasts that it will continue to fall in the coming decades. A survey of global economies provides plenty of examples of economies that struggle with stagnant or even negative population growth, and illustrates how difficult it is to generate sustainable economic growth when human capital is in short supply. Japan—an economy relatively closed to immigration—stands out as the clearest example of these challenges.[23] As the global population ages, countries will also compete to attract migrants as a solution for labor shortage. Figure 1.4 illustrates how the composition of the global population has changed by age group.

The global workforce has also become a more gender and ethnically diverse workforce. Country of origin or ethnicity no longer determines a worker's geographical scope, particularly in developing countries that now produce at least as many skilled, educated workers and managers as developed countries. While these changes have positive implications for firms and workers alike, they also carry negative repercussions. The scarcity of experienced

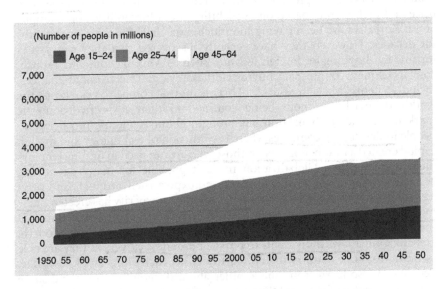

Figure 1.4 Shifts in Distribution of the Global Workforce Population by Age Group

Source: The World Population Prospects: The 2012 Revision, Medium Variant.

leaders, lack of cultural knowledge, inconsistent educational standards, and greater risk exposure all indicate new challenges not encountered in previous decades.[24]

4. Information

We now feel the impact of the Internet at every moment of our lives. It conveys distant information in real time and connects everything around us. Police officers are wearing cameras and companies are using big data software to conduct marketing research. Overwhelmed by the enormous influence of overflowing data, some people have started to feel information claustrophobia. Thanks to the convergence of information and telecommunication technology, new "smart" machines help us learn, improve, and understand task-specific contexts; home-helper robots and hand-held interactive assistants are just a few examples. This coming era of non-human aid will have a profound effect on the way we work, live, and play.[25]

V. Benefits and Costs of Globalization

I. Benefits of Globalization

What are the main benefits of globalization? Proponents for globalization highlight the following benefits. First, consumers can benefit from increased competition and easy access to a variety of products and services. Intense competition among countries is supposed to not only drive prices down but also offer differentiated products. Accordingly, consumers can choose a product or service that provides them with the best combination between low price and high quality based on availability and affordability. For example, South Koreans have been paying too much, especially for their local goods, for decades. However, they have recently discovered that they can save a fortune by shopping on foreign websites such as Amazon.com and Taobao. com, its Chinese counterpart, buying clothes, toys, and electronic appliances, including items "Made in Korea."[26] This means that companies can target the worldwide market without being confined to their respective domestic markets. Second, globalization has brought about economic prosperity to people in developing countries where the infusion of technology and foreign capital created a number of jobs for those who are not used to finding employment opportunities. Globalization made it possible for many developing countries to tap into overseas markets and export their products and services. Third, optimists believe that such economic prosperity has created a new middle class in emerging economies such as China and India and thus laid the foundation for political stability and even democratization. Fourth, globalization allows individuals to pursue borderless careers as they are able to move from one country to another to market their skills and knowledge. People can also learn from one another about different cultures and share concerns about environmental issues, etc., since they are frequently exposed to an opportunity to work with diverse groups of people.

2. Costs of Globalization

While the benefits of globalization are substantial, negative impacts of globalization should not be overlooked in order to seek a balanced perspective about globalization.

First, globalization has shifted jobs from developed to developing countries. The first and the second wave of offshoring moved many manufacturing jobs from wealthy, advanced countries to poor, developing countries. In particular, offshore outsourcing has caused the loss of jobs not only among unskilled workers but also skilled workers in developed countries. In order to compete for the jobs with people in developing countries, wage rates of unskilled workers in developed countries continued to decline. According to conservative estimates by Robert Scott of the Economic Policy Institute, China's most favored nation status took away 3.2 million jobs from the U.S., including 2.4 million manufacturing jobs.[27] Second, as a result of migration of jobs, income disparity between haves and have-nots has worsened both internationally and within countries. "The UN Development Program reports that the richest 20 percent of the world's population consume 86 percent of the world's resources while the poorest 80 percent consume just 14 percent."[28] Income and wealth inequality are a threat to any economy and have become a moral issue for us to tackle. Political reaction against perceived negative impacts of growing inequality may trigger social unrest in some countries and expand into larger-scale regional or global conflicts.

Third, as globalization allows companies to easily move their operations to countries with lax labor and environmental regulations, environmental degradation has become more serious. Critics increasingly accuse MNCs of social injustice, unfair working conditions as well as environmental degradation, exploitation of natural resources, and ecological damage. The U.N. has warned "preventing, managing and resolving natural resource-induced conflicts may well come to define global peace and security in the 21st century."[29] An increased flow of people across borders may make us more vulnerable to pandemics as we have recently seen in the cases of Zika virus and Ebola virus.

Finally, globalization may even result in loss of sovereignty. MNCs tend to control the dynamic sectors of a host country with their advanced technology and powerful human and financial resources. Countries that signed international trade or investment agreements are required to comply with rules and regulations that may adversely affect the lives of their constituencies and MNCs exert an increasing influence on the important political decisions of a country.

When evaluating the pros and cons of globalization, two different views exist about the impact of globalization. First, market globalism is based on the assumption that globalization is driven by the free market and its supporters naively believe that globalization will benefit everyone. Therefore, we need to encourage the free flow of trade and investment through deregulation and breed increased competition through market fundamentalism. However, the recent global credit crisis taught us a lesson that unbridled capital flow across borders may bring about undesirable and unexpected consequences to the global economy. It is probably true that globalization is irreversible but there are many policies and strategies we can use to make it more equitable. This perspective is called justice globalism.[20] Justice globalism claims that the widening global disparity should be recognized and corrected through redistribution of wealth and power. To achieve this goal, fair trade, not free trade, should be promoted and capital flow across borders needs to be adequately controlled. At the same time, environmental protection, human rights improvement, and labor unions deserve more attention. While globalization has certain benefits, we also need to recognize its downsides in order to have a balanced and comprehensive view about globalization.

This book consists of 13 chapters grouped into three sections addressing the questions of why, what, where, and how in the context of international business. Section one includes the first three chapters. In Chapter 1, we have seen why companies are interested in expanding their businesses abroad to take advantage of globalization. Chapter 2 and Chapter 3 address the two main contents of global business: trade and FDI, i.e. what constitutes global business. These two chapters explain the concepts and theories of international trade and FDI along with the government policies and company practices involving international trade and FDI. Section two consists of four chapters, Chapter 4 through Chapter 7 that discuss the key contexts that MNCs should be aware of when they screen and assess business opportunities in foreign markets. They include political, economic, sociocultural, and monetary environments. Section three concerns how companies pursue their competitive strategies and manage their primary and secondary value creation activities engaged in global business. Chapter 8 discusses the entry and exit modes and chapters 9 through 12 cover both strategic decisions and practices of MNCs' production, accounting, finance, marketing, and human resource management. Chapter 13, the final chapter of this book, covers how companies deal with sustainability, corporate social responsibility, and business ethics.

Key Terms

Globalization, demand perspective, supply perspective, multinational corporations (MNCs), global supply chain, offshore outsourcing, reshoring, taskification, BRICs, IMF, Non-tariff Barriers (NTBs), multilateral trade negotiations (MTNs), Trans-Pacific Partnership (TPP), KORUS FTA, global connectedness index, trade liberalization, foreign direct investment (FDI), global workforce, market globalism, justice globalism

Review Questions

1. Explain what globalization means and how it has affected people's lives.
2. What are the key drivers of globalization, both positive and negative? Which one of these drivers do you think has the most powerful impact on globalization and why?
3. What are the mega trends that will have a significant impact on globalization in the future? Which one of these trends will exert the most and the least favorable influence on globalization?

4. Evaluate the benefits and costs of globalization. How do you think that globalization has affected your country's economic growth and improvement in its standard of living?
5. Compare and contrast between market globalism and justice globalism. What is our own perspective on these two different ideologies of globalization?

Internet Exercise

Please visit the following website: www.globaleducation.edu.au/teaching-activity/whats-globalisation-got-to-do-with-me.html#activity1 and answer the questions in Activity 1 (How close is the world to me?) to understand your connections to the rest of the world based on the music you listen to and Activity 2 (Globalisation: swings and roundabouts?) to understand the advantages and disadvantages of global trends, technologies, and economies.

Notes

1 Schlossberg, M. (2015, December 19). This Spanish retailer with the "best business model" in apparel is scaring Gap, Abercrombie & Fitch, and J. Crew. Retrieved January 22, 2016, from www.businessinsider.com/zara-has-the-best-business-model-2015-12
2 Murphy, E. (2016, January 11). A.T. Kearney predicts the end of offshoring as we know it. *Forbes*. Retrieved January, 2016, from www.forbes.com/sites/erikamorphy/2016/01/11/a-t-kearney-predicts-the-end-of-offshoring-as-we-know-it/#1b9255ff61a7
3 Conerly, B. (2014, September 2). Reshoring or offshoring: U.S. manufacturing forecast 2015–2016. *Forbes*. Retrieved December, 2015, from www.forbes.com/sites/billconerly/2014/09/02/reshoring-or-offshoring-u-s-manufacturing-forecast-2015-2016/#7f3689487419
4 Murphy, E. (2016, January 11). A.T. Kearney predicts the end of offshoring as we know it. *Forbes*. Retrieved January, 2016, from www.forbes.com/sites/erikamorphy/2016/01/11/a-t-kearney-predicts-the-end-of-offshoring-as-we-know-it/#1b9255ff61a7
5 Ghemawat, P. and Altman, S. A. (2014, October). DHL Global Connectedness Index 2014: Analyzing global flows and their power to increase prosperity. Retrieved from www.dhl.com/content/dam/Campaigns/gci2014/downloads/dhl_gci_2014_study_low.pdf
6 Jones, G. (2013). *Entrepreneurship and Multinationals: Global Business and the Making of the Modern World*. Northampton, MA: Edward Elgar Publishing.
7 Dobbs, R., Manyika, J., and Woetzel, J. R. (2015, April). *No Ordinary Disruption: The Four Global Forces Breaking All the Trends*. New York: McKinsey Global Institute, McKinsey and Company.
8 Ibid.
9 Ibid.
10 Ibid.
11 Ibid.
12 Ibid.
13 Ghemawat, P. and Altman, S. A. (2014, October). DHL Global Connectedness Index 2014: Analyzing global flows and their power to increase prosperity.

Retrieved from www.dhl.com/content/dam/Campaigns/gci2014/downloads/dhl_gci_2014_study_low.pdf

14   M. G. J. (2015, September 15). What slowing trade growth means for the world economy. *Economist*. Retrieved from www.economist.com/blogs/economist-explains/2015/09/economist-explains-10

15   Persio, S. L. (2015, September 24). Five trends that will shape the future of trade. *Global Trade Review* (GTR). Retrieved from www.gtreview.com/news/global/five-trends-that-will-shape-the-future-of-trade/

16   Ibid.

17   Ibid.

18   Ibid.

19   Ibid.

20   *Economist*. (2015, June 27). Foreign direct investment. Retrieved from www.economist.com/news/economic-and-financial-indicators/21656180-foreign-direct-investment

21   OECD, 1–12 (2015, October). FDI continues to rise in the first half of 2015. Retrieved from www.oecd.org/daf/inv/investment-policy/FDI-in-Figures-October-2015.pdf

22   Meehan, M. (2015, January 16). The five big ideas (and the trends behind them) that will shape 2015. *Forbes*. Retrieved from www.forbes.com/sites/marymeehan/2015/01/06/the-five-big-ideas-and-the-trends-behind-them-that-will-shape-2015/#46a302e13975

23   Clemons, S. (2014, September 4). The unsung economics of immigration. *Forbes*. Retrieved from www.forbes.com/sites/realspin/2014/09/04/the-unsung-economics-of-immigration/#7895bed73ec3

24   SHRM Foundation/The Economist Intelligence Unit, 1–50 (2015, February). Global trends impacting the future of HR management: Engaging and integrating a global workforce. Retrieved from www.shrm.org/about/foundation/documents/3-15 eiu theme 2 report-final.pdf

25   Persio, S. L. (2015, September 24). Five trends that will shape the future of trade. *Global Trade Review* (GTR). Retrieved from www.gtreview.com/news/global/five-trends-that-will-shape-the-future-of-trade/

26   *Economist*. (2015, January 17). Won over: Locals, fed up of paying over the odds, are shopping abroad. Retrieved from www.economist.com/news/business/21639579-locals-fed-up-paying-over-odds-are-shopping-abroad-won-over?zid=293

27   Collins, M. (2015, May 6). The pros and cons of globalization. *Forbes*. Retrieved from www.forbes.com/sites/mikecollins/2015/05/06/the-pros-and-cons-of-globalization/#a82959f2170a

28   Ibid.

29   Meehan, M. (2015, January 16). The five big ideas (and the trends behind them) that will shape 2015. *Forbes*. Retrieved from www.forbes.com/sites/marymeehan/2015/01/06/the-five-big-ideas-and-the-trends-behind-them-that-will-shape-2015/#46a302e13975

30   Steger, M. B. (2003). *Globalization: A Very Short Introduction*. New York, NY: Oxford University Press.

2 Trade

Rhetoric and Practice

Learning Objectives

1. Recognize the emerging trends in global trade.
2. Understand why international trade occurs and how it benefits the countries involved in trade.
3. Compare and contrast old and new trade theories.
4. Explain the rationales behind government intervention in free trade.
5. Understand global trade governing systems and the emergence of regional free trade agreements.

Cases

Case 2.1 Fast Track Authority Rendered to President Obama
Case 2.2 U.S. Olympic Uniforms and Comparative Advantage
Case 2.3 The Fight for Flight: Boeing vs. Airbus Trade Dispute
Case 2.4 The Influence of U.S. Foreign Policy toward China on Trade
Case 2.5 Trade Facilitation Deal at the WTO Bali Meeting

Case 2.1 Fast Track Authority Rendered to President Obama

After countless months, President Barack Obama was finally given authority to expedite negotiations for a landmark agreement with Pacific Rim countries that will reshape the global economy. The Republican-controlled Senate passed legislation on Wednesday, June 24, 2015 providing the president with the power to "fast-track" negotiations with the 11 other countries partaking of the Trans-Pacific Partnership (TPP). The vote, which passed 60–38, was a significant victory for MNCs. They had been lobbying hard for a trade agreement aimed to reduce tariffs and create new regulations for diverse sectors such as agriculture, banking, and the pharmaceutical industry. The outcome of the vote was expected to increase the prospects for the swift ratification of the Transatlantic Trade and Investment Partnership (TTIP), a European trade agreement in the early stages of negotiation.

During Obama's tenure as president, pro-growth policies were few. The victory means the U.S. reasserted itself as a trade leader after a decade of being on the sidelines. The trade negotiation among 12 Asia-Pacific nations was able to focus on making difficult choices, as other countries became aware of Congress's inability to rewrite the deal; Congress will only have to vote yes or no. Fast-track authority lasts six years, so the next President will be afforded greater flexibility to pursue further trade agreements.

While the victory was bipartisan, it was clear that the bill could only pass when Republicans control Congress. The three bilateral trade pacts remaining from the Bush administration (Colombia, Panama, and South Korea) were ratified only after Nancy Pelosi stepped down as House Speaker in 2010, and trade authority moved only when Harry Reid lost the Senate in 2014. The same Republicans that Mr. Obama condemned as cynical partisans put their partisanship aside to help the country.

Democratic Leader Nancy Pelosi released the following statement after the Senate voted to send Trade Promotion Authority legislation to the President:

> Throughout the debate on Fast Track, House Democrats have been united in our concern over the impact trade agreements will have on America's hard-working families. Any trade agreement must be judged by whether it will create good-paying jobs, whether it will increase the paychecks of American families, and whether it recognizes the fundamental connection between commerce and climate. We know we must put America's workers first for our economy to grow and our nation to succeed. The Senate's final passage of Trade Promotion Authority ends one phase, but it does not end our fight for working families.[a]

The White House spent months trying to persuade skeptical labor union leaders and Democrats who were wary of a replication of the North American Free Trade Agreement (NAFTA) with Canada and Mexico concluded in 1994. The overall impacts of the NAFTA have been disputed, but many economists contend that it increased the U.S. trade deficit resulting in the movement of manufacturing jobs overseas. A multitude of major labor unions threatened to freeze campaign contributions to members of Congress to pressure them to oppose the fast-track trade legislation that President Obama pursued. These actions were part of the unions' campaign against the TPP. The unions were concerned that the TPP could send more jobs to low-wage countries, such as Vietnam and Malaysia. The Obama administration refuted these allegations by maintaining that the deal would level the playing field for American workers and raise standards abroad. His administration branded the pact as "the most progressive trade agreement in history."[b]

The Democrats' persistent fight against trade reflects a broader retreat of liberal economic and intellectual ideologies. It's remarkable how many leading voices on the left have walked away from the free-trade support they provided as recently as the 1990s. For decades through the 1920s, Republicans were the protectionist party. Hoover signed the Smoot–Hawley Tariff to catastrophic effect, and during the Great Depression the Roosevelt administration worked to rebuild a global trade order, starting with bilateral trade deals. These grew into multilateral pacts after World War II that John F. Kennedy (JFK) and Bill Clinton supported. The liberal trade flip-floppers claim that tariffs are now so low that gains from free trade are overstated. But while U.S. tariffs are low, that isn't true everywhere. The average tariff in Vietnam and Malaysia is three times the U.S. average, and tariffs range up to 70 percent on cars, 35 percent on chemicals, and 75 percent on consumer goods in Southeast countries. American exports would gain in these markets, as they have in countries where the U.S. has bilateral free trade agreements.

The U.S. recently withdrew from this landmark agreement, TPP, with the issuance of an executive order by the new President Donald Trump. However, the conclusion of the TPP was crucial to breaking down cartels in Japan and elsewhere that block U.S. competition in services. American companies are highly competitive in finance, retail, insurance, and software—yet they face higher barriers overseas than U.S. goods do. New protections for intellectual property, such as drug patents, will also help prevent countries from robbing America's most creative industries. It's funny that liberals complain about low American wages but then sneer at trade deals that would increase the number of highly paid American skilled jobs. Liberals who oppose free trade are harming the high-wage, high-tech industries in which U.S. companies have a comparative advantage.

Notes

a.   Pelosi statement on Senate passage of Trade Promotion Authority, June 24, 2015. Retrieved from https://pelosi.house.gov/news/press-releases/pelosi-statement-on-senate-passage-of-trade-promotion-authority

b.   *The Guardian* (2015, June 24). Barack Obama given "fast-track" authority over trade deal negotiations. Retrieved from www.theguardian.com/us-news/2015/jun/24/barack-obama-fast-track-trade-deal-tpp-senate

Sources

1.   *Wall Street Journal.* (2015, June 24). Lessons from a trade victory, Eastern edition (New York, NY): A.12.

2.   Trottman, M. (2015, March 11) U.S. news: New step by unions to block trade pact. *Wall Street Journal*, Eastern edition (New York, NY): A.4.

3.   *The Guardian* (2015, June 24). Barack Obama given "fast-track" authority over trade deal negotiations. Retrieved from www.theguardian.com/us-news/2015/jun/24/barack-obama-fast-track-trade-deal-tpp-senate

Questions for Case Discussion

1.   What is fast-track authority and why is it important for the U.S. government and President Barack Obama to have this privilege?

2.   What are the expected impacts of providing President Obama with fast-track authority on the negotiation of the TPP?

3.   Why do you think that Democrats have recently been opposed to signing another free trade agreement? Do you think that trade policies are necessary to save jobs for the American people?

Case 2.2 U.S. Olympic Uniforms and Comparative Advantage

British economist David Ricardo changed how people think about trade when he developed the theory of comparative advantage. Countries do best, he said, by concentrating on their strengths, and then trading with others for everything else. In 1817, when countries were striving for self-sufficiency, Ricardo's notion of comparative advantage challenged a traditional view. Over time, Mr. Ricardo's insight into trade proved to be accurate: The U.S., which is more efficient at producing sophisticated products, such as software and power-plant generators, is better off importing textiles from developing, lower-wage countries, such as Bangladesh and Pakistan. Similarly, Japan is better off by specializing in and exporting automobile production while importing agricultural products from resource-rich countries such as Brazil and China.

The intuition behind the principle of comparative advantage, which drives globalization and its economic benefits, is that Americans or Japanese are not going to excel at everything. Comparative advantage allows each country to concentrate its energies and resources on the particular goods and services that it is most efficient and productive at compared to the rest of the world. The countries then export those overseas, and in exchange import other goods and services produced relatively more efficiently in other countries.

In a perfect world, Sen. Harry Reid and Rep. John Boehner, when confronted with the revelation that China stitches together U.S. Olympic uniforms, might have stated:

> "Small potatoes. Call us back after we've fixed the deficit, the economy, Iran, and our real problems with China."
>
> Unfortunately, Democrat Reid said "we should burn the clothes." Republican Boehner said, "They should have known better." Several senators spent their time and the public's money, introducing the 'Team USA Made in America Act,' which would require that future Olympic uniforms be made – guess where? (China).[a]

Election seasons often bend sensibility and populism gains votes. The political process also distracts from predominant issues challenging U.S. businesses: protection of intellectual property rights, market access, forced transfer of U.S. technology to China, and the ability of China's state-owned enterprises to defeat competitors. These days that agenda has not received priority. An executive with a U.S. manufacturer that has operations in China stated:

> The comments reflect either a lack of understanding of comparative advantage and how trade works (the Chinese are really good at producing low-cost uniforms, the U.S. is really good at innovative technology and advanced manufacturing—which would you rather be?), or cynical politics. More likely both.
>
> He doesn't want to be named and get his company in trouble with the politicians. It's just "grandstanding," says another manager with a tech

multinational. "There are far more important bilateral business and trade issues for both countries." The flap over the uniforms has a lot to do with U.S.-China relations. A feeling echoed by Americans that the country is losing the race to this "commercial juggernaut." Ask the average man on the street what percentage of goods sold in the U.S are produced in China, including those Olympic uniforms, and you'll most likely receive double digit estimates.[b]

Yet researchers at the Federal Reserve Bank of San Francisco calculate that in 2010 goods labeled "Made in China" accounted for just 2.7 percent of U.S. personal-consumption expenditures on goods and services that include all the things we purchase in a given year, from cars to clothing to health care. (Services account for about two-thirds of our spending and are primarily produced locally.) U.S. businesses transport, sell, and market those Chinese goods. Remove that value, and the percentage attributed to the actual cost of Chinese imports drops to just 1.2 percent. Products that are made in America occasionally include "Made-in-China" components. When researchers added those components into their calculations, the final figure incrementally increased to just 1.9 percent.

"Although globalization is widely recognized these days, the U.S. economy actually remains relatively closed," the researchers said in their report. "The vast majority of goods and services sold in the U.S. are produced here." Ralph Lauren, which designed the U.S. Olympic uniforms, won't mention which factory in China manufactured the uniforms. One company making clothes for Ralph Lauren is Hong Kong-based Luen Thai, which has operations in southern China. This company produces millions of garments and accessories a year for several American and global retailers. China can clearly make clothes and Olympic uniforms less expensively in comparison to the U.S. However, Ralph Lauren used employees in the U.S. to design the uniforms. Additionally, if the San Francisco Fed's calculations are correct, more than half of the value of any U.S. public sale of "Made-in-China" clothing will flow to American companies.

"Across the business community there's a recognition that we need to talk about trade in a more sophisticated way – that global value chains can't be boiled down to three words: 'Made in China' or 'Made in America,'" says John Murphy of the U.S. Chamber of Commerce. "I think the debate reflects the current economic and unemployment concerns in the U.S.," adds John Frisbie, head of the U.S.-China Business Council.[c]

Criticizing foreigners during election cycles and economic downturns is a familiar political game in America. Mr. Bill Clinton famously campaigned against the "butchers of Beijing" when he ran for president. Once elected, however, he championed China's entry into the World Trade Organization. Mitt Romney once advocated for a "Confront China" policy and stated he would declare China a currency manipulator if elected president. More recently, although Barack Obama imposed tariffs on certain Chinese goods, there was little progress regarding more complex issues.

"The relationship at this point is a bit stalled," says Charlene Barshefsky, the chief U.S. trade negotiator in the Clinton administration. She believes that the relationship will change after U.S. elections and a transition in Chinese leadership. "Both countries will go back to trying to find elements over which they can cooperate. That's been the pattern over the last 30 years." This is based on the assumption that America can overcome the critical issue of who should sew the country's Olympic uniforms.

Notes

a.   Bussey, J. (2012, July 20). The business: Does it matter China made the U.S. Olympic uniforms? *Wall Street Journal*: B.1.
b.   Ibid.
c.   Ibid.

Sources

1.   Bussey, J. (2012, July 20). The business: Does it matter China made the U.S. Olympic uniforms? *Wall Street Journal*: B.1.
2.   Slaughter, M. J. (2011, January 26). Comparative advantage and American jobs. *Wall Street Journal*: A.17.
3.   Lahart, J. (2011, September 27). U.S. news: An early argument for the specialization of nations (comparative advantage). *Wall Street Journal*: A.5.

Questions for Case Discussion

1.   What is comparative advantage and why is it important in trade?
2.   Do you think that the U.S., not China, should produce the Olympic uniforms for the U.S. Olympic athletes? If so, please explain your rationale.
3.   What is the general perception about the dominance of "Made in China" products among the American people? Is there any myth about it?

Case 2.3 The Fight for Flight: Boeing vs. Airbus Trade Dispute

The U.S. and the EU filed counter-claims at the WTO after the administration of former President George W. Bush walked out of an aircraft-aid accord with the EU in 1992. According to the 2004 filing, the U.S. claimed Airbus unfairly benefited from no or low-interest loans from the U.K., French, German, and Spanish governments to launch new aircrafts. If a particular aircraft did not do well, the U.S. claims Airbus was not obligated to repay the loan.

In 2012, WTO appellate judges partially sustained the EU claims that tax breaks from the state of Washington were specific and harmful subsidies, meaning they were aimed at a company or group of companies, and had adversely impacted Airbus's sales by allowing Boeing to lower prices. However, the judges rejected EU claims that these subsidies should be categorized more severely as illegal export subsidies. In a comparable case, WTO judges discovered that Airbus benefited from aid in the form of government development loans that included illegal export subsidies affecting Boeing sales. Airbus' jumbo-sized A350 and Boeing's enlarged 777X were not part of the WTO case but were expected to be raised in compliance procedures that would determine what, if any, sanctions would be imposed.

The Washington state tax break for Boeing extends to over 20 years and only partially lowers the sales tax on Boeing aircrafts. Boeing receives tax benefits only after it invests its own funds into development and delivering aircrafts to customers. It is Boeing that bears all of the development and investment risk upfront. In contrast, Airbus has enjoyed launch aid that basically shifts risk away from the market. Since 1970, Airbus has been able to utilize $15 billion USD in government loans, specifically $3.2 billion USD for the A380. The launch aid has protected Airbus from the same market risks that Boeing and other commercial competitors have to deal with. The greatest benefit conferred to Airbus is that the company is not required to pay back the loans if the aircraft program proves to be unsuccessful. Between 2010 and 2012, the WTO ruled against Boeing and Airbus receiving billions of dollars of aid. This decision was viewed as a victory for both the EU and the U.S. New aircraft development by both companies has sparked new debates over whether they are obeying the WTO case rulings or disregarding the courts decision and continuing to receive financial support.

The EU has contemplated whether to pressure the U.S. by challenging tax incentives accorded to Boeing. These incentives encouraged Boeing to keep production of its latest jet in Washington state. The potential movement of production would have created tension between parties in what was deemed the largest ever, decade-old formal trade dispute over aircraft industry aid. Both Brussels and Washington continued to accuse one another of failing to comply with the WTO rulings and encouraged the imposition of sanctions as punishment for the guilty party.

The European Commission and its member states have also been accused of financing the development, expansion, and upgrade of manufacturing facilities at certain Airbus subcontractors through the European Investment Bank. According to Boeing, at least $15 billion USD in launch aid has assisted Airbus in developing new aircrafts without the company having to incur full commercial risk. If the company had secured the loan on commercial terms, it would have additional debt exceeding $100 billion USD.

In return, European officials, ministers from Britain, France, Germany, and Spain, disputed the $8.7 billion USD tax break issued by Washington state.

European Commission trade spokesman John Clancy called Washington's actions "the largest targeted state tax incentive for the civil aerospace industry in U.S. history. The EU is very concerned about the extension of these subsidies which indeed figure—originally and as extended—in the EU's WTO case on subsidies to Boeing, but it declines to comment further on the ongoing litigation."[a]

The latest maneuvers risk deepening an already bitter industrial and trade fight between the two plane makers as the 406-seat Boeing 777X and a large version of the A350 compete for billions of dollars of sales. Washington's state legislature agreed in November 2014 to implement tax break as Boeing considered whether to build the newest version of a successful 777 wide body jet in the Seattle area. The package exceeds the estimated cost of developing the 777X, suggesting Boeing is getting an aircraft "fully funded by the U.S. taxpayer," Airbus spokeswoman Maggie Bergsma said.

> Boeing said tax decisions by Washington were meant for the whole industry in the state, including some Airbus suppliers, and have been designed to comply with WTO rulings. "The $8.7 billion figure that's mentioned is the state's estimate of the total value of its incentives for the entire commercial aerospace industry over 16 years," Boeing spokesman Charlie Miller said. "The benefit to Boeing will only be a fraction of that amount." The WTO was expected to report on whether Europe had obeyed WTO rulings in the summer 2014, followed by a similar report on the U.S. track record that was expected about six months later. Those findings were to include a level of damage that would set the bar for possible sanctions, but most trade analysts say that in practice these could be years away.[b]

Notes

a.   Hepher, T. (2014, May 19). EU may challenge $8.7 billion U.S. tax breaks in Boeing-Airbus trade dispute. *Reuters*. Retrieved from www.reuters.com/article/us-trade-aircraft-subsidies-exclusive-idUSBREA4I03W20140519
b.   Ibid.

Sources

1.   Hepher, T. (2014, May 19). EU may challenge $8.7 billion U.S. tax breaks in Boeing-Airbus trade dispute. *Reuters*. Retrieved from www.reuters.com/article/us-trade-aircraft-subsidies-exclusive-idUSBREA4I03W20140519
2.   Stearns, J., Freedman, J. M., and Rothman, A. (2010, September 15). WTO rules Boeing got illegal U.S. aid, officials say. *Bloomberg Business Week*. Retrieved from   www.bloomberg.com/news/articles/2010-09-15/wto-rules-boeing-got-illegal-u-s-government-development-aid-france-says
3.   Holmes, S. (2005, March 20). Boeing vs. Airbus: Time to escalate. *Bloomberg Business Week*. Retrieved from www.bloomberg.com/news/articles/2005-03-20/boeing-vs-dot-airbus-time-to-escalate

Questions for Case Discussion

1.   What was the ruling of the WTO regarding the trade dispute between Boeing and Airbus?
2.   How was the form of subsidies by Airbus different from that by Boeing? Who do you think has more substantially subsidized the manufacturing of new airplanes and why?
3.   Why do think that the EU and the U.S. government have been supporting the production of commercial airplanes?

Case 2.4 The Influence of the U.S. Foreign Policy toward China on Trade

U.S. foreign policy has reached a turning point, as analysts from across the political spectrum dust off Cold War-era arguments and instead advocate for the implementation of a containment policy against China. Previous sentiments from Washington supporting a "constructive engagement" with Beijing have disappeared. President Obama's "pivot to Asia" strategy is designed to both calm American allies and recognize the continent's great strategic importance in the twenty-first century. This is why the U.S. is bringing advanced American combat ships to Singapore, Marines to Australia, and military advisers to the Philippines. Japan, America's key partner in Asia, is rearming and has adjusted its pacifist postwar constitution to allow its forces to play a bigger role in the region. The country has decided to increase its activity to help preserve the independence of smaller Asian nations who fear they might have no choice but to yield to China's ambitions of territorial extension and thus its regional influence.

Former President Barack Obama was determined to sell his trade agenda, like the Trans-Pacific Partnership, by warning that failure to reach an agreement would help China overshadow the U.S. as the global trade arbitrator. Even some of the president's supporters on trade claimed he was exaggerating the Chinese threat, which may weaken relations with Beijing. The Chinese suspected that the U.S. would attempt to constrain China and Mr. Obama's trade argument seemed to reaffirm these suspicions.

> The president's "message is designed for a domestic audience, but it can feed the perception in Asia that the U.S. is trying to limit China's ambitions," said Matthew Goodman, a former Obama White House economic aide. China is completely convinced the U.S. is pursuing a containment policy. Mr. Kevin Rudd, the former Australian prime minister, in a recent Harvard study, summarized Beijing's outlook toward the U.S.'s proposed trade agenda in five bullet points: to isolate China, contain it, diminish it, internally divide it and sabotage its political leadership. China believes this is evidenced in the U.S.'s conclusion of the TPP, a 12-nation trade deal, that included the U.S., Vietnam, Australia, Japan but not China. Mr. Rudd made China a key piece of his pitch for concluding the trade deal, "We've got to make sure that we're writing those trade rules in Asia as opposed to having China write those rules for us," he said. "If China comes out ahead," he added, "American businesses as well as American workers will lose." He stressed that the U.S. wants China to be successful and play a leading role in the global economy.[a]

It is not difficult to see that foreign-policy rationales have been used to sell trade deals. Constituents can more easily understand the political rhetoric than the tedious details of trade agreements. President Bill Clinton argued that the NAFTA would strengthen Mexico and contain Japan's ambitions in the Western hemisphere. Japan, not China, was once viewed as the U.S.'s main economic foe. The Bush administration argued that Colombia needed a free trade agreement with the U.S. to boost the country's embattled democratic principles. When President Nixon was in office, he could not have envisioned China's transformation into a major global player. Trade and technology were the main drivers for this change that has resulted in China and the U.S. becoming each other's second largest trading partners. Furthermore, China is the U.S.'s biggest creditor but trade deals are ultimately about economic benefits. The U.S. and China approach trade expansion differently. Mr. David Dollar, a former Obama administration official who served as the Treasury representative in Beijing and a Brookings Institution scholar, states that:

> China focuses on the "hardware of trade." China provides financing to developing countries so that they can build ports, airports, roads and other infrastructure, which are necessary for global trade. China's recent push for the creation of the Asian Infrastructure Investment Bank (AIIB), without U.S. involvement, and Chinese megaprojects across Central Asia to boost trade over land and by sea are part of the country's overarching expansion strategy. "Those projects will continue whether or not the U.S. wraps up the trade deals it seeks," said He Fan, an economist at the Chinese Academy of Social Sciences. But when trade rules are concerned, what Mr. Dollar refers to as "the software of trade," the U.S. is the undisputed champion with China a distant laggard. Trade rules are extremely important since they determine when tariffs can be imposed on goods, the level of protection afforded to intellectual property and investments, which subsidies have been approved, and how government make purchases, among many other issues. Since World War II, the U.S. has largely set those rules and persuaded other nations to accept them in regional and global trade pacts.[b]

The former Obama administration acquired congressional approval for fast-track authority, which obliges Congress to vote "yes" or "no" on a trade deal but not amend it. This achievement definitely expedited the conclusion of the TPP negotiation, which in turn the U.S. wanted to use to expand the countries covered by these trade rules. Washington argued that the new TPP standards, specifically e-commerce and the conduct of state-owned industries, could ultimately influence Chinese behavior because they would become the new criteria. Whether China accepts TPP standards or not, it is not demanding an alternative agenda on the U.S. Instead, the U.S. encouraged China to be more aggressive in formulating its trade policy. U.S. Trade Representative Michael Froman urged China to be aggressive in reducing tariffs to help complete multilateral agreements in information technology and environmental goods, and to cut agricultural subsidies to help revitalize negotiations for a global trade deal, i.e. Doha Round.

Since China was excluded from the TPP deal, the country has joined negotiations for another trade talk, the 16-nation Regional Comprehensive Economic Partnership (RCEP). The RCEP is a proposed free trade agreement (FTA) between the ten member states of the Association of Southeast Asian Nations (ASEAN) and the six states with which ASEAN has existing

FTAs. RCEP negotiations were formally launched in November 2012 at the ASEAN Summit in Cambodia. Trade experts predicted that as China has taken a back seat in those talks to Southeast Asian nations and India, the results of these negotiations are expected to be modest: perhaps a slight reduction in tariffs. The aforementioned agreement is hardly comparable to the TPP. Now that the U.S. has pulled out of the TPP with the installation of the new Trump government, the remaining countries may consider China as an important option for expanded trade. It is noteworthy that Chinese President Xi Jinping has recently claimed to assume the mantle of market globalism.

Notes

a.   Davis, B. (2015, May 4). The U.S.–China disconnect on trade deals. *Wall Street Journal*. Retrieved from www.wsj.com/articles/the-u-s-china-disconnect-on-trade-deals-1430681997
b.   Ibid.

Sources

1.   Davis, B. (2015, May 4). The U.S.–China disconnect on trade deals. *Wall Street Journal*. Retrieved from www.wsj.com/articles/the-u-s-china-disconnect-on-trade-deals-1430681997
2.   Browne, A. (2015, June 13). The China rethink: As tensions with China rise, U.S. foreign policy thinkers are dusting off ideas from the Cold War and starting to reconsider the decades-long consensus behind 'constructive engagement' with Beijing. *Wall Street Journal*: C.1.

Questions for Case Discussion

1.   How does U.S. foreign policy influence its trade policy in East Asia, particularly in the context of U.S.–China relations?
2.   What is China's response to the U.S. suggestion of linking China's foreign policy to its trade policy?
3.   How is the U.S. approach to trade expansion different from the Chinese approach?

Case 2.5 Trade Facilitation Deal at the WTO Bali Meeting

The collapse of a global trade agreement centered on simplifying customs rules will make it extremely difficult for the World Trade Organization (WTO) to complete its much-delayed Doha round of negotiations. Doha Round multilateral trade negotiation (MTN) has been dealing with a trade agenda to reduce tariffs and lower trade as well as non-tariff barriers (NTBs).

In December 2013 at a meeting in Bali, the Indonesian island, the WTO's 160 members agreed to improve customs procedures by "reducing red tape"—a trade facilitation deal that some analysts estimate could increase trade and thus add $1 trillion USD to the global economy. The WTO had set July 31, 2014 as the deadline to finalize the agreement. At the Bali meeting, the countries had also agreed that by the end of 2017 they would renegotiate existing rules regarding agricultural subsidies. India is concerned that the current regulations are overly restrictive and could hurt the nation's ability to store grains to ensure food security.

The trade facilitation deal is aimed primarily at developing and emerging economies, and attempts to encourage these economies to set and implement required standards to improve ports and customs to world class status. Yet, numerous legal loopholes and broad use of language and terms such as "as soon as possible," "to the extent practicable," and "as appropriate" has weakened the overall structure and enforceability of the agreement and allowed developing countries to delay its implementation.

Moreover, the agreement requires that rich countries finance the improvement of customs and trading procedures in poorer ones. Thus, the deal would operate less like a traditional reciprocal WTO agreement and more as a half-hearted aid program. Undefined terms stating when aid will be provided displays a lack of commitment, which has inevitably caused developing countries to delay adoption of the aforementioned measures. India vetoed the final agreement on customs rules, stating the effort to promote global trade should be linked to food security. A similar issue negated the enactment of a deal at the Doha Round negotiations in 2008.[a]

Recently, India has insisted that the WTO expedite negotiations over agricultural subsidies. Under WTO rules, agreements must be adopted unanimously before they can be sent to the legislature of each country for ratification; two-thirds of the countries have to ratify trade deals for them to become effective. India's actions prompted criticism from WTO members, some of whom claim that India's brinkmanship could undermine the international trading system, the country has essentially used trade talks to focus and force a change on a domestic issue.[b]

India has expanded its food subsidy program. Under this program, the government purchases wheat and rice from farmers at above-market prices, hoards the grain, and sells a portion to consumers at much lower prices. WTO rules on food stockpiling and subsidizing create a problem for India. The WTO has a formula that defines how much money a country can spend creating a safety food stockpile to support both farmers and citizens. India wants the rules modified so that it can exceed predefined limits. Other countries such as the U.S. and Pakistan, have complained that the program distorts trade. One of the major concerns is that India is storing so much grain, with millions of tons rotting due to lack of storage space, that the country in response will dump some of it onto the world market, depressing global prices, and hurting farmers in other countries.

The Bali pact, which India's previous government supported, included an agreement by the U.S., the EU, and other nations that stated no countries could challenge the food policies of India and other developing nations while the food subsidy rules were being renegotiated. The outlines of the agreement detailed methods on how to improve access to global trade markets, by 2014, and solve food security issues (stockpiling and subsidies), by 2017. Countries whose current stockpiles exceed WTO guidelines would get a reprieve until 2017. Originally, India agreed to grant the WTO four years to find a permanent solution, but it appears now that the country wants a solution before it will approve the trade facilitation package. It is disappointing that Prime Minister Modi's cabinet, which was elected in part because it promised to revive India's economy, did not fully support the proposed agreements in Bali.

Indian officials downplayed their veto of the agreement, stating that July 31, 2014 was an arbitrary deadline and that trade negotiators could sign the agreement by September. Anjali Prasad, India's ambassador to the WTO, said,

> This is important so that the millions of farmers and the poor families who depend on domestic food stocks do not have to live in constant fear. The adoption of the (trade facilitation) protocol should be postponed until a permanent solution on public stockholding for food security is found.[c]

The Bali agreement was supposed to represent a package of "low-hanging-fruit" or policies to which every country could easily agree upon. It was an attempt to rejuvenate the long-stalled WTO talks of the Doha Round that began in Qatar in 2001. The Doha Round was an ambitious plan to open up more trade sectors within the global economy but progress has been hindered because the WTO depends on consensus for decisions and countries can't agree on many of the controversial issues such as agricultural subsidies and anti-dumping. This latest failure will further erode confidence in the MTN, and it will encourage officials in the U.S., the EU, China, and Japan to pursue more regional and bilateral trade deals. Unfortunately, those deals often leave out the smallest and poorest nations, as mentioned by Roberto Carvalho de Azevêdo, the general director of the WTO. It remains to be seen whether the Doha negotiations will be revitalized.

Notes

a.   Beattie, A. (2014, July 17). Smoothing rough trade without the WTO. *Financial Times*. Retrieved from http://blogs.ft.com/beyond-brics/2014/07/17/smoothing-rough-trade-without-the-wto/
b.   *New York Times*. (2014, August 3). Global trade talks suffer another setback. Retrieved from www.nytimes.com/2014/08/04/opinion/global-trade-talks-suffer-another-setback.html?_r=0
c.   Bellman, E. and Kenny, P. (2014, July 27). India blocks WTO agreement to ease trade rules. *Wall Street Journal*.

Sources

1.   Beattie, A. (2014, July 17). Smoothing rough trade without the WTO. *Financial Times*. Retrieved from http://blogs.ft.com/beyond-brics/2014/07/17/smoothing-rough-trade-without-the-wto/
2.   Bellman, E. and Kenny, P. (2014, July 27). India blocks WTO agreement to ease trade rules. *Wall Street Journal*. Retrieved from www.wsj.com/articles/india-blocks-wto-agreement-to-ease-trade-rules-1406471335

3.   Ayres, A. (2014, July 30). India: Tough talk and the Bali Trade Facilitation Agreement. *Forbes*. Retrieved from www.forbes.com/sites/alyssaayres/2014/07/30/india-tough-talk-and-the-bali-trade-facilitation-agreement-2/#7177029f2b95
4.   *New York Times*. (2014, August 3). Global trade talks suffer another setback. Retrieved from www.nytimes.com/2014/08/04/opinion/global-trade-talks-suffer-another-setback.html?_r=0

Questions for Case Discussion

1.   What was the trade facilitation deal signed at the Bali WTO meeting in 2013? What does the implementation of this deal signify?
2.   Why did India veto the final agreement on this deal?
3.   What is the likely impact of the failure of the trade facilitation deal on the agreement of the WTO's Doha Round negotiation?

Trade

Rhetoric and Practice

I. The Recent Trend in Global Trade

The continued growth in free trade contributes not only to national economic development but also world economic growth. As mentioned in Chapter 1, increase in international trade and FDI have been the two main drivers of the global economy. However, world trade, which used to grow faster than GDP, seems to have slowed down. It has registered less than 3 percent of annual growth rate in real terms from 2013 to 2015.[1] Figure 2.1 shows the largest global exporters as of 2014. According to the WTO data, the 1960s were the peak decade for world trade mainly due to an extended global supply chain. Trade growth slowed after that, until the 1990s when China started participating in the global economy. Growth in global trade volumes, however, has slowed again in recent years, due to a sluggish economic recovery from the global financial crisis and the changing structure of the Chinese *2008* economy.[2] During rapid economic growth periods for the past three or four decades, China used to import in large volume not only raw materials to build its infrastructure but also intermediary products to assemble finally

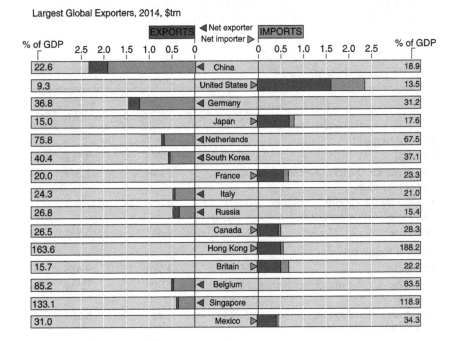

Figure 2.1 Trade Flows

Source: IMF.

manufactured goods. Now China makes the parts and components and assembles them itself, reducing the dependence on trade, shifting to a more consumption-based economy.

As Table 2.1 indicates, the slowdown in international trade has been noted mainly in manufacturing, not in services, which makes the supply chain argument more compelling. In fact, services account for a larger share of global GDP than ever before, Cross-border trade in services accounts for one-fifth of global trade, even without including international transactions through foreign affiliates and the temporary movement of people.[3]

> The trade of services is the future and the way we define world trade volumes will need to be changed as a result. If we look at smartphones, only a percentage of the work that goes into this product is hardware. The services which are provided in terms of software updates also need to be accounted for.[4]

As Case 2.1 illustrates, the fast-track authority accorded to President Obama expedited negotiations for a huge trade deal with countries on the Pacific Rim, i.e. the Trans-Pacific Partnership (TPP) agreement. Although its future becomes uncertain with the recent withdrawal of the U.S., the recently signed TPP agreement would increase freer trade in services, which account for most of developed countries' GDP but only a small share of trade. Opening up trade in services could help reduce the cost of everything from shipping to banking, education, and health care. Pharmaceuticals are subject to the same testing regimes, and standards on everything from car design to chemical

Table 2.1 Global Trade Statistics

	% Change 2010 to 2014	% Change 2013 to 2014	% Change 2012 to 2014
Global Imports			
Services	25.981	3.484	9.562
• Charges for the use of intellectual property n.i.e.	30.079	6.944	12.874
• Telecommunications, computer, and information services	29.079	0.880	12.702
Products	22.947	0.837	2.814
Global Exports			
Services	26.70	4.188	9.878
• Charges for the use of intellectual property	22.29	2.009	5.734
• Telecommunications, computer, and information services	33.73	0.721	9.509
Products	23.95	0.576	3.138

Source: ITC, UNCTAD, WTO.

labeling are harmonized or mutually recognized. Labor markets, too, stand to become loosened, and workers' rights more accessible. Exposing professional occupations to the same global competition that factory workers have faced for decades could even help reduce the income inequality that former president Obama so often used to decry.[5]

Reflecting the increased importance of service trade,

> the WTO and the World Bank have agreed to jointly develop and maintain a database on trade in services. The joint database covers various sectors in more than 100 countries, such as financial, transportation, tourism, retail, telecommunications, and business services, including law and accounting. Transparency is particularly important in the dynamic area of trade in services because the regulatory framework is complex and little information is publicly available.[6]

In the following section, we will review the old trade theories first.

II. Neoclassical Trade Theories

A single country cannot produce everything it needs. Benefits from trade are rather obvious as exchanging goods and services between countries will benefit both countries. Trade leads to specialization and specialization is more efficient. In other words, international trade will allow countries to gain access to each other's products that one or the other country cannot produce efficiently. The origin of the trade theory goes back to the sixteenth century where then European superpowers Great Britain, Spain, and the Netherlands fiercely competed in searching for colonies that would provide them with treasures such as gold and silver. As the accumulation of national wealth was determined by the amount of treasure, mercantilism promoted exports while discouraging imports. As such, mercantilism is based on the premise that trade is not a positive sum but a zero-sum game in which only those exporting countries benefit from it while importing countries do not gain anything. Japan's attempt to accumulate a trade surplus in the 1970s and 1980s and the similar effort of China since the 1990s have been described as new mercantilism.

1. Absolute Advantage

Recognizing the shortcomings of the intellectual foundation of mercantilism, in the late eighteenth century, British economist Adam Smith advanced the theory of absolute advantage in his seminal book *The Wealth of Nations*, arguing that any country can find a product that it can produce more efficiently than another country. For example, Bangladesh produces textiles, garments, and clothing more efficiently than Ethiopia while the latter produces shoes more efficiently than the first. Adam Smith corrected the logical flaw of the mercantilist assumption that trade is a zero-sum game in which only one country gains at the expense of the other country. He proved that trade is a positive sum game that allows both countries to benefit from trade as the consumption in each country increases after trade.

2. Comparative Advantage

Case 2.2 explains why it would make more sense for China to manufacture U.S. Olympic uniforms based on the comparative advantage theory. David Ricardo advanced the comparative advantage theory that refined the logical reasoning of the absolute advantage theory by answering a question that the absolute advantage theory could not.[7] What if a certain country can produce multiple products more efficiently than other countries? According to the absolute advantage theory, this particular country is supposed to produce all the products while the other countries produce nothing, which will defeat the very purpose of trade. Based on the concept of opportunity cost, Ricardo argued that even the country that does not have any absolute advantage could have a comparative advantage. The following example in Table 2.2 illustrates the difference between absolute advantage and comparative advantage.

In this example, the U.S. has absolute advantages in producing both cars and smart phones while China has no absolute advantage in either of these two products. According to the theory of absolute advantage, the U.S. should produce both products since American workers are more productive in producing both items. However, using the notion of opportunity cost, the theory of comparative advantage arrives at a different conclusion. While the opportunity cost of producing cars is four smart phones in the U.S., China has to give up 15 units of smart phones in order to produce one more car. Since the opportunity cost of producing cars is much lower in the U.S. than in China, the U.S. should produce and export cars to China and import smart phones from China. Meanwhile, China can also benefit from trade with the U.S. by exporting smart phones whose opportunity cost is lower than in the U.S. Accordingly, the theory of comparative advantage emphasizes that any country can benefit by participating in free trade even though it does not have an absolute advantage.

Does the comparative advantage still hold in this global economy? Thanks to the rapid dissemination of technology, it has become a matter of time before developing countries such as China and India are capable of producing products of almost the same quality as those in developed countries where they were originally invented. If multiple countries are capable of producing a more or less identical product in terms of quality and function, it will make the price of exports steadily decrease. This phenomenon, known as immis-erating effect, questions the validity of the intellectual foundation of the comparative advantage theory since the countries involved in trade cannot gain from it as export prices get caught in a downward spiral.[8]

Table 2.2 Absolute Advantage vs. Comparative Advantage

Country/Product	Cars	Smart Phones
U.S.	8	40
China	2	30

3. Factor Endowment Theory

While both absolute and comparative advantage theories focus on efficiency and productivity of workers in a specific country, the factor endowment theory advanced by Heckscher and Ohlin, two Swedish economists, attributes the cause of trade to the existence of different factors across countries. Countries are endowed with different resources; while countries such as China and India are endowed with an abundant supply of labor, other countries such as Russia and Canada are endowed with massive land. Simply put, this theory argues that a country should produce a product in which it intensively uses the factors that it has in abundant supply. According to this theory, it makes sense that while China takes advantage of its huge supply of labor to produce labor-intensive products, Canada produces agricultural products making the best use of its extensive arable land. In a nutshell, they contend that differences in national factor endowments are the main source of comparative advantage.[9]

4. International Product Life Cycle (IPLC)

Raymond Vernon introduced this theory in the mid-1960s.[10] According to Vernon, a product goes through a life cycle just like a human being as Figure 2.2

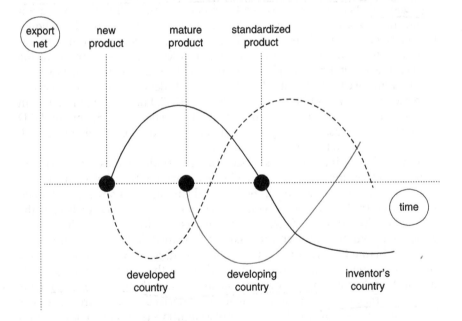

Figure 2.2 International Product Life Cycle

Source: Adapted from Vernon, R. International Investments and International Trade in the Product Life Cycles. Quarterly Journal of Economics, May 1966. 190–207.

illustrates. A product is born, grows and matures, and dies. At the introductory stage, a product is invented and introduced in a developed country like the U.S. Then at the growth stage, the product is introduced to other developed countries that are capable of producing their own products. Afterwards, as the product gets mature and standardized, even developing countries can produce the very same product that the developed country invented first. It is at this stage that the inventing country becomes a net importer of the very same product its company invented. Finally, a new product will replace the existing product as it gets old. This theory was once useful in explaining the trade pattern between developed and developing countries. However, the validity of the IPLC theory has become weaker and weaker as the product life cycle gets shorter and as more companies market and sell their products targeting consumers in the global market, not confined to their respective domestic markets. In other words, we seldom observe the sequential introduction of the products from developed to developing countries in this integrated global economy.

III. Is a Trade Deficit Bad?

Neoclassical trade theories assume that trade is not a zero-sum but a positive-sum game. When countries reduce trade barriers, they all benefit because it allows them to buy and produce goods inexpensively. If this is true, there should be no serious concern about the rising trade deficit since it is a natural phenomenon that will self-correct. However, there is a legitimate concern about the rising trade deficit. For example, a country like the U.S. has continued to accumulate a massive trade deficit. The total U.S. trade deficit in goods and services increased from $476.4 billion USD in 2013 to $505.0 billion USD in 2014, an increase of $28.6 billion USD (6.0 percent). This reflected a $6.5 billion USD (2.9 percent) increase in the services trade surplus and a $35.2 billion USD (5.0 percent) increase in the goods trade deficit.[11]

Meanwhile, China continues to accumulate a trade surplus, amounting to almost $600 billion USD in 2015. This is a stark contrast between the two largest economies of the world, the U.S. and China, also known as G2. Such imbalanced trade leads many Americans to naively believe that China is the principal culprit of the U.S. trade deficit, accusing China of its exchange rate policy manipulation to keep the yuan undervalued. While China might be partly to blame for the chronic U.S. trade deficit, it is not the root cause for this development. If not China, then, what are the main sources of trade deficit? Simply put, when a country consumes more than it produces, it ends up with a trade deficit. The following formula derived from macroeconomics neatly summarizes the two key sources of a country's trade deficit: low savings rate in the private sector and large spending in the government sector.

$$X - M = (S - I) + (T - G)$$ (X: Value of exports, M: Value of imports, S: Savings, I: Investment, T: Taxes, G: Government spending)

A country's trade deficit can be attributed to two major sources: low savings rate from the private sector and large expenditures by the government. A country with a low savings rate and huge government spending ends up with a deficit. A budget deficit combined with a trade deficit is called a twin deficit. Therefore, in order to reduce a country's trade deficit, either domestic savings or tax revenue should increase. Since these options are not easy to implement, a government typically tries to reduce its expenditures, which represents unpopular policy among the middle class who often lose social welfare programs. If the domestic savings rate is not high enough to finance the investment amount required for economic growth, a country has no option but to either borrow money from other countries or attract foreign direct investment to bring in needed capital. The U.S. economy is a case in point. According to Warren Buffett, the U.S. has continued to accumulate a trade deficit because Americans want to consume more than they produce at home. Using the metaphor of squanderville vs. thriftvilles, Buffett warned that the U.S., an example of squanderville, might have to give up its land and other properties to other countries if the country continues to accumulate trade deficits beyond its means.[12] People living in squanderville like to keep spending money in purchasing imported items produced in thriftville and pay their bills by issuing squanderville bucks. Since thriftville people possess all the financial instruments issued by squanderville, they can sell them whenever they start losing confidence in the American economy and can purchase its assets with the proceeds. It is not very likely that such a scenario will become a reality. However, the continued accumulation of the U.S. trade deficit will eventually result in the precipitation of the U.S. dollar value, nullifying its effectiveness as key international currency.

IV. New Trade Theory

The key premise of old or neoclassical trade theory is an argument for free trade that all the countries participating in international trade will be better off. However, free trade critics contend that in the real world, where governments protect and promote industries, things are a lot more complex and complicated than in David Ricardo's model. The key question is, "Is free trade best to exploit comparative advantage?" As some economists question the validity of comparative advantage as discussed above, it becomes increasingly evident that government can play a critical role in changing the terms and conditions of trade in favor of its domestic companies and reap greater trade benefits. In the early 1970s, Paul Krugman advanced a new trade theory that contended not all countries will gain the same degree of benefit from trade as the role of government would make a significant difference in determining how much benefit is accrued from trade.[13] The intellectual foundation of this argument is based on two key concepts: first mover advantage and economies of scale. While old trade theories assume constant returns to specialization, the new trade theory presumes increasing returns to specialization. This means that the units of resources required to produce a certain good are assumed to decrease over a period of time due to first mover advantage and economies of scale. The first mover advantage refers to the benefits that an early entrant into a new industry can enjoy over latecomers, particularly when the industry can accommodate only a few competitors. In this type of industry, e.g. the commercial aircraft industry, late entrants will face a tough challenge in matching the efficient cost structure of the first mover. As we will discuss later, in the acute competition between Boeing and Airbus, they are the only two major companies in the commercial aircraft industry since its industry structure would not allow a third competitor. As Case 2.3 illustrates, both the U.S. and the EU governments recognize how critical a role they play in helping domestic companies gain first mover advantage by providing subsidies such as low-interest loans and tax breaks. Economies of scale describes economic advantages generated when a large scale of output results in substantial savings in unit production costs mainly by spreading fixed costs over a larger volume. The first mover advantage often allows a firm to exploit economies of scale, as it usually dominates the market without the existence of competitors. The significance of new trade theory makes us realize that trade will open a new opportunity for a company to increase volume across countries and thus achieve economies of scale which would have been unavailable without trade. Consumers will benefit from free trade as different companies can now produce different types of products even in the same industry as long as sufficient demand exists for each product to enable the company to attain economies of scale. As such, the new trade theory can explain why intra-industry trade occurs while old trade theories only focused on the phenomenon of inter-industry trade. While companies such as Mercedes-Benz and BMW can produce high-quality, luxurious cars targeting affluent consumers across countries, other automobile companies can serve the needs of consumers in developing countries who can only afford low-end cars.

V. Government Intervention in Free Trade

Although the benefits of free trade have been well recognized, the reality is that government intervention in free trade is almost inevitable. What are the typical arguments used to support government protectionist measures from both political and economic perspectives?

I. Political Argument

The rationale behind protectionism is often driven by political objectives rather than economic reasons. Government may justify its intervention in free trade for the following reasons.

(1) Saving Jobs and Industries

Although this argument is related to an economic reason at first glance as it concerns the loss of jobs and industries, it indeed represents one of the most commonly cited political reasons. Many politicians often use this argument in order to seek political support from their electorates in exchange for promising to keep the jobs for those who are engaged in industries whose comparative advantage is eroding. Steel and textile industries are a case in point as the U.S. continues to lose its comparative advantage. While it argues that countries are better off for trading, that isn't always true for all people—such as the U.S. textile workers who were adversely affected by the conclusion of the NAFTA. It is not difficult to understand why these workers expect the government to save their jobs through protectionist measures. Enormous amounts of farming subsidies prevailing in developed countries such as U.S. and Japan can also be interpreted as politically motivated government efforts to gain support from the farmers.

(2) Protecting Consumer Health

Some governments use the protection of consumer health as an excuse for justifying its intervention in free trade. The advances in biotechnology have allowed great progress in producing genetically modified agricultural and meat products. Hormone-treated beef is a well-publicized case in point. When the EU banned the importation of hormone-treated beef from the U.S. in 1989, U.S. exports declined from $231 million USD in 1988 to $98 million USD in 1994. In response, the U.S. filed a complaint with the WTO in 1995 and the WTO panel ruled that the EU's ban on hormone-treated beef was illegal. As a result, the WTO allowed the U.S. to impose punitive tariffs valued at $120 million USD on hundreds of EU products in 1999. In 2012, the EU reached a deal with the U.S. to continue with the ban but to increase its import quota of high-quality non-hormone treated beef from the U.S.[14]

While Europeans are very reluctant to accept genetically modified organism (GMO) products, Americans seem to be more tolerant about them. Since different people have different attitudes and preferences toward GMO products, a trade dispute is expected to occur whenever there is a cultural clash between two countries involved in trading GMO products.

(3) National Security

Certain items are not allowed to be exported to or imported from other countries for security reasons. For example, the Japanese government has been trying very hard to minimize rice imports from other countries since the country does not want to be dependent upon other countries for their main staple, rice. Most governments of developed countries prohibit defense-related industries from trading key parts or finished products that contain embedded confidential information regarding national security. In this Information Age, the U.S. government is concerned about China's massive cyber campaign to steal trade secrets and intellectual property from American companies.[15] The U.S. government may impose restrictions on trade if it believes that China continues to commit cyber theft of American companies' intellectual property. Chinese officials believe that national security and economic security are inextricably connected.

(4) Supporting Foreign Policy

Trade policy is also used to further government diplomacy. As Case 2.4 indicates, the Obama government used its foreign containment policy against

China to leverage trade policy in Asia as implied by the elimination of China from the TPP. The U.S. government placed a similar trade embargo on Cuba for more than 50 years before it recently normalized its diplomatic relationship with Cuba in 2014. American companies have long been prohibited from exporting to and importing from Cuba to support the U.S. government's diplomacy tactic aimed at removing Fidel Castro, then Cuban dictator. The U.S. has also long maintained trade sanctions against countries such as Iran, Iraq, and North Korea, the so-called axis of evil, in the hope that applying such harsh economic pressures will result in the downfall of totalitarian government and replacement with a democratic government.

(5) Human Rights Protection

Human rights issues in developing countries are often cited to leverage protectionism by developed countries. Before China became a member of the WTO, the U.S. Congress used to annually discuss human rights issues in China to determine whether the most favored nation (MFN) status should be renewed or not, criticizing the Chinese government's lack of effort to improve its domestic human rights situation. The U.S. government took a similar approach to handling human rights issues in Myanmar by linking these issues to its trade policy highlighted by the economic embargo on the country until 2013 when the new democratic government was installed.[16]

2. Economic Arguments

(1) Infant Industry Arguments

This represents the oldest argument that justifies government intervention of developing countries to protect its new industry that cannot compete with well-established competitors from developed countries. Intuitively, it makes sense to nurture and support a new industry until it grows to become strong enough to match the cost structure and quality of counterparts from developed countries. However, this argument has two pitfalls. First, a government should be able to select the right industry that it believes has high growth potential to become internationally competitive. It is not always easy to accurately forecast and predict successful industries. Second, determining when to remove protectionist policies is just as difficult as choosing which industry to protect at first. The removal of government protection often faces strong resistance from an industry that has long enjoyed government protection. This is why the infant industry argument often defeats its original purpose, resulting in inefficient and unviable companies who cannot survive in the global market.

(2) Strategic Trade Policy

While developing countries often use the infant industry argument to defend their protectionist measures, strategic trade policy is a typical argument employed by developed countries. This trade policy reflects the rationale behind the new trade theory that emphasizes the first mover advantage and benefits from economies of scale. Strategic trade policy provides the intellectual foundation for a more sophisticated trade policy that a developed country's government can devise in order to help its domestic companies gain first mover advantage. The government can construct a strategy to change the terms and conditions of the competition to favor its domestic companies over foreign competitors. Case in point, the recent trade dispute between Boeing and Airbus at the WTO as described in Case 2.3. Boeing and Airbus filed complaints with the WTO accusing one another of violating the WTO's free trade provisions. The WTO concluded that the subsidies both companies had been receiving from their respective governments to build commercial airplanes were illegal. The U.S. had used federal government grants and state taxes to support the development of the Boeing 787 while the EU had provided launch aid, risk free loans to finance the upfront costs necessary to build the Airbus 380.

VI. Porter's Diamond Model

Michael Porter, Professor at Harvard University, created the diamond model in which he explains why a certain country continues to sustain a competitive advantage in a particular industry.[17] For example, Germany continues to enjoy a strong position in high-end automobiles while Japan is known for producing excellent consumer electronic appliances, appealing to consumers around the world. More recently, South Korea joined Japan as a global competitor of consumer electronic appliances; Samsung has become the largest producer of smart phones and LG has also gained a solid position in the global market for refrigerators and LED TVs. How can we explain the remarkable success of each of these industries from different countries? As Figure 2.3 illustrates, Porter attributes this achievement to the following four elements: factor conditions; demand conditions; supporting and related industries; and firm strategy, structure, and domestic rivalry.

Factor conditions: While Heckscher and Ohlin first advanced the factor endowment theories, Porter refined their theory by classifying the factors into two different categories: basic factors and advanced factors. While basic factors consist of natural factor endowment such as labor, land, and climate, advanced factors are created by the provision of quality education and effective training. A government can play a critical role in developing advanced factors such as software engineers and microchip designers. As advanced factors have become significantly more important than basic factors in this era, in the knowledge economy AKA the Information Age, countries without basic factor endowment can overcome disadvantages by creating specialized and sophisticated factors. The success of made-in-Japan or made-in-Korea products in the global market provides a good testimony to this claim.

Demand conditions: Two important components influence the shape of different demand conditions across countries. First, consumers are likely to demand certain types of products and/or services due to the specific physical

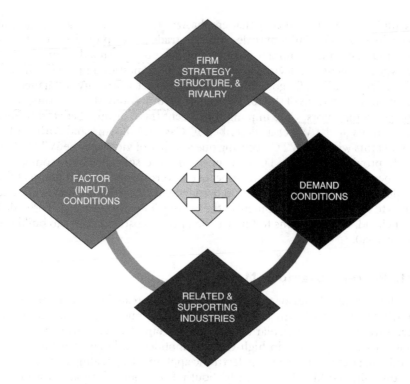

Figure 2.3 Porter's Diamond Model

Source: Porter, Michael E. (1990). *The Competitive Advantage of Nations.* New York: Free Press, p. 136.

countenance and unique environment in which they are living. For example, it is not a coincidence why Nokia was the forerunner of manufacturing mobile phones. Because Finland gets large amounts of snow in the winter, telephone lines put underground may not function properly during cold seasons. This creates a natural demand for mobile phones that work in any weather conditions. In other words, the weather conditions created a demand for mobile phones so that Finns could communicate with one another. Similarly, Japanese companies invented miniature consumer electronic appliances and fuel-efficient compact cars to accommodate Japan's small living spaces and narrow streets. Second, demanding and sophisticated consumers continue to apply pressures on producers to keep improving existing products to satisfy their unfilled needs and wants. Korean and Japanese consumers are known for being selective. They have access to a variety of high-quality products that are widely available. For example, Korean consumers continually demand that new features be added to their cellular phones and automobiles. This explains why Samsung and LG put out new products in the market every six months or so.

Supporting and related industry: Another key element of Porter's model emphasizes the development of supporting and related industries that provide high-quality parts and components to final manufacturers. It highlights the importance of the existence of an industry cluster that creates both forward and backward linkages. For example, in order to establish a competitive automobile industry, a country should develop computer, steel, and rubber industries that produce critical parts and components to manufacture cars. Without the strong presence of these supporting industries, the development of an auto industry is almost impossible. A heavy reliance on imported parts and components from another country would hamper the successful growth of the auto industry. Hyundai and Kia Motors producing key automobile parts and components such as the engine and transmission, reducing their dependence on Japanese suppliers, signified the rise of the South Korean automobile industry in the global market. This element also explains why countries such as Japan and Germany continue to lead the global automobile market.

Firm strategy, structure, and rivalry: First, Porter noted that management philosophy and the profile of top management influence a firm's strategy and structure. If people with financial backgrounds mainly occupy top management, they are likely to emphasize short-term profitability to meet the expectations of shareholders. Meanwhile, top managers with engineering backgrounds tend to put higher priority on long-term market share and product improvement over short-term profitability. U.S. companies represent the former case while Japanese and German counterparts illustrate the latter. Fierce competition among rival companies is also critical to sustain pressure on domestic companies to deliver high-quality products at reasonable prices. Products that have already survived intense domestic competition are likely to be readily accepted in the global market. This is how Japanese consumer electronic appliances and German automobiles have established strong reputations in the global market.

Porter's diamond model is not a trade theory in itself yet it offers critical insights into the significance of key elements that a country should advance in order to sell its products to global consumers. However, Porter's diamond has been criticized as a home-based model since he fails to incorporate the effects of multinational activities occurring across borders in his model. For example, in this Global Age, consumer demand is not limited to the domestic market but expanded globally. Likewise, firms can procure key parts and components from global suppliers who provide the best mix between low cost and differentiation. Such an offshoring option will allow them strategic flexibility without solely relying on domestic suppliers although their strong establishment at home contributes to enhancing the competitiveness of their local manufacturers. Overcoming the limitation of Porter's home-based model, scholars have extended his model into the double diamond model by incorporating multinational activities.[18] For example, scholars argue that both inbound and outbound FDI are important in improving a country's factor conditions, advanced factors in particular.

Finally, we will briefly take a look at the evolution of global organizations that have served as the vanguards of free trade.

VII. Global Trade Governing Systems: GATT and WTO

1. General Agreement on Tariffs and Trade (GATT) and the Uruguay Round

The GATT was created in 1947 by 23 countries to promote free trade after the end of World War II. Since its foundation, it has sponsored the multilateral trade negotiations (MTNs), called "Rounds", in order to reduce and ultimately eliminate tariffs through the application of the most favored nation (MFN) clause. Overall, while tariff barriers have been substantially reduced since the establishment of the GATT, non-tariff barriers (NTBs) are on the rise. Starting with the Geneva Round, the GATT sponsored eight rounds of MTNs from 1947 to 1993. The Uruguay Round was the last and the most comprehensive MTN that brought about remarkable success in reducing trade barriers. The key achievements of the Uruguay Round include an adequate protection of intellectual property rights, reduction of agricultural subsidies, and the creation of the WTO. First, developed countries wanted to assure that their intellectual property rights, such as patents copyrights and trademarks, were adequately protected. Second, the WTO was created as an umbrella organization that took over all the domains of the GATT and two additional functions: first, promotion of free trade on services and second, assurance of adequate protection of intellectual property rights. The Agreement on Trade-related Aspects of Intellectual Property Rights (TRIPS) is an effort to harmonize different standards across countries by introducing intellectual property law into the international trading system for the first time. Finally, the EU was the main opponent to the agricultural subsidy issue but the GATT member countries eventually agreed to substantially reduce agricultural subsidies.

2. World Trade Organization and Doha Round

As mentioned above, the WTO was created under the Uruguay Round of the GATT in 1995 as an umbrella organization that took over all the functions of the GATT. Its purpose is to oversee the rules of trade among the member countries, with the goal of promoting free trade. The WTO continued to increase its membership to 162 countries, as of December, 2015. Overall, the track record of the WTO has been encouraging. Because the WTO's mandate extended to the promotion of free trade in services, remarkable achievements were made in the telecommunication and financial services sectors. The WTO has also strengthened its mechanism through which trade disputes are settled. While the GATT handled a total of roughly 200 trade dispute cases over almost half a century, the WTO dealt with more than 400 cases between 1995 and 2013.[19]

The Doha Round represents the very first MTN sponsored by the WTO. The WTO launched the Doha Round discussion in 2001 but unfortunately has not been able to reach an agreement to date due to conflicting interests among the member states. From a procedural perspective, the impasse partly results from the requirement that all WTO members are expected to settle trade negotiation by consensus. It is understandable that 162 member countries is too many to easily reach an agreement. From a substance perspective, conflicts of interest involving various intractable issues remain not only between developed and developing countries but also among developed countries. For example, the U.S. and Japan blame each other for subsidizing agricultural industries while India has its own agenda to protect its domestic farmers as indicated in Case 2.5.

Agricultural subsidies: Developed countries have provided a significant amount of subsidies to their farmers. In aggregate, they spend more than $300 billion USD a year to subsidize their farmers. Government subsidies account for 21 percent of the cost of agricultural production in the U.S., 35 percent in the EU, and 59 percent in Japan.[20] These subsidies create surplus production, which in turn leads to dumping and depressed prices. The U.N. estimates that producers in developing countries lose $50 billion USD export revenue due to depressed prices.[21] Similarly, developing countries such as India and Brazil also overproduce agricultural products to feed a number of people living in poverty, resulting in substantial decreases in agricultural products.

Anti-dumping issues: Many developing countries have blamed the U.S. for abusing its anti-dumping act to penalize companies who allegedly market their products below production costs or fair market price. 4,230 cases of dumping charges were filed at the WTO between 1995 and 2012.[22] Among the developing countries, India and China rank very high in terms of the number of dumping practices with which they were charged. Developing countries are asking the U.S to clarify what constitutes as dumping. These countries are also assessing how they can reduce dumping incidents.

Intellectual property rights: While developed countries want to strengthen the protection of their use and sale of intellectual property, developing countries want greater access to public use of intellectual property. For example, patients afflicted with AIDS need serious treatment. Adequate protection of intellectual property rights is critical in order to keep the incentives for pharmaceutical companies to conduct research to develop new medicines to cure fatal diseases like AIDS. However, the prices of original products are too expensive for people in developing countries to purchase. Developing countries want to produce generic products to substitute expensive original products. So, the challenge remains as to how we can harmonize the interests of MNCs with those of the general public that a society is responsible for taking care of.

In addition to these issues, the finalizing trade agreements has become more difficult as developed countries increasingly want to link trade issues to non-trade issues such as labor and environment protection. For example, the TPP agreement is based less on dismantling tariff barriers and more on tackling tough issues such as intellectual property, labor, and environmental standards which many developing countries are trying to avoid.

A glimpse of hope to save the Doha Round was revived at the Bali meeting held in December 2013 when WTO members agreed to facilitate trade by streamlining the customs process. The Organization for Economic Cooperation and Development (OECD) estimates that the saving from streamlining procedures could be 2–15 percent of the value of the goods traded.[23] However, since the new Indian government refused the implementation of the signed agreement as illustrated in Case 2.5, future prospects to reach any kind of agreement among the WTO members has become increasingly uncertain.

VIII. Regional Trading Agreement vs. Multilateral Trading Agreement

As the MTN of the Doha Round was caught in impasse, bilateral or regional free trade agreements (RFTAs) have substantially increased. As Figure 2.4 illustrates, the number of RFTAs has risen from around 70 in 1990 to more than 270 today.[24] As an example of bilateral free trade agreement, the U.S. and Korea signed the KOREA-US Free Trade Agreement (KORUS FTA) in March 2012. KORUS FTA made South Korea open its domestic market of automobiles and agricultural products, two of its most restricted areas, to foreign competition. Average agricultural tariffs were 49 percent while average non-agricultural tariffs were 12.2 percent before the conclusion of the KORUS FTA. Upon KORUS FTA's entry into force, almost two-thirds of Korea's agricultural imports from the United States have become duty free. South Korea also immediately cut its tariffs on U.S. auto imports from 8 percent to 4 percent and will fully eliminate the tariff by 2017. Overall, U.S. passenger vehicle exports to Korea have increased 80 percent following the implementation of the KORUS FTA. By 2013, the number of imported cars sold in Korea had risen 250 percent to 156,497 units, accounting for 12.1 percent of the 1,137,027 vehicles sold in that year.[25]

The most comprehensive RFTA is the Trans-Pacific Partnership (TPP) concluded in October 2015. The TPP was intended to encompass 12 econo-

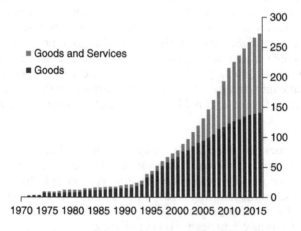

■ Goods and Services

■ Goods

1970 1975 1980 1985 1990 1995 2000 2005 2010 2015

Figure 2.4 Cumulative Number of Regional Free Trade Agreements

Source: UNCTAD; WTO.

mies of the Pacific Rim including the U.S. and Japan. These 12 countries together account for 40 percent of world GDP and one-third of world trade. American trade negotiators predicted that by 2025 the TPP would increase $220 billion a year adding roughly 1% to world GDP.[26] The U.S. government has also been working hard to conclude another similar mega free trade deal, the Transatlantic Trade and Investment Partnership (TTIP), with the EU.

Two competing perspectives exist with regard to the RFTA. The progressive view includes the following arguments. First, regional deals can act as bridges to wider liberalization. Second, the RFTA will create incentives for other nations to join or encourage other nations to negotiate their own RFTA. Third, trade barriers around the world would fall, one by one, and political support for multilateral deals would increase. However, negative impacts should not be overlooked. RFTA member countries would discriminate against outsiders and lose interest in Multilateral Free Trade Agreements (MFTAs), undermining the authority of the WTO. As member countries may benefit from the regional trade agreements they signed, non-member countries are increasingly concerned about the erosion of the non-discrimination clause at the WTO. They would divert as much trade as they create and introduce distortions. As a result, these nations might be labeled as least favorable instead of most favorable. Overall, it is critical to keep support for the Doha Round alive. It is noteworthy that plurilateral agreements within MTNs were suggested as alternatives to RFTAs.[27]

Key Terms

Mercantilism, absolute advantage, comparative advantage, factor endowment theory, international product life cycle, new trade theory, first mover advantage, economies of scale, diamond model, infant industry argument, strategic trade policy, General Agreement on Tariffs and Trade (GATT), Uruguay Round, World Trade Organization(WTO), Doha Round, regional free trade agreement.

Review Questions

1. What are the major trends in global trade? Are there any particular phenomena to which we need to pay close attention?
2. How is comparative advantage theory different from absolute advantage theory? Why do some economists believe that comparative advantage theory may no longer hold in this global economy?
3. What are the key elements of new trade theory? Are you convinced that new trade theory is more powerful than old trade theory in explaining the current developments in international trade?
4. Discuss the key political and economic arguments that justify government protectionism. Identify and explain one recent case for each of these arguments.
5. What are the key remaining issues that the Doha Round needs to deal with to reach an agreement? Do you think that regional free trade agreements such as the TPP will continue to be drafted in the future? If so, please explain your reasoning.

Internet Exercises

Please visit the following website (www.nytimes.com/2016/01/26/business/ international/trans-pacific-pact-would-lift-us-incomes-but-not-jobs- overall-study-says.html?_r=0) and discuss the key positive and negative impacts of the Trans-Pacific Partnership (TPP) on the U.S. economy.

Notes

1   Buttonwood. (2015, June 25). World economy: Globalisation's retreat? *The Economist*. Retrieved from www.economist.com/blogs/buttonwood/2015/06/ world-economy

2   *Economist*. (2014, December 13). International trade: Troubling trajectory. Retrieved from www.economist.com/news/finance-and-economics/21636089- fears-are-growing-trades-share-worlds-gdp-has-peaked-far

3   *Economist*. (2015, October 6). Why everyone is so keen to agree new trade deals. Retrieved from www.economist.com/blogs/graphicdetail/2015/10/global-trade- graphics

4   Persio, S. L. (2015, November 24). Five trends that will shape the future of trade. *Global Trade Review*. Retrieved from www.gtreview.com/news/global/five- trends-that-will-shape-the-future-of-trade/

5   *Economist*. (2015, October 6). Why everyone is so keen to agree new trade deals. Retrieved from www.economist.com/blogs/graphicdetail/2015/10/global- trade-graphics

6   The World Bank. (2013, August 13). World Bank to develop services trade data- base. Retrieved from www.worldbank.org/en/news/press-release/2013/08/06/ wto-world-bank-to-develop-services-trade-database

7   Ricardo, D. (1967). *The Principles of Political Economy and Taxation*. Homewood, IL: Irwin, first published in 1817.

8   Bernstein, A. (2004, December 5). Shaking up trade theory. *Bloomberg Business Week*. Retrieved from www.bloomberg.com/news/articles/2004-12-05/shaking- up-trade-theory

9   Ohlin, B. (1933). *Interregional and International Trade*. Cambridge, MA: Harvard University Press.

10   Vernon, R. (1966, May). International investments and international trade in the product life cycles. *Quarterly Journal of Economics*, 190–207.

11   The U.S. Census Bureau (2014). US Bureau of Economic Analysis: U.S. interna- tional trade in goods and services.

12   Buffett, W. (2003, October 26). America's growing trade deficit selling the nation out from under us. *Fortune Magazine*. Retrieved from http://archive.fortune. com/magazines/fortune/fortune_archive/2003/11/10/352872/index.htm

13   Krugman, P. (1992). Does the new trade theory require a new trade policy? *World Economy*, 15(4), 423–442.

14   Andrews, E. L. (1997). In victory for U.S., European ban on treated beef is ruled illegal. *New York Times*, p. A1; Miller, S. (2004, February 26). EU trade sanctions have dual edge. *Wall Street Journal*, p. A3; and Reilhac, G. (2012, March 14). "Vote ends EU-U.S. hormone-treated beef row." Reuters. Retrieved from www. reuters.com/article/eu-trade-beef-idUSL5E8EE50620120314

15   Harris, S. (2015). U.S. poised to indict China's hackers for cyber blitz. *The Daily Beast*. Retrieved from www.thedailybeast.com/articles/2015/09/09/u-s-poised- to-indict-china-s-hackers-for-cyber-blitz.html

16   Tandon, S. (2013). U.S. heads to end Myanmar sanctions after landmark visit. Retrieved from www.mysinchew.com/node/86667

17   Porter, M. E. (1990). *The Competitive Advantage of Nations*. New York: Free Press. Retrieved from www.hbs.edu/faculty/Pages/item.aspx?num=189

18   Moon, H. C., Rugman, A., and Verbeke, A. (1998). A generalized double diamond approach to the global competitiveness of Korea and Singapore. *International Business Review, 7*(2), 135–150.

19   Information provided on WTO Website, www.wto.org

20   World Trade Organization. (2003). *Annual Report by the Director General 2003*, Geneva.

21   Pango. Instruments of trade policy. www.slideshare.net/PANGO/instruments-of-trade-policy-presentation

22   Information provided on WTO Website, www.wto.org

23   Information provided on WTO Website, www.wto.org/english/news_e/brief_tradefa_e.htm

24   *Economist.* (2015). Why everyone is so keen to agree new trade deals. Retrieved from www.economist.com/blogs/graphicdetail/2015/10/global-trade-graphics

25   *Wall Street Journal.* (2013, January 22). Benefits of free trade: Opening up Korean auto market, B.4.

26   *Economist.* (2015). Why everyone is so keen to agree new trade deals. Retrieved from www.economist.com/blogs/graphicdetail/2015/10/global-trade-graphics

27   Nakatomi, M. Plurilateral agreements: A viable alternative to the World Trade Organization? Retrieved from https://ideas.repec.org/p/eab/tradew/23716.html

Foreign Direct Investment

3

Learning Objectives

1. Understand the key concepts of foreign direct investment (FDI).
2. Know the general trends and current conditions of FDI.
3. Describe the main theories that explain the reasons for and patterns of FDI.
4. Identify the main benefits that companies seek from FDI.
5. Comprehend the impacts of FDI on the host country and the home country.

Cases

Case 3.1 Vodafone's Success in Africa
Case 3.2 Huawei's Journey in the U.S.
Case 3.3 GM and Ethanol Fuel in Brazil
Case 3.4 The Evolution of FDI in China
Case 3.5 Microsoft's Relocation: China vs. Vietnam

Case 3.1 Vodafone's Success in Africa

In August 2015, *Fortune* magazine published its "Change the World" list, featuring companies that have made a sizable impact on social and environmental issues. It was probably the first ranking of companies' achievements in aligning business innovation and social responsibility. The number one position on the list was awarded to U.K.-based Vodafone and Safaricom from Kenya for their mobile-phone based micro-financing service, M-Pesa. M-Pesa allows people without bank accounts to use their smart phones to save and transfer money, receive pensions, and pay bills.

When Vodafone and Safaricom first launched M-Pesa in Kenya in 2007, they only had a modest expectation. However, M-Pesa gained staggering popularity. In 2012, M-Pesa had more than 17 million registered users in Kenya and 42 percent of Kenya's GDP flowed through M-Pesa. The mobile money platform soon spread across Africa, Afghanistan, India, and Eastern Europe. As of 2014, M-Pesa was available in nine countries with about 20 million users. The mobile system has become extremely convenient, allowing people to pay hospital bills, taxi bills, satellite bills, and other various bills.

M-Pesa has helped reduce transactional costs and risks in an otherwise largely cash-based society. "It has been revolutionary," says World Bank economist Wolfgang Fengler. "It has changed lives, businesses, and the perception of Africa, and brought substantial flows into the financial system that would have otherwise been lying literally under mattresses."ᵃ M-Pesa brought not only a trophy to Vodafone but also positive cash flows and high returns on investment. It has become a major source of revenue for Vodafone.

The success of M-Pesa showed that Vodafone's strategy of growth in emerging markets has paid off. As a British company, Vodafone has come a long way. For years, the company was under pressure due to declining revenues from its traditional European telecom markets. Vodafone estimated that intensifying competition contributed to price declines of around 15 percent per annum. Pressures from regulators for lower mobile termination rates and roaming prices further squeezed Vodafone's margin. In 2006, the company launched a new strategy to focus on emerging markets. Vodafone made it clear that emerging markets with growing populations and demand represent long-term potential for the company.

Stronger performance was recorded in the following years. From 2007 to 2008, Vodafone reported a significant global presence through equity interest and a 14.1 percent increase in its revenue. While growing only 6.1 percent in Europe, revenue in other regions increased 45.1 percent. On an organic basis, Europe recorded a growth of 2.0 percent, while other regions delivered an increase of 14.5 percent, accounting for 62.1 percent of the organic growth for the company.

Particularly, with the spectacular rise of Africa's mobile telecommunications industry, Vodafone, as one of the first movers in that region, has made significant investments. In May 2000, Vodafone acquired a 40 percent stake and management responsibility of Safaricom, the leading mobile operator in Kenya. In November 2006, Vodafone increased its share in Vodafone Egypt, a joint venture with the Egyptian fixed-line monopoly Telecom Egypt, to 55 percent. In August 2008, Vodafone spent $900 million USD acquiring 70 percent equity in Ghana Telecom and later renamed it Vodafone Ghana.

Vodafone's biggest business in Africa is the Johannesburg-based Vodacom Group Ltd., a joint venture between Vodafone and Telkom in South Africa. In May 2009, after taking a 65 percent majority holding, Vodafone listed Vodacom on the Johannesburg Stock Exchange. Vodacom then became Vodafone's exclusive investment vehicle in Sub-Saharan Africa. Its profit surpassed the profit of Vodafone's U.K. subsidiary in 2010, and that of the subsidiary in Spain in 2011.

Beyond traditional cellular and network services, Vodafone and other telecom companies were able to do more. With a blank slate on the continent, they could develop and construct infrastructures that were even better and more capable than those in developed markets. In countries with little infrastructure but high growth, Vodafone has not only built modern networks from scratch but also provided Internet, banking, and many other services. As of 2015, Internet penetration in Africa was about 20 percent while the average rate for the world was over 40 percent. "There's a massive opportunity in penetration that we need to drive forward on," said Nick Read, the head of Vodafone's African operations, "Everyone in Africa wants to be on Facebook. They want e-mail. They want social networks."[b] In fact, the African region has witnessed one of the strongest increases in mobile data use in the world. Forecasts suggest that mobile Internet traffic across Africa may see a twenty-fold increase by the end of the decade.

Vodafone has become the second largest mobile telecommunications company in the world with about 93,000 employees. It is listed on both the London Stock Exchange and NASDAQ, and also part of the Financial Times Stock Exchange 100 Index. Vodafone's business activities are spread across Africa, Asia Pacific, Europe, and the Middle East. By the end of 2014, Vodafone had 446 million mobile customers and 12 million fixed broadband users. Its 2014 revenue reached 42.2 billion GBP and the EBITA was 11.9 billion GBP. Vodafone has stated that it would keep generating revenue growth by driving penetration and accelerating data services in attractive emerging markets. Although it must comply with a wide range of regulations on construction, licensing, and operation of telecommunications networks and services, Vodafone has been growing quickly and getting financial rewards in emerging markets. Today, over 60 percent of Vodafone customers are from emerging markets.

Notes

a.   *Fortune*. (2015) Vodafone and Safaricom. Retrieved from http://fortune.com/ change-the-world/2015/vodafone-and-safaricom-1/
b.   Thomson, A. (2013, January 9). Vodafone Africa becomes profit machine via banking. *Bloomberg*. Retrieved from www.bloomberg.com/news/2013-01-09/ vodafone-africa-becomes-profit-machine.html

Sources

1.   Thomson, A. (2013, January 9). Vodafone Africa becomes profit machine via banking. *Bloomberg*. Retrieved from www.bloomberg.com/news/2013-01-09/ vodafone-africa-becomes-profit-machine.html
2.   Vodafone. About us. Retrieved from www.vodafone.com/content/index/investors/ about_us/background_history/where_we_are.html
3.   Zekaria, S. (2014, April 10). Vodafone lines up emerging markets. *Wall Street Journal*. Retrieved from http://blogs.wsj.com/corporate-intelligence/2014/04/10/ vodafone-lines-up-emerging-markets/

Questions for Case Discussion

1.   What internal and external factors drove Vodafone's international expansion?
2.   How would you rate Africa as an investment destination for Vodafone? Why?
3.   What can be learned from the success of M-Pesa in Africa?

Case 3.2 Huawei's Journey in the U.S.

On a late February night in 2011, Mr. Hongkun Hu, the Deputy Chairman of Huawei Technology, was sitting at his desk in his office suite in Shenzhen,

China, the home city of Huawei. From his window, he could see the lights set over the silhouette of a busy and rapidly growing city. Mr. Hu picked up a letter from his desk and carefully read through it one more time. The letter stated, "We would like to provide the basic facts behind the recent 3Leaf matter that has been the subject of much attention and discussion about Huawei."

This letter was prepared in response to a notice from the Committee on Foreign Investment in the United States (CFIUS), an inter-agency committee of the U.S. government that reviews the national security implications of foreign investments. A few days earlier, CFIUS had informed Huawei that they recommended against Huawei's acquisition of assets and technology from 3Leaf Systems, a California-based cloud computing company. 3Leaf's technology would enable groups of computers to work together, thus creating more powerful machines. In May 2010, Huawei paid $2 million USD to acquire some of 3Leaf's intellectual property and assets. Since it did not acquire the whole company and the deal was only $2 million USD, Huawei reportedly thought the deal should not warrant a CFIUS review.

CFIUS typically reviews acquisition deals before they are completed. When Pentagon officials found out about the Huawei-3Leaf deal, they took an unusual step to ask the company to file for a review retroactively. Huawei did so voluntarily in November 2010. According to the Exon–Florio Amendment, if a foreign investment is deemed to pose a threat to national security, the President may block the investment. After their investigation, CFIUS suggested Huawei divest the newly acquired assets from 3Leaf, otherwise the committee would recommend the President to reverse the transaction.

Executives of Huawei, including Mr. Hu, needed to resolve this issue. Initially, they wanted to press on and await the President's decision. In the end, after considering various tradeoffs, Huawei made the decision to back away from this acquisition. On February 21, 2011, Huawei issued a brief statement.

> It was a hard decision. However, we have decided to accept the recommendation of CFIUS to withdraw our application to acquire specific assets of 3Leaf. The significant impact and attention that this transaction has caused were not what we intended. Huawei will remain committed to long-term investment in the United States.[a]

The 3Leaf deal was not the only failure Huawei encountered in the U.S. In 2008, Huawei's proposal to acquire 16 percent equity of 3Com Corp was also rejected by CFIUS. In 2010, Huawei reportedly lost a major equipment supply contract with Sprint Nextel after the U.S. Commerce Secretary expressed some concerns to Sprint Nextel executives. In a letter to U.S. government officials, eight Republican senators also raised national security concerns in relation to the contract. All these disappointments prompted Huawei to post an open letter inviting the U.S. government to investigate the company regarding security concerns and intellectual property disputes.

In addition, several other Chinese companies' acquisitions were blocked by CFIUS. In December 2009, CFIUS stopped a Chinese government-controlled company's deal to acquire 51 percent of Firstgold Corp., a Nevada gold mining company. An alleged reason was that Firstgold's mining facilities were close to a naval air station and other sensitive military installations. In June 2010, CFIUS expressed concerns about New Mexico-based EMCORE's sale of its fiber optics business to China's Tangshan Caofeidian Investment Corporation. The deal was eventually withdrawn. Since all CFIUS proceedings are kept confidential, there may be other Chinese investment deals that have been blocked by CFIUS.

The Chinese government questioned the decisions of CFIUS. China's Ministry of Commerce issued a statement urging the U.S. government to make national-security reviews more transparent, avoid protectionist measures, and treat investments from China fairly. In the United States, CIFUS' rejection of Huawei's small $2 million USD acquisition also caused an uproar. ZDNet posted an article asking, "How a bankrupt U.S. company [3Leaf] could give China a powerful new superweapon development system?"[b]

Despite the setbacks in the U.S., Huawei has expanded globally and become the largest telecommunications equipment manufacturer in the world. Their total global revenue was CNY 238 billion ($39.6 billion USD) in 2013 and CNY 288 billion ($46.5 billion USD) in 2014. In 2014, Huawei recorded profits of CNY 34.2 billion ($5.5 billion USD). Its products and services have been deployed in more than 140 countries and it currently serves 45 of the world's 50 largest telecom operators and about two-thirds of Huawei's revenue comes from outside its homeland. In 2014, Huawei was the first Chinese company entering Interbrand's "Best Global Brands" list and ranked the ninety-fourth most valuable brand at $4.3 billion USD. In 2015, Huawei went up to the eighty-eighth position on the list.

Most of Huawei's success has come from offering customers top-quality products at a low cost. This strategy has forced multinationals such as Nortel, Alcatel-Lucent, and Cisco to compete on an ever-improving product mix with razor-thin margins. Ericsson CEO Carl-Henric Svanberg described Huawei, which surpassed Ericsson in sales in 2012, as "pretty brutal" on pricing and innovation. In order to keep up with global competition and continue sales growth, Huawei has invested heavily in research and development of higher-end products. It spent $5 billion USD on R&D expenses in 2013, increased the amount to $6.4 billion USD in 2014, and made commitments to invest more in the future. As of September 2015, Huawei had 21 R&D centers all over the world. Among the over 170,000 employees of Huawei, 76,000 were engaged in R&D.

Even in the U.S., where the company had trouble with acquisitions, Huawei has invested a lot in R&D. Its first R&D center in the U.S. was set up in Plano, Texas in 2001 with only five employees. The following decade witnessed notable growth. Its R&D investment in the United States grew 66 percent per year and reached $62 million USD in 2010. Huawei's U.S. operations expanded to seven R&D centers and 12 branch offices. Their employees grew to 1,100. Almost all of them are senior-level technical staff, and about 75 percent locally hired.

In 2012, the company announced plans to invest about $3.6 billion USD to build a research and development facility in Santa Clara, California, in the middle of Silicon Valley. Huawei's press release stated that, "The

200,000 square-foot facility includes multiple state-of-the-art research labs and focuses on the research and development of next generation communications solutions for U.S. customers while supporting Huawei's global R&D research efforts." This expansion also included the relocation of Huawei's North American Headquarters from Plano, Texas to Santa Clara. The move was intended to further enhance Huawei's global R&D, on which the company spends nearly $4 billion USD a year. Charles Ding, President of Huawei North America and Co-president of Huawei USA said, "With our Santa Clara R&D facility, we will continue to focus on groundbreaking research that addresses customer needs and creates new growth opportunities for the company."c

Notes

a.   Reuters. (2011, February 19). Huawei backs away from 3Leaf acquisition. Retrieved from www.reuters.com/article/us-huawei-3leaf-idUSTRE71I38920110219
b.   Gewirtz, D. (2011, February 10). How a bankrupt U.S. company could give China a powerful new superweapon development system? ZDNet. Retrieved from www.zdnet.com/article/how-a-bankrupt-u-s-company-could-give-china-a-powerful-new-superweapon-development-system/
c.   Huawei. (2011, April 5). Huawei celebrates ten years in the U.S.; Opens new R&D facility in Silicon Valley. Retrieved from www.huawei.com/us/about-huawei/newsroom/press-release/hw-u_103584.htm

Sources

1.   Adams, S. (2011, April 13). A U.S.–China M&A cold war? Not so fast. *Business Insider*. Retrieved from www.businessinsider.com/a-us-china-ma-cold-war-not-so-fast-2011-4
2.   Scott, H. (2012, February 14). Huawei gets serious about U.S. market, sets up shop in Silicon Valley. Phone Arena. Retrieved from www.phonearena.com/news/Huawei-gets-serious-about-U.S.-market-sets-up-shop-in-Silicon-Valley_id26886
3.   Huawei. (2011, April 5). Huawei celebrates ten years in the U.S.; Opens new R&D facility in Silicon Valley. Retrieved from www.huawei.com/us/about-huawei/newsroom/press-release/hw-u_103584.htm
4.   Lawson, S. (2011, April 22). Huawei open to more U.S. acquisitions. *PC World*. Retrieved from www.pcworld.com/article/226093/article.html
5.   Osawa, J. and Mozur, P. (2014, January 16). The rise of China's innovation machine. *Wall Street Journal*. Retrieved from http://online.wsj.com/articles/SB10001424052702303819704579320544231396168
6.   Rice, S. and Dowell, A. (2011, February 22). Huawei drops U.S. deal amid opposition. *Wall Street Journal*. Retrieved from www.wsj.com/articles/SB10001424052748703407304576154121951088478

Questions for Case Discussion

1.   Do you agree with CIFUS' decision on Huawei's acquisition of 3Leaf? Why?
2.   What are the impacts of Chinese companies' investments in the U.S.?
3.   What factors drove Huawei to invest in Silicon Valley? Was it a smart move?

Case 3.3 GM and Ethanol Fuel in Brazil

October 28, 2014 was a big day for car fans in Brazil. It was the opening day of the Sao Paulo International Motor Show, the biggest automotive event in South America that takes place every two years. By nine o'clock, thousands of fans had arrived despite the sweltering heat. The exhibition hall was filled with people even when temperatures inside the venue rose above 80 °F degrees. Shiny new cars looked triumphant on expansive stages under blinding spotlights, people bustled throughout the hall and samba music could be heard everywhere. General Motors (GM) was going to introduce four concept cars on that day. The most exciting among them was the Onix Track Day concept. It was based on the Onix hatchback, which GM had been offering exclusively in Latin America since 2012. Other automakers were unveiling some new cars as well. It was clear that Brazil's auto market was booming.

Since the market opened up in the 1990s, it has been displaying impressive growth. By the end of 2010, when Brazil's gross domestic product per capita exceeded the significant $10,000 USD benchmark, Brazil's car sales totaled over $100 billion USD. The country's fast-growing middle class has demonstrated strong purchasing power, making Brazil the largest consumer market in South America. The country's car sales were expected to increase from 3.4 million units in 2011 to 5.7 million by 2016. Brazil became the fourth largest car market in 2014 and could overtake Japan to become the third, trailing behind only China and the U.S. In terms of production, Brazil ranks seventh in the world. But this too will change with multiple automakers collectively investing billions of USD in new research, engineering, and production facilities. Along with its competitors, GM is also betting on the long-term growth of Brazil.

GM, an American multinational corporation headquartered in Detroit, Michigan, designs, manufactures, markets, and distributes vehicles and vehicle parts and sells financial services all over the world. In 2014, GM's U.S. operation exported 233,145 vehicles, with Canada being its largest export market (almost 158,000 vehicles), Middle East the second (44,356 units), followed by Mexico (16,420). GM's export from the U.S. to Brazil is rather limited. Most GM cars sold in Brazil were manufactured locally by GM do Brasil, a wholly owned subsidiary that GM set up in 1925. As one of the first foreign automakers in Brazil, GM do Brasil has been manufacturing and selling vehicles for more than 90 years. It has three vehicle assembly plants and a modern R&D facility with full capacity to design new vehicles. It is also the largest subsidiary of GM in South America and the second largest operation outside the U.S.

Many of GM do Brasil's vehicles are tailored specifically for the Brazilian market. For instance, Onix, a hatchback vehicle, was launched exclusively in South America and won the trophy "vehicle of the year" in Brazil in 2012. Chevrolet Cruze, which was part of GM's aggressive new-product push in Brazil, won the Best National Car of the Year and the thirteenth annual Automotive Press Award in 2013. A large majority of their vehicles are ethanol flexible, a unique feature of the Brazilian automobile industry. Over the years, both political and technological developments have led Brazil to become the world leader in the development and use of ethanol fuels. The rise of ethanol can be attributed to Brazil's National Alcohol Program—Pró-Álcool. This government-financed program, launched two years after the 1973 oil crisis, aimed to replace fossil fuels with ethanol produced from sugar cane. The Brazilian government made it mandatory to blend ethanol fuel with gasoline. All the major automakers in Brazil started to work on flexible-fuel vehicles that can use any blend of gasoline and ethanol or even 100 percent ethanol. In 2003, Volkswagen launched the Golf 1.6 Total Flex, Brazil's first commercial flexible-fuel vehicle. Two months later, GM do Brasil launched the Chevrolet Corsa 1.8 Flexpower. Soon all the major automakers began producing flexible-fuel vehicles in Brazil. Flexible-fuel vehicles gained 22 percent of new car sales in 2004 and soon reached a record 94 percent market share in 2009. In recent years, the sales of flexible-fuel vehicles declined due to fluctuating oil and ethanol prices, but the market share remained above 80 percent.

While serving the Brazilian market, GM do Brasil has been exporting vehicles from Brazil to other countries. In 2005, GM do Brasil produced over 559,000 units with 365,000 vehicles sold in Brazil. The remaining over 156,000 vehicles were exported to some 40 countries around the world, a total value of $1.6 billion USD. In 2014, GM do Brasil exported 3.15 million units valued at $11.5 billion USD. These numbers were actually lower than prior years due to economic woes in Argentina, a main market for GM do Brasil. The company also exports to Mexico, Venezuela, other Latin American countries, and South Africa.

Despite its past success, GM faces many challenges in Brazil. First, Brazil has a history of rollercoaster economy, with booms followed by busts. For instance, the fluctuation of the Brazilian real has created many uncertainties and risks. While GM do Brasil's export might benefit from a weak real, its production relies on a significant number of imported auto parts, whose costs could be raised by a weak real. Meanwhile, GM faces intense competition. GM, along with Fiat, Ford, and Volkswagen, the so-called "Big Four" in Brazil, have been producing cars in Brazil for so long that many locals consider them domestic brands. The big four have dominated the Brazilian market for years. Their total market share reached 84 percent in 2007. However, according to market research by J.D. Power and Associates, their market share has dropped to around 70 percent as more and more players enter Brazil.[a] Their competitors include not only established automakers like BMW, Honda, Hyundai, Kia, and Nissan but also newcomers like China's Chery, Geely, JAC, Hafei as well as India's Tata and Mahindra. Even GM's new products could not stop the company's market share decreasing. Its share of total retail vehicles sales volume in South America in 2015 was 16.6 percent, a drop from 17.7 percent in 2014, 18.0 percent in 2013, and 18.8 percent in 2012.

In order to strengthen its market position, GM has decided to pump more capital into Brazil. From 2009 to 2014, GM do Brasil received about $3 billion USD for plant upgrades and new vehicle development. In 2013, GM acquired equity interests in Ally Financial Inc.'s auto finance business in Brazil. In August 2014, GM announced it would invest 6.5 billion Brazilian real ($1.9 billion USD) in Brazil over the next five years to focus on new products and technologies as well as plant maintenance, reaffirming the automaker's long-term commitment. In July 2015, GM announced a plan to double its investment in Brazil to $3.8 billion USD (13 billion real). The additional $1.9 billion USD investment would be used to create an all-new global Chevrolet vehicle family for Brazilian customers. GM also stated that, as a global leader in flexible-fuel vehicles, it would offer more of such vehicles in Brazil.

Note

a.   Muller, J. (2012, October 22). Why the World's Automakers Love Brazil. *Forbes*. Retrieved from www.forbes.com/sites/joannmuller/2012/10/05/why-the-worlds-automakers-are-loving-brazil/

Sources

1.   De Paula, M. (2012, October 31). Brazil rising: Why the Sao Paulo Auto Show is unlike any other. *Forbes*. Retrieved from www.forbes.com/sites#/sites/matthewdepaula/2012/10/31/brazil-rising-why-the-sao-paulo-auto-show-is-unlike-any-other/2/
2.   General Motors. (2014). General Motors Company and Subsidiaries Supplemental Material. Retrieved from http://media.gm.com/content/dam/Media/gmcom/investor/2010/Q1FinancialHighlights.pdf.
3.   General Motors. (2015). Q4 financial highlights. Retrieved from http://media.gm.com/content/dam/Media/gmcom/investor/2015/feb/4th-qtr-earnings/GM-2014-Q4-Financial-Highlights.pdf
4.   Higgins, T. (2012, October 22). GM introducing seven models into Brazil to reverse loss. Retrieved from www.bloomberg.com/news/2012-10-22/gm-introducing-seven-models-into-brazil-to-reverse-loss.html
5.   Rapoza, K. (2012, June 7). In Brazil, General Motors car sales beat rival Volkswagen. *Forbes*. Retrieved from www.forbes.com/sites/kenrapoza/2012/06/07/in-brazil-general-motors-car-sales-beat-rival-volkswagen/
6.   U.S. Department of Commerce, Office of Transportation and Machinery. (2015, August). Trends in U.S. vehicle exports. Retrieved from www.trade.gov/td/otm/assets/auto/ExportPaper2015.pdf.
7.   GM Heritage Center. GM Do Brasil milestones: 2000–2008. Retrieved from https://history.gmheritagecenter.com/wiki/index.php/GM_do_Brasil_Milestones:2000_-_2008

Questions for Case Discussion

1.   Why would GM set up production in Brazil rather than export vehicles from the U.S.?
2.   What are the advantages and disadvantages of Brazil as an investment destination for GM?
3.   What do you think of GM's increased commitment to Brazil? Was it a smart move?

Case 3.4 The Evolution of FDI in China

China has been continuously recognized as a top destination for foreign direct investment (FDI). Most of the world's largest multinational companies have invested in the country. Its huge domestic market, cheap labor force, established infrastructure, and government incentives have made China highly attractive to foreign investors. According to China's National Bureau of Statistics, its annual utilized FDI inflow averaged $73 billion USD between 1995 and 2015, and reached above $120 billion USD in 2015 (see Figure 3.1 below).

After China started its economic reform in the late 1970s, FDI began to flow into the country. Recognizing FDI as an important vehicle to access new technology, capital as well as export market, the Chinese government introduced a range of policies and procedures characterized by setting up Special Economic Zones (SEZs) for foreign investors and allowing the formation of joint ventures. During the 1980s, FDI inflows grew steadily but remained relatively low. Most investments came from small and medium-sized enterprises in Hong Kong and were highly concentrated in southern provinces. They were primarily undertaken to take advantage of low labor costs and to create a base for exports to other countries. The share of foreign-invested enterprises in total exports increased from 1.88 percent in 1986 to 12.58 percent in 1990. Meanwhile, many restrictions existed. For instance, foreign investors were largely confined to joint ventures with state-owned enterprises. To cover foreign exchange expenses, they had to export and maintain a foreign exchange balance. Limited convertibility of Chinese currency made it difficult to repatriate profits. In addition, foreign investors were often concerned about policy uncertainty, lengthy bureaucratic processes, and the lack of property rights protection.

FDI inflow began to surge after China reaffirmed its commitment to economic reforms and open policies in early 1990s. More SEZs were established across the country, with some designated to promote technology transfer. More favorable policies were adopted to attract FDI, such as simpler registration and approval procedures, less restrictions on capital requirement and equity structure, more freedom to import equipment and materials, and more flexibility to swap foreign currencies. Foreign companies, especially those export-oriented and technologically advanced, could receive tax benefits, privileged access to utilities, and low-interest loans. Meanwhile, government policies favored FDI in certain industries and regions. Priorities were

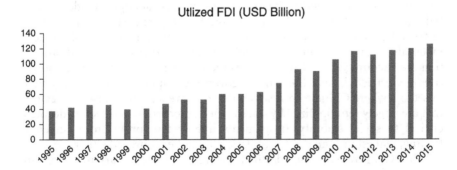

Figure 3.1 Trends of FDI in China

Data Source: National Bureau of Statistics of China.

given to agriculture, basic raw materials, energy, telecommunication, transportation, and high-technology industries as well as less developed central and western provinces.

FDI flows into China, especially those from developed countries, increased steadily. By the end of the 1990s, China had become the largest recipient of FDI among developing countries. Its annual actual inward investment rose from $4.4 billion USD in 1991 to $40.7 billion USD in 2000. By 2000, the total amount of actual investment reached $348.3 billion USD. The contribution of foreign-invested firms to China's total exports increased from 16.75 percent in 1991 to 47.93 percent in 2000. The share of foreign-invested firms in total industrial output also increased from 5.29 percent in 1991 to 22.51 percent in 2000. In terms of sector distribution, the majority of FDI went into manufacturing. Among the FDI in manufacturing sectors, about half flowed into labor-intensive ones (e.g. textile and clothing, food processing, furniture), while technology-intensive (e.g. medical and pharmaceuticals, electrical machinery and equipment, electronics) and capital-intensive (e.g. chemical materials, petroleum refining) sectors accounted about a quarter each. As many foreign investors were motivated to take advantage of the country's low labor costs, China was quickly becoming a key location for low-cost production.

FDI inflow continued to grow in the following years. Especially after China joined the World Trade Organization (WTO) in December 2001, many restrictions on foreign investment were removed or loosened. By the end of 2003, China had accumulated more than $500 USD billion of FDI, and wholly owned enterprises had replaced joint ventures to become the most popular form of FDI. China remained the top recipient of FDI among developing countries. Its actual inflow reached $117 billion USD in 2013. In 2014, while global FDI declined 8 percent due to economic fragility and geopolitical risks, FDI inflows to China continued to rise to $119 billion USD, making China the world's largest recipient of FDI. In 2015, China utilized $126 billion USD FDI, up 5.6 percent from the previous year.

During this period of time, in order to upgrade its economic structure, China took deliberate measures to encourage or restrict FDI in select industrial sectors. The Chinese government published a catalogue to guide FDI in 1997 and has been amending it every five years. The catalogue divides potential industrial sectors for FDI projects into four types: encouraged, allowed, restricted, and prohibited. For instance, investments in high technology, new materials, clean production, renewable energies, and environmental protection are encouraged. FDI in resource-intensive and highly polluting industries are restricted. Also, the Chinese government appears to discourage FDI in sectors where Chinese companies already have a strong presence, sectors that are largely monopolized by state-owned enterprises, and sectors deemed critical to social stability. Investments intended to profit from currency trading, real estate, and asset speculation are not encouraged either.

While China remains a top destination for FDI in recent years, many foreign investors have started to worry about China's long-term prospects. After decades of double-digit growth, China's economic development is slowing down. China's GDP grew by 6.9 percent year-over-year in 2015, the slowest since 1990, and down from 7.4 percent in 2014 and 7.7 percent in 2013. Despite its sheer volume, the growth of FDI inflow to China seems to have slowed down. From 2001 to 2011, the average annual FDI growth rate was 10.3 percent. The average rate dropped to about 2.2 percent between 2012 and 2015.

Meanwhile, FDI in China has shown some new features and the motives of foreign investors have changed. First of all, China's low-cost labor advantage is declining. According to China's National Bureau of Statistics, the average monthly wage for migrant workers at the end of 2013 was 2,609 yuan ($420 USD), a 13.9 percent increase over the previous year. And the year-over-year rise was 11.8 percent in 2012 and 21.2 percent in 2011. In comparative terms, China is no longer a low-wage economy. According to World Bank data, only 30 percent of the world's population lives in countries with a higher GDP per capita than China. In Southeast Asia and South Asia, every developing country except Malaysia now has a lower GDP per capita than China.[a] While rising labor costs, along with increasing energy costs and industrial property prices, may hinder FDI, China is offering something else to attract investment—its unrivaled capacity and skillset in manufacturing. Over the last few decades, China has developed flexible and experienced workforces as well as gigantic factories and fully fledged supply chains. It offers a one-stop solution for manufacturing, which can ramp up production capacity on short notice. Although other countries may offer lower labor costs, China still excels in manufacturing speed, flexibility, and know-how.

Moreover, many foreign investors have switched their focus from export to local markets. Historically, foreign-owned companies have been a strong exporting force. For instance, among the top 200 exporting firms in 2009, 153 were foreign-invested. Nonetheless, while remaining an export-driven economy, China has become a gigantic and fast-growing market. Many FDI projects today aim to take advantage of China's domestic demand. Especially, an increasing amount of FDI has flown into service sectors, which primarily serve local customers. In 2013, China's service sectors attracted 52 percent of inward FDI, surpassing manufacturing sectors for the first time. In 2014, while FDI in manufacturing was lower than the previous year, FDI in service continued to increase. Similarly, in the first half of 2015, China's service sectors attracted $43.4 billion USD of FDI, up 23.6 percent from a year ago, while FDI in manufacturing dropped 8.4 percent to $20.9 billion USD.

Note

a. World Bank. (2013). World Development Indicators. Retrieved from http://databank.worldbank.org/data/download/WDI-2013-ebook.pdf

Sources

1. BBC News (2015, January 30). China overtakes U.S. for foreign direct investment. Retrieved from www.bbc.com/news/business-31052566
2. *Wall Street Journal.* (2014, June 17). Foreign direct investment in China declines. Retrieved from www.wsj.com/articles/foreign-direct-investment-in-china-declines-1402980999

3. Long, G. (2005). China's policies on FDI: Review and evaluation. In T. H. Moran, E. M. Graham, and M. Blomstrom (Eds.), *Does Foreign Direct Investment Promote Development*, 315–336. Peterson Institute for International Economics.
4. Ross, J. (2014, October 16). China's changing pattern of FDI. Retrieved from www.china.org.cn/opinion/2014-10/16/content_33783694.htm
5. Singh, T. (2012). China: Reasons for being a top FDI destination. Institute of Peace and Conflict Studies. Retrieved from www.ipcs.org/article/china/china-reasons-for-being-a-top-fdi-destination-3767.html
6. Sweeney, P. (2014, August 26). China foreign investment pattern changes as challenges grow. Retrieved from www.reuters.com/article/2014/08/26/us-china-investment-idUSKBN0GQ26M20140826

Questions for Case Discussion

1. What impact did FDI inflows have on China's economic development?
2. What are the key features of Chinese government policies for FDI?
3. What factors drove the changing patterns of FDI flows into China?

Case 3.5 Microsoft's Relocation: China vs. Vietnam

In September 2013, in an attempt to mimic Apple/Google's strategy of owning an ecosystem of hardware, software, and services, Microsoft announced a $7.2 billion USD deal to acquire Nokia's handset business including the "Lumia" and "Asha" brands. Prior to the acquisition, Microsoft mainly focused on software in the mobile phone industry. Its Windows phone operating system had been used on various handsets such as Nokia's Lumia devices. In fact, Nokia contributed 87 percent of all Windows phone sales. However, sales of Windows phone handsets had become sluggish. According to a report by International Data Corporation, as of the second quarter of 2014, Windows phone made up 2.5 percent of the worldwide smart phone market, while Google's Android accounted for 84.7 percent and Apple's iOS had 11.7 percent. Microsoft was hoping to use Nokia's assets to catch up with iPhone and Android. Meanwhile, the deal brought some relief to Nokia. Despite its stronghold in the feature phone business, Nokia had just a 3 percent share of the smart phone handset market. This acquisition was expected to vertically integrate Microsoft products and Nokia devices, thus creating a strong ecosystem and increasing profits.

In early 2014, Satya Nadella became the CEO of Microsoft. In his vision, all different Windows systems would eventually merge into one integrative platform. Thus, app developers would be able to write universal apps that work across Windows computers, Windows phone handsets, and Xbox game consoles. Amid this major strategic shift, Microsoft started restructuring its Nokia unit. In July 2014, the company announced a plan to close down two Nokia manufacturing plants in China. The manufacturing function would be relocated to Vietnam, Brazil, and Mexico. Microsoft would also scale back engineering efforts in Beijing, China, but keep a team focused on affordable devices. In total, 9,000 jobs would be cut in China. The plan triggered protests among Nokia employees in China. Protesters said that Microsoft broke its promise not to cut jobs within the first year following its acquisition of Nokia's handset business.

Some of the manufacturing equipment in China was scheduled to be shipped to Microsoft's factory in Bac Ninh, Vietnam. The Bac Ninh factory was designed to carry out almost all Nokia handset production starting from November 2014. After obtaining production capacity from China, it would have 39 assembly lines, triple its outputs, and export about 76.4 million devices per year. Having more than 10,000 employees, the factory was already the largest U.S. business in Southeast Asia. Given its growth plan, the factory would need many more professional engineers and technicians.

Microsoft was not the first tech giant to scale back manufacturing in China. Google sold off the handset unit it had acquired from Motorola, which once had a large operation in China. Panasonic shut down its LCD television production in China. Citizen closed a watchmaking factory and laid off over 1,000 workers. Given China's aging population and fast increasing wages, Chinese labor has grown older and costlier. Other Asian countries such as Indonesia, the Philippines, and Vietnam have become increasingly attractive destinations for manufacturing plants. Particularly, Vietnam has emerged as the replacement for China. According to JETRO (Japan External Trade Organization), a factory worker in Hanoi, the capital of Vietnam, makes $145 USD a month on average, compared to $466 USD in Beijing. Also, more than 60 percent of the Vietnamese population is under 30 years old. Intel has invested $1.3 billion USD in Vietnam to take advantage of low-cost labor. Samsung's $3.38 billion USD investment has transformed the tea-growing Thai Nguyen province into a manufacturing hub. LG, another electronic giant, has also built manufacturing plants in Vietnam.

Vietnam is opening up markets and pushing for economic reforms that will lead to a market economy. It has been aggressively courting technology companies and aims to derive 30 percent of its industrial production from high-tech sectors. Local governments have also been making infrastructure investments, hoping to increase investors' confidence and become a high-tech hub like India. Various incentives like tax breaks are offered to foreign investments. For instance, Intel's Vietnam operation does not need to pay corporate taxes for the first four years of operation and will enjoy a 50 percent tax break in the following nine years. That's less than 10 percent per year, while the standard rate is 28 percent.

Gaurav Gupta, chairman of the American Chamber of Commerce in Vietnam, once said:

> The transitions taking place in China—including rising labor costs and the shift toward an economic model that is less reliant on exports—are creating a window of opportunity for Vietnam to capture a greater share of global manufacturing, especially from multinationals that are seeking a lower cost base.[a]

As one of the world's fastest-growing economies, Vietnam is also a good base for expanding into other Southeast Asian countries such as Cambodia, Laos, and Myanmar. Many companies are looking at this new investing hot spot.

Microsoft has also explored other opportunities in Vietnam. In March 2015, Microsoft announced a plan to invest $3 million USD in Vietnam over the next three years, as part of the tech giant's YouthSpark program. The YouthSpark program in Vietnam focuses on three areas: development of employees, broadening investment in youth across the country, and supporting young leaders. In June 2015, Microsoft set up the first authorized local retail store in Hanoi. The Microsoft Store offers a variety of Microsoft products, including Windows phone handsets, surface devices, computer software, and laptops and tablets made by Microsoft's partners. In the store, customers can test out the latest Windows platform that integrates various Microsoft applications, devices, and services.

Note

a.   Vietnamcolors.net (2014, Dec. 24). Vietnam inherits factories from manufacturers fleeing China. Retrieved from www.vietnamcolors.net/2014/12/vietnam-inherits-factories-from-manufacturers-fleeing-china/

Sources

1.   Hill, C. (2015, March 2). Microsoft closing two China factories and relocating to Vietnam; Another 9,000 jobs lost. *China Daily Mail*. Retrieved from http://chinadailymail.com/2015/03/02/microsoft-closing-two-china-factories-and-relocating-to-vietnam-another-9000-jobs-lost/
2.   Matthew, J. (2015, February 27). Microsoft to lay off 9,000 employees in China as it shuts down two former Nokia plants. *International Business Times*. Retrieved from www.ibtimes.co.uk/microsoft-layoff-9000-employees-china-it-shuts-down-two-former-nokia-plants-1489730
3.   Tuoi Tre News. (2015, June 19). Microsoft opens first authorized reseller store in Vietnam. Retrieved from http://tuoitrenews.vn/business/28788/microsoft-opens-first-authorized-reseller-store-in-vietnam
4.   Nath, T. (2014, December 3). Why Microsoft's acquisition of Nokia makes sense. Retrieved from www.investopedia.com/articles/investing/120314/why-microsofts-acquisition-nokia-makes-sense.asp
5.   Zeman, E. (2013, September 2). Microsoft's Nokia deal, analyzed. *Information Week*. Retrieved from www.informationweek.com/mobile/mobile-devices/microsofts-nokia-deal-analyzed/d/d-id/1111372?

Questions for Case Discussion

1.   What factors drove Microsoft to relocate phone production from China to Vietnam?
2.   What do you think of Vietnam as an investment destination?
3.   What role should the government play in attracting foreign investments?

Foreign Direct Investment

I. Concepts of FDI

To tap into international markets, many companies have established or acquired productive assets overseas. For instance, General Motors invested billions of dollars in plants in Mexico, Italy-based Fiat acquired Chrysler—an American automaker, Wal-Mart set up sourcing centers in China, and IBM established research labs in India. Such cross-border spread of investment enables companies to directly control or influence business operations such as production, procurement, marketing, service, and R&D in other countries. This phenomenon is known as foreign direct investment (FDI), an investment made to acquire lasting interest in enterprises operating in a foreign country.[1] Once engaging in FDI, a firm becomes a multinational corporation (MNC), also known as multinational enterprise (MNE), that operates in more than one country.

The entity that makes FDI is called direct investor. Its overseas enterprise is called direct investment enterprise. Investments that are classified as FDI include equity capital, the reinvestment of earnings, and the provision of intra-company loans. FDI implies the investor has effective influence on the management of the overseas enterprise, which usually requires some degree of equity ownership. According to the OECD benchmark definition of FDI, the direct investor generally owns 10 percent or more of the voting power of the enterprise, unless it can be proven that less than 10 percent ownership enables an effective voice in management. [2]

A key feature of FDI that distinguishes it from portfolio investment is that FDI is a long-term investment with the intention of exercising control over an enterprise. For cross-border portfolio investments, investors mostly focus on profiting from the purchase and sales of shares and other financial instruments. While FDI often leads to long-term financing and knowledge transfers, portfolio investors usually do not have a long-term relationship with the enterprises in which they invest. For instance, when mutual funds include stocks from international markets in their portfolio, they usually do not expect to influence the operations of the enterprises underlying such investments.

When examining FDI activities in a country or region, we often look at the flow of FDI and the stock of FDI. FDI flow records the value of FDI transactions during a given period of time, usually a quarter or a year. Specifically, FDI inflow refers to the value of inward direct investment made by foreign investors in the reporting country or region, and FDI outflow refers to the value of outward direct investment originated from the reporting country or region.[3] FDI stock refers to the total accumulated amount of FDI in a country or region. It reflects the total value of foreign-owned assets in the reporting country or region at a given point of time.

II. Types of FDI

I. Greenfield Investment vs. Merger & Acquisition (M&A)

FDI has two main forms—greenfield investment in which a direct investor establishes a new venture by constructing new facilities from the ground up, and cross-border M&A in which a direct investor acquires or mergers with an existing firm in a foreign country. For example, Volkswagen used greenfield investment in Kaluga, a Russian city, by building a new auto-making facility; it also acquired Skoda, a Czech-based automaker, to expand its operation in Eastern Europe. The essential difference between greenfield investment and cross-border M&A is that the former adds new productive capacity while the latter requires a change of assets from domestic to foreign hands.[4] In some cases, acquisitions involve extensively restructuring existing operational facilities for new production activities, and such acquisitions are labeled "brownfield investment."[5]

When conducting FDI, companies face the choice between acquiring an existing entity and starting up something new. Comparatively, M&A has two main advantages: access to proprietary resources and speed of entry. The investor will be able to keep the acquired firm's physical assets (such as plant and equipment), experienced employees and managers, access to current customers and suppliers, as well as brand names and reputation. The investor may also generate extra gains by pooling complementary resources from the acquired firm. Moreover, M&A represent a fast means of building up a strong position in a foreign market. Existing operations simplify a lot of potentially tedious details for the investor. Especially in relatively saturated markets, which are hard for newcomers to enter, investors tend to favor M&As.

By contrast, greenfield investment usually requires longer time and greater efforts. However, it allows the investor to build business operations the way it likes, whereas M&A often requires difficult integration with the acquired firm. Sometimes, it is easier to start everything from the ground up than to takeover and change an existing operation. A direct investor may also choose greenfield investment when there is not a suitable target to acquire in a foreign country. This is why many companies favor greenfield investment in developing and underdeveloped markets. Furthermore, greenfield investment, compared to M&A, usually brings new constructions, creates new jobs, and facilitates knowledge transfer. Such investment may get preferential treatments from local governments, such as tax breaks and utility subsidies.

2. Vertical vs. Horizontal FDI

Based on the activities of the overseas enterprise, FDI can be classified into vertical and horizontal FDI. Vertical FDI reflects a company's strategy of vertical integration whereby it owns or seeks to own different stages of the value chain of a product or service in foreign countries. Forward vertical FDI is where the company engages later-stage or downstream activities of the value chain. Backward vertical FDI is where the company engages preceding-stage or upstream activities of the value chain. For instance, GM, a U.S. automaker, conducts forward vertical FDI when it builds or acquires a car distributor overseas, or backward vertical FDI when it owns an auto parts manufacturer abroad. Horizontal FDI is an investment through which a company carries out the same activities abroad as at home. For example, Hyundai, a Korean automaker, assembles cars in both Korea and the U.S.; Microsoft owns software development operations not only in the U.S., its home country, but also several other countries.

The choice between vertical and horizontal FDI depends on the investor's motives for locating production overseas. If a firm focuses on selling goods or services in a foreign country, it may pursue horizontal FDI by locating production near customers, thus circumventing trade barriers and lowering transportation costs.[6] On the other hand, if a firm focuses on seeking efficiency in the value chain, it may choose vertical FDI by replacing outside suppliers or buyers with its own operations.[7] Vertical FDI usually results in intra-company trade among the company and its affiliates.

3. Wholly Owned vs. Partially Owned

In FDI, the investor can choose to have full or partial ownership of its overseas enterprise. Wholly owned FDI is an arrangement in which the investor has 100 percent ownership of the overseas enterprise. Consequently, the investor has full control over the assets and operations of the enterprise. For example, when Honda built its first auto plant in North America, the Marysville Auto Plant in Ohio, it contributed all the investments and had full ownership. Partially owned FDI is an arrangement in which the investor has a part of the overseas enterprise's total equity, and shares its ownership with one or more partners. Such an enterprise is known as joint venture, in which a partner may hold majority, equal (50–50), or minority ownership.

The main difference between wholly owned subsidiaries and joint ventures lies in the level of control. While full ownership allows complete control, joint venture partners have to share control and collaborate on management, which may not be easy due to potential mistrust and conflicts. Certainly, joint venturing can be beneficial as partners bring complementary resources and share risks and costs. In some situations, in order to protect local industries, governments may require foreign direct investors to form joint ventures with local firms. For instance, when entering the Chinese market, Honda set up Guangqi Honda, a 50–50 equal ownership joint venture with Guangzhou Auto Group, a state-owned enterprise.

III. Trends in Global FDI

Over the last several decades, the world has witnessed a significant increase of FDI activities. In the 1990s, the annual average amount of global FDI inflow was about $425 billion USD. In the 2000s, the annual average was $1,153 billion USD. From 2010 to 2014, the annual average reached $1,439 billion USD.[8] Despite a few downturns, the global FDI is expected to continuously grow with the global economy.

It should be noted that FDI is quite reactive to political and economic changes in the world. For instance, FDI declined dramatically after 2000 because of an economic recession in developed countries. The burst of the dot-com bubble in the late 1990s played a major role in this recession. FDI flows later recovered and peaked in 2007, but then plunged again due to the global financial crisis of 2007–8. In general, firms are likely to adjust their overseas investments in response to economic turbulence, policy changes and geopolitical risks.[10]

Historically, the majority of global FDI has flowed into developed countries in most years (as shown in Figure 3.2). Meanwhile, FDI inflows to developing countries have been steadily increasing, even surpassing FDI inflows to developed economies in recent years. In 2014, while developed countries experienced a decrease of inward FDI, FDI inflows to developing economies rose to $681 billion USD and accounted for 55 percent of the global FDI. Among the top ten FDI recipients in 2014, five were developing economies, with developing Asia leading the pack (see Table 3.1). China was ranked the world's largest recipient of FDI, a position previously held by the U.S. for many years. Thanks to continuous FDI flows, the world's FDI stock increased from $7,202 billion USD in 2000 to $26,039 billion USD in 2014, and the share of FDI stock in developing countries increased from 23 percent to 32 percent.

Companies from developed countries remain active in overseas investments and have contributed the majority of FDI outflows. The U.S. has been the number one FDI contributor for many years. Nonetheless, outward FDI from developing countries, especially developing Asia, has seen significant growth in recent years. In 2014, FDI outflows from developing economies

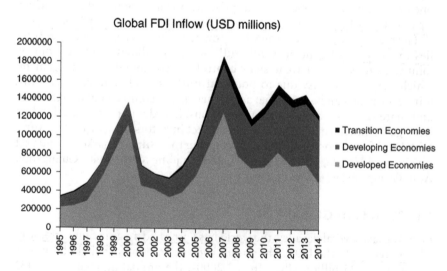

Figure 3.2 Global FDI Inflow

Data Source: UNCTAD, World Investment Report, various years. Retrieved from http://unctad.org/en/pages/DIAE/World%20Investment%20Report/WIR-Series.aspx

Table 3.1 Top 20 Destinations of FDI Flows

Country	Rank in 2014	2014 FDI Inflow (billion USD)	Rank in 2013	2013 FDI Inflow (billion USD)
China	1	129	2	124
Hong Kong, China	2	103	3	74
United States	3	92	1	231
United Kingdom	4	72	9	48
Singapore	5	68	6	65
Brazil	6	62	7	64
Canada	7	54	4	71
Australia	8	52	8	54
India	9	34	15	28
Netherlands	10	30	14	32
Chile	11	23	21	17
Spain	12	23	12	41
Mexico	13	23	10	45
Indonesia	14	23	19	19
Switzerland	15	22	187	−23
Russia	16	21	5	69
Finland	17	19	185	−5
Colombia	18	16	22	16
France	19	15	11	43
Poland	20	14	148	0

Source: UNCTAD, World Investment Report 2015. New York: United Nations.

increased 23 percent from the previous year and reached $468 billion USD. Their share in global FDI outflows reached 35 percent, up from 11 percent in 2004 (see Figure 3.3). Nine of the 20 largest source countries were developing or transition economies, including Hong Kong, China, Russia, Singapore, the Republic of Korea, Malaysia, Kuwait, Chile, and Taiwan.

FDI is generally financed by equity capital, reinvested earnings, and other capital (primarily intra-company loans). Equity capital is a major means of FDI financing, which typically results in new investments and capital expenditures. Reinvested earnings have been rising in recent years. Many direct investors, especially those from developed countries, reinvest their retained earnings in their FDI projects rather than distribute them as dividends. In 2014, the share of reinvested earnings reached a record 81 percent of FDI outflows from developed economies. Intra-company loans usually account for no more than 10 percent of FDI flows. Interest expenses may be used to offset capital gains, thus reducing income tax payments.

As for the sector distribution of FDI, there has been a shift from manufacturing to services. The share of services in global FDI stock increased from 49 percent in 1990, to 58 percent in 2001, and 63 percent in 2012, while the share of manufacturing sectors decreased and the share of primary sectors

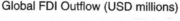

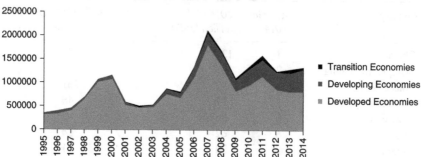

Figure 3.3 Global FDI Outflow

Data Source: UNCTAD, World Investment Report, various years. Retrieved from http://unctad.org/en/
pages/DIAE/World%20Investment%20Report/WIR-Series.aspx

remained below 10 percent. This shift reflects a similar trend in the global GDP, in which service sectors' contributions have been growing. Deregulation has also encouraged FDI in service sectors, especially in those traditionally restricted areas such as finance and telecommunication.

The distribution of FDI flows between greenfield projects and cross-border M&As is also worth noting. In terms of total value, greenfield projects surpassed M&As in most years except 2007, when an M&A boom was fueled by cheap debt financing. As FDI sources, while developed countries contribute more in both greenfield projects and M&As, developing countries have been gaining strength steadily. Between 2005 and 2014, developing-country firms' share in greenfield FDI projects increased from 20 to 30 percent, while their share in cross-border M&As jumped from 10 to almost 40 percent. When talking about FDI destinations, the value of greenfield projects in developed countries is much less than that in developing countries (see Table 3.2). Conversely, the value of M&A deals in developed countries is greater than that in developing countries. These patterns suggest that greenfield projects are usually preferred in developing countries while M&As are more common in developed economies.

IV. Theories of FDI

Why would a firm invest overseas? Where and when would a firm conduct direct investment? With the rise of FDI, scholarly theories have addressed these questions from various perspectives. This section presents a few general theories and frameworks explaining FDI flows and their patterns.

I. Monopolistic Advantage Theory

According to Stephen H. Hymer, the pioneer of monopolistic advantage theory, a company pursues FDI because it has firm-specific advantages that

Table 3.2 Value of Announced Greenfield Projects and Cross-Border M&As

Year	Greenfield Projects (billion USD)				M&As (billion USD)			
	Sources		Destinations		Sources		Destinations	
	Developed	Developing	Developed	Developing	Developed	Developing	Developed	Developing
2008	982	351	412	845	480	114	474	118
2009	710	243	322	602	191	80	236	44
2010	599	206	290	489	225	100	260	83
2011	610	253	289	534	432	101	437	84
2012	432	188	237	356	184	124	267	55
2013	479	209	226	452	179	120	238	79
2014	481	208	222	448	228	152	275	120

Source: UNCTAD, World Investment Report 2015. New York: United Nations.

others do not in that country.[11] Firm-specific advantages, such as superior knowledge and economies of scale, are relatively monopolistic, allowing the firm to compete abroad against local firms. Compared to local firms, foreign investors usually lack familiarity with local business contexts (including culture, language, market condition, legal system, etc.) and are exposed to the fluctuation of foreign exchange rates. In order to offset these disadvantages, foreign firms must establish market power from their monopolistic advantages. In addition to suppressing competition, monopolistic advantages also enable investors to generate greater returns. Superior knowledge, such as advanced technology and managerial expertise, can be further exploited via direct investments in more than one country. The increase of operational scale following FDI may lead to a decrease in unit cost, i.e. economies of scale. For instance, GM's overseas plants not only enable the company to transfer and exploit its auto technologies, manufacturing know-how, and brand reputation in multiple countries but also spread the costs of procurement, R&D, and other functions over a global scale of production. This theory highlights the distinction between FDI and portfolio investment. While portfolio investments are driven by short-term financial returns, direct investments are capital flow associated with business operations, in which firms exercise control to profit from monopolistic advantages.

2. Product Life Cycle Theory

Raymond Vernon's product life cycle theory provides explanations for both international trade and FDI. By adding a time dimension to the monopolistic advantage, this theory addresses why a firm in an advanced economy shifts from exporting to FDI.[12] When the firm initially innovates a new product, it gains a monopolistic advantage, enabling export to other countries. As foreign demand increases, the firm may shift production abroad in order to achieve economies of scale and bypass trade barriers. As the product matures and becomes standardized, its original advantage based on product features declines. The firm begins to focus on cost reduction and shifts production to countries with lower production costs. For instance, many personal computer (PC) technologies were invented in the U.S. and the U.S. was initially the major manufacturing country of PCs. With the maturity of PC technologies and the increase of foreign demand, many American PC manufacturers cut their production at home and opened up plants in low-cost countries like China. The product life cycle theory outlines how innovating firms start their international production. It highlights the interplay of technology innovation and location-specific factors and explains why multinational companies may prefer FDI to exporting. However, with the increasing speed and globalization of innovations, companies do not necessarily follow the sequential stages of the product life cycle.[13] Many firms develop new products in offshore research centers and quickly transfer new knowledge across the world. Instead of pacing their international production as a new product matures, they are able to utilize a globalized network of R&D and production from the beginning.

3. Internalization Theory

The internalization theory suggests that FDI enables a firm to internalize and control the transactions of intermediate products or services, thus replacing external transactions with more efficient organizational arrangements.[14] This theory helps explain why a firm prefers direct investment to licensing or franchising in international markets. In a licensing or franchising agreement, the firm receives a royalty fee without bearing the costs of investing in and managing an overseas entity in an unfamiliar setting. However, according to the internalization theory, firm advantages based on tacit knowledge, such as technical know-how and managerial expertise, are more amenable to FDI than they are to licensing or franchising. Those advantages require hands-on training and learning-by-doing, and thus cannot be easily or fully transferred via an arm's-length deal in the market. Also, FDI allows a firm to have more control over international operations than licensing or franchising does. The exploitation of firm-specific advantages may require the coordination of manufacturing, marketing, and other business functions. But the foreign licensee (or franchisee), out of its own interests, may act in a way against the licensor's (or franchiser's) objectives. Furthermore, FDI enables a firm to better protect its intellectual property rights. When licensing or franchising, the firm may give away its valuable knowledge to a foreign company, who then may become a potential competitor. Even though restrictions are often included in licensing (or franchising) contracts to protect the licensor's (or franchiser's) interests, such contract clauses can be difficult to enforce. Given the limitations of licensing and franchising, a firm may find it more efficient to directly control international operations than to work with a foreign licensee or franchisee. Through FDI, the firm internalizes the transactions between entities in different countries, thus circumventing the limitations of licensing and franchising. For instance, after licensing its first overseas theme park (Tokyo Disney) to a Japanese company, Disney shifted to partial-ownership FDI in Paris, Hong Kong, and Shanghai in an effort to better utilize and protect its brand and reputation. Although Hyundai could license its car models to other companies, it decided to set up its own production in Europe as the company's competitive advantages mainly derive from its manufacturing expertise.

4. The Eclectic Paradigm

The eclectic paradigm, also known as the OLI model, is a theoretical framework developed by John Dunning.[15] It provides a holistic approach to explaining FDI and its pattern. The paradigm includes three sets of components:

- Ownership advantages (O) refer to firm-specific characteristics that enable a firm to gain competitive advantages in international markets, such as brand name, technology, managerial skills, organizational structure and process.
- Location advantages (L) refer to location-specific conditions that facilitate a firm's business operations in a country, such as factor endowments (e.g.

land, raw materials, labor, capital, and knowledge), market conditions, government policies, as well as political, legal, and cultural environments.
- Internalization advantages (I) refer to benefits gained through owing and controlling foreign operations rather than producing via market transactions such as licensing and franchising.

This paradigm integrates different theories about FDI. Ownership advantages, corresponding to the monopolistic advantage theory, suggest that firms seek to utilize their assets through international expansion. Similar to the product life cycle theory, location advantages indicate that firms are motivated to locate operations in certain countries rather than conduct those activities at home. As per the internalization theory, internalization advantages answer why it is advantageous for firms to internalize certain operations via FDI. According to the OLI model, all three types of advantages are important to firms' FDI activities. For instance, Vodafone invested in Africa not only because it has advanced mobile technologies and Africa is a booming market but also because the company needs direct control to transfer and utilize its core competencies.

5. The Linkage-Leverage-Learning Framework

In recent years, the increasing FDI outflow from emerging markets has imposed a new challenge to FDI theories. Unlike traditional MNCs from developed countries, multinational firms from emerging markets are typically latecomers and they rarely possess monopolistic advantages. To account for their rapid rise, the linkage-leverage-learning framework addresses FDI from a dynamic perspective.[16] This framework views FDI as a process of resource deployment, utilization, and development. Linkage is about how the latecomers link up with existing knowledge networks and sources of advantage. The international expansion of emerging-market firms is focused on the advantages that can be acquired externally rather than their own existing advantages. By tapping into resources and capabilities in foreign markets, a firm may use FDI to mitigate the disadvantages of being a newcomer or latecomer. Leverage is about turning access to new knowledge into leverage opportunities. For instance, emerging-market firms may use their newly acquired resources and capabilities to upgrade and expand their product portfolio. Learning is the result of repeated applications of the linkage and leverage processes. The success of emerging-market firms depends on the integration of the newly acquired knowledge into their existing knowledge portfolio. For instance, Geely, a Chinese automaker, acquired Volvo to access Volvo's technology base and develop new products through collaboration with Volvo; Huawei's R&D center in Silicon Valley has allowed the company to tap into local talent pool and knowledge spillover.

V. FDI Motives and Benefits

Firms pursue FDI in order to enhance firm competitiveness in the global marketplace. Various specific motives can be derived from the aforementioned theories—market seeking, resource seeking, efficiency seeking, and strategic asset seeking.[17] These motives are not exclusive. Some may apply simultaneously to a given FDI venture.

Market-seeking FDI is intended to meet market demand in a particular foreign market. First, attractive overseas opportunities may pull companies to expand internationally. Local production is utilized to meet local customers' preferences and adapt to local market conditions. Second, when a firm's key customers invest abroad, the firm may need to follow them overseas. Such FDI allows the firm to preempt other vendors from serving its customers. Third, a company may be pushed by competition to invest abroad. In order to maintain its global presence and market share, the firm may need to venture into the markets served by its current or potential competitors.

Resource-seeking FDI is focused on gaining access to certain production factors at a lower cost in foreign countries. Such FDI is supply oriented, i.e. that firms tend to invest where certain resources are more abundant and less costly. They may seek physical resources (like natural resources and raw materials), human labor (skilled or unskilled), as well as technological and managerial skills.

Efficiency-seeking FDI is focused on gaining efficiencies, such as economies of scale and economies of scope, by owning and organizing business activities in geographically dispersed locations. In other words, it is intended to promote a more efficient division of labor and specialization among the foreign and domestic operations of an MNC. For instance, the MNC may set up a global procurement network to lower sourcing costs, or concentrate manufacturing in a few locations to optimize production and distribution. Through its internal network of subsidiaries, the MNC may also avoid trade barriers and tap into favorable government incentives.

Strategic asset-seeking FDI is intended to acquire the assets of foreign firms so as to develop long-term competitive advantages. Unlike resource-seeking motives, which stress location advantages, the purpose of strategic asset seeking is to augment ownership advantages. Firms with this intention are usually active in forming cross-border partnerships and/or pursuing international acquisitions.

These motives correspond to potential benefits that can be obtained from FDI. On the one hand, firms can achieve cost savings by accessing location-specific advantages and optimizing their business operations in different countries. On the other hand, they can increase returns by exploiting overseas opportunities and ensure learning by acquiring new knowledge from international markets. Certainly, these benefits are not guaranteed. Additional risks and costs arise when an MNC operates in unfamiliar political, legal, economic, and cultural systems of a foreign country.

VI. Country Impacts and Government Policies

I. The Host Country

FDI flows generate impacts on the national welfare of both host and home countries. The host country is the destination or receiving country of FDI.

Along with capital flow, other resources such as technology and management skills are often transferred into the host country. MNCs bring not only additional capacity but also efficient production to serve local customers. They may increase local competition and force local incumbents to be more innovative and productive. Also, they may spillover new knowledge to local companies, thus increasing the overall productivity of the host country. Meanwhile, FDI has positive employment effects when MNCs launch or expand overseas business operations. They not only directly hire more people in their own operations but also indirectly create new jobs through sourcing from local suppliers and communities. Even in acquisition deals where job cuts are common, foreign investors often inject capital for expansion after initial restructuring.

Other than these benefits, FDI flows also have adverse effects. Competition from MNCs may hurt local incumbents' market performance, thus reducing employment in those businesses. In some cases, powerful foreign firms may achieve monopolies in local markets, allowing them to hike up prices for customers and harm the economic welfare of the host country. Furthermore, the host country government may be concerned about the loss of economic independence when MNCs dominate the supply of certain critical products.

In order to maximize the benefits and minimize the drawbacks, most host countries have both promotional and restrictive policies toward FDI. In the last several decades, government policies are predominantly geared toward promoting and encouraging FDI. For instance, in 2014, more than 80 percent of investment policies were aimed at improving entry conditions and reducing restrictions.[18] Various incentive measures, such as tax breaks, low-interest loans, grants and subsidies, are offered to attracted foreign investments. For instance, in order to attract Microsoft's investment, the Vietnamese government significantly lowered tax burden for the company. With the progress of globalization, many sectors traditionally closed to foreigners, like infrastructure and services, are increasingly open. Meanwhile, restrictions on FDI still exist in many countries. Foreign companies are often excluded from areas with national security concerns or restricted in industries with strategic importance to the host country, such as transport, energy, and defense. Equity restraint is the most common restrictive measure. For instance, foreign firms are not allowed to own more than 25 percent of an airline in the U.S.; in China, foreign ownership is restricted to 50 percent in auto manufacturing and media businesses. In addition, some governments have operational requirements for foreign companies, such as local content (mandatory sourcing from local suppliers), export (certain percentage of products must be exported), and technology transfer (advance technologies must be transferred to local operations).

2. The Home Country

The home country is the origin or source country of FDI. For the home country, the main benefits of FDI outflows derive from the repatriation of profits and the acquisition of resources and strategic assets. Once an MNC becomes profitable in a foreign market, it can send foreign earnings back to its headquarters, increasing the national income of the home country. Also, the MNC may acquire valuable resources and strategic assets from its international operations. For instance, in order to secure the supply of certain natural resources, many companies have invested in extraction and mining businesses in foreign countries. Through partnership with or acquisition of foreign firms, companies can learn valuable skills and utilize them in home country operations.

The major concern about outward FDI flows is the loss of employment in the home country. In many cases, FDI involves the relocation of production from the home country to the host country, which may result in job loss in production. However, if such relocation enables an MNC to lower costs and increase sales, the expansion of its business may create new jobs in other functions, such as marketing and administration.

Similarly, home country governments have both encouraging and restricting policies. Many countries have government-backed programs to support firms' international expansion, such as insurance policies covering foreign investment risks, government funding for FDI, and tax breaks for foreign incomes. For instance, to help Chinese firms gain global competitiveness, the Chinese government has initiated a "Go Out" policy to promote investment abroad, which includes such measures as simplified approval process, foreign currency exchange support, government funding and low-interest loans, tax incentives, insurance support, as well as information, training, and legal support. Moreover, home country governments can negotiate international investment treaties with other countries to remove host country restrictions on FDI flows. Meanwhile, many countries have some control over outward FDI. They may prohibit investment in certain countries due to political reasons, apply foreign exchange restriction to limit capital outflows, and use tax incentives to encourage investment at home rather than abroad.

Key Terms

FDI flow, FDI stock, multinational corporation (MNC), portfolio investment, greenfield investment, merger & acquisition (M&A), ownership advantage, location advantage, internalization advantage, strategic asset seeking, host country, home country, resource transfer, knowledge spillover, FDI incentives, FDI restrictions

Review Questions

1. What are the key characteristics of FDI? How is it different from portfolio investment?
2. What are the main trends of global FDI? How do these trends affect the global economy?
3. How do monopolistic advantage theory, product life cycle theory, and internalization theory differ from one another?
4. Can the eclectic paradigm completely explain FDI activities? Does the linkage-learning-leverage framework add new insights about FDI?
5. What are the main benefits MNCs seek from FDI?

6. What impacts do FDI inflows have on the host country economy?
7. What impacts do FDI outflows have on the home country economy?
8. How can governments encourage or restrict FDI?

Internet Exercises

1. Please visit the website of United Nations Conference on Trade and Development (www.unctad.org) and review the latest World Investment Report. Identify the countries that are most active in FDI and explain why. Find the newest developments of FDI and discuss your findings with your classmates.
2. Please go to A. T. Kearney's website (www.atkearney.com/gbpc/foreign-direct-investment-confidence-index) to review the consulting firm's Foreign Direct Investment Confidence Index. Suppose you are in charge of researching prospective destinations for a company's direct investment. What can you learn from this index? You may select a few countries and compare them.

Notes

1   UNCTAD. (n.d.). Definition of FDI. Retrieved from http://unctad.org/en/Pages/DIAE/Foreign-Direct-Investment-(FDI).aspx
2   D Statistics. (n.d.). Retrieved from www.oecd.org/daf/inv/investmentstatisticsandanalysis/40193734.pdf
3   United Nations. (n.d.). FDI net inflows and net outflows as share of GDP. Retrieved from www.un.org/esa/sustdev/natlinfo/indicators/methodology_sheets/global_econ_partnership/fdi.pdf
4   UNCTAD. (2000). World Investment Report 2000. New York: United Nations.
5   Meyer, K. E. and Estrin, S. (2001). Brownfield entry in emerging markets. *Journal of International Business Studies*, 32(3), 257–267.
6   Ramondo, N., Rappoport, V., and Ruhl, K. J. (2013). Horizontal versus vertical foreign direct investment: Evidence from U.S. multinationals. *UC San Diego Typescript Manuscript.*
7   Lankhuizen, M. (2014). The (Im)possibility of distinguishing horizontal and vertical motivations for FDI. *Review of Development Economics*, 18(1), 139–151.
8   UNCTAD. World Investment Report, various years. New York: United Nations.
9   Poulsen, L. S. and Hufbauer, G. C. (2011). Foreign direct investment in times of crisis. *Peterson Institute for International Economics Working Paper*, (11–3).
10 UNCTAD. (2015). World Investment Report 2015. New York: United Nations.
11 Hymer, S. H. (1960). The international operations of national firms: A study of direct foreign investment. PhD Dissertation. Published posthumously. The MIT Press, 1976. Cambridge, MA.
12 Vernon, R. (1966). International investment and international trade in the product cycle. *The Quarterly Journal of Economics*, 80(2), 190–207.
13 Dhalla, N. K. and Yuspeh, S. (1976). Forget the product life cycle concept. *Harvard Business Review*, 54(1), 102–112.
14 Buckley, P. J. and Casson, M. (1976). A long-run theory of the multinational enterprise. In *The future of the multinational enterprise* (32–65). London: Palgrave Macmillan; Hennart, J. F. (1982). *A theory of multinational enterprise*. Ann Arbor, MI: University of Michigan Press.

15 Dunning, J. H. (1988). The eclectic paradigm of international production: A restatement and some possible extensions. *Journal of International Business Studies, 19*(1), 1–31.
16 Mathews, J. A. (2006). Dragon multinationals: New players in 21st century globalization. *Asia Pacific Journal of Management, 23*(1), 5–27.
17 Meyer, K. E. (2015). What is "strategic asset seeking FDI"? *The Multinational Business Review, 23*(1), 57–66.
18 UNCTAD. (2015). World Investment Report 2015. New York: United Nations.

The Context of Global Business

Economic Environment

Learning Objectives

1. Recognize world economic development trends and compare economic growth across different regions.
2. Understand regional economic integration efforts and trends on major continents.
3. Identify the pros and cons of different measurements of a country's economic development.
4. Explain indices that measure the degree of a country's globalization, openness and competitiveness.

Cases

Case 4.1 Economic Development Trends in BRICS
Case 4.2 Singapore's Economic Growth
Case 4.3 Brexit's Effect on the Global Economy
Case 4.4 Economic Impact of the TPP Agreement

Case 4.1 Economic Development Trends in BRICS

Over the past two years, economic growth in emerging markets including BRICS (Brazil, Russia, India, China, and South Africa) has considerably weakened. In 2014, experts predicted that the weighted gross domestic product (GDP) growth of BRICS would be lower than the annual average growth of 8 percent between 2000–2008. A key issue lies in figuring out whether the stagnation in emerging economies is cyclical or temporal and to what extent is the slowdown structural and continual. The former means that economic growth of emerging markets could return to earlier high growth levels experienced before the global financial crisis if cyclical conditions, like external demand from developed countries, improve. Conversely, the latter implies that economic growth in emerging markets will have long-term recessional patterns and maintain lower economic growth levels as experienced after the crisis. The growth decomposition of BRICS between 1996 and 2012 shows several noteworthy features regarding the growth slowdown in these countries. In terms of production function, GDP growth rate can be broken down into three contributing factors: labor input, capital accumulation, and total factor productivity (TFP).

The main causes for the decline in GDP growth that superseded the 2008 global financial crisis can be attributed to a decrease of total factor productivity, the measurement of the overall efficiency of the economy resulting from the transformation of labor, and capital into output. However, in recent years, contributions from labor and capital growth have also been declining. One thing to note is that, in the aftermath of the financial crisis, a significant part of variation reflected cyclical movement due to changes in aggregate demand as opposed to structural changes in technological advances or supply factors.

Many studies that utilize sophisticated techniques such as series analysis and the structural modeling approach provide more information. Comparisons of the estimates of potential output and output gaps for actual GDP growth and potential growth in BRICS suggest some interesting results. First, prior to the crisis, potential output in 2005–2008 grew slower than real gross domestic product (GDP), creating a substantial positive output gap during the crisis. The output gap increase correlated with a significant increase of inflation in all emerging countries, except Brazil. The output gap is most likely largest in Russia and South Africa. Second, the growth of potential GDP has declined in all five economies in the aftermath of the crisis. In particular, China and India's GDP declined the most. Lastly, economists estimated small negative output gaps for these economies, the largest gap being in India. The projected decline of growth potential with small negative output gaps reveals that the relative speed of economic expansion in BRICS will fall below pre-crisis levels. A moderate cyclical upturn in the short term is expected, particularly in India. However, a more sustainable growth process will depend on policies and reforms to eliminate bottleneck on the supply side. Strong efforts are required to stimulate capital accumulation, promote technological development, strengthen human capital, and improve the function of labor markets in most emerging economies.

Almost all emerging economies including Brazil, India, Indonesia, Mexico, Russia, South Africa, and Turkey are expected to experience modest economic growth recovery in 2015 and 2016. However, there are significant risks of further stagnation, and slow and weak long-term growth. Broad slowdown in emerging economies, especially rapid slowdown in China, results in developing countries experiencing low economic growth. Low economic growth also makes economic recovery difficult for developed countries, particularly in the Euro zone. The combination of weak growth and tighter financial constraints present a hazard. The current economic risks affecting many emerging economies is due to negative feedback loops between weak activity in the real sector and domestic financial conditions tightening in accordance with an expected rise in interest rates in U.S.

Situations similar to the 2014–15 financial crisis show the dynamics of the feedback loop and illustrate the policy dilemmas that emerging countries are facing. During the crisis, global investors showed concerns about global growth, high uncertainty and country-specific shock. This resulted in strong portfolio capital reversals and currency depreciation in emerging markets, especially in Brazil, Indonesia, South Africa, and Turkey. Thus, these countries have a strong need for external funding.

The central banks of these countries faced significant downward pressure of domestic asset price and currency. Interest rates were raised even when economic growth was slow. Even though these moves stabilized the financial markets, real economy activities were further slowed down and developed economies produced lower than expected performances due to geopolitical tensions between Russia and the Ukraine. China's moderate economic growth negatively affected real economic activity in emerging economies.

The current growth rate is less than half the annual average of 8.5 percent from 2004–2007. With the exception of China, economic downturn, indicated by the size of the recent recession, is more pronounced. Without China, emerging-market growth in 2014 is only 2.3 percent, compared to 6.5 percent from 2004–2007. Most of the recent slowdown in emerging economies outside of Asia is due to weak growth in investment and total factor productivity. Since 2011, many countries displayed slow investment in fixed capital.

As a result, gross fixed investment showed negative or low contribution to GDP in most emerging economies outside Asia for the past two years. Investment-to-GDP ratios were below 20 percent in several economies including Argentina, Brazil, South Africa, and Turkey. Emerging economies having the lowest levels of total factor productivity in two decades face challenges to achieve technological progress and efficiency improvements.

With expected monetary policy in the United States, emerging markets are likely to see tightening financial conditions in the future. The absence of a push for new reforms may weaken real investment growth in the private sector. An important question in this regard is the degree that U.S. interest rates affect the cost of borrowing in emerging markets. While fixed capital formation has not changed significantly in recent years, many emerging countries showed credit growth with increased leverage in corporate and household sectors. Corporate sector debt as a share of GDP is high in fast-growing East Asian countries including China and Malaysia. Less dynamic economies such as Brazil, Russia, South Africa, and Turkey are in a similar situation. Preliminary evidence indicates that a portion of the new loan was used to increase corporate cash holdings. Rising interest rates and stagnant economic growth may place significant pressure on companies' balance sheets weakening earnings.

Although most Chinese debt is held domestically and is less affected by global financial conditions, a high and rapidly growing level of total debt is subject to significant risks. South Africa and Turkey have large current account deficits. Among economies with large external financing needs, countries with weak economic fundamentals and large open capital markets seem to be most vulnerable to global financial situations.

Sources

1.   DESA Development Policy and Analysis Division. (2015). World Economic Situation and Prospects, 2015. Retrieved from www.un.org/en/development/desa/policy/wesp/

Questions for Case Discussion

1. Explain whether recent slowdowns in emerging economies are cyclical or temporary.
2. Describe the reasons for the decline in GDP growth in emerging economies.
3. Discuss how the economic slowdown in China would affect the growth rate in transitional and developing countries.
4. Estimate potential output and output gaps between actual GDP growth and potential growth in BRICS.

Case 4.2 Singapore's Economic Growth

Fifty years ago, the per capita gross domestic product of Singapore was less than $320 USD. Today, however, it is among the fastest-growing economies in the world. For a country that lacks geographic size and is scarce in natural resources, Singapore's economic growth is remarkable. Singapore has been able to overcome geographical disadvantages and has emerged as a global commerce leader by embracing globalization, free market capitalism, and education, as well as introducing meticulous pragmatic policy. This case shows how Singapore achieved its economic growth and the resulting consequences including income inequality.

Singapore was under the control of the U.K. for more than 100 years. When the U.K. failed to defend Singapore from the Japanese during World War II, a strong anti-colonial sentiment emerged among the Singapore citizens eventually leading to the country's independence. In 1963, Singapore quickly merged with Federation of Malaysia denouncing British rule. Although Singapore was not the under the U.K.'s rule, for two years, various ethnic groups in Malaysia struggled to coexist as assimilation efforts proved to be unsuccessful. Street riots and violence became common occurrences. The Chinese population in Singapore was three times higher than the Malay population. Malay politicians in Kuala Lumpur were afraid that the increasing number of Chinese citizens would threaten their heritage and political ideologies. The Malaysian Parliament responded by voting to oust Singapore from Malaysia in order to lift the domestic communist sentiment and ensure a Malay majority resided within the country. Singapore gained its formal independence on August 9, 1965, with the election of the influential Lee Kuan Yew as prime minister. After gaining independence, Singapore continued to experience difficulties. The majority of the country's three million people were unemployed and more than two-thirds of the population were living in ghettos and unauthorized settlements on the outskirts of the city. Singapore was stuck in the middle between two large and uncooperative countries, Malaysia and Indonesia. The country was also short of natural resources, sanitation, proper infrastructure, and adequate water supply. In order to facilitate development, Lee sought international support, but there was no response.

As a small, resource-deprived city-state without an adequately large domestic market to create sufficient jobs and economic growth, Singapore had no strategy for long-term survival and prosperity that would enable it to integrate into the global economic system. After achieving independence, politicians, academics, and other leaders continuously advocated for the nation to globally integrate. In response, lawmakers revised policies encouraging Singapore to integrate into regional and global networks. In 1972, in a speech titled "Global City in Singapore," Singapore's first Foreign Minister S. Rajaratnam emphasized that Singapore's survival depended on the ability to become a "global city."

In general, globalization means the greater interdependence of national, regional, and global economies by reducing barriers to the international flow of goods, capital, labor, technology, and ideas. For example, technological development, infrastructure and policy reforms such as trade and capital liberalization have facilitated globalization. It was important for Singapore, through foreign investment, to develop manufacturing and production facilities and generate financial capital.

To facilitate globalization, Singapore continued to act as the international hub connecting the international trade and commerce system through its ports, airports, and technological systems. It also needed to attract multinational corporations (MNCs) and take a central role in the international financial network. In 1961, the Singaporean government established the Economic Development Board (EDB) to attract foreign investors. The board allowed the government to adopt Free Trade Zones (FTZs) and Export Processing Zones (EPZs). EPZs are industrial sites with first-class physical infrastructures and allowed duty-free entry for the re-export of goods. Tax benefits were also offered to foreign investors and labor costs were controlled to help sustain a competitive advantage.

Singapore pursued tourist dollars as part of its economic growth strategy. In 1964, the government created the Singapore Tourism Promotion Board (STPB) in order to promote Singapore as a tourist destination. STPB sought tourism strategies that focused on garden attractions and modern hotels. In 1968, Singapore liberalized migrant workers to enter with temporary work permits. In 1970, migrant workers accounted for 3.2 percent of the labor force. In the 1980s, the Singaporean economy transformed from labor-intensive industries to high-technology and service industries. This transition was the beginning of a long-term redirection toward Singapore becoming a business services gateway to firms operating in the region.

In 1979, policymakers implemented a high-wage policy to push firms to transform themselves to compete in more capital-intensive and productive industries. However, in 1985, increased costs led to an economic slump. Additionally in 1985, the economic crisis led to a reversal of the high-wage policy and mandated employers to open retirement funds for workers. This period also demonstrated a significant change in Singapore's tourism strategy that shifted toward a greater emphasis on the preservation of cultural heritage. Cultural sites such as Chinatown and Little India were preserved and redeveloped as important landmarks.

In addition to the construction of various economic structures in the 1990s, Singapore's service industries grew. In 1991, the government set a vision for the long-term development trajectory of Singapore stating that a clear end goal of Singapore is to become a global city. To compete effectively, Singapore should have an international perspective and only utilize internal human resources. Therefore, Singapore was opening its doors to anyone with talent or skills, and who could adapt to the local lifestyle. Highly talented people have high mobility; as a result, Singapore should have leveraged its strengths as an international metropolis to attract talent in Asia. In the late 1990s, Singapore deregulated the banking and financial sectors to compete with Hong Kong and other financial hubs. Capital markets were liberalized to allow foreigners to access foreign stocks and future exchanges. A tax exemption scheme was introduced to entice risk management companies while MNCs were prompted to install regional financial centers in Singapore.

Singapore's reaction to globalization demands was not unique. Numerous countries and cities had adopted similar strategies focused on taking advantage of globalization to promote economic growth and enhanced living standards.

Despite the economic downturn triggered by regional and global events from 1997 to 2009, Singapore's commitment to attain greater global integration remained intact. Currently, Singapore has grown into a global and regional hub with high-skilled industries, R&D, export services, global talent, and a rich creative arts cluster. The Urban Redevelopment Authority (URA) in Singapore adopted a greater outward approach.

Economic Growth and Job Creation

Overall, the strategy of the government was to strengthen the global integration of Singapore to spur economic growth and create jobs. The introduction of multinational companies in Singapore in the 1960s created many jobs for Singaporeans. Until 1973, multinational corporations had drastically reduced unemployment by absorbing 10 percent of the labor force. The unemployment rate fell from 10 percent in 1965 to 2 percent in 1990, and the current unemployment rate is lower than the unemployment rate of 6 percent over the past 20 years. These figures show the success of Singapore's global economic orientation strategy. The real GDP growth rate between 1960 and 1969 doubled and the real GDP rate between 1966 and 1973 grew to reach double digits.

Furthermore, Singapore's open economy and integration into global markets means it is vulnerable to economic instability. It has been proven that globalization cannot be a "panacea." Instead, side effects such as increased income inequality are prevalent. For example, the devaluation of the Thai baht in 1997 caused a domino effect in many countries, including Singapore. Like the economic downturns from 2001 to 2003 and subsequently in 2008, financial crises triggered by U.S. subprime mortgage defaults had an adverse impact on Singapore's economy.

Over time, Singapore's employment has shifted from the manufacturing to the service sector. In 2013, about 80 percent of the domestic labor force was engaged in services, compared to 67 percent in 1990. During the same period, the share of manufacturing labor force significantly decreased from 26 percent in 1990 to 14 percent in 2013. Specifically, the share of the workforce engaged in financial and business industries rose from 12 percent in 1990 to 21 percent in 2013. On the other hand, the GDP share of the financial services industry underwent a slight rise from 23 percent in 1985 to 27 percent in 2013.

Fall and Rise of Income Inequality

An economic strategy focused on export-led employment significantly reduced unemployment and moderately reduced income inequality. Income inequality is measured by the Gini coefficient; the coefficient declined from 0.498 in 1966 to 0.448 in 1975. Since 1975, income disparity in Singapore has increased. Wages of top earners steadily increased while those of low-income workers remained almost the same. Furthermore, in 1974–1997, the top 5 and 1 percent of income earners has remained fairly constant but in recent decades this number has increased. Local scholars have offered a possible explanation for the increase in wage inequality in Singapore. They pointed out a global decrease in middle skilled jobs that were replaced by automation and IT technology. On the other hand, the proportion of high-skilled personnel was only 1.6 percent in 2010.

Sources

1. DESA Development Policy and Analysis Division. (2015). World Economic Situation and Prospects, 2015. Retrieved from www.un.org/en/development/desa/policy/wesp/.
2. Ghesquiere, H. (2006, September). *Singapore's Success—Engineering Economic Growth*. Singapore: Thomson Publishing, p. 40.
3. Bhanoji Rao, V. V. and Ramakrishnan, M. (1980). *Income Inequality in Singapore*. Singapore University Press, pp. 25–26.
4. Teo, Leslie (2014, January 28). Presentation "Divergence: The paradox of global convergence," Singapore Perspectives 2014. Retrieved from http://lkyspp.nus.edu.sg/ips/wp-content/uploads/sites/2/2013/12/Leslie-Teo-Slides_website.pdf
5. Department of Statistics. Household income by work. Retrieved from www.singstat.gov.sg/statistics/browse-by-theme/population-and-population-structure
6. Lee Kuan Yew School of Public Policy at the National University of Singapore (2014). http://lkyspp.nus.edu.sg/wp-content/uploads/2014/11/Case-Study-Singapore-as-a-Global-City.pdf

Questions for Case Discussion

1. Describe the advantages and disadvantages of the globalization strategy in Singapore.
2. Investigate inequality problems resulting from Singapore becoming a global hub. How can the country overcome these problems?
3. Explain the potential pitfalls of continuing Singapore's "global hub" strategy.
4. Examine the possibilities of applying Singapore's globalization strategy to other countries.

Case 4.3 Brexit's Effect on the Global Economy

If Britain decides to leave the European Union, the economic ramifications and consequences will be felt across the global economy, especially in the U.K. There are three potential results of Britain's exit: a "Booming Britain," in which the British economy will experience tremendous economic growth and be unaffected by the severance from the EU; "Troubled Transition" Britain will experience a period of financial instability and turmoil; and "Disastrous Decision" Britain's economy will suffer long-term damage.

Those in favor of a Brexit believe in the "Booming Britain" approach. These individuals believe that Britain will experience a major growth period in which the country can negotiate and establish new free trade agreements that would serve the country's economic interest. They also believe that with this separation the country will be able to control migrant movement in and out of the country, regulate the markets, and gain access to specific markets. Critics of a Brexit believe in both the "Troubled Transition" and "Disastrous Decision." These individuals believe Britain's exit from the EU would prevent the country from taking advantage of a growing global economy and utilizing the EU's influence on the rest of the world. If Britain were to exit and attempt to negotiate a free trade agreement, the country would be unable to access the same goods and services.

Furthermore, there are multiple ways in which a Brexit will impact domestic GDP. Foremost, Britain will experience losses from lower trade. The Center for European Reform recently published a study concluding that Britain's inclusion in the EU has actually boosted trade by 55 percent. This contradicts proponents of a Brexit who believe that trade decreased due to EU membership. Additionally, Britain would lose a large portion of foreign investment, especially in the financial services industry. As Britain voted to leave the EU, it is estimated that 100,000 financial service jobs could be lost. PricewaterhouseCoopers (PwC) in its latest report warned that an exit would cause a serious impact on the British economy leading to significant job loss. As a result, there would be between 70,000 and 100,000 fewer jobs in 2020 as the sector declines by 9.5 percent compared to estimated job numbers if Britain remained.

Reputable firms from around the world come to London to gain access to the European single market bringing jobs and infusing investment. Brexit risks damaging the financial services sector, delaying investment decisions, and reducing activity. It also threatens the overall competitiveness of Britain as it loses location advantage for conducting business. Some have argued the financial sectors would still experience growth but at a decreasing rate; instead of 45 percent in 2020 it would most likely be between 35–38 percent. PwC believe Britain's financial sector is more vulnerable than the rest of Britain's economy because the country relies heavily on access to European markets. The financial sector is closely linked to the condition of the economy and susceptible to slow economic growth.

Furthermore, Britain's trading relationships with the EU and the rest of the world are at risk. Britain could retrieve some of the loss by creating new FTAs with EU partners and other countries but it is not assured and could take several years to negotiate. Finally, proponents of a Brexit believe that, as an independent nation, the country would be able to enforce tighter regulations preventing the number of foreign workers from entering the country. Critics are quick to point out that an imposition of tighter controls on migrants would actually require the country to recruit and attract skilled employees from other countries and regions such as India and Africa instead of Eastern Europe. An exit would have no net effect on migration.

In a larger context, Britain's exit would also affect those remaining members in the EU. In 2014, Britain contributed 14.1 billion euros to the EU. After rebates and contributions to customs and duties this amount equates to approximately 7 billion euros, which constitutes 5 percent of the EU's budget. If Britain did decide to leave, this amount would have to be supplemented by Germany since they are the largest shareholder in the EU. Furthermore, Britain's exit would affect the EU's trade reducing the surpluses in the service industry, specifically financial services. Regardless, economists have forecasted that Britain's exit will have negative short- and long-term economic implications. The British pound would weaken and the euro-based earnings of European companies with businesses in Britain would decrease, triggering a potential financial crisis. British household earnings will diminish by $4,300 USD a year per household and after 15 years outside of the EU, U.K. GDP would decline by 6.2 percent. Additionally, outside of the EU, Britain would receive $36 billion USD less in tax receipts, equivalent to 35 percent of the annual budget raising basic income tax to 28 pounds. Furthermore, economic losses related to leaving the EU would significantly outweigh any potential gain from contributing less to the EU. If Britain leaves the EU and instead joins the European Economic Area (EEA), it would be worse off; the economy would contract by 3.8 percent ($2,600 USD per household). Lastly, if the U.K. left the EU and adopted WTO rule, the U.K. economy would shrink by 7.5 percent ($25,000 USD per household); the WTO model is perceived as the worst alternative to EU membership.

The IMF already warned that Britain's economy would suffer if the U.K. were to leave the EU. A British departure would threaten to impose "severe" damage on the U.K. and world economy. Christine Lagarde, Managing Director of the IMF, has expressed her opposition to the U.K.'s leaving the EU warning that it's the first time the IMF has expressed a view ratified by all board members. Proponents state that the break with Brussels would spur greater economic dynamism. The IMF is wrong in its forecast about the U.K. and other countries. There is no compelling evidence that the referendum had produced market uncertainty. The IMF countered by stating the referendum was lowering investment in the U.K. economy. If Britain remains in the EU, the IMF forecasts the country will remain one of the world's stronger and more advanced economies, behind the U.S. but ahead of Japan and France. In 2016, U.K. growth was expected to be driven by domestic private demand supported by lower energy prices and a thriving property market; offsetting fiscal consolidation; and heightened uncertainty. The result of Britain leaving the EU would also cause post-exit arrangements and negotiations that would raise uncertainty. This uncertainty would weigh heavily on investors' confidence while increasing market volatility. Brexit would disrupt and reduce mutual trade and financial flows stifling key benefits from economic cooperation and integration resulting from economies of scale and efficient specialization.

Sources

1. FT.com (n.d.). IMF warns Brexit could wreak 'severe' damage in U.K. and beyond. Retrieved April 24, 2016, from www.ft.com/intl/cms/s/0/ad066f38-008f-11e6-ac98-3c15a1aa2e62.html#axzz46cOwhFwc

2. FT.com. (n.d.). What are the economic consequences of Brexit? Retrieved April 24, 2016, from www.ft.com/intl/cms/s/2/70d0bfd8-d1b3-11e5-831d-09f7778e7377. html#axzz46cOwhFwc
3. *Economist*. (2016, April 9). The economic consequences. Retrieved April 24, 2016, from www.economist.com/news/britain/21696517-most-estimates-lost-income-are-small-risk-bigger-losses-large-economic
4. Reuters (2016, April 14). From budget to banks: How Brexit could impact the EU economy. Retrieved April 24, 2016, from http://uk.reuters.com/article/ uk-britain-eu-impact-idUKKCN0XB124
5. Treanor, J. and Farrell, S. (2016, April 14). Brexit could lead to loss of 100,000 financial services jobs, report warns. Retrieved April 24, 2016, from www. theguardian.com/business/2016/apr/14/brexit-could-lead-to-loss-of-100000-financial-services-jobs-report-warns
6. Allen, K. (2016, April 18). Treasury analysis of effects of Brexit on U.K. economy: Key points. Retrieved April 24, 2016, from www.theguardian.com/politics/2016/ apr/18/treasury-analyses-impact-brexit-scenarios-uk-economy

Questions for Case Discussion

1. What is Brexit? What are three possible scenarios?
2. What would be the global impact and the potential domestic repercussions of a Brexit?
3. What are Britain's alternatives to leaving the EU?
4. If you were voting on the Brexit referendum what would you decide? (Consider implications on various sectors.)

Case 4.4 Economic Impact of the TPP Agreement

The Trans-Pacific Partnership (TPP) is a free trade agreement to unify a group of Pacific Rim countries varying in size and level of economic development. It binds them to a set of high-standard rules and intends to provide a positive effect to its members. As the U.S. recently left the TPP, the agreement now consists of 11 Asia-Pacific countries including Australia, Brunei, Canada, Chile, Japan, Malaysia, Mexico, New Zealand, Peru, Singapore, and Vietnam. On February 4, 2016, they signed the TPP, a high-standard comprehensive agreement that closes a number of "missing links" in the global FTA network. It addresses the need for convergence among overlapping FTAs already in place. The TPP seeks to remove tariffs and non-tariff barriers to trade in goods, services, and agriculture, and to institute or expand rules on a broad range of issues regarding intellectual property rights, foreign direct investment, and other trade-related issues. Ultimately, the TPP attempts to construct a twenty-first-century agreement to deal with new concerns presented by an increasingly globalized economy.

Details of the TPP

Once ratified, the TPP will be the largest trade pact in recent history. It rewrites the rules that affect how 40 percent of the global economy conducts business and intends to promote trade and investment. The TPP is similar to the NAFTA but has been improved in numerous facets. The TPP includes the strongest labor standards of any trade agreement; it requires the protection of freedom to form unions and bargain collectively, prohibits exploitative child and forced labor, and defends against employment discrimination. The agreement has also adopted laws concerning acceptable working conditions, minimum wage, work hours, and occupational health and safety. It contains the highest environmental commitment standards prohibiting harmful fishery subsidies, using new tools to combat wildlife trafficking, and improving the enforcement of conservation laws. Lastly, it includes terms to ensure state-owned enterprises (SOEs) compete on a commercial basis and ensures that the advantages SOEs receive from governments (subsidies) do not adversely impact American workers and businesses.

According to the World Bank, the average tariffs in both developed and developing countries have decreased. Without the withdrawal of the U.S., the TPP was expected to eliminate 1,800 tariffs levied by 11 other countries, most of which are inconsequential. The majority of terms in the TPP consist of new rights and privileges for MNCs and constraints on government regulation. The TPP makes it easier for companies to move jobs offshore, take control of natural resources and prevent regulation of financial services. It is mandatory that all disagreements be decided by an "Investor State Dispute Resolution" conducted by TPP tribunals staffed by private-sector lawyers. These attorneys are empowered to force governments to pay limitless fines to corporations that claim they are losing profits.

The Evolution of the TPP

The original idea of the Trans-Pacific Strategic Economic Partnership was conceived by Singapore, New Zealand, and Chile in 2003 to expand trade in the Asia-Pacific region. In 2005, Brunei joined the discussions; the Trans-Pacific Strategic Economic Partnership (P-4) contract was completed in 2006. In March 2008, the U.S. joined the negotiations in order to conclude investment and financial service provisions. Then President Bush explained his intentions to negotiate with existing P-4 members and other countries including Australia, Peru, and Vietnam on September 22, 2008.

After a review of U.S. trade policy, the Obama administration decided to continue the TPP negotiations. On December 14, 2009, President Obama officially addressed Congress in regards to the U.S. government's intention to negotiate with TPP countries. In October 2010, TPP participants agreed unanimously to include Malaysia as a negotiating partner. Subsequently, Canada, Japan, and Mexico began to consult with existing TPP partners about joining the dialogue. After several months of intense bilateral consultations with existing TPP countries, they were admitted by consensus. Finally, in December 2012, Mexico and Canada were added as negotiating partners.

Japan began to conduct internal debates on whether participation in the TPP negotiations was in the country's best interest. In March 2013, Prime Minister Abe officially announced Japan's interest and in July 2013, Japan began full participation in negotiations. In early 2014, South Korea began the discussion with TPP negotiating partners to join the TPP. However, the

Korean government did not formally make a request. Furthermore, all current members of the TPP negotiations are also members of APEC.

China has expressed concern with the TPP because of the possible inclusion of Japan and Australia. President Xi Jinping has advocated for a new brand of nationalism that highlights the predominance of Chinese power in Asia. China's alignment with Syria, Iran, and Russia have placed it in an unfavorable position with the Obama administration's strategy in the Middle East. Chinese leaders who were once worried about losing influence in the region with the ratification of this agreement are now relieved to learn that Trump's new U.S. government decided to leave the TPP. Chinese moderates view the TPP as a means to encourage Chinese leaders to enact systemic reforms. The TPP contains clauses regarding progressive environmental policies that could influence and benefit the Chinese system. Furthermore, China is trying to push the Regional Comprehensive Economic Partnership (RCEP), its own multilateral trade agreement. This proposal is regarded as China's TPP; it involves ten member states of the Association of Southeast Asian Nations (ASEAN) and will affect 40 percent of the global economy.

Economic Significance

Potential economic effects of the TPP agreement depend on many factors including potential growth of trade, investment, and the degree of trade liberalization between TPP members. The TPP would have been quite significant and influential as it represented the largest U.S. FTA in terms of trade flow. Although potential areas not covered in previous FTAs can be important in certain sectors from the point of view of the U.S., a significant share of liberalization has already transpired in existing FTAs with six out of the 11 TPP member countries. Japan's participation in TPP negotiations has raised the potential economic significance of the agreement. In 2014, Japan ranked as the fourth largest exporter of goods to the U.S. ($67 billion USD) and importer ($134 billion USD). U.S.-Japan trade between high-income countries differs considerably from U.S. trade with other negotiating partners given that many of the TPP partners are low- and middle-income nations. Thus, Japan's participation in this agreement has received extensive attention from many U.S. industries, including agriculture, automobile, and service. It would have brought trade and investment relations between these two countries under a formal legal framework that establishes rules for fairer and more effective trade practices. It also set a precedent for future negotiations between the two countries that may not have pursued partnership opportunities due to their prior history.

The TPP will also bring together developed and developing countries. Making connections is important given the global shift in trade patterns that have occurred in the last five to ten years. Among the TPP countries without existing U.S. FTAs, Malaysia and Vietnam stand out as candidates in terms of their current trade and investment with the U.S. and their potential growth. These countries' populations have exceeded 120 million and, in recent years, have experienced rapid growth. In addition, most-favored nation tariffs of Malaysia and Vietnam are 6 percent and 9.5 percent, respectively, the highest levels among TPP countries. Additionally, certain U.S. industries will benefit from the TPP. Cotton exports will no longer face a 10 percent tariff in Vietnam. Tariffs on American frozen beef and U.S. automobiles will be reduced by 40 percent and 75 percent, respectively. Conversely, Americans will no longer have to deal with Malaysia's shark fin tariffs, Vietnam's whale meat tariffs, and Japan's ivory tariffs. Furthermore, the agreement would benefit Japan and Vietnam who would both stand to gain tariff-free access to North America for apparel, footwear, and textiles. Vietnamese support for the TPP is growing because they believe increased U.S. trade will help the country offset China's economic leverage in the region.

Sources

1. Ferguson, I. F., McMinimy, M. A., and Williams, B. R. CRS (Congressional Research Service) Report (2014). The Trans-Pacific Partnership (TPP) Negotiations and Issues for Congress.
2. Estevadeordal, A. (2016, March 9). What the TPP means for Latin America and the Caribbean. Retrieved April 26, 2016, from www.brookings.edu/research/opinions/2016/03/09-tpp-latin-america-caribbean-estevadeordal
3. Zhou, S. (2015, November 6). OPINION: The TPP risks making U.S.–China relations worse. Retrieved April 26, 2016, from america.aljazeera.com/opinions/2015/11/the-tpp-risks-making-us-china-relations-worse.html
4. Devoss, D. (2016, April 18). Trans-Pacific Partnership under fire from both right and left in America. Retrieved April 26, 2016, from http://atimes.com/2016/04/trans-pacific-partnership-under-fire-from-both-right-and-left-in-america/
5. The Trans-Pacific Partnership @ USTR.gov. (n.d.). Retrieved April 24, 2016, from https://ustr.gov/tpp/

Questions for Case Discussion

1. What is the TPP? How does it differ from the NAFTA?
2. Describe the evolution and economic significance of the TPP and its impact on employment and welfare.
3. Compare and contrast the various countries' perspectives on the TPP.
4. Explain the potential long-term impact of the TPP on members and non-members.

Economic Environment

I. World Economic Growth Trends

In 2014, the global economy grew at a modest rate due to market suffering and adjustment resulting from the lingering effect of the global financial crisis.[1] World economic recovery has been hampered by unexpected shocks and geopolitical conflicts in many parts of the world. The overall growth of world GDP (WGP) in 2014 was slightly better than in 2013, with 2.6 percent growth rate. According to the WGP, the growth of world output is expected to increase by 3.1 and 3.3 percent in 2015 and 2016, respectively, as shown in Table 4.1. Six years after the global financial crisis, the gross domestic product growth rate in the global economy is significantly lower than the pre-crisis level. Even excluding 2008–10 during which the aftermath of the global financial crisis was still at work, the average growth rate in 2011–2014 was lower than the rate from 2004–2007.[2]

It still remains to be seen whether low growth rates in most countries will become a long-term trend or not. The major developed economies, from a skeptical point of view, could fall into a cyclical economic stagnation whereas Chinese policymakers estimate a growth rate of 7.0–7.5 percent, which is much lower than 10 percent average economic growth over the last three decades. Many other emerging economies, especially Asian countries, have also shown a much slower growth trajectory in recent years.

Table 4.1 Growth of World Output, 2008–2016

Annual percentage change	2008–11[a]	2012	2013[b]	2014[b]	2015[c]	2016[d]
World	**1.9**	**2.4**	**2.5**	**2.6**	**3.1**	**3.3**
Developed economies	**0.1**	**1.1**	**1.2**	**1.6**	**2.1**	**2.3**
United States	0.2	2.3	2.2	2.3	2.8	3.1
Japan	−0.7	1.5	1.5	0.4	1.2	1.1
European Union	−0.1	−0.4	0	1.3	1.7	2
EU-15	−0.2	−0.5	−0.1	1.2	1.5	1.9
New EU members	1.2	0.7	1.1	2.6	2.9	3.3
Euro area	−0.2	−0.8	−0.5	0.8	1.3	1.7
Other European countries	0.7	1.9	1.4	1.4	2.2	2.3
Other developed countries	1.5	2.6	2.2	2.6	2.6	2.6
Economies in transition	**1.9**	**3.3**	**2**	**0.8**	**1.1**	**2.1**
South-Eastern Europe	1.6	−0.9	2.4	0.7	2.7	3
Commonwealth of Independent States and Georgia	1.9	3.5	2	0.8	1.1	2.1
Russian Federation	1.4	3.4	1.3	0.5	0.2	1.2
Developing economies	**5.6**	**4.8**	**4.8**	**4.3**	**4.8**	**5.1**
Africa	3.5	5.6	3.5	3.5	4.6	4.9
North Africa	1.8	6.6	1.4	1.6	3.9	4.3
East Africa	6.2	6.1	6.3	6.5	6.8	6.6

Central Africa	3.9	5.3	2.2	4.3	4.7	5
West Africa	5.9	6.9	7	5.9	6.2	6.1
Nigeria	6.4	6.7	7.3	5.8	6.1	5.9
Southern Africa	3.3	3.4	3	2.9	3.6	4.1
South Africa	2.2	2.5	1.9	2	2.7	3.3
East and South Asia	7.2	5.6	5.9	5.9	6	6
East Asia	7.4	6.3	6.4	6.1	6.1	6
China	9.6	7.7	7.7	7.3	7	6.8
South Asia	6.2	2.9	4.1	4.9	5.4	5.7
India	7.3	4.7	5	5.4	5.9	6.3
Western Asia	4.3	4.5	4	2.9	3.7	4.3
Latin America and the Caribbean	3.2	2.7	2.6	1.3	2.4	3.1
South America	3.8	2.2	2.8	0.7	1.9	2.8
Brazil	3.7	1	2.3	0.3	1.5	2.4
Mexico and Central America	1.6	4.2	1.8	2.6	3.5	3.8
Mexico	1.4	4	1.4	2.4	3.4	3.8
Caribbean	2.5	2.8	3	3.8	3.8	3.8
High-income countries	0.4	1.4	1.4	1.7	2.2	2.4
Upper-middle-income countries	5.7	4.9	4.9	4.3	4.8	5.2
Lower-middle-income countries	5.6	4.8	5.2	4.6	5.3	5.7
Low-income countries	5.7	4.9	4.9	4.4	4.9	5.3
Least developed countries	5.6	5	5.3	5.3	5.7	5.9
World trade[e]	2.5	2.5	3	3.4	4.5	4.9
World output growth with PPP-based weights	2.7	2.9	3	3.1	3.5	3.8

Source: United Nations New York. (2015). Retrieved from www.un.org/en/development/desa/policy/wesp/wesp_archive/2015wesp_chap1.pdf

a Average percentage change.

b Actual or most recent estimates.

c Forecast, based in part on Project LINK and baseline projections of the UN/DESA World Economic Forecasting Model.

d See United Nations World Economic Situation and Prospects 2014.

e Average of exports and imports of goods and services.

During 2014, North America, Europe, and all of developed Asia except Japan displayed an upward growth trajectory for the first time since 2011. During 2014, developing countries and transitional economies showed different patterns of growth rates. Latin America and the Commonwealth of Independent States (CIS) witnessed a rapid economic decline. These countries encountered country-specific challenges including structural imbalances, infrastructure bottlenecks, increasing financial risk, and ineffective macroeconomic management as well as geopolitical and political tension. In contrast, East Asia, including China, registered a relatively strong growth rate while India led South Asia's respectable economic growth. Overall, the growth rate in developing countries is expected to grow 4.8 and 5.1 percent in

2015 and 2016, respectively. The transitional economies are expected to grow by 1.1 percent in 2015 and 2.1 percent in 2016. However, these figures are still unpredictable since many developing countries and transitional economies are vulnerable to tightening global financial conditions and high geopolitical tensions, further deteriorating risks.

II. How to Measure a Country's Economic Development

A country's economic development, growth performance, and market potential can be measured in a number of ways. Yet, income and wealth are the most common measures of a country's economic development. The World Bank classifies countries with less than $2,963 USD per capita as low-income countries. People in the majority of these countries have limited public access to services and suffer from a low standard of living. According to the World Bank, 151 countries constitute developing countries and these economies represent the largest share of the global population with 5.5 billion people.

Those countries that have experienced the fastest economic growth are called emerging economies or emerging markets. There are about 30 emerging economies worldwide including Brazil, Russia, India, China, and South Africa (BRICS), as illustrated in Case 4.1. BRICS have greater market size than the other emerging economies and set an example for economic reform. Other emerging economies are likely to follow the economic development model of the BRICS. Countries whose per capita income exceeds $37,970 USD in 2009 are categorized as developed countries. People in developed countries have easy access to various goods and services and enjoy a high standard of living. Developed countries consist of Japan, Australia, New Zealand, Canada, the U.S., and many Western European countries.

I. GNP

Gross National Product (GNP) refers to income that combines the value of final goods and services produced in a country in a given year and income earned abroad minus income foreigners earned in the country. Simply put, GNP equals gross domestic product (GDP) plus net property income from abroad, which typically includes dividends, interest, and profit. In other words, GNP includes the value of all goods and services produced by nationals whether in the country or not.

2. GDP

Gross Domestic Product (GDP) means that the sum of the market value of the goods and services produced in a country during a certain period, usually measured on the basis of one year. GNP has mainly been used as an indicator of national income representing the economic size of a country until the 1980s. As GDP is a more appropriate measure to assess the actual welfare of a people living in the country, GDP is now more widely used than GNP. GDP per capita is often used to measure the standard of living of people in a certain country. As GDP at Purchasing Power Parity (PPP) takes different living costs across countries into account, it represents a more accurate reflection of actual living standards in countries. PPP theory will be explained in detail in Chapter 7.

3. GNI

The World Bank defines Gross National Income (GNI) as the sum of value added by all resident producers plus any product taxes (minus subsidies) not included in the valuation of output plus net receipts of primary income (compensation of employees and property income) from abroad.[3] For example, both the value of a Samsung TV produced in Korea and that of a Samsung TV produced in Japan are included in the GNI of Korea. Conceptually, the value of GNI and GNP should be very close to each other since GNI is based on a principle similar to GNP.

4. Growth Rate

Monitoring the economic growth rate may provide a more dynamic picture about a country's market potential than by simply measuring its income level, which just presents a static picture of development. If economic growth outpaces population growth, the standard of living improves. For example, China has achieved a remarkable economic growth with a double-digit growth rate over the past 30 years. China is one of the fastest countries in

Table 4.2 Gross National Income (GNI) per capita, Ranking 2015

Rank		GNI (Purchasing power parity, international dollars)
1	Qatar	138,480
2	Macao SAR, China	102,480
3	Kuwait	84,360
4	Brunei Darussalam	82,140
5	Singapore	81,360
6	Luxembourg	70,750
7	United Arab Emirates	70,020
8	Bermuda	66,670
9	Norway	64,490
10	Switzerland	62,590
11	Hong Kong SAR, China	57,860
12	United States	57,540
13	Saudi Arabia	54,840
14	Ireland	51,920
15	Germany	48,410

Source: The World Bank. (2015). GNI per capita, PPP. Retrieved from http://databank.worldbank.org/data/download/GNIPC.pdf

history to escape from poverty as its phenomenal economic growth created the middle class which leads the increase in consumer demand. It does not always have to be a large country endowed with an abundant supply of production factors to attain economic growth. Singapore is a good example as illustrated by Case 4.2 that explains how the country has successfully integrated its economy with the rest of the world.

5. HDI

The GNI, GNP, or GDP captures only one aspect of current economic performance or long-term growth potential. Furthermore, those who insist on sustainable development require economic activity to address current needs without limiting the ability to meet the needs of future generations.[4] Thus it is desirable that other indicators should be included in order to assess the economic status and prospect more accurately and comprehensively. The current method used for measuring sustainable economic growth is the Human Development Index (HDI) that the United Nations has developed. The supporting argument for HDI is that if the human condition gets better, economic performance will also improve. HDI consists of life (life expectancy), knowledge (literacy and primary, secondary, and tertiary education enrollment), and living standards (PPP and GNI per person).

6. Happiness Index

Whereas HDI is an indicator of a country's economic sustainability, the happiness index measures stability. People in rich countries are not necessarily happier than those in poor nations. According to *Science of Happiness*, 70 percent of happiness is determined by the quality and quantity of relationships rather than economic output or income. GNI has been criticized as it contains many drawbacks as a measure of a country's economic activity.[5] The assessment of a country's overall performance and market potential depend on whether measurements of happiness (well-being) that go beyond financial performance are included or not. For example, the total amount of financial capital in the United States is much greater than in France and Germany. However, if life expectancy, leisure time, and income equality are considered, the standard of living in France and Germany is equivalent to the U.S. The following lists various indices measuring the happiness of people.

(1) Gross National Happiness (GNH): GNH is a yardstick that measures the ability to preserve and promote the cultural values and promote social and economic development while protecting and establishing a sustainable natural environment.

(2) Happy Planet Index (HPI): This index reflects the utilitarian view that most people wish to live a healthy and happy life. Thus, achievement and potential of a country can be determined by how much government can help people live healthy and happy lives without diminishing opportunities for future generations.

(3) Your Better Life Index (YBLI): This index measures the standard of living and happiness. It is composed of housing, income, employment, social relations, education, environment, health, general satisfaction, safety, and work and family balance.[6] The OECD has developed this index to measure economic performance, based on a range of topics deemed important to the world as opposed to financial measures.

III. Regional Economic Integration

Regional economic integration refers to an attempt to harmonize economic policies between different countries by promoting free flows of trade and investment through a partial or complete elimination of tariff and non-tariff barriers to trade. Regional economic integration is expected to lower prices for both consumers and producers leading to an increased level of welfare.[7] We have recently seen an expansion of regional economic integration not only across continents but also within a continent, whether in Europe, America, or Asia.

The level of economic integration can be categorized into five stages as Figure 4.1 illustrates.[8] Regional economic integration ranges from a free-trade area to the most complete integration that is likely to involve political integration. First, a free-trade area (FTA) represents the lowest level of integration in which two or more countries partially or completely abolish tariffs on their inner borders. While member countries attempt to remove all barriers to the trade of goods and services, it is still up to each country to determine its own trade policy. One step closer toward complete economic integration, a customs union imposes the same tariffs on exterior borders of the union. The

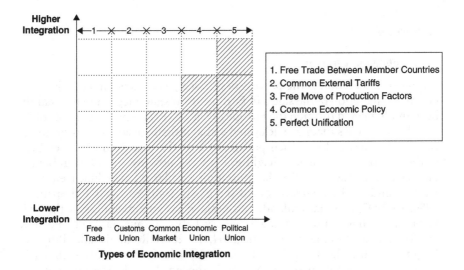

Figure 4.1 Types of Economic Integration

Source: Polina Voronevica. (2015). The Three Economists. Retrieved from http://threeeconomists.blogspot.kr/2015_10_01_archive.html

participating countries set up a common external trade policy, but in some cases, use different import quotas. The purpose behind setting up a customs union is usually to increase economic efficiency and establish closer political and cultural relations between member countries. The EU started as a customs union but now has grown into an economic union as it will be explained later.

The next level of economic integration, a common market, allows free movement of production factors such as capital and labor between member countries, in addition to the free trade of goods and services. It also sets a common external tariff among member countries. The Treaty of Rome was signed in 1957 to establish a common market in Europe before the Maastricht Treaty created the EU in 1992. Today, EU citizens have a common passport and can work in any EU member country and may invest in a member country without restriction. An economic union involves even deeper economic integration than a common market by allowing the free flow of goods and services as well as production factors, the adoption of a common external trade policy, and a common currency. The EU represents an economic union, albeit imperfect. The majority of member countries use the euro as a single common currency to harmonize monetary policy across nations.

As the final stage, a complete economic integration has unified economic policies, including complete or nearly complete fiscal and monetary policies. A complete economic integration results in a federal system of governance that is necessary for political integration to function as a single economy. The U.S. represents a political union since the single nation consists of 50 independent states whose economic, social, and foreign policies are integrated at the federal level. In the following sections, we will examine the progress of regional economic integration in each region.

I. Europe

(1) European Integration

European integration is the process of political, legal, economic, social, and cultural integration of the states in Europe. European integration has mainly been implemented through the European Union (EU). The EU consists of 28 member countries that have delegated some of their sovereignty to common institutions to coordinate their policies in several areas.[9] Founding members of the EU are six countries: Belgium, France, Germany, Italy, Luxembourg, and the Netherlands. In 1973, the communities enlarged to include Denmark, Ireland, and the U.K. Greece joined the EU in 1981, Portugal and Spain in 1986. In 1995, Austria, Finland, and Sweden became members of the EU. Cyprus, Czech Republic, Estonia, Hungary, Latvia, Lithuania, Malta, Poland, Slovakia, and Slovenia entered in 2004. In 2007, Romania and Bulgaria became EU members and in 2013, Croatia became the twenty-eighth EU member. The adoption of the Single European Act laid the groundwork to complete one unified market by December 1992 before introducing a common currency, the euro, in 1999. Within the institutions of the EU, its parliamentarians, judges, commissioners and secretariat, the governments of

Table 4.3 European Union Member Nations (in 2015)

Country	Joined EU	Euro Zone Member	Country	Joined EU	Euro Zone Member
Austria	1995	Yes	Italy	1957	Yes
Belgium	1957	Yes	Latvia	2004	Yes
Bulgaria	2007	No	Lithuania	2004	Yes
Croatia	2013	No	Luxembourg	1957	Yes
Cyprus	2004	Yes	Malta	2004	Yes
Czech Republic	2004	No	Netherlands	1957	Yes
Denmark	1973	No	Poland	2004	No
Estonia	2004	Yes	Portugal	1986	Yes
Finland	1995	Yes	Romania	2007	No
France	1957	Yes	Slovakia	2004	Yes
Germany	1957	Yes	Slovenia	2004	Yes
Greece	1981	Yes	Spain	1986	Yes
Hungary	2004	No	Sweden	1995	No
Ireland	1973	Yes	United Kingdom	1973	No

Source: Tutor2u (2015) Economics: European Union Enlargement.
Retrieved from www.tutor2u.net/economics/reference/european-union-enlargement

its member states all play a part in European integration, the most common and critically disputed question concerns which party plays a key role. As Case 4.3 illustrates, Britain will soon leave the EU. The country held a referendum on its EU membership on June 23, 2016 and the majority of constituents voted in favor of departing the EU.

(2) The Transatlantic Trade and Investment Partnership (TTIP)

The Transatlantic Trade and Investment Partnership (TTIP) was proposed as a free trade agreement between the EU and the U.S. The TTIP is an ambitious, comprehensive, high-level trade and investment agreement between the U.S. and the EU. The European Commission estimates that the TTIP will increase up to 50 percent of trade between the economic blocs. The U.S. and the EU are each other's largest trading partner and account for one-third of the flow of world trade. Because tariff barriers between the two blocs are already low, the success of these agreements depends on removing non-tariff barriers. The TTIP is expected to provide an export opportunity for American farmers and ranchers through increased access to the European market for Made-in-USA goods and services. Enhanced competitiveness, job creation and economic growth in both the U.S. and the EU are also expected. The TTIP aims to boost economic growth and add more than 13 million jobs for American and EU citizens. "Proponents argue that the agreement would result in multilateral economic growth. However, critics worry that it would strengthen corporate power and make it more difficult for governments to regulate markets for public benefit."[10]

2. America

(1) NAFTA

The North American Free Trade Agreement (NAFTA) is a free trade agreement signed by Canada, Mexico, and the U.S. to make a trilateral trading bloc in North America. It came into force on January 1, 1994.[11] NAFTA has two supplements including the North American Agreement on Environmental Cooperation (NAAEC) and the North American Agreement on Labor Cooperation (NAALC). The NAFTA aims to eliminate barriers to trade across the U.S., Canada, and Mexico. Tariffs on more than one-half of Mexico's exports to the U.S. and more than one-third of U.S. exports to Mexico were eliminated. The NAFTA also seeks to protect intellectual property rights and eliminate non-tariff trade barriers. Thanks to the NAFTA, Canada and Mexico have now become not only among the top three trading partners of the U.S. but also strong political allies. This suggests that regional economic integration is also likely to improve the political relationship among the member countries.

(2) Mercosur

Mercosur originated with an agreement enacted by the Argentina-Brazil formal program of economic and political cooperation called the Program for Integration and Economic Cooperation (PICE) in 1986. Mercosur was established in 1991 by the Treaty of Asuncion, which was later updated by the 1994 Treaty of Ouro Preto.[12] Members of Mercosur are Argentina, Brazil, Paraguay, Uruguay, and Venezuela and associate member countries include Chile, Bolivia, Peru, Colombia, and Ecuador. New Zealand and Mexico are observer countries. The purpose of this regional economic integration is to promote free trade and the fluid movement of goods, people, and currency. Spanish, Portuguese, and Guarani are the official languages.[13] The agreement has been amended and is now a full customs union. Customs unions, such as Mercosur and the Andean Community of Nations, advance the continuing process of South American integration connected to the Union of South American Nations.

3. Africa

"The Southern African Customs Union (SACU) was founded in 1910 to form a Customs Union Agreement between the then Union of South Africa and the High Commission Territories of Bechuanaland, Basutoland and Swaziland."[14] "Five African countries including Botswana, Lesotho, Namibia, South Africa and Swaziland signed to form The Southern African Customs Union (SACU), the oldest existing customs union in the world."[15] The agreement was relaunched on December 11, 1969 with the signing of an accord among the Republic of

South Africa, Botswana, Lesotho, and Swaziland. March 1, 1970, officially marked the enforcement of this new regional economic integration. Namibia joined SACU as its fifth member after it separated from South Africa in 1990.

4. Asia-Pacific

(1) APEC

Asia-Pacific Economic Cooperation (APEC) is a forum to help 21 Pacific Rim countries promote free and open trade and investment throughout the Asia-Pacific region.

With the growing interdependence of Asia-Pacific countries and regional trade advent in other parts of the world, APEC was established in 1989 to promote and accelerate regional economic integration by encouraging economic and technical cooperation, enhancing human security, and facilitating a favorable and sustainable business environment. 12 APEC members have signed the Trans-Pacific Partnership (TPP), a trade agreement that would achieve many of APEC's goals. [16]

This raises the question, if the TPP is ratified, what would be APEC's role? Since China was excluded from the TPP deal, APEC's fate seems to largely depend on China's approach to regional economic integration.

The 21 APEC economies are forecast to grow 3.4 percent in 2016, the same as world GDP growth. This is up from 3.1 percent growth in APEC in 2015, which was undermined by a contraction in regional trade. Keeping trade and investment barriers in check and taking next steps to enable more people and businesses to take advantage will be an important determinant of future prosperity.[17]

(2) TPP

The purpose of the TPP is to establish a common framework for intellectual property rights, lower tariffs and other trade barriers, stronger labor laws and environmental laws, and the enforcement of standards for investor-state dispute settlement mechanisms among 12 countries in the Asia-Pacific region.[18] Stated goals of the agreement are mentioned as follows: enhance trade and investment among TPP partner countries, promote innovation, economic growth and development, and support the creation and retention of jobs.[19] Case 4.4 describes the evolution and significance of the TPP. "Historically, the TPP was an extension of the Trans-Pacific Strategic Economic Partnership Agreement (TPSEP or P4) signed by Brunei, Chile, Singapore, and New Zealand in 2006. In early 2008, Australia, Canada, Japan, Malaysia, Mexico, Peru, the U.S., and Vietnam joined the agreement, increasing the number of member countries to 12. These countries signed a trade agreement in Auckland, New Zealand, in February 2016, after seven years of negotiations. Finalizing the TPP was one of the main trade agendas for the Obama administration. During his tenure in office Mr. Obama battled to win bipartisan support from both Republicans and Democrats. However, the U.S. recently withdrew from the TPP with the instatement of the new Trump government.

IV. Measurement of a Country's Globalization, Openness, and Competitiveness

I. Globalization Index

(1) DHL index

As briefly mentioned in Chapter 1, the DHL Global Connectedness Index consists of 12 types of interactions that can be grouped into four pillars: trade, capital, information, and people.[21] The aim of the DHL Global Connectedness Index is to provide the most comprehensive and timely explanation of global connectivity around the world. It is measured by the depth and breadth of a country's integration with the rest of the world. Depth of global connectedness is measured by the ratio of international and domestic activities or flows. For example, the depth of Hong Kong can be measured by the ratio of exports compared to its GDP. The export-to-GDP ratio of Hong Kong's merchandise is 196 percent, the highest level in the world. The breadth of global connectedness is measured by the distribution of a given type of activity across countries. For example, the Bahamas' case shows the importance of incorporating breadth into global connectedness measurement. Although the Bahamas ranks second in the world in terms of depth of global connectedness based on the number of inbound tourists per capita, its breadth is limited as more than 80 percent of tourists come from the U.S.

In addition to depth and breadth of measuring globalization, the third metric is directionality. Inbound and outbound flows are qualitatively different in significance. We have observed the biggest differences between countries' inward and outward flows in terms of international education. For example, Australia has 22 percent of college students from abroad, but less than one percent in Australia studies overseas. In Botswana, 50 percent of students study overseas, but only 4 percent of domestic university students are from abroad. This data clearly shows a significant difference between the tertiary education systems of both countries.

The DHL Global Connectedness Index ranks the world's most globally connected countries. The Netherlands ranks at the top in terms of overall global connectedness, followed by Ireland, Singapore, Belgium, Luxembourg, Switzerland, the U.K., Denmark, Germany, and Sweden. Nine of the ten most connected countries are in Europe and overall they received the highest scores on the trade and people pillars of the index. North America ranks second overall and earned high marks in the capital and information pillars. Emerging economies typically lag advanced economies in the global connectedness index. However, growing participation of emerging economies in international flows changes the situation. The ten most increased global connectedness countries in 2013 are from emerging economies, eight of them are located in two regions including South and Central America and the Caribbean and Sub-Saharan Africa.

(2) Global Connectedness Trends

The fact that global connectedness was lowered by the financial crisis in 2008 and 2009 shows that globalization can indeed both rise and fall. Figure 4.2 displays that global connectedness recovered most of its losses but has yet to surpass its 2007 peak.

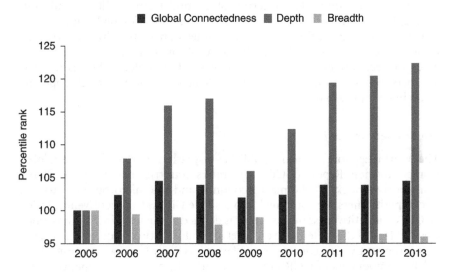

Figure 4.2 Global Connectedness, Depth and Breath 2005–2013

Source: DHL Global Connectedness Index 2014.

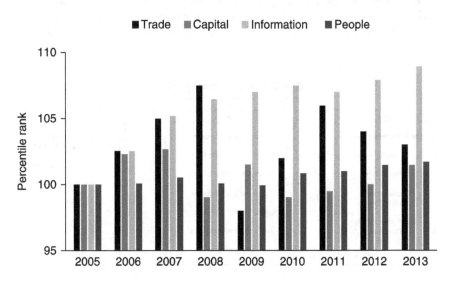

Figure 4.3 Global Connectedness Pillar 2005–2013

Source: DHL Global Connectedness Index 2014.

Over the course of 2014, the depth of global connectedness continued to increase, but the breadth continued to decrease. More than 40 percent of all international interaction has taken place within intra-regions. More than half of merchandise trade and telephone calls are also intra-regional. Declining breadth at the global level is not necessarily positive or negative as international interaction tends to focus on neighboring countries that share proximity and similarity in terms of administrative/political, cultural, geographical, and economic aspects. Further investigation on breadth trends indicates that the decline of global connectedness breadth occurred in advanced economies while the breadth of international interaction in emerging economies continues to increase. This reflects the reality that advanced economies face significant challenges to capture growth opportunities in emerging markets.[22]

(3) Competitiveness Index

The World Economic Forum publishes a yearly report called The Global Competitiveness Report (GCR), and ranks countries based on the Global Competitive Index.[23] "The macroeconomic and the micro/business aspects of competitiveness are combined into a single Global Competitiveness Index (GCI). Competitiveness in this report is defined as the set of institutions, policies and factors that determine the level of productivity of a country. Thus, the more competitive an economy is, the faster it is likely to grow over time."[24]

The components of GCR are grouped into 12 pillars of competitiveness: Institutions, infrastructure, macroeconomic environment, health and primary education, higher education and training, goods market efficiency, labor market efficiency, financial market development, technical market development, technological readiness, market size, business sophistication and innovation. The GCR evaluates important factors that determine economic growth and levels of present and future prosperity in a country.

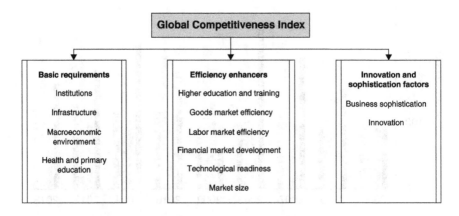

Figure 4.4 The Global Competitiveness Index Framework

Source: World Economic Forum. (2016). The Global Competitiveness Report 2015–2016.

The report aims to help stakeholders understand the strengths and weaknesses of each country so that they can shape economic agendas to address challenges and create opportunities. Although the relationship between productivity, social development and environmental factors is rather complex, the forum has continued its research into how sustainability relates to competitiveness and economic performance.[25]

Highly advanced Western economies and several Asian "Tiger" economies continue to dominate the ranks. In particular, Switzerland has topped the Global Competitiveness Index for six years in a row and Singapore ranks as the second most competitive economy in the world. It is impressive to see how stable and consistent Switzerland's competitiveness is across the board, ranking in the top ten in eight of the pillars. Singapore ranked second due to its stable competitiveness across all dimensions of the GCI. In particular, it is the only economy that ranks top three in seven out of the 12 pillars. The United States regained third place due to improvements in a number of areas including institutional framework, business sophistication, and innovation. Finland ranked fourth and Germany dropped to fifth.

This chapter described the trend of world economic development in developed, emerging, and developing economies. The chapter then defined regional economic integration and illustrated the major regional economic trends in Europe, America, Africa, and Asia-Pacific countries. To better assess business opportunities in foreign markets, global managers need to carefully measure a country's economic development, growth performance, and market potential. The most commonly used metrics, which were addressed in this chapter, to better understand business opportunities include GNP, GDP, GNI, and economic growth rate. However, these measures have limitations as they only capture economic dimensions. Furthermore, the chapter introduced more comprehensive measures of economic development such as the HDI and the Happiness Index. Finally, the chapter examined the Global Connectedness Index as well as the Global Competitiveness Index.

Key Terms

Economic development, Singapore, regionalization, economic integration, GNP, GDP, GNI, economic growth, Human Development Index, Happiness Index, globalization, openness, competitiveness, DHL Index, Global Competitive Index.

Review Questions

1. Compare and contrast the current economic development trends among developed, emerging, and developing countries.
2. What is regional economic integration and why is it significant? Identify and discuss the five different levels of economic integration.
3. What is the significance of signing TPP for the U.S. and the Japanese economy? How do you think that China will react to this agreement?
4. How is a country's economic development measured? Why is it critical for an MNC to understand the level of a host country's economic

development using various methods including HDI and Happiness Index?

5. Explain how DHL measures a country's global connectedness. Select your own country of research interest and discuss how it is globally connected.

Internet Exercise

Visit the following website and listen to the CAFTA case study and discuss the pros and cons of this agreement with your group members. http://globaledge.msu.edu/content/onlinecoursemodules/43/regionalization-and-trading-blocs/player.html

Notes

1 DESA Development Policy and Analysis Division. (2015). World Economic Situation and Prospects, 2015. Retrieved from www.un.org/en/development/desa/policy/wesp/

2 United Nations. (2014). World economic situation and prospects as of mid-2014 (E/2014/70). Retrieved from www.un.org/en/development/desa/policy/publications/ecosoc/e_2014_70_wesp_mid.pdf

3 The World Bank. (2015). GNI per capita, PPP. Retrieved from http://data.worldbank.org/indicator/NY.GNP.PCAP.PP.CD

4 United Nations. (1983). Process of preparation of the environmental perspective to the year 2000 and beyond. Retrieved May 27, 2007, from www.un.org/documents/ga/res/38/a38r161htm

5 Eric, W. (2008, April 23). The happiest places in the world. Forbes. Retrieved July 16, 2009, from 2011 www.forbes.com/2008/04/23/happiest-places-world-opendex_ewe_0423happiest.html

6 OECD. (2016). OECD Better Life Index. Retrieved from www.oecd.org/betterlifeindex

7 Brou, D. and Ruta, M. (2011). Economic integration, political integration or both? Journal of the European Economic Association, 9(6), 1143–1167.

8 Balassa, B. (2013). The Theory of Economic Integration. New York: Routledge.

9 Richardson, J. and Mazey, S. (Eds.). (2015). European Union: Power and Policy-making. London: Routledge.

10 Rt.com (2014). 'No to TAFTA': France celebs campaign against EU–U.S. trade deal, sign petition. Retrieved from www.rt.com/news/172012-france-celebrities-protest-tafta/

11 Office of the United States Trade Representative. (2014). North American Free Trade Agreement (NAFTA). Retrieved from https://ustr.gov/trade-agreements/free-trade-agreements/north-american-free-trade-agreement-nafta

12 ABACC. (n.d.). Tratado de Integración, Cooperación y Desarrollo entre Brasil y Argentina. Retrieved from www.abacc.org.br/?p=3417&lang=es.

13 El País. (2012). Venezuela irrumpe en el Mercosur. Retrieved from http://internacional.elpais.com/internacional/2012/07/31/actualidad/1343729834_339776.html.

14 El-Agraa, A. M. (2011). The European Union: Economics and Policies. Cambridge University Press.

15 WTO. (2003). Continued economic reforms would attract more foreign investment. Retrieved from www.wto.org/english/tratop_e/tpr_e/tp213_e.htm.

16 Asia-Pacific Economic Cooperation. (2016). Member economies. Retrieved from www.apec.org/about-us/about-apec/member-economies.aspx

17 Asia-Pacific Economic Cooperation. (2016). Member economies. Retrieved from www.apec.org/Press/News-Releases.aspx

18 BBC News. (2015). Trans-Pacific free trade deal agreed creating vast partnership. Retrieved from www.bbc.com/news/business-34444799

19 The Tico Times News. (2015). 12 Pacific countries seal huge free trade deal. Retrieved from www.ticotimes.net/2015/10/05/trans-pacific-partnership-12-pacific-countries-seal-huge-free-trade-deal

20 U.S Department of State. (2014). Transatlantic interests in Asia. Retrieved from www.state.gov/p/eap/rls/rm/2014/01/219881.htm

21 DHL. (2014). Global Connectedness Index 2014. Retrieved from www.dhl.com/content/dam/Campaigns /gci2014/downloads/dhl_gci_2014_study_low.pdf.

22 Ghemawat, P. and Altman, S. (2014). *DHL Global Connectedness Index 2014: Analyzing Global Flows and Their Power to Increase Prosperity.* Bonn, Germany: Deutsche Post DHL, Headquarters Corporate Communications and Responsibility.

23 Sala-i-Martin, Xavier and Elsa V. A. (2004). The Global Competitiveness Index. *Global Competitiveness Report.* Global Economic Forum.

24 World Economic Forum. (2016). *The Global Competitiveness Report 2015–2016.* Retrieved from http://reports.weforum.org/global-competitiveness-report-2015-2016/

25 Ibid.

Political and Legal Environment

Learning Objectives

1. Explain different political systems and the political risks associated with them.
2. Discuss different economic systems and economic risks that affect an MNC's profitability.
3. Describe different legal systems and identify legal risks that originate from either the home or host country.
4. Understand how MNCs can manage country risk before and after entering foreign markets.

Cases

Case 5.1 Political Risk in South America: The Cases of Cuba, Bolivia, and Brazil
Case 5.2 Transition from Planned Economy to Market Economy: Lessons from China
Case 5.3 The Foreign Corrupt Practices Act: The Case of U.S. Companies
Case 5.4 The "Panama Papers"

Case 5.1 Political Risk in South America: The Cases of Cuba, Bolivia, and Brazil

Nationalization, as a type of political risk, was mainly analyzed in Cuba, Bolivia, and Brazil. Fidel Castro succeeded Cuba's revolution in 1959 and immediately began confiscating land and limiting foreign MNCs' ownership of land. Additionally, the land was redistributed to farmers by farm land reform in Cuba. In particular, Cuba discarded the U.S' profit making rights in October 1959 and limited capital exploitation. In 1960, Cuba nationalized American assets equivalent to $10 billion. Castro first declared Cuba as a socialist state on April 16, 1961; after two years, the Cuban revolution achieved success.

The next day, April 17, the U.S. Central Intelligence Agency (CIA) played a pivotal role in an attack on Cuba, known as the Bay of Pigs, utilizing "Brigade 2506," a group of 1,500 Cuban refugees. However, the U.S. Air Force's showdown ended in failure due to a lack of support. The failed invasion resulted in

Cuba's decision to strengthen its relations with the Soviet Union and bolstered Castro's leadership. The U.S. invasion led to the Cuban Missile Crisis of 1962 creating a major issue for American foreign policy. U.S. President John F. Kennedy ordered an internal investigation into Latin America. After the failed Bay of Pigs attack in 1960, Cuba froze diplomatic relations with the U.S.

Eisenhower decided to cancel 700,000 tons of sugar imports from Cuba to the U.S. and denied the export of oil to Cuba. As a result, Cuba had to rely on Russian crude oil and decided to nationalize its refineries. On February 7, 1962, the embargo expanded to include almost all imports. Currently, the Cuban embargo is based on six types of law: the Trading with the Enemy Act of 1917, the Foreign Assistance Act of 1961, the Cuban Assets Control Regulations of 1963, the Cuban Democracy Act of 1992, the Helms–Burton Act of 1996, and the Trade Sanctions Reform and Export Enhancement Act of 2000. The stated objective of the Cuban Democracy Act of 1992 was to keep sanctions against Cuba as long as Cuba refuses to change direction in respect to greater democracy and human rights. As a further step, the Helms–Burton Act restricted U.S. citizens from doing business with Cuba or in Cuba. In addition, until the Cuban government met certain requirements, a mandate was issued restricting public and private support to the succeeding government in Havana ruled by Raul Castro. President Bill Clinton did not even allow foreign subsidiaries of U.S. companies to trade with Cuba as the measures of the trade embargo expanded in 1999. In 2000, Clinton approved the sale of "humanitarian" U.S. products to Cuba.

On April 11, 2015, the relationship between U.S. and Cuba changed. Presidents Barack Obama and Raúl Castro secured the first meeting between the U.S. and Cuban head of state since the two countries severed ties in 1961. The meeting was held four months after the presidents announced the restoration of U.S.-Cuba relations. In March 2016 President Obama made the first visit to Cuba by an incumbent president in over 85 years.

On May 1, 2006, Bolivia announced the nationalization of natural gas. Immediately after Bolivia declared nationalization, the Bolivian military seized 56 natural gas facilities. The Bolivian government announced the ownership of natural resources and complete control over the sale. The Bolivian government's nationalization policies are as follows: 1) the Bolivian government has complete and absolute ownership regarding all natural resources in Bolivia; 2) foreign companies are allowed to produce only 18 percent and the remaining 82 percent of production is owned by the national oil company (YPFB); and 3) foreign companies including Petrobas, BP, Total, and other U.S. companies were required to sign a new contract within six months or they must leave Bolivia.

Petrobras, Brazilian Petroleum Corporation, is headquartered in Rio de Janeiro, Brazil. It is one of the largest companies in Latin America in terms of revenue. It was founded in 1953 and remains a significant oil producer, producing more than two million barrels (320,000 m^3) of oil per day. However, Petrobras faced a colossal bribery scandal in 2015. Ms. Dilma Rousseff, the Brazilian President, struggled to resurrect her political career as a result of an ongoing investigation known as "Operation Car Wash." The Petrobras scandal may be the largest corporate corruption scandal in Brazil's history. On November 14, 2014, prominent Brazilian politicians and businessmen were interrogated in regards to suspicious contracts worth $22 billion USD. The Petrobras scandal placed Brazil at political risk. Ms. Rousseff was eventually impeached and removed from office due to the extensive scandal at Petrobras in August 2016, although she was officially charged with allegations that she manipulated the federal budget to disguise a growing deficit.

Sources

1. Quiroga, C. A. (2006, May 2). Bolivia's military takes control of gas fields. *NZHerald*. Retrieved from www.nzherald.co.nz/business/news/article.cfm?c_id=3&objectid=10379942
2. Harder, C. (2015, May 22). Petrobras scandal pressures Brazil leader. *Wall Street Journal*. Retrieved from http://blogs.wsj.com/moneybeat/2015/05/22/petrobras-scandal-pressures-brazil-leader-energy-journal
3. Schepers, E. (2015, March 18). Brazil: Amid coup talk, massive demonstrations for and against Dilma. People's World. Retrieved from http://peoplesworld.org/brazil-amid-coup-talk-massive-demonstrations-for-and-against-dilma
4. Renwick, D. (2016, March 24). U.S.–Cuba Relations. Council on Foreign Relations. Retrieved from www.cfr.org/cuba/us-cuba-relations/p11113

Questions for Case Discussion

1. Explain the timeline that led to the deterioration of the political relationship between the U.S. and Cuba.
2. How can MNCs use the recent change in diplomatic relations between U.S. and Cuba to their advantage? Examine the opportunities and challenges facing U.S. companies if they decide to enter the Cuban market.
3. What do you think are the major political risks that MNCs have to cope with in conducting businesses overseas?

Case 5.2 Transition from Planned Economy to Market Economy: Lessons from China

China's economic reform refers to the Chinese socialism program that was launched in December 1978 by the reformist, Deng Xiaoping, of the People's Republic of China (PRC). The success of China's economic policy and its implementation changed Chinese society. While large-scale government plan programs with market characteristics minimize poverty, income and income inequality have increased. Scholars discussed the reasons behind the success of the "dual-track" economy in China comparing the country to the Eastern Bloc and the Soviet Union. Increased efficiency in China's industries represents success in competitive world markets. Although national income growth may not be the sole criterion for evaluating the success of a country's economic policy, it is the most common measure of success. China had greater obstacles to overcome and transition from given that education levels were much lower in China than in Eastern Europe. How did China successfully transform from a planned economy to a market economy?

The contributing factors to China's successful economic transition include competition, investment in new firms, price reform, restructuring of the tax system, decentralization, and export-led growth. Competition, not privatization, was critical in transforming from a centrally planned economy to a market economy in China. Many Western economists argue that the fast transfer of ownership from state to private hands is required in order to achieve economic development. China's experience illustrates that rapid privatization is not necessary as the centerpiece of reform policy because of a lack of economic resources and management expertise. Several reasons can be offered to delay privatization. The fact that entrepreneurs invest in new companies for profit is the most powerful force that reform can harness. One of the most dynamic areas of China, especially since 1984, was non-state-owned industrial enterprises. These companies were mainly located in rural areas and have a range of formal organizational structures, but are mainly profit-seeking firms. Price distortion is one of the most disputed issues in a planned economy. If prices bear little relationship to the production costs of demand, a serious misallocation of resources is expected. China is often criticized for neglecting a price reform system. This criticism is wrong; China did not introduce rapid and comprehensive price reform, however, gradual marketization accompanied by the continued entrance of new producers realigned the price.

Another success factor attributed to Chinese economic reform is the decentralization of state authority that allowed local leaders to experiment with various ways to privatize the state sector and stimulate the economy. Officials at local and provincial government levels had strong internal incentives to generate high economic growth because these officials are more likely to be promoted based on their contribution to increased economic growth. Therefore, they were anxious to compete to reduce regulation and barriers to investment to boost economic growth. Another key factor in China's economic success was the implementation of an export-led growth strategy that the Four Asian Tigers as well as other newly industrialized countries have adopted.

Many economists favor the "big bang" approach of quick reform based on a comprehensive plan. According to this view, partial reforms are useless. The big bang reform theory has been influential in Poland, Czechoslovakia, and Russia who have used plans to rapidly transition to a capitalistic system. This is based on the assumption that evolutionary reform is not innately superior to big bang reform because a government needs to swiftly create an efficient, market-based economy.

In order to reform a centrally planned economy, the price management, fiscal and monetary policy, ownership, and legal systems must be altered. Rapid transition by "big bang" can cause a monolithic socialist system to collapse, because in all planned economies institutions are mutually interdependent. Given that China's reforms were gradual but remarkably successful, China's experimentation offers some valuable lessons on what types of reforms can work elsewhere and serves as a counter-example to the "big bang" reform theory's claim that gradual reform is likely to fail.

The paradox of the "big bang" reform theory is that obstacles to comprehensive reform plan are similar to those encountered in economic planning. Central planning does not work because it tries to control the uncontrollable.

Planners need incredibly large amounts of information and decision-makers' lack of crucial information causes inefficiencies within socialist economies. The problems that planners face in "big bang" reforms are similar. They must decide at what time and in what sequence prices are to be freed, enterprises privatized, trade barriers removed, and financial systems revamped. For example, reformers must decide how to allocate the ownership rights to state-owned enterprises and what type of financial system to adopt. Of course, evolutionary reform also requires these types of choices. However, it is much easier to make such a decision in a piecemeal fashion than all at once. China's successful transformation into a market economy provides compelling evidence that nothing was more important than competition to stimulate economic growth, notably absent in socialist planned economies. As Schumpeter pointed out, competition disciplines firms by making them operate efficiently. The massive entry of non-state firms created competition in China while state firms' willingness and ability to participate in free markets, against other producers, enhanced it.[a]

Note

a. Liberty Fund, Inc. (2007, October 8). Joseph Alois Schumpeter: Biography. Econlib.org. Retrieved from www.econlib.org/library/Enc/bios/Schumpeter. html

Sources

1. Brandt, L. and Rawski, T. G. (Eds.). (2008). *China's Great Economic Transformation*. Cambridge: Cambridge University Press.
2. Lipton, D. and Sachs, J. (1992). *Privatization in Eastern Europe: The Case of Poland* (pp. 169–212). UK: Palgrave Macmillan.

Questions for Case Discussion

1. Explain the key success factors of China's economic transition from a planned economy to a market economy. Discuss if these success factors can be applied to other planned economies.
2. Compare the experience of China with those of Poland, Czechoslovakia, and Russia in their efforts to transform into a market economy.
3. Why is it difficult to successfully implement "big bang" reforms as we have seen in the case of the former Soviet Union and its former satellite countries in Central and Eastern Europe?

Case 5.3 The Foreign Corrupt Practices Act: The Case of U.S. Companies

Multinational corporations (MNCs) that enter into foreign markets are still influenced by their home country's legal system, e.g. the Foreign Corrupt Practices Act (FCPA) that the U.S. Congress passed in 1977. The FCPA has two main provisions. One concerns accounting transparency requirements under the Securities Exchange Act of 1934. The other is about bribery of foreign officials. The act was amended twice, in 1988 and in 1998. The purpose of the Foreign Corrupt Practices Act (FCPA) is to make it illegal for companies to influence others through personal payment or rewards. The FCPA applies to a person associated with some degree of foreign corrupt practice or who has a connection to the U.S. The act also applies to any action by U.S. businesses, American nationals, foreign corporations trading securities in the U.S., and citizens whether they are physically present in the U.S. or not.

Businesses that are engaged in unethical behavior will incur severe consequences including high financial penalties and any individual who violates this law may face prison time. This law makes it illegal for specific classes and entities to make payments to foreign government officials with the intention of obtaining or retaining business. The Act can not only be applied to payment to foreign officials, candidates, and parties, but can also be applied to any other recipient of a bribe that is ultimately attributable to a foreign official, candidate, or party. Given that a growing number of American MNCs confirm that briberies do exist, the act appeared to have a positive effect. Although more action needs to be taken to eradicate bribery that still prevails in many countries, the fact of the matter is that both the government and companies have taken important steps toward solving the problem.

Wal-Mart, the giant retailer, was accused of regularly bribing Mexican officials to quickly obtain permits to open its stores. However, Wal-Mart is not the only U.S. company under investigation. John Deere, Qualcomm, Hewlett-Packard, Las Vegas Sands, and many other companies have also been under investigation for violations of the U.S. FCPA. The Securities and Exchange Commission (SEC) charged a former Morgan Stanley executive, Garth Peterson, with bribing a state-owned Chinese company's official in order to obtain business for the investment firm. He negotiated a deal with a Chinese official for the purchase of a $3.4 million USD Morgan Stanley property and arranged to split $1.8 million USD in secret payments with the Chinese official.

A media conglomerate, News Corp, was also subject to a U.S. bribery investigation. As of April 2012, the SEC and the Department of Justice (DOJ) were investigating at least 81 public companies for violations of the Foreign Corrupt Practices Act, which punishes those who are engaged in bribery in foreign countries. Although many companies do their best to prevent their employees from violating the FCPA, their financial documents display that their employees may at times violate U.S. overseas bribery law. The company that does not pay bribes for greasing the wheels of commerce encounters disadvantages compared with companies that pay bribes. Lakeland Industries, a Long Island, New York, manufacturer of industrial safety garments, allegedly claims that its inability to pay bribes, unlike its competitors, has lowered its sales.

The SEC has also contacted News Corp's 20th Century Fox, Disney and DreamWorks Animation. In 2011, the DOJ announced that there were 150 open investigations conducted by the department regarding foreign corrupt practices. Many companies have already paid large fines for violating this Act. For example, Johnson & Johnson paid $78 million because it violated the UN's Oil for Food program and Halliburton paid over $550 million to settle claims that officials at a former division provided bribes to officials in Nigeria while building a gas plant there in 2009. Bribes at German conglomerate Siemens were so pervasive around the world that the company was forced to pay $800 million dollars, the largest FCPA fine yet, to settle charges. Altogether, FCPA violation cases increased from two cases in 2002 to 20 in 2010.[a]

Many of the cases under investigation for many years never lead to actual charges or fines. In one case, there was evidence that a company attempted to hide wrongdoing. In March 2012, Qualcomm, a telecom giant, revealed that a whistle-blower approached the company's board of directors back in late 2009. The company had already completed an internal investigation into the matter and found no wrongdoing. However, the company admitted later the allegations related to bribery. Hewlett-Packard was also under investigation for bribery, embezzlement, and tax evasion. Employees of the company were accused of attempting to help a former German subsidiary of the company secure an IT contract in Russia. The money was given to the General Prosecutor's Office of the Russian Federation for five years from 2001 to 2006. In addition, the SEC and DOJ investigated casino giant, Las Vegas Sands, for possible FCPA violations. John Deere was under investigation by the SEC for allegations relating to bribery in Russia. It was also reported that a European subsidiary of Koch Industries bribed government officials and others to secure contracts in India, Africa, and the Middle East.

Another recent incident in relation to the FCPA involves a Chilean chemical and mining company, SQM. The company disclosed that in 2015 it was conducting an internal investigation into certain payments made by the company between 2009 and 2015 that may not have been properly supported or that may not have been necessary to generate corporate income. The company also reported that there was evidence of payments made without significant documentation but no evidence that directly demonstrated the payments were made to influence public officials.

Another violation of the FCPA involved Avon Products, the world's largest door to door seller of cosmetics, in which the company agreed to pay $4 million in legal fees and implement compliance reforms to settle a shareholder derivative action arising from a subsidiary bribery of Chinese foreign officials. In 2010, claims were made that directors and officers breached fiduciary duties and proxy disclosures related to bribery allegations. In 2014, the company ended a six-year U.S. probe that it engaged in overseas bribery with a guilty plea by its Chinese subsidiary. The company also spent at least $344 million on an internal investigation into corrupt payments and agreed to pay $135 million to settle U.S. criminal and civil claims. In the settlement, Avon agreed to adopt an international anti-corruption policy and code of conduct as well as implement specific FCPA tests. The company will also integrate in each business unit a compliance staff dedicated to FCPA matters. These individuals will conduct quarterly checkups for compliance and take steps to ensure the company's chief ethics officer and audit committee have access to hosting and gift request forms.[b]

More recently, the DOJ announced that under the new initiative, companies that self-report violations of the FCPA can take other remedial measures and may be eligible for a 50 percent reduction in sanctions.

The goal of this program is to encourage companies to self-disclose violations and increase the department's ability to file charges against individual wrongdoers. Federal prosecutors will be able to offer the reduction to companies that self-report violations and disclose all known facts and remediate bad acts; including the receipt and concealment of improper benefits. Under the new policy, cooperation after officials determine a violation occurred will not be viewed the same as voluntarily reporting. These changes come after the department had been publicly scrutinized for failing to punish wrongdoers during the financial crisis.[c]

Notes

a.   Gandel, S. (2012, April 26). Not just Wal-Mart: Dozens of U.S. companies face bribery suspicions. *Fortune*. Retrieved from http://fortune.com/2012/04/26/not-just-wal-mart-dozens-of-u-s-companies-face-bribery-suspicions

b.   Odom, C. (2016, April 20). Avon agrees to settle investor action over FCPA breaches. BNA.com. Retrieved April 26, 2016, from www.bna.com/avon-agrees-settle-n57982070108/

c.   Odom, C. (2016, April 7). New DOJ program aims to beef up FCPA prosecutions. BNA.com. Retrieved April 26, 2016, from www.bna.com/new-doj-program-n57982069556/

Sources

1.   Gandel, S. (2012, April 26). Not just Wal-Mart: Dozens of U.S. companies face bribery suspicions. *Fortune*. Retrieved from http://fortune.com/2012/04/26/not-just-wal-mart-dozens-of-u-s-companies-face-bribery-suspicions

2.   Funk, T. M. (2010, September 10). Getting what they pay for: The far-reaching impact of the Dodd-Frank Act's 'whistleblower bounty' incentives on FCPA enforcement (PDF). *White Collar Crime Report* (Bureau of National Affairs). Retrieved from www.perkinscoie.com/images/content/2/2/v2/22172/comm-10-09-whitecollarcrimereport.pdf

3.   Posadas, A. (2000). Combating corruption under international law. *Duke Journal of Comparative & International Law, 10*(2), 345–414.

4.   Odom, C. (2016, April 7). New DOJ program aims to beef up FCPA prosecutions. BNA.com. Retrieved April 26, 2016, from www.bna.com/new-doj-program-n57982069556/

5.   Dockers, S. (2016, April 22). Chilean company notifies U.S. of foreign corruption probe results. *Wall Street Journal*. Retrieved April 26, 2016, from http://blogs.wsj.com/riskandcompliance/2016/04/22/chilean-company-notifies-u-s-of-foreign-corruption-probe-results/

6.   Odom, C. (2016, April 20). Avon agrees to settle investor action over FCPA breaches. BNA.com. Retrieved April 26, 2016, from www.bna.com/avon-agrees-settle-n57982070108/

Questions for Case Discussion

1. Explain the background and significance of the Foreign Corrupt Practices Act.
2. Explain a recent FCPA lawsuit. How did the company or individual violate the act? What were the consequences or results if any?
3. What changes have been made to the FCPA? Why?

Case 5.4 The "Panama Papers"

In April 2016, the world witnessed the largest data leak in history, an unidentified employee at the Panamanian law firm Mossack Fonseca disclosed more than 11 million documents to German newspaper Suddeutsche Zeitung who then forwarded the 2.6 terabytes of data to the International Consortium of Investigative Journalists (ICIJ) who dissected it and released it in over 100 publications to the general public. The files cover over 40 years and unveil offshore accounts and shell companies of individuals in tax havens such as the British Virgin Islands, Seychelles, and Panama. Documents show how money was circulated and hidden by at least 33 people and companies banned by the U.S. for allegedly conducting business with rogue states, terrorists, or drug barons.

These accounts and companies are owned by current and former world leaders (Russian President: Vladimir Putin, Pakistani PM: Nawaz Sharif, and British PM: David Cameron), celebrities (Jackie Chan, Amitabh Chan, and Lionel Messi), and global business executives. Connections to these offshore entities is not illegal and the law firm, Mossack Fonseca, has denied any wrongdoing although some of those documented have used the firm's services to set up offshore companies in tax havens for illegal purposes and to confer illegitimate benefits.

British PM David Cameron who was revealed to have an offshore account in Panama has been publicly scrutinized. Cameron admitted to benefiting from an offshore trust established by his deceased father in which he owned shares in the tax haven fund that he sold before becoming PM in 2010. Some members of the British Parliament demanded Cameron's resignation claiming he misled the public. Iceland's PM, Sigmundur Gunnlaugsson, another figure named in the "Panama Papers" leak is facing calls to resign. Mr. Gunnlaugsson has insisted he will not resign after the documents disclosed that he and his wife in 2007 set up a paper company in the British Virgin Islands. Iceland's residents are still angry from the effects of the 2008 financial crisis, which hit the country hard. When the bubble burst, its three private banks became bloated and could not defend short-term debts and repay depositors. The company that Mr. Gunnlaugsson created was claiming about $4.2 million USD from these collapsed banks. Ultimately, Iceland suffered a deep economic depression from this financial crisis which caused the country to request emergency loans from the IMF. Finally, Pakistani PM Nawaz Sharif is also feeling the repercussions of being named in the "Panama Papers" as opposing politicians are calling for his resignation. The documents revealed his three children controlled shell companies in which they owned expensive residential properties in London. Mr. Sharif rejected money laundering allegations and claims his children have legitimate business abroad. These accusations come at a bad time in Pakistan as political tensions are rising high and the political infrastructure is weak. Military intervention may step in and political opposition are using these allegations to promote their own agendas.

Overall, the Panama Papers have addressed a global problem with economic transparency, specifically with tax havens. There are valid reasons for using offshore companies or bank accounts. Offshore accounts and shell companies can be used when two firms need to set up a cross-border joint venture and need to incorporate on neutral turf and when citizens in unstable countries seek a location to place their savings in case of a political or economic crisis within their country. Unfortunately, cleaning up tax havens will not deter the practice and create financial transparency. The responsibility to enforce compliance and create transparency belongs to a country's national government but it is difficult for these entities to enforce a practice they themselves do not exercise. Corruption increases inequality making the world poorer and widening the wage gap. When politicians steal from their constituents they reduce the amount of public cash that can be used for public services and the public good. Many of the shell companies under anonymous identities in "Panama Papers" involved "nominees" or individuals who would represent the real owners. It was found that these vehicles were used for tax avoidance and money laundering.

German Chancellor Angela Merkel and the EU have offered solutions on how to prevent this practice and ensure transparency in the aftermath of these publications. The EU plans to intensify its combat against tax evasion and money laundering as a result of the leak. Members of the EU are vying over a location for the creation of a central registry open to tax officials, law enforcement, and the public. Law firms and other intermediaries that construct offshore companies and trusts to circumvent government regulations will be subject to strict penalties, e.g. criminal charges for lying or enabling tax evasion.

Sources

1. Booth, R., Watt, H., and Pegg, D. (2016, April 7). David Cameron admits he profited from father's Panama offshore trust. *The Guardian*. Retrieved April 24, 2016, from www.theguardian.com/news/2016/apr/07/david-cameron-admits-he-profited-fathers-offshore-fund-panama-papers

2. Min-ho, J. (2016, April 22). AmorePacific founder's children named in Panama Papers. *Korea Times*. Retrieved April 22, 2016, from www.koreatimes.co.kr/www/news/nation/2016/04/116_203196.html

3. Erlanger, S. (2016, April 4). 'Panama Papers' leaks put Iceland prime minister under pressure to quit. *New York Times*. Retrieved April 24, 2016, from www.nytimes.com/2016/04/05/world/europe/panama-papers-leaks-put-iceland-leader-under-pressure-to-quit.html

4. *Economist*. (2016, April 9). The lesson of the Panama Papers. Retrieved April 24, 2016, from www.economist.com/news/leaders/21696532-more-should-be-done-make-offshore-tax-havens-less-murky-lesson-panama-papers

5. Wishart, I. (2016, April 19). EU cites panama papers as underscoring urgency in tax reform. Bloomberg.com. Retrieved April 24, 2016, from www.bloomberg.com/news/articles/2016-04-19/eu-cites-panama-papers-as-underscoring-urgency-in-tax-reform

6. Associated Press (2016, April 5). Germany wants to create a 'transparency register' after the Panama Papers leaks. Retrieved April 24, 2016, from www. businessinsider.com/germany-wants-a-transparency-register-after-panama-papers-leaks-2016-4

Questions for Case Discussion

1. What are the Panama Papers? What are the legitimate and illegitimate ways offshore accounts and companies can be used?
2. What are some methods the EU and other countries would employ to prevent political and economic corruption?
3. What institutions do you feel are responsible for enforcing economic transparency and preventing corruption?

Political and Legal Environment

I. Political Systems and Risks

1. Types of Political Systems

(1) Democracy

Democracy can be defined as a principle in which all people in a country are politically and legally equal. Abraham Lincoln's expression "Government of the people, by the people, for the people" is a basic overview or description of democracy. It means all of the citizens in a nation have equal rights; the right to an opinion, religion, speech, and assembly. Various types of democracies exist as shown in Table 5.1. Democracy creates a business environment that promotes the expansion of trade and simplifies exchanges between domestic and international business.[1] It also creates a productive business environment based on a non-bureaucratic regulated market. Managers and consumers can engage in activities that meet their freedoms.

(2) Totalitarianism

A totalitarian system puts the overarching goal of the nation over the interests of its individual citizens. Individuals, parliament, political parties, or certain institutions monopolize political power and control the majority of public and private life. A totalitarian government blocks opposing values and ideals through brainwashing, persecution, surveillance, propaganda,

Table 5.1 Types of Democracy

Representative	It is based on the constitution protecting freedom. The law treats equally all citizens, public and private. Elected representatives exercise its sovereignty on the basis of the interests of the people. Representative democracy includes the United States and Japan.
Multiparty	A system where more than three parties govern the nations independently or through an alliance. No single party can legislate policy. Canada, Germany, Italy, and Israel are examples in this category.
Parliamentary	The people's parliament elects the legislative representation to exercise political authority. India and Australia belong to this category.
Social	A system where capitalism transforms into socialism through democratic procedures. The government restricts and regulates so that capitalistic ideals does not create an unfair system. Norway and Sweden can be put in this category.

Source: Smith, M. A. (2000). *American Business and Political Power: Public Opinion, Elections, and Democracy.* Chicago and London: University of Chicago Press.

Table 5.2 Forms of Totalitarianism

Authoritarianism	It does not allow ideological deviation from the country. Obedience to the authorities is reflected in daily life. Resistance to government will be punished. Though the government regulates the political environment, it does not have any great interest in social economy or social structures. Kazakhstan, Republic of Chad in Africa, and Turkmenistan belong to this category.
Fascism	Fascists seek to organize a country according to corporatist perspectives, values, and systems. The people in these countries have their mind, spirit, and daily lives controlled by the forces and brainwashing of the single party system. North Korea and Myanmar belong to this category.
Secularism	A single party regulates and restricts elections. When the country is not challenged, objections are tolerated. However, other ideologies are suppressed. Individual freedom is allowed when the government is not challenged and social harmony is not harmed. China, Vietnam, and Venezuela belong to this category.
Theocratic	The government represents God. Leaders argue that they represent the interests of the world. Society is strictly regulated and controls the social gender roles. Iran, Afghanistan, and Saudi Arabia belong to this category.

Source: Economist. (2011, June 25). China's future: rising power, anxious state. Special Report: China.

censorship, and other measures. The system does not accept free thought, benefits, or behaviors that oppose the national ideology. For example, bookstores in China are allowed to stock only those books that have been approved by the Chinese Communist Party (CCP).[2] Table 5.2 explains various forms of totalitarianism.

Approximately one-third of the world population or 2.5 billion people live in totalitarian systems. Two of the totalitarian governments include Afghanistan and North Korea; only a few people in these nations enjoy individual freedom. Totalitarian governments support measures that control and manage economic resources. Managers must learn how to cope with a strong government influence. For example, GE has established a 50–50 joint venture with the Chinese jet manufacturer, Aviation Industry, to produce key components for the company's aircrafts. Despite the potential political risk, GE decided to form a partnership with a state-owned company to seek a long term benefit and build a relationship with the Chinese government. Problems may arise if GE's Chinese partner becomes a potential competitor after acquiring GE's proprietary technology and information.

(3) Socialism

The basic doctrine of socialism is that capital and wealth belong to the country. These items should be utilized for production methods rather than profit making.[3] Such an ideology is based on the assumption that the collective welfare of people should take precedence over individual welfare. Socialists argue that capitalists gain excessive wealth within a society as compared to laborers. Since laborers receive compensation below their labor value, the government believes that they must regulate basic production, dispersion, and other commercial activities.

In most socialist countries, socialism is known as social democracy, which has been successful in Western Europe. Social democracy also plays a critical role in the political system of major emerging economies such as Brazil and India. The French and Norwegian governments, under social democratic systems, intervene in the private sector and enterprise activities.[4]

2. Political Risks

Political risks tend to be higher in a country that practices totalitarianism or socialism instead of democracy. They are classified into two types: macro and micro political risks. While macro political risks affect the performance of all the industries and companies in a country, micro political risks only impact a certain industry or a specific firm. As shown in Case 5.1, the former may include corruption, riot, change in the hands of government; the latter contains local content requirement, pricing regulation, etc. For example, a newly elected president might introduce unwelcoming policies toward international trade and FDI. Under these circumstances, these newly implemented regulations can adversely affect the macroeconomic environment. Similarly, government regulations may target industries that are dominated by foreign companies. In addition, public-sector corruption and a partisan judicial system often observed in developing countries may increase the costs of conducting business. For example, foreign firms may have to pay higher customs or licensing fees or taxes. A host country government may also put a restriction on the repatriation of profits if an MNC sends back all the profit to its headquarters at home without leaving much surplus in its country. In the worst case, the host country government may expropriate an MNC's assets or properties usually without compensation. However, an outright expropriation is seldom exercised as it builds a negative reputation about the country. Instead, a creeping expropriation has become more common by forcing an MNC to gradually give up its ownership to a local company.

II. Economic Systems and Risks

1. Types of Economic Systems

(1) Market economy

A market economy is comprised of two important units: individuals and firms. While a company uses its resources to create products, individuals own resources and purchase products. The market mechanism is based on interactions between price, quantity, supply and demand of resources and products. If a company provides the appropriate wage, labor is supplied. If the price is within a certain range, the product will be consumed. The company bases its wage on quantity of labor available for a job. Resources are allocated as a result of actions between firms and households. Important factors that help market economies function are the ability of companies to freely act in the market and consumer sovereignty. As long as the two units, individuals and households, are free to make decisions, the interaction of supply and demand can ensure the appropriate allocation of resources.

(2) Centrally planned economy (command economy)

A centrally planned economy or command economy is an economic system in which a government allocates resources directly. Case 5.2 illustrates how China successfully transformed from a centrally planned economy to a market economy. The government in a centrally planned economy tries to control the activities of all the economic sectors. The government determines how much is produced for whom and by whom. The basic assumption is that the government is more capable of determining how resources should be allocated than the market. Planned economies are generally classified as variants of socialism.

(3) Mixed economy

In reality, it is rare to see either a pure market economy or a completely planned economy. A mixed economy takes on a hybrid form between free market and government planning. Government intervention in the free market can be done in two ways: influence over economic decision-making and ownership over the means of production. Many industrialized countries in Europe such as Germany and France have maintained a relatively low level of government ownership, while traditionally emphasizing social welfare. The Scandinavian countries such as Sweden and Denmark have also maintained a strong social welfare system supported by high taxes.

2. Economic Risks

As a centrally planned economy usually goes hand-in-hand with totalitarianism, firms operating in the command economy tend to be more susceptible to economic risks. High inflation, increasing unemployment rate, widening trade deficit, and accumulation of government debt are all symptoms of a looming economic or financial crisis. Inflation refers to the phenomenon where price levels steadily rise as compared to purchasing power. High inflation is likely to result in depreciation of the value of a local currency, reducing the profitability of an MNC operating in a host country as well as eroding the purchasing power of consumers, thus increasing economic and financial risks. Countries that are unable to create jobs suffer from slow growth, social pressure, and political instability. A high unemployment rate reflects the government's inability to manage the country's human resources properly, thus raising political risks.[5] In addition, the financial debt of a government is indicative of a country's economic well-being. The accumulated public debt reflects a high level of uncertainty regarding a country's economic performance.[6] A high debt service burden will reduce consumer confidence and contract government fiscal activities, resulting in higher economic risks. A widening trade deficit also often results in devaluation of a local currency, triggering capital flight into a foreign country.

III. Legal Systems and Risks

1. Legal Systems

Countries practice different types of laws: common law, civil law, theocratic law, customary law, and mixed law.

(1) Common law

The common law system is generally uncodified as it is based on custom, tradition, and precedent. Common law respects previous cases and legal history in resolving conflicts and disputes. One of the key characteristics of common law is the *stare decisis* principle. In a common law society, the precedents of earlier cases prevail as sources of law rather than codes of law. This allows more discretion to judges in a common law system in interpreting the law in accordance with the unique circumstances of an individual case. The common law system, has its heritage in Anglo-American society, is accepted in Canada, the U.S., India, Hong Kong, the U.K., New Zealand, and Australia. Since common law is uncodified or ill specified, business contracts in these countries tends to be long and detailed, specifying all the contingences.

(2) Civil law

The civil law system relies on systematic codes of laws. In contrast to the *stare decisis* principle, the civil law system is not constrained by the judges' previous precedents. Instead, judges are often described as "investigators." In a civil law system, the judge's role is to establish the facts of the case and to apply the provisions of the applicable code. The judge's decision is consequently less influential in shaping civil law than the decisions of legislators who write and interpret the codes. Approximately 150 countries including Germany, France, Mexico, and Japan practice various types of civil law systems. Since civil law covers many issues through specific codes, a business contract in these countries tends to be short and succinct.

(3) Theocratic law

The theocratic law system is based on the religious doctrine, precepts, and beliefs of the country. Thus, religious leaders have the legal authority to interpret religious doctrines and regulate business deals and social relations.[7] Theocratic law does not separate religion from state. The government, law, and religion are considered as one unit. Islamic law is the most widely practiced theocratic legal system adopted mostly in the Middle East and North

Africa. The Islamic laws have an emphasis on the Koran, Sunnah (The Prophet Muhammed's word and judgment), Islamic scholars' books, and law specialists' opinions.[8] However, modernism (Turkey and Indonesia), traditionalism (Kuwait and Malaysia), and fundamentalism (Iran and Saudi Arabia) provide different interpretations of Islamic laws.

(4) Customary law

The customary law system reflects the wisdom of daily life, spiritual heritage, and philosophical tradition. The customary system is founded in laws that regulate the members' rights and responsibilities in many indigenous communities. Violation of this law corresponds to "Civil law tort." It is not considered a crime toward nations and societies, but as individual criminal behavior or damage. This law system is widely adopted in developing countries in Africa.[9] However, few countries fully rely on the customary law system; most countries adopt a mixed law system.

(5) Mixed law

The mixed law system refers to particular nations utilizing more than two systems of aforementioned laws. It is the most commonly adopted in Africa and Asia. For instance, Nigeria has adopted and maintained a mix of common law, theocratic law, and customary law. Pakistan uses common laws, British colonial heritage, and theocratic law. Indonesia has a system of civil combined with theocratic law. The U.S. officially adopted the common law system; however, it can be considered a mixed system since both the French civil law and English criminal law were adopted in Louisiana.

2. Legal Risks

(1) Host Country Origin

FOREIGN DIRECT INVESTMENT LAW

Foreign investment law not only affects the type of entry strategies for MNCs but also their activities and performance.[10] Many countries put restrictions on foreign direct investment. For example, the Japanese Daitenhoo (Law to restrict large-scaled retailing enterprises) once banned warehouse stores and large retailers like Wal-Mart and Toys "R" Us from entering the market to protect small retailers.

RESTRICTION ON EQUITY OWNERSHIP AND OPERATION

Many countries enact laws and regulations to restrict MNCs' production, marketing, and distribution activities. Such regulations reduce both the efficiency and effectiveness of the companies. Complex regulations disturb distribution activities and restrict entrance strategies.[11] For instance, in the Chinese telecommunications market, the Chinese government requires foreign companies to enter only as a joint venture with local firms and prohibits foreign investors from possessing 100% ownership. Such a restriction on full ownership by a foreign company is also applied to the Chinese auto industry.

INTELLECTUAL PROPERTY PROTECTION LAWS

Intellectual property is probably the most important asset for many companies in this information and digital age and includes any product as a result of a firm's intellectual activity such as a music CD, computer software, car design, a screenplay, etc. Some common types of intellectual property rights are patents, copyrights, and trademarks. MNCs may lose their critical proprietary knowledge when they conduct business in a host country where an adequate protection of intellectual property is not provided. Therefore, they have to come up with an effective strategy on how to deal with the violations of intellectual property rights before entering a host country. Under the umbrella of the United Nations (U.N.), the World Intellectual Property Organization (WIPO) was created in 1967 to promote the protection of intellectual property throughout the world.

LAWS RELATED TO MARKETING AND DISTRIBUTION

This law regulates what measures of advertisement, promotion, and distribution are allowed.[12] For example, Finnish, French, Norwegian, and New Zealand law restricts cigarette advertisements on TV. In Germany, so-called comparative advertising that compare specific products and promote the advantages of one brand over another are prohibited. Many countries limit price increases for food and health products and services. These limitations certainly restrict marketing and profitability.

PROFIT REMITTANCE LAWS

MNCs generate revenue in host countries and generally attempt to transfer earnings to their home country. However, in some countries, the government enacts a law prohibiting such income transfers. Restrictions on the remittance of dividends and net income of MNCs limit transfers to headquarters. These restrictions sometimes block the inflow of MNCs and such situations are often seen in countries where the foreign exchange reserve is low.

ENVIRONMENTAL LAWS

The government wants to preserve natural resources. To secure health and safety, laws are made to avert the abusive use and pollution of air, soil, and water resources. For instance, Russian law imposes a "recycling fee" on imports from foreign auto makers. The charge is meant to pay for the future costs of scrapping or recycling an imported car and doesn't apply to domestic cars. However, "many believe that the aim of Russia's recycling fee is not to protect the environment but discriminate arbitrarily and unjustifiably against imported vehicles."[13] In another case, MNCs have to obey the thorough recycling regulations in Germany. The pressures of packaging recyclable products transfer from manufacturers to distributors. However, the government tries to seek a balance between environmental laws and their potential adverse effect on employment, entrepreneurship, MNCs' investment, and economic growth.

INTERNET AND E-COMMERCE REGULATION

Such regulations are new to the current law systems.[14] Amazon.com acquired a patent in September 1999 and also owned the "1-Click" trademark. Just 23 days after Amazon.com was granted its 1-Click patent, Amazon filed a lawsuit against Barnes & Noble, a rival online bookseller and largest competitor, in the federal district court of Seattle because Barnes & Noble introduced a very similar ordering system. This case shows new debates on cyber patents including standards for patents, time frames, and criteria. Firms operating e-commerce businesses in countries with lax regulations are facing serious economic or financial risks. For instance, due to the rapid spread of the Internet and e-commerce, the Chinese government has enacted laws to protect individuals' private lives and improve both personal and cyber security.

(2) Home Country Origin

THE FOREIGN CORRUPT PRACTICES ACT (FCPA)

The FCPA (The Foreign Corrupt Practices Act) passed by the U.S. government in 1977 stipulates that offering bribes to foreign governments for the purpose of protecting and maintaining foreign business is illegal. The FCPA was introduced after more than 400 U.S. enterprises admitted to offering bribes to foreign government administrators and politicians. As Case 5.3 indicates, the FCPA also requires publicly listed companies follow accounting regulations. The FCPA distinguishes the difference between payments, bribery, and business promotions. Under the law, payments for business promotion are allowed if they are allowed under local law. Case 5.3 shows how MNCs have recently responded to effectively deal with the FCPA.[15]

ACCOUNTING AND INSPECTION LAWS

Accounting standards differ from one country to another. Separate standards pose challenges but may also create opportunities for a firm.[16] For example, when stock prices and other marketable securities are determined, most countries choose the lowest market price. However, Brazil recommends that Brazilian stockholding firms and companies modify the value of their stock to account for the country's historically high inflation rate. Canada and the U.S. adopt the acquisition cost when computing the value of physical assets such as factories and facilities.

FINANCIAL REPORT TRANSPARENCY

The frequency and transparency of financial reports differ greatly throughout the world. Transparency refers to the degree of divulgence of considerable periodical information related to a firm's financial state and accounting. For instance, public enterprises in the U.S. should allow the Securities and Exchange Commission to review their financial performance reports every quarter. However, numerous countries around the world divulge these reports only annually or more rarely. There is a lack of transparency. The more transparency, the more enhanced the decision-making becomes at the firm and the more people are likely to understand these enterprises. As Case 5.4 describes, the recent publications of the "Panama Papers" illustrates how difficult it is to control illegal practices of a country's resident who is trying to avoid the scrutiny of a financial transparency requirement in the home country.

IV. Managing Political Risks

An accurate assessment of political risks can predict potential political changes in the future and evaluate how these changes will affect an MNC's business operation. Political risks can be managed prior to or after entry into a host country.

1. Before Entering Foreign Markets

Governments have developed and operated insurance systems to protect domestic firms from political risks.[17] Starting in the U.S. in 1948, many countries' governments including the Japanese and German have adopted similar systems. The U.S. Overseas Private Investment Corporation (OPIC) is well known as the U.S. government development finance institution that provides investors political risk insurance. Private insurance companies developed various insurance products in order to help MNCs hedge against political risks. Private insurance companies like Lloyds of London offer standard insurance products that account for specific types of political risk.[18]

Investment guarantee programs including investment funds from the host country's government, investment protection, and tax concessions can be ensured when MNCs in a host country have huge influences on the host country's economy or when the government of the host country provides incentives to foreign investment. Such guarantees are more likely to be offered when MNCs make substantial contributions to the host country's government. Such guarantees are also more likely to be rendered to MNCs that possess a proprietary technology, have well-known brands, and enter into joint ventures with local enterprises.[19]

2. After Entering Foreign Markets

Ethical business practices are essential because MNCs may potentially avoid or reduce the consequences of political risks through ethical conduct. Corporate Social Responsibility (CSR) refers to how businesses should be run to meet moral, legal, commercial, and public expectations toward stake-holders (consumers, shareholders, employees, and communities). The belief that firms should not only be good citizens, by providing jobs and paying taxes, but also engage in ethical business practices prevails around the world.[20] A host country is less likely to intervene in business activities of those companies that make a good contribution to its economy.

When MNCs integrate their operations across countries, they are more likely to avoid political risks in a host country since it makes it difficult for the host country government to intervene in its globally integrated operations, whether vertical or horizontal. Entering into foreign markets as a joint venture with a reliable local partner is another practical strategy to reduce political risk.[21] The qualified local partner has an insightful understanding of local situations and can help an MNC cultivate trustful relations with the local government. MNCs should also be familiar with the legal contexts of a host country so that they can pursue an appropriate legal remedy when disputes arise with local partners.

Key Terms

Political systems, democracy, totalitarianism, socialism, political risks, economic systems, transition economy, centrally planned economy, market economy, mixed economy, legal systems, civil law, common law, theocratic law, customary law, legal risks, Foreign Corrupt Practices Act (FCPA)

Review Questions

1. Discuss the differences between macro and micro political risks.
2. Describe different economic systems and explain how a country can successfully transform from a command economy to a market economy.
3. Explain the Foreign Corrupt Practice Act. How can American MNCs maintain their competitive advantage without violating it in a foreign market?
4. Describe differences between common law and civil law and discuss their implications for a business contract.
5. How can an MNC manage political risks before and after entering a foreign market?

Internet Exercise

Please visit the website of the World Intellectual Property Organization (www.wipo.int/portal/en/index.html) and find out the materials that would be of assistance to a company contemplating the international licensing of intellectual property rights.

Notes

1   Smith, M. A. (2000). *American Business and Political Power: Public Opinion, Elections, and Democracy*. Chicago: University of Chicago Press.

2   *Economist.* Special Report: China. (2011). China's future: Rising power, anxious state. Retrieved from www.economist.com/node/18866989.

3   Schumpeter, J. A. (2013). *Capitalism, Socialism and Democracy.* London and New York: Routledge.

4   Pontusson, J. (2011). Once again a model: Nordic social democracy in a globalized world. In James E. Cronin, George W. Ross, and James Shoch (Eds.), *What's Left of the Left: Democrats and Social Democrats in Challenging Times* (pp. 89–115). Durham, NC: Duke University Press. ISBN 0822350793.

5   Friedberg, R. M. and Hunt, J. (1995). The impact of immigrants on host country wages, employment and growth. *The Journal of Economic Perspectives, 9*(2), 23–44.

6   Bordo, M. D. and Meissner, C. M. (2006). The role of foreign currency debt in financial crises: 1880–1913 versus 1972–1997. *Journal of Banking & Finance, 30*(12), 3299–3329.

7   Heer, N. (1990). *Islamic Law and Jurisprudence.* Seattle, WA: University of Washington Press.

8   Media Monitors Network. (2003). Islamic law: Myths and realities. Retrieved from http://mediamonitors.net/wiechmankendall&azarian1.html

9   Theodor, M. (1987). The Geneva Conventions as customary law. *The American Journal of International Law, 81*(2), 348–370.

10   List, John A. and Co, Catherine Y. (2000). The effects of environmental regulations on foreign direct investment. *Journal of Environmental Economics and Management, 40*(1), 1–20.

11   Van der Vorst, J. G. and Beulens, A. J. (2002). Identifying sources of uncertainty to generate supply chain redesign strategies. *International Journal of Physical Distribution & Logistics Management, 32*(6), 409–430.

12   An, D. (2007). Advertising visuals in global brands' local websites: A six-country comparison. *International Journal of Advertising, 26*(3), 303–332.

13   Europa.eu. (2013, July 9). EU challenges Russian 'recycling' fee in WTO. Retrieved from http://europa.eu/rapid/press-release_MEMO-13-671_en.htm

14   *Forbes.* (2012). Amazon loses 1-click patent. Retrieved from www.forbes.com/sites/timworstall/2011/07/07/amazon-loses-1-click-patent/#47c7336c788e

15   *Fortune.* (2012). Not just Wal-Mart: Dozens of U.S. companies face bribery suspicions. Retrieved from http://fortune.com/2012/04/26/not-just-wal-mart-dozens-of-u-s-companies-face-bribery-suspicions/

16   Miller, P. and Power, M. (1992). Accounting, law and economic calculation. In M. Bromwich and A. Hopwood (Eds.), *Accounting and the Law* (pp. 230–253). Englewood Cliffs, NJ: Prentice Hall.

17   *Economist.* (2007). Of coups and coverage: Political turmoil is costly. Unless you are fully insured. Retrieved from www.economist.com/node/896722

18   Mishra, K. C. (2006). For political risk, insurance isn't all. DNA India. Retrieved from www.dnaindia.com/money/report_for-political-risk-insurance-isnt-all_1027950.

19   Neumayer, E. and Spess, L. (2005). Do bilateral investment treaties increase foreign direct investment to developing countries? *World Development, 33*(10), 1567–1585.

20   Eisingerich, A. B. and Bhardwaj, G. (2011). Does social responsibility help protect a company's reputation? *MIT Sloan Management Review, 52*(3), 18.

21   Lu, Y. (1998). Joint venture success in China: How should we select a good partner? *Journal of World Business, 33*(2), 145–166.

6 Social and Cultural Environment

Learning Objectives

1. Describe the definition of culture.
2. Identify the various aspects of social and cultural environments.
3. Understand and compare the major national cultural models.
4. Understand why cultural changes occur over time.
5. Recognize cultural differences across countries and their implications.

Cases

Case 6.1 Europe's Vehicle Color Preferences
Case 6.2 The Global Appeal of Gangnam Style
Case 6.3 Kia Hajj Bus in Saudi Arabia
Case 6.4 Islamic Banking in the U.S.
Case 6.5 Groupon's Struggle in China

Case 6.1 Europe's Vehicle Color Preferences

Not long ago, Ford released the results of a study it had conducted to examine which vehicle colors were popular in Europe (see Table 6.1). Recognizing color preferences across European countries has really helped Ford meet customer demand with the right vehicles.

The results from the survey indicated that the most popular colors were white, black, and silver in general. Specifically, people in Turkey showed greater preference for white cars than any other color. Black was most popular in Denmark and Norway. Surprisingly, the Irish chose silver more than any other shade, despite the country's national identification with green. These observations offered practical knowledge about sales trends in specific countries, so that Ford managers could plan for production and manage inventory accordingly.

At a glance, it seems that car buyers' color preferences are just personal preferences. In fact, a country's geographical location and climate may play a major role in local consumers' color choices. For instance, since local weather is often sweltering, Turkish car buyers preferred white most and liked black least. In contrast, black was the most popular vehicle color in Denmark while white was the least popular one. Certainly, geographical borders and climate

Table 6.1 Top Five Countries in Each Color (by Percentage of Ford Vehicles Sold in 2010)

Rank	Black	Blue	Brown
1	Denmark (37.8%)	Czech Republic (24.5%)	Finland (1.4%)
2	Norway (31.6%)	Romania (21.9%)	Norway (1.3%)
3	Portugal (26.7%)	Great Britain (19.7%)	Belgium (1.2%)
4	Germany (26.6%)	Finland (16.2%)	Poland (0.9%)
5	Russia (24.9%)	Poland (14.9%)	Hungary (0.9%)

Rank	Cream	Green	Grey
1	France (4.1%)	Hungary (2.9%)	Belgium (20.8%)
2	Italy (1.2%)	Czech Republic (2.1%)	Italy (17.6%)
3	Greece (0.8%)	Austria (1.8%)	Portugal (16.7%)
4	Netherlands (0.6%)	Germany (1.7%)	France (16.4%)
5	Hungary (0.5%)	France (1.6%)	Netherlands (16.4%)

Rank	Orange	Red	Silver	White
1	Sweden (0.8%)	Czech Republic (15%)	Ireland (37%)	Turkey (49%)
2	Romania (0.6%)	Finland (12.8%)	Romania (30.2%)	Hungary (32.2%)
3	Hungary (0.4%)	Greece (12.7%)	Finland (29.4%)	Switzerland (31.3%)
4	Austria (0.3%)	Spain (12.5%)	Poland (28.8%)	Spain (28.8%)
5	Poland (0.28%)	Belgium (9.1%)	Sweden (28.3%)	France (27.5%)

Source: Autoblog.com. (2011, April 1). Ford reveals Europe's color preferences by country. Retrieved from www.autoblog.com/2011/04/01/ford-reveals-europes-color-preferences-by-country

are not the only determinants of consumer color preference. For example, Norway and Portugal shared the same six favorite colors but do not share a geographical border or climate pattern.

For some countries, patriotism may explain their car buyers' color preferences. For instance, buyers in the Czech Republic showed a much stronger preference for blue cars than any other color. In fact, it was the only country in which the most popular color was not black, white, or silver. Among all vehicles Ford had sold in 2010, blue and red ones accounted for a bigger share in the Czech Republic than they did in other countries. These two color choices were consistent with the dominant red and blue colors of the Czech national flag. But then again, not all countries showed this pattern. The Netherlands didn't show any preference for orange vehicles, while green was one of the least liked colors in Ireland.

Moreover, general color preferences do not necessarily correspond to color choices for different car models. For example, following German customers' color preferences, Ford should make cars in darker colors. However, two colors of Ford Fiesta—bright red (Hot Magenta) and bright green (Squeeze)—have sold extremely well in Germany. Ford needs to cautiously interpret the findings from the color study. It may be necessary to offer a variety of unique colors for different car models and for different customer groups.

Additionally, vehicle color trends change over time, just like trends in fashion markets. For example, red was once the most popular color, but its position has been replaced by white in recent years. According to Axalta Coating Systems, a supplier of liquid and powder coatings, white was the most popular car color in 2013 not only in Europe but also in the U.S., Asia, and South America.[a] People also show strong preferences for dark greys, blacks, and blues just like they do for clothing. In recent years, car colors appear to follow the latest trends in technology. While flashier colors dominated in the 1990s, silver was prevalent in the 2000s due to the popularity of stainless appliances, and Apple's iPhone has made white particularly popular.

Obviously, it is important for Ford to recognize and respond to rising color trends by designing, manufacturing, and stocking the right colored vehicles at the right time. If Ford adopts a color trend too early, customers may be unresponsive to the company's efforts. If Ford adopts a color trend too late, the popularity of a particular vehicle color may have already peaked, squandering a solid sales opportunity.

Notes

a. Business Wire. (2014, Oct. 30). Axalta releases global automotive 2014 color popularity report and future trends. Retrieved from www.businesswire.com/news/home/20141030006776/en/Axalta-Releases-Global-Automotive-2014-Color-Popularity

Sources

1. Autoblog.com. (2011, April 1). Ford reveals Europe's color preferences by country. Retrieved from www.autoblog.com/2011/04/01/ford-reveals-europes-color-preferences-by-country
2. Forttrell, Q. (2014, June 17). Why white is No.1 car color. Blame Apple, not O.J. Marketwatch.com. Retrieved from www.marketwatch.com/story/white-cars-are-no-1-blame-the-iphone-not-oj-2014-06-12

Questions for Case Discussion

1. How should a company like Ford adapt its products to the color preferences of foreign markets?
2. Compare the vehicle color preferences of Europe with those of your country. Do you see any differences? Please explain why.
3. Other than color, what other cultural differences do you see in the global auto market?

Case 6.2 The Global Appeal of Gangnam Style

"Gangnam Style," a music single released by South Korean musician Psy in July 2012, was the first YouTube video to reach one billion views. It has been viewed more than 2.5 billion times ever since. The music video went viral beyond Asia and became a global sensation. By the end of 2012, the song had topped music charts in more than 30 countries including Australia, Canada, France, Germany, Italy, Russia, Spain, and the U.K. The title of the song was even named one of the "words of 2012" by the Collins English Dictionary. Psy's signature dance moves have been imitated by many notable political leaders such as the then British Prime Minister David Cameron, the then U.S. President Barack Obama, and the then U.N. Secretary-General Ban Ki-moon.

Many people were puzzled by the success of Gangnam Style. What is Gangnam Style anyway? The song title refers to the lifestyle associated with Gangnam District, a fancy community in Seoul, the capital city of South Korea, where wealthy young people hang out. The song's refrain "Oppa Gangnam style" can be translated as "big brother in Gangnam style." Korean girls often call their boyfriends "Oppa" (i.e. big brother). The refrain actually implies that your boyfriend is a rich kid.

How come such a culture-specific song gained worldwide popularity? First of all, Psy, the singer, should thank the Internet. Social media websites such as YouTube, Facebook, and Twitter have made it easier for Korean musicians to reach a much wider audience outside of East Asia. Korean pop culture has grown into a popular subculture among teenagers and young adults around the world, a phenomenon known as the "Korean Wave." The fans of the "Korean Wave" not only discovered Gangnam Style but spread it all over the world by sharing, "liking," and "following" on social media. Thanks to the Internet, the "Korean Wave" has been amplified and become a transnational phenomenon.

Another factor that contributed to Gangnam Style's success was Psy's somewhat wacky dance performance in the music video, which transcended national cultural barriers. To some extent, the song's popularity was based more on the performer's unique body movements rather than its lyrical content. For instance, in Western countries, the song brings a carnivalesque appeal; people are amused by imitating the dance moves. Similarly, many people in Brazil think the dance moves are ridiculous and funny, and the moves resonate with the tradition of carnival, which encourages absurdity and wildness. In an interesting experiment, a group of Brazilian children were asked to watch different versions of the Gangnam Style music video. They showed little excitement when watching the original music video of Psy, but started dancing crazily when they saw Mickey Mouse doing the dance moves.

In fact, tens of thousands of people have mimicked the dance moves and posted their own videos online, which further spread the song to many more viewers. The Gangnam Style music video is probably the most parodied music video ever. Despite their wacky style, the dance moves are relatively easy to imitate. To many people, making a parody is not only fun but also a way to engage in collective effervescence and to create social bonds. Some even adapted the song to local customs and traditions. For example, young students at Eton, an English boys' boarding school, adopted the dance but changed the lyrics to express the Eton lifestyles. One of the most watched videos in Saudi Arabia depicted male performers dancing to the song in traditional clothing.

According to YouTube's trend manager Kevin Allocca, videos go viral because of three important factors: the influence of trend makers, community participation, and unexpectedness.[a] While trend setters make a video noticeable, community participation pushes its dispersion. Popular news media and celebrity endorsements helped Gangnam Style gain fame early on. Its somewhat wacky dance moves were catchy and unexpected. People participate in this global trend by utilizing social media websites to distribute their own versions of Gangnam Style. Parodies and imitations from all over the world cemented its role as a global trans-cultural phenomenon.

Notes

a.   Allocca, K. (2012). Why videos go viral. TED Talks. Retrieved from www.ted. com/talks/kevin_allocca_why_videos_go_viral/transcript

Sources

1.   Allocca, K. (2012). Why videos go viral. TED Talks. Retrieved from www.ted. com/talks/kevin_allocca_why_videos_go_viral/transcript
2.   Cho, W.-S. (2012). Riding the Korean Wave from 'Gangnam Style' to global recognition. *Global Asia*, 7(3), 35–39.

Questions for Case Discussion

1.   How did you get to know the song Gangnam Style? Was it popular among your peers? Explain why.
2.   Name several other cultural phenomena that have gained global popularity.
3.   What business implications can we draw from the global acceptance of popular culture?

Case 6.3 Kia Hajj Bus in Saudi Arabia

Kia Motors Corporation is a Korean automobile company located in Seoul, South Korea. It is the second largest car manufacturer in South Korea, following Hyundai Motor Company. It manufactured 2.7 million vehicles in 2012 and 2.75 million in 2013. Kia has exported various vehicles to international markets and is a top exporter of South Korea. One of its exports is a bus called "Hajj", a new type of vehicle developed for the Middle East market.

In Arabic, "Hajj" refers to Muslims' pilgrimage to Mecca. Fulfilling this pilgrimage or Hajj is one of the five pillars of Islam. To Muslims, visiting Mecca, a city where many sacred Islamic buildings are located, is a lifetime goal. According to the Islamic calendar, the Hajj period is usually held between January and March every year. Muslims from all over the world travel to Mecca to attend events during this period (see Figure 6.1).

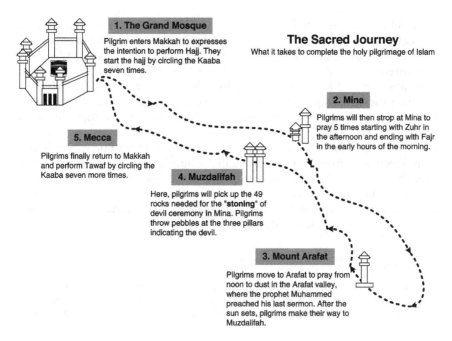

Figure 6.1 The Sacred Journey

Source: McDermott, H. V. (2013, October 13). Rivers flowing in paradise: My journal through Islam. Retrieved from https://riversflowinginparadise.com/2013/10/13/hajj-the-sacred-journey/

More than one million pilgrims visit Mecca each year. The Saudi government and local Hajj transport associations arrange bus transportations for the visitors. Kia's market research showed that there were more than ten Hajj bus transportation associations and over 11,000 buses in operation. Also, there was demand for new buses every year. However, when Kia initiated its Hajj bus development project in 1991, most Saudis did not even know the Korean brand. Local Hajj bus transportation associations had been importing buses from leading bus enterprises such as Benz and Scania.

Kia also learned that local transportation associations require buses to be furnished with components like fire extinguishers, first aid kits, and tire inflation pressure gauges. Fire extinguishers are necessary because bus engines have a tendency to overheat and catch fire due to high temperatures in local areas. To prevent fire hazard, Kia also equipped their buses with heat-resistant engines. Moreover, buses need to have strong rust prevention since people in water-scarce areas like Saudi Arabia often wash vehicles with sea water which can cause rust over time. The pilgrimage-oriented Hajj buses also need to have sinks installed for passengers to wash their hands prior to religious ceremonies. For long trips in the desert, air conditioners and fans must be installed to prevent passengers from succumbing to heat stroke or exhaustion. In addition, the religious custom of Shia Muslims requires them to look to the sky and pray during the pilgrimage. In response to this custom, Kia installed adjustable roofs, so passengers could perform the religious act.

In addition to customizing products for local markets, Kia needed to adapt to local business culture. When first entering Saudi Arabia, Kia failed to meet sales objectives due to a lack of demand. Kia then turned to local transportation enterprises and cooperated with them to sell Kia products. Such relationships required Kia to understand local business traditions. For instance, Saudi businessmen typically do not have a rigid concept of time and schedule. It is common for them to be interrupted and discuss multiple business matters simultaneously. Strong trust must be established first, which may take some time. One cannot rush into a business agreement or appear impatient. Meetings are often loosely scheduled around prayer times. In a meeting, Saudi businessmen like to have small talks before discussing serious business matters. When Kia started working with local transportation associations, there were a few incidents in which transactions were cancelled or delayed due to cultural misunderstandings.

Sources

1. Korean Trade Association. (2004). Product differentiation across countries (in Korean). Retrieved from www.kyobobook.co.kr/product/detailReviewKor.laf?mallGb=KOR&barcode=9788983930668&linkClass=13210104&ejkGb=KOR

Questions for Case Discussion

1. What religious and cultural factors have affected the business operations of Kia in Saudi Arabia?
2. What has Kia changed to adapt to the Saudi Arabian market?
3. Can you identify other products or services that require adaptation to Saudi Arabian culture?

Case 6.4 Islamic Banking in the U.S.

Twenty years ago, shopping for a mortgage was almost a mission impossible for Muslims in the U.S. because conventional loans were not compatible with Islamic principles. Nowadays a number of banks are offering various programs for Islamic clients to follow the Islamic guidelines of the Quran. Buying a home in the U.S. is getting easier for Muslims.

According to Islamic principles, all finance activities should be shariah-compliant. Shariah is the divine ideal of justice and compassion, which includes three principal rules. The first rule is the absence of interest, i.e. commodity (including money) should not increase in value by being lent to others. The lender should not accept interest and the borrower should not pay it. Nevertheless, shariah allows investors to gain return on capital if they assume the risks of a productive enterprise. The second is a prohibition on making money from certain products. Parties involved in a transaction should spend money on activities that promote social good. Investments in alcohol, gambling, tobacco, and pornography are not acceptable. The third rule is the validity and transparency of contracts. Parties involved in a transaction should ensure that all terms and conditions are detailed enough to prevent future disputes. Contracts containing "gharar" (unacceptable uncertainty) are considered void.

Given these requirements, it can be challenging to establish banking services in shariah-compliant marketplaces. As of 2009, Muslims accounted for about a quarter of the world's population but less than 1 percent of the world's financial assets were considered shariah-compliant. In 2015, there were about 3.3 million Muslims living in the U.S. but Islamic financing was rare compared to conventional financing. This disconnection between demand and supply suggests growth opportunities. While worldwide shariah-compliant financing has reached more than $1.6 trillion USD in assets over the past three decades, many analysts expect even greater future growth. The Malaysia International Islamic Financial Centre (MIFC) estimated the Islamic finance industry would expand to above US$4 trillion USD by 2020. Malaysia, Saudi Arabia, UAE, Kuwait, and Qatar are the leading countries in this industry.

In the U.S., the Muslim population is expected to reach 8.1 million, or 2.1 percent of the total population by 2050. The Islamic financing section is already growing at 15–20 percent a year and may grow even faster. Many financial institutions are looking into this opportunity. Those with an Islamic culture origin usually have advantages over others. American Finance House LARIBA is one of the largest providers of Islamic financing in the U.S. The company's founder, Dr. Yahia Abdul-Rahman, came to the U.S. from Egypt in 1968. He started LARIBA in 1987 to serve customers who had avoided using conventional banks for religious reasons. The company quickly expanded and bought the Bank of Whittier in California in 1998. Abdul-Rahman said that LARIBA's services allowed people to participate in the "American dream" without over indulging money through the abuse of credit cards and loans. Other financial institutions have also set up Islamic financing to target this market. For instance, University Bancorp, a community bank in Michigan, took four years to develop a home loan product that complied with the strict rules of Islamic financing. Its Islamic financing subsidiary generated roughly 20 percent of the company's revenue, and it planned to open at least five more offices outside its home state. The shariah-compliant services of those firms include:

- Seller Financing—Seller financing would include all creative financing done by the seller to sell his or her property. This type of financing could also include lease options.
- Ijara or Declining Rent Schedule—Ijara is where the bank buys the home and rents the home back to the borrower for a certain term of years. Once the home is paid in full, the title is placed in the owner's name.
- Murahaba—With this type of financing, the bank purchases the home, and then for an inflated price, the borrower is allowed to purchase the home. The amount owed is amortized over a certain number of years and the word interest is never used.

Outside the U.S., Islamic financing is also making huge strides. The U.K. became the first Western nation to issue Islamic bonds, known as "sukuk." To comply with shariah, the bonds are tied to specific physical assets.

Instead of earning interests, investors share the profits generated from the assets. In 2014, Luxembourg issued a $254 million USD, five-year Islamic bond. Later in the same year, Hong Kong completed its first sale of Islamic debt raising $1 billion USD.

Sources

1. PwC. (2009). Shariah-compliant funds: a whole new world of investment. Retrieved from www.pwc.com/gx/en/industries/financial-services/islamic-finance-programme/shariah-compliant-funds.html
2. Mohamed, B. (2016, January 6). A new estimate of the U.S. Muslim population. Pew Research. Retrieved from www.pewresearch.org/fact-tank/2016/01/06/a-new-estimate-of-the-u-s-muslim-population/
3. Permatasari, S. (2010, October 13). Shariah U.S. loans left to guidance, Lariba: Islamic finance. Bloomberg News. Retrieved from www.bloomberg.com/news/articles/2010-10-13/shariah-mortgages-left-to-guidance-lariba-in-u-s-market-islamic-finance
4. Malaysia International Islamic Financial Centre. (2014, December 26). 2014—A landmark year for the global islamic finance industry. Retrieved from www.mifc.com/index.php?ch=28&pg=72&ac=106&bb=uploadpdf.

Questions for Discussion

1. What business opportunities and challenges have been brought by Islamic principles?
2. What are the main characteristics of the Islamic banking system?
3. Discuss the impacts of other religious beliefs on business practices in different parts of the world.

Case 6.5 Groupon's Struggle in China

In February 2011, Groupon's Chinese site went live and started offering daily deals, marking its long-awaited entry to the world's most populous Internet market. However, at the end of August in the same year, Groupon closed 13 of its Chinese locations and laid off over 400 full-time staff. The move marked an abrupt reversal of the company's expansion into China. What happened?

Groupon, a Chicago-based daily discount website, opened in 2008. The company partnered with local businesses to offer deep discounts to group buyers through mass emailing. Groupon grew quickly in the U.S. and expanded to more than 35 countries by 2010. Groupon decided to enter China's large e-commerce market in 2010. At that time, China had over 450 million Internet users, more than any other country. It was estimated that the group-buying market had 19 million users and $300 million USD in revenue. In addition, group purchasing behavior seemed compatible with China's collective culture. Many Chinese make an effort to get a good deal. For instance, in September 2010, 200 Mercedes-Benz Smart cars discounted by 33 percent sold out in three and a half hours. Therefore, investors and analysts were optimistic about Groupon's business expansion in China.

To tackle the Chinese market, Groupon partnered with a team of elite companies: Tencent, China's second largest Internet company; Rocket Asia, whose owner helped Groupon's entry into the European market; and Yunfeng Capital, whose investors include Jack Ma, the founder of China's e-commerce giant Alibaba Group. Groupon invested $8.6 million for a 40 percent stake in the joint venture. A new website, GaoPeng.com, was set up. During its peak time, the company had about 80 offices and more than 3,000 employees around the country. However, the company went into a downfall very quickly. It fell way behind two other group-buying websites Lashou.com and Meituan .com. Even after adding more investments, the situation did not improve.

Groupon started its operations in China by using expatriate managers and copying its U.S. business model. Its early management team was mostly composed of foreigners. Even operations in some remote parts of China were run by foreigners with limited understanding of local language and culture. Those managers' Western-style management was not well received by their local subordinates, resulting in low efficiency and high turnover. When building up partnerships with local vendors, Groupon strictly followed its business model in the U.S. and insisted on split profits 50–50 with partnering vendors. However, China had a different demand-supply condition. Local vendors usually had the upper hand and gave only 10 percent of the profits instead of 50 percent to other group-buying sites. They were shocked by Groupon's aggressive sales approach. Groupon also tried to replicate its U.S. marketing strategy in China. As it did in the U.S., Groupon sent daily emails about deals to customers. However, Chinese consumers are less responsive to mass emailing. Most of them seldom read that type of email.

In fact, Groupon's local partner, Tencent, had warned the company about these problems. But Groupon insisted on its own way of doing business. Very soon, its relationship with Tencent went sour due to internal conflicts. Groupon failed to take advantage of Tencent's local market expertise. And for Tencent, the joint venture with Groupon was not its priority. The company had highly successful instant messaging and social network services, and GaoPeng.com was only one of several group-buying portals it operated in China.

Groupon's lack of local knowledge was also revealed in its recruiting process. Its initial recruitment of sales force focused on consultants and investment bankers with MBA degrees. Much attention was paid to academic credentials and consulting experience rather than local experience and knowledge. This approach might work in the U.S. but was probably not right for China. Also, Groupon reportedly offered to pay salaries several times higher than local competitors were paying. The huge wage increase was meant to attract outstanding candidates, but was strongly opposed by other companies. In an attempt to negate Groupon's offers to new hires, several local group purchase sites formed a mutual agreement to never hire a former Groupon employee.

Some industry observers also attributed Groupon's failure to intense competition. The number of groups buying websites in China surged to over 2,500 in 2011. GaoPeng was number eight among group-buying websites in China. Its 15 million unique visitors per month were less than 30 percent of the visitors of the top website, Lashou.com, which operated in more than 500 cities. Lashou.com was founded by an experienced local entrepreneur and backed by seasoned venture capital firms. In order to quickly expand in China, Groupon actually offered to acquire Lashou.com. Acquisitions had proven to be successful when Groupon entered other markets such as Hong Kong, Taiwan, Singapore, and Germany. But its offer was rejected by Lashou .com.

Sources

1. Chao, L. (2011, August 24). Groupon stumbles in China, closes some offices. *Wall Street Journal*. Retrieved from www.wsj.com/articles/SB10001424053 111904279004576526283328853022
2. Zhu, J. (2011, November 3). 4 mistakes behind Groupon's failure in China. TechinAsia.com. Retrieved from www.techinasia.com/4-mistakes-behind-groupons-failure-in-china
3. Mangalindan, J. P. (2011, February 23). Can Groupon crack the China puzzle? *Fortune*. Retrieved from http://fortune.com/2011/02/23/can-groupon-crack-the-china-puzzle/

Questions for Discussion

1. What cultural factors drove Groupon's entry into China?
2. What cultural challenges did Groupon face in China?
3. In order to achieve success in China, what should have Groupon done differently?

Social and Cultural Environment

I. Definition of Culture

There are over 160 definitions for the term culture.[1] The number and variety of those definitions show how complicated culture is. In this textbook, culture is defined as the shared beliefs, norms, and values that cause individuals to conform to a society or group and provide mechanisms for the survival of the society or group.[2] Cultural norms tell us what we should do and what we cannot do by prescribing and proscribing behaviors. For example, norms prescribe what clothes we can and cannot wear to a funeral.[3] Cultural beliefs show our understandings about the truth. Cultural values tell us what is right and desirable. These beliefs, norms, and values are shared by members of a society and are transferred to the next generation through the process of socialization. The socialization process indicates how parents, friends, educators, and other members of a particular society influence an individual and how interactions within these societal groups cultivate an individual's value system.

People in different societies have developed different cultures in response to their natural and social environments. For example, Eskimos have many words to describe the nature of snow, a cultural adaptation resulting from unique weather patterns. From an international business perspective, national culture refers to the shared value system of a country. Individuals in a country share values, belief, behaviors, customs, and attitudes that distinguish one country from another. Such culture is transmitted from one member of a society to another through socialization and learning. For example, Japanese culture stresses social harmony and teamwork. A priority of Japanese preschools is to teach students to adhere to a harmonious and group-oriented culture, so that they can grow up to be collaborative societal members.

II. Various Aspects of Social and Cultural Environment

Globalization has significantly increased interactions between countries. It is extremely important for international firms to understand other countries' cultures. However, it can be difficult to understand another culture because of the various aspects it entails. Many scholars have used metaphors to describe culture. For example, Geert Hofstede introduced the Onion model to illustrate the different layers of culture.[4] The outer layers encompass cultural artifacts or symbols such as architecture, color, languages, or traditional clothing. Heroes make up the next layer which represents highly prized characteristics within the society. The third layer is composed of common rituals and traditions, such as greetings, etiquette, ceremonies, and religious practices. In the center of the onion are the underlying cultural values and assumptions. Since this is the most hidden layer, its components are difficult to recognize and require deep analysis and thorough understanding.

Culture as an Iceberg

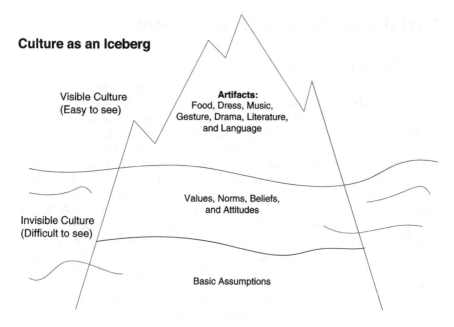

Visible Culture
(Easy to see)

Artifacts:
Food, Dress, Music,
Gesture, Drama, Literature,
and Language

Values, Norms, Beliefs,
and Attitudes

Invisible Culture
(Difficult to see)

Basic Assumptions

Figure 6.2 Culture as an Iceberg

Source: Adapted from Hall, E. T. (1976). *Beyond Culture*. New York, NY: Anchor Books.

Another popular model of culture is the iceberg by Edward T. Hall, presented in Figure 6.2. The small visible part above the water and the much larger portion below the surface indicate the multiple layers of culture.[5] The upper portion of the iceberg illustrates the easily noticeable elements of culture such as clothing, language, gestures, food, music, and rituals. The less visible components of culture—values, beliefs, and attitudes—are shown in the lower portion of the iceberg. The visible part of the culture is what you are first exposed to and become aware of in a new environment. However, this is probably just the tip of an iceberg. A greater portion of culture is not easily visible and lies below the water.

In this chapter, we combine these two metaphors and examine three aspects of national culture:

1. Artifacts and Symbols

Cultural artifacts are the outermost or most visible parts of culture. They are created by humans and provide information about people's values, beliefs, and norms. Symbols are words, gestures, pictures, or objects that represent particular meanings that are recognized and shared by a group or society. This aspect of culture includes languages, numbers, colors, dresses, hairstyles, flags, status symbols, etc. For example, people may associate specific numbers with different meanings. In China, the number eight is preferred because the pronunciation of "eight" in Cantonese sounds like the word "Fa," which means prosperity, wealth, and success.[6] Many Chinese pick lucky numbers for business addresses, residences, telephone numbers as well as dates of important events. It is not a coincidence that the 2008 Beijing Olympics Opening Ceremony began at 8:08 pm on August 8, 2008. On the other hand, Chinese people generally dislike the number four, similar to Westerners' cultural aversion to the number 13. The number four is pronounced "Si," sounding like the word "death" in Chinese. Therefore, many buildings, especially hotels and hospitals, do not have the fourth and the fourteenth floor. They also do not like to have the number four in their telephone numbers or vehicle identification numbers.

Color preference is also an important cultural symbol. It arises from a person's psychological tendency to choose one color over another.[7] Color preference widely varies across countries. Table 6.2 lists the color preferences of select countries. For instance, Chinese extensively use the red color, as red represents happiness, beauty, success, and good fortune in its culture.[8] People wear red at weddings, festivals, and other celebrations. During the Chinese New Year, red envelopes with money inside are given to children as gifts. However, in Nigeria and Germany, red has a negative connotation and represents the exact opposite. In the U.S., white indicates purity and peace, but the same color symbolizes sadness and mourning in many Asian countries. As discussed in Case 6.1, automakers need to adapt product offerings to Europeans' vehicle color preferences.

As one main element of culture, language is essential for people to express, exchange, and record their values, beliefs, and opinions. Members within a society use their common language to communicate thoughts, feelings, knowledge, and information. There are about 3,000 different languages and 10,000 distinct dialects worldwide. Without a good understanding of local language, international companies are likely to run into various communication problems, or even big blunders in business dealings. For example, when GM's Chevrolet division launched its Chevrolet Nova in Spanish-speaking markets, it encountered marketing challenges as "No va," the name of the vehicle, means "No go" in Spanish. General Motors later renamed the car Caribe (piranha) after the voraciously carnivorous freshwater fish. Electrolux once had a slogan saying "Nothing sucks like an Electrolux" for its vacuum cleaners. The slogan worked successfully in the U.K., but did not resonate well with Americans as "suck" has an informal meaning of "very bad" in North America.

Music also belongs to this cultural category because people can perceive it by hearing. For instance, the popularity of Korean pop music has greatly promoted Korean culture around the world. Korean musicians and performers not only have large followings in Asia but also have extended their influence to other countries like the U.S. In particular, as shown in Case 6.2, Gangnam Style became a global sensation that showcased the success of Korean pop culture.[9] The Korea entertainment industry has worked towards this moment for more than 20 years by strenuously recruiting and transforming young talents.

Table 6.2 The Cross-Cultural Spectrum of Meanings and Associations of Color

Color	Country-Culture Cluster								
	Anglo-Saxon	Germanic	Latin	Nordic	Slavic	Chinese	Japanese	Korean	ASEAN
White	Purity; Happiness	–	–	–	–	Death	Death	Death	Death
Blue	High quality; Corporate; Masculine	Warm; Feminine	–	Cold; Masculine	–	Mourning; High quality; Trustworthy	Mourning; High quality; Trustworthy	Mourning; High quality; Trustworthy	Mourning; Cold; Evil (Malaysia)
Green	Envy; Good taste	–	Envy	–	–	Pure; Reliable	Love; Happy	Pure; Adventure	Danger; Disease (Malaysia)
Yellow	Happy; Jealousy	Envy; Infidelity	Envy; Infidelity	–	Envy	Pure; Good taste; Royal; Authority	Envy; Good taste	Happiness; Good taste	–
Red	Masculine; Love; Lust; Fear; Anger	Fear; Anger; Jealousy	Masculine	Positive	Fear; Anger; Jealousy	Love; Happiness; Lucky	Love; Anger; Jealousy	Love; Adventure; Good taste	–
Purple	Authority; Power	–	–	–	Anger; Envy; Jealousy	Expensive; Love	Expensive; Sin; Fear	Expensive; Love	–
Black	Expensive; Fear; Grief	Fear; Anger; Grief	Fear; Anger; Grief	–	Fear; Anger	Expensive; Powerful	Expensive; Powerful	Expensive; Powerful	–

Source: Singh, S. (2006). Impact of color on marketing. *Management Decision, 44*(6), 783–789.

2. Religions, Rituals, and Traditions

There are a variety of religions in the world. Religious rituals and traditions have profound influence on people's behavior.[10] They set certain principles in regard to how people view various aspects of life, such as work, saving, material goods, consumption, responsibilities, and planning for the future. Thus, it is very important to understand how a country's religious practices influence business practices.[11] For instance, the Protestant work ethic was believed to be a main factor in the development of capitalism in nineteenth-century Europe. This Protestant code emphasizes individual hard work, frugality, and achievement, encouraging people to constantly strive for efficiency and reinvest profits for future productivity. Islam emphasizes individuals' obligation to the society. While supporting profits earned in fair business dealings, profiting from exploitation or deceit is forbidden. Thus, payment or receipt of interest is prohibited because the practice is considered as exploiting the less fortunate. Buddhism and Hinduism generally stress spiritual accomplishment rather than material success. Believing in reincarnation, the rebirth of the human soul at the time of death, these religions encourage people to lead ascetic and pure lives. Thus, capitalistic activities such as investment, wealth accumulation, and constant quest for higher productivity and efficiency are not particularly encouraged.

Specifically, religions, rituals, and traditions may directly affect consumer behavior. Traditions often develop norms of a society that guide acceptable behaviors in a certain situation. For instance, most Hindus do not eat beef because they consider cows to be sacred animals. Therefore, McDonald's has removed all beef products from its menu and offers vegetable and fish products instead in India. It also sells the Maharaj Mac, made of lamb for Indians who eat red meat. Islamic teachings impose constraints on alcohol and pork consumption. Substitutes for alcohol include soda pop, coffee, and tea. Popular pork substitutes are lamb, beef, and poultry, which have to be slaughtered in a prescribed way. Case 6.3 (Kia Hajj Bus) and Case 6.4 (Islamic Banking in the U.S.) also illustrate the importance of understanding religious traditions.

3. Values and Basic Assumptions

Cultural values reflect underlying societal emphases on how things should be. They indicate desirable end-states or behaviors, thus guiding peoples' selection and evaluation of business activities. For example, if a culture stresses ambition and success then it tends to support those legal, market, and educational systems that are conducive to competition.[12] Values often concern the core issues in our lives such as personal and social relationships, morality, gender and social roles, race, social classes, and societal organizations. Assumptions are unquestioned standards about the way things are. People brought up in the same community tend to share certain assumptions about morals and ethics (e.g. what is right or wrong, what is desirable or undesirable). They likely also share assumptions about human nature and social relationships. The next section presents several models that highlight key national differences in cultural values and assumptions.

III. National Cultural Differences

I. Hofstede Model

Geert Hofstede's cultural dimensions theory is probably the most influential model that quantifies cultural differences across countries.[13] By surveying the employees of IBM, a major multinational company, in its oversea branches and subsidiaries located in over 70 countries, Hofstede found four cultural value dimensions: individualism vs. collectivism, masculinity vs. femininity, power distance, and uncertainty avoidance. Hofstede further validated the dimensions in his studies on commercial airline pilots, students, civil service managers, and other professionals in different countries. Later, based on more recent research on world culture, two additional dimensions—long-term orientation vs. short-term orientation and indulgence vs. restraint—were added to the Hofstede model.

Individualism-Collectivism (IDV)

This dimension refers to the degree to which a person sees himself or herself as an individual or a member of a group. In individualistic cultures, people tend to value personal achievement and privacy, and tend to prioritize individual autonomy over group obligations. In collectivist cultures, people recognize that they are part of an organization, family, or group so there is an emphasis on loyalty and devotion to the organization, one's own family, or the group. Therefore, in individualistic cultures, active expression is associated with personal creativity; whereas in collectivist cultures, active expression is the process of exchanging feelings with others. If a country features an individualistic orientation, it has a high score on the individualism dimension. A country gets a lower score if it leans toward collectivism. On this index, a clear gap has been found between developed Western countries and most other countries (see Table 6.3). North America and Europe usually have strong individualistic values. For instance, Canada and Hungary scored 80 points. In contrast, most Asian, African and Latin American countries are considered collectivist societies with relatively low scores on this dimension. For example, Colombia scored 13 points and Indonesia 14 points. The greatest contrast is found when comparing the U.S. and Guatemala, which are at opposite ends of the spectrum. Guatemala scored six points while the U.S. scored 91 points on this dimension.

Masculinity-Femininity (MAS)

People in masculine cultures stress acquiring power, success, and fortune. They tend to be more aggressive, competitive, and goal-driven. People in feminine cultures place higher value on quality of life and relationships with others. They are generally more caring and considerate. Therefore, a workplace in masculine societies often features a competitive atmosphere, in which tension and conflict prevail. In contrast, in feminine cultures, there is an emphasis on equality between men and women, and the workplace atmosphere encourages

Table 6.3 Hofstede's Cultural Values Scores

Country	PDI	IDV	MAS	UAI	LTO	IND
Africa East	64	27	41	52	32	40
Africa West	77	20	46	54	9	78
Arab countries	80	38	53	68	23	34
Argentina	49	46	56	86	20	62
Australia	36	90	61	51	21	71
Austria	11	55	79	70	60	63
Bangladesh	80	20	55	60	47	20
Belgium	65	75	54	94	82	15
Belgium French	67	72	60	93		
Belgium Netherl	61	78	43	97		
Brazil	69	38	49	76	44	59
Bulgaria	70	30	40	85	69	16
Canada	39	80	52	48	36	68
Canada French	54	73	45	60		
Chile	63	23	28	86	31	68
China	80	20	66	30	87	24
Colombia	67	13	64	80	13	83
Costa Rica	35	15	21	86		
Croatia	73	33	40	80	58	33
Czech Rep	57	58	57	74	70	29
Denmark	18	74	16	23	35	70
Ecuador	78	8	63	67		
El Salvador	66	19	40	94	20	89
Estonia	40	60	30	60	82	16
Finland	33	63	26	59	38	57
France	68	71	43	86	63	48
Germany	35	67	66	65	83	40
Great Britain	35	89	66	35	51	69
Greece	60	35	57	112	45	50
Guatemala	95	6	37	101		
Hong Kong	68	25	57	29	61	17
Hungary	46	80	88	82	58	31
India	77	48	56	40	51	26
Indonesia	78	14	46	48	62	38
Iran	58	41	43	59	14	40
Ireland	28	70	68	35	24	65
Israel	13	54	47	81	38	
Italy	50	76	70	75	61	30
Jamaica	45	39	68	13		
Japan	54	46	95	92	88	42
Korea South	60	18	39	85	100	29
Latvia	44	70	9	63	69	13
Lithuania	42	60	19	65	82	16

(Continued Overleaf)

Table 6.3 Continued

Country	PDI	IDV	MAS	UAI	LTO	IND
Luxembourg	40	60	50	70	64	56
Malaysia	104	26	50	36	41	57
Malta	56	59	47	96	47	66
Mexico	81	30	69	82	24	97
Morocco	70	46	53	68	14	25
Netherlands	38	80	14	53	67	68
New Zealand	22	79	58	49	33	75
Norway	31	69	8	50	35	55
Pakistan	55	14	50	70	50	0
Panama	95	11	44	86		
Peru	64	16	42	87	25	46
Philippines	94	32	64	44	27	42
Poland	68	60	64	93	38	29
Portugal	63	27	31	104	28	33
Romania	90	30	42	90	52	90
Russia	93	39	36	95	81	20
Serbia	86	25	43	92	52	28
Singapore	74	20	48	8	72	46
Slovak Rep	104	52	110	51	77	28
Slovenia	71	27	19	88	49	48
South Africa	49	65	63	49	34	63
Spain	57	51	42	86	48	44
Suriname	85	47	37	92		
Sweden	31	71	5	29	53	78
Switzerland	34	68	70	58	74	66
Switzerland French	70	64	58	70		
Switzerland German	26	69	72	56		
Taiwan	58	17	45	69	93	49
Thailand	64	20	34	64	32	45
Trinidad and Tobago	47	16	58	55	13	80
Turkey	66	37	45	85	46	49
U.S.A.	40	91	62	46	26	68
Uruguay	61	36	38	100	26	53
Venezuela	81	12	73	76	16	100
Vietnam	70	20	40	30	57	35

Source: Geert-hofstede.com. (n.d.). National culture. Retrieved from https://geert-hofstede.com/national-culture.html

harmonious interactions between co-workers. Additionally, an individual's career is considered relatively less important as greater emphasis is placed on maintaining stable employment and creating a tension-free work environment. A country gets a high score on the masculinity dimension when it embraces a masculine culture, or a low score when it favors a feminine culture. The masculinity scores of Nordic countries are relatively low, with Norway and Sweden scoring eight and five respectively. In contrast, Japan and certain European countries like Hungary, Austria, and Switzerland show very high scores. The U.S. and the U.K. have moderately high scores on this dimension (see Table 6.3).

Power Distance (PDI)

Power distance refers to the degree to which people in a society accommodate unequal distributions of power. People in high power distance cultures tend to conform to the power structure as they are more likely to accept the imbalance of power. On the other hand, in low power distance cultures, people are less likely to accept the concentration of power. Hence, managers in such workplaces should use their power carefully and strive to build trust relationships with employees. The power distance dimension has important implications for management control in an organization. Scores on the power distance dimension are relatively high in many Latin American, Asian, African, and Arabic countries where social hierarchy is more visible. For instance, due to large power distance, young people in Ghana are unwilling to speak up in front the elders.[14] On the other hand, Anglo and Germanic countries usually have small power distance scores, with Austria scoring 11 and Denmark 18.

Uncertainty Avoidance (UAI)

Uncertainty avoidance refers to the degree to which people want to stay away from uncertain or ambiguous situations. People in cultures that have low uncertainty avoidance tend to care less about traditional institutions and prescribed rules. They are more likely to believe that risks are inevitable and success can be achieved by taking chances. In contrast, people in high uncertainty-avoidance cultures prefer to have stable and predictable work environments so that they take fewer and lower risks. Pre-defined routines, manuals, and procedures are considered as ways to reduce uncertainty. Latin American countries, Southern and Eastern European countries, and Japan show relatively high scores in the uncertainty avoidance dimension. In contrast, the scores for Anglo, Nordic, and Chinese cultures are relatively low. Interestingly, while Belgium has a high uncertain avoidance score of 94, Sweden and Denmark score much lower at 29 and 23, despite their geographic proximity.

Long-Term Orientation (LTO)

The fifth cultural dimension accounts for time orientation, indicating that people in countries may have different points of view with respect to their use of time. This dimension distinguishes countries by whether people focus on short-term or long-term results when pursuing their endeavors in life. In a long-term oriented culture, people tend to emphasize long-term goals and achievements such as saving, thriftiness, patience, and persever-ance. They tend to focus on time-honored traditions, stress personal stability, and view societal change with suspicion. In a short-term oriented culture, people have a narrow and temporary perspective. East Asian countries typi-cally receive high scores on long-term orientation, with China and Japan scoring 118 and 88 respectively. While Eastern and Western Europe have moderate to low scores, the Anglosphere, Africa, Latin America, and the Muslim world tend to score low on this dimension, meaning they generally favor short-term orientation.

Indulgence-Restraint (IND)

The sixth cultural dimension focuses on indulgence versus restraint, which indicates to what extent a society allows people to enjoy life and have fun.[15] Indulgence is a cultural value that allows societal constituents to freely undertake activities that result in human gratification, such as leisure activi-ties. In contrast, restraint culture tends to suppress and regulate people's need for gratification with strict social norms. A high score on this dimension means the country is more inclined toward the indulgence culture. The indulgence scores are relatively high in the Anglosphere, Nordic countries, Latin America, and parts of Africa. In comparison, East Asia, Eastern Europe, and the Muslim world have low scores, suggesting that they belong to restraint cultures.

2. Hall Model (High-Context vs. Low-Context)

The Hall model, developed by American anthropologist Edward T. Hall, focuses on how cultural context influences communication between commu-nity members.[16] In the Hall model, the term context indicates to what extent the context of a message is important as the message itself. In other words, it concerns what inferences are drawn from similar experiences and expecta-tions of a society or group.

High context refers to a situation where members of a society or group have close connections over a long period of time, and have developed implicit understandings about what to do and what to think. For example, one's family is usually a high-context environment. In a high-context culture, many things are not explicitly expressed; signals or meanings can only be fully understood within that specific culture. A few words can carry a compli-cated message embedded in the culture. Even without using words and tones, body gestures can be interpreted correctly by members of the same culture. For people outside of the culture, such communication becomes vague and ineffective. Typically, Asian, African, Arabic, and Latin American countries are regarded as high-context cultures.[17] On the other hand, in low-context societies, people tend to have shorter connections with one another. Lacking implicit mutual understandings, communication needs to be more direct and specific. In a low-context culture, values and beliefs need to be expressed explicitly so that people know how to behave appropriately in this culture. Switzerland, Germany, Scandinavian, and Anglosphere countries are often

Table 6.4 High and Low Context Culture

Factor/Dimension	High Context	Low Context
Lawyers	Less important	Very important
A person's word	In his/her bond	Is not reliable
Responsibility for organizational error	Taken by highest level	Pushed to the lowest level
Space	People breathe on one another	Private space maintained
Time	Polychronic	Monochronic
Competitive bidding	Infrequent	Common

Source: Hall, Edward T. (1976). Beyond culture. New York: Anchor Books.

viewed as low-context cultures. Table 6.4 lists several main differences between high-context and low-context cultures.

The Hall model suggests cultural context significantly influences people's points of view toward the world. For instance, Figure 6.3 shows two pictures, each with a boy in the center, surrounded by people with different moods. When asked about the emotional state of the two boys, Asians tend to answer that the boy in the picture on the left is unhappy while the boy in the picture on the right is happy. However, Westerners tend to answer that the boys in both pictures are happy. It seems that Asians are more likely to judge each boy's emotional state by assessing the overall situation, including the boy and his peers in the background. Because people surrounding the boy on the left seem unhappy, many Asians think the boy smiles because he feels awkward. Conversely, Westerners are more likely to judge each boy's emotional state strictly by his own appearance and situation.

In another example, when asked whether the flower at the bottom of Figure 6.4 should be placed in Group A or B, most people in high-context cultures would choose Group A while most in low-context cultures tend to choose Group B. More specifically, many Asians answered Group A because the flower at the bottom has rounded petals and a leaf like the majority of flowers in Group A. Many Westerners chose Group B because the flowers at the bottom have a straight stem just like all the flowers in Group B. A possible explanation is that, in low-context cultures, people tend to see the world as being divided into separate objects. Westerners with developed analytical abilities would find the only similarity among the flowers in Group B is a straight stem. The flower at the bottom also has a straight stem. Therefore, it belongs to Group B. Differently, in high-context cultures, people tend to see the world in a broader context. Although there is no single common similarity among the four flowers in Group A and the flower at the bottom, Asians are more likely to notice that the follower at the bottom generally looks similar to the majority of flowers in Group A.

In addition to context, the Hall model also considers personal space and time. National cultures vary in terms of how much people are comfortable sharing personal space with others. In some countries, like the U.S. and Japan, people need to clearly delineate personal space among themselves. In

Figure 6.3 Pictures Illustrating the Different Points of Views between East and West

Source: Korea Educational Broadcasting System (EBS). (2008). *East and West,* EBS Documentary. Retrieved from www.youtube.com/watch?v=RnyaDIZjS-s

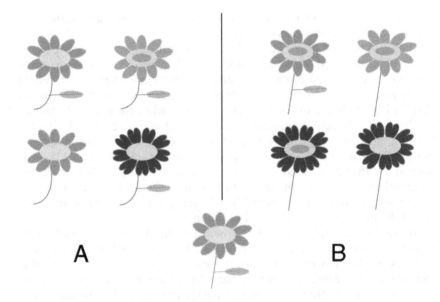

Figure 6.4 Differences between East and West in Perspective of Looking at Things

Source: Korea Educational Broadcasting System (EBS). (2008). *East and West,* EBS Documentary. Retrieved from www.youtube.com/watch?v=RnyaDIZjS

other countries, like Latin American and Arabic states, people are more comfortable sharing space with others. Meanwhile, countries show different cultural preferences toward time. Some countries such as the U.S. and Germany prefer a monochronic approach, in which time is viewed as linear. People are expected to do one thing at a time and finish individual tasks on time. They have a precise concept of time and tend to separate work and pleasure. Other countries, like France, Spain, Mexico, and Brazil, seem to favor a polychronic approach, in which people do multiple tasks simultaneously. Attention is given to multiple goals at the same time, and work and personal life are often integrated.

3. Schwartz Model

The Schwartz model, developed by Israeli scholar Shalom Schwartz and his colleagues, maps out world cultures using ten universal values (see Figure 6.5): power, achievement, hedonism, stimulation, self-direction, universalism, benevolence, tradition, conformity, and security. This model indicates the mixed relationships among the ten values. Although some values conflict with one another, others are compatible. For instance, the activity of pursuing achievement may conflict with seeking benevolence, while seeking achievement and seeking power are usually compatible. Stimulation values such as novelty and change tend to be incompatible with traditional values, which are often consistent with pursuing conformity. The Schwartz model believes the essential distinction between national cultures is the motivational goals they express.[18] As shown in Figure 6.5, tradition and conformity are located in the

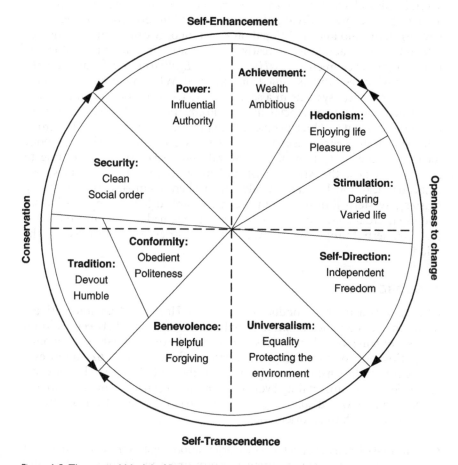

Figure 6.5 Theoretical Model of Relations Among Ten Motivational Types of Value

Source: Schwartz S.H. (1992). Universals in the content and structure of values: Theoretical advances and empirical tests in 20 countries. Advances in Experimental Social Psychology, 25, 1–65. EBS Documentary, East and West 2008.

same wedge because they share the same broad motivational goal. But tradition is located further away from the center because it is more likely to conflict with opposing values than conformity.[19]

Figure 6.5 also shows two dimensions. One dimension indicates the tension between openness to change and conservation. This dimension suggests that some values (self-direction and stimulation) emphasize change and action, while others (security, conformity, and tradition) tend to resist change and preserve order. The other dimension is self-enhancement versus self-transcendence. This dimension demonstrates that some values (power, achievement) emphasize the pursuit of one's own interests, while others (universalism, benevolence) stress interests of others. Hedonism is a value that combines openness to change and self-enhancement.

Different societies put varied weights on the ten values. After analyzing people's responses to those values in different countries, Schwartz identified several cultural clusters in three pairs: (1) *Embeddedness vs. Autonomy* addresses the degree individuals are integrated into groups. Embeddedness stresses status quo and traditional order. Autonomy can be further divided into intellectual autonomy (creativity, curiosity) and affective autonomy (stimulation, excitement). (2) *Hierarchy vs. Egalitarianism* focuses on the extent to which equality is valued and expected. While hierarchy stresses the role of hierarchical systems in a society, egalitarianism focuses on the transcendence of self-interest, social justice, and equality. (3) *Mastery vs. Harmony* is about the extent to which people seek changes to advance personal or group interests. Mastery encourages active efforts to surpass others, while harmony focuses on the protection of the natural and social world. According to Schwartz's study, the Middle East and most Asian countries had strong embeddedness and hierarchy while Anglosphere countries stressed strong mastery. Western European countries were ranked high on egalitarianism and intellectual autonomy, while Eastern Europe had higher embeddedness than Western Europe. South American countries were clustered in the middle.

4. GLOBE Model

GLOBE was a project, conducted by Robert House and an international team, that systematically investigated the relationship between cultural values, organizational practices, conceptions of leadership, economic competitiveness of societies, and human conditions across 62 countries.[20] Nine cultural dimensions were found from the GLOBE research: performance orientation, uncertainty avoidance, in-group collectivism, institutional collectivism, power distance, gender egalitarianism, assertiveness, future orientation, and human orientation.

- The first dimension, performance orientation, reflects the degree to which a culture encourages performance improvement and innovation. Societies with a strong performance orientation tend to value results, competitiveness, and materialism. These societies expect direct, explicit communication and view feedback as a necessity to improve performance. Societies with a low performance orientation value harmonious environments and emphasize societal and family relationships. Such societies are more likely to engage in indirect, subtle communication.

- Uncertainty avoidance refers to the degree a society relies on social norms, rules, and procedures to mitigate future uncertainty. Societies with high uncertainty avoidance show such characteristics as emphasis on formal interactions with others, reliance on formalized policies and procedures, and strong resistance to change. Societies with low uncertainty avoidance display informality in interactions with others, reliance on informal norms, and moderate resistance to change.
- In-group collectivism refers to the extent individuals express pride, loyalty, and cohesiveness in their families or organization.[21] High in-group collectivism cultures usually have a strong distinction between in-groups and out-groups and emphasize group relatedness and obligations. Societies with low in-group collectivism often place greater weight on personal needs and have a smaller distinction between in-groups and out-groups.
- Institutional collectivism refers to the degree organizational and societal institutions emphasize collective distribution of resources and collective action. High institutional collectivism societies tend to encourage group loyalty, interdependence, and collective interests. Critical decisions are largely made by groups. The characteristics of societies with low institutional collectivism include high individual independence within the organization, the pursuit of individual goals, and the maximization of individual interests. In such societies, critical decisions are mainly made by individuals.[22]
- The notion of power distance here is similar to that in Hofstede's cultural dimensions. High power distance societies have class differentiation; power distribution provides social order; there is limited upward social mobility; and resources are available to only a few. Low power distance societies tend to have a large middle class; power is viewed as linked to corruption and coercion; upward social mobility is common; and resources are available to the majority.
- Gender egalitarianism is about the degree of gender equality in a society. Societies that have high gender egalitarianism usually have more women in powerful positions and less gender segregation at work.[23] In these societies, women often attain a similar level of education as men do. In contrast, low gender egalitarianism suggests fewer women in power and more gender segregation. These cultural features restrict women's decision power in community affairs.
- Assertiveness is the extent to which individuals are assertive, confrontational, and aggressive toward others. Societies with high assertiveness stress competition, success, and progress. They tend to encourage direct, unambiguous communication and control over the environment. Societies with low assertiveness are characterized by warm relationships, cooperation, indirect communication, and harmony within the environment.
- Future orientation is the degree to which a society encourages future-oriented behaviors, such as planning beforehand and delayed gratification. Societies with high future orientation have a propensity to save now for the

future, emphasize working toward long-term success, and encourage flexible and adaptive organizations. In contrast, low future orientation cultures tend to favor instant gratification and prefer spending now to saving for the future.

- Humane orientation refers to the degree a society encourages individuals to be generous, fair, and kind to others. Societies that have high humane orientation tend to stress the interests of others. Members of such societies have a sense of belonging and are willing to work for the well-being of others. Societies with low humane orientation tend to stress the importance of self-interest. Their members demand support for self-sustainment, and stress personal power and material wealth.

The GLOBE researchers have found systematic differences in leadership across cultures. For instance, an American leader is expected to listen to his/her subordinates and apply participatory decision-making, while such activities are not viewed as effective in East Asia, where managers stress paternalistic leadership and group maintenance activities. While Malaysians prefer leaders that are humble and modest, Indian leaders are expected to be assertive and bold. Specifically, the GLOBE researchers have identified ten cultural clusters: Anglo cultures (e.g. the U.S., the U.K., Canada, Australia), Arab cultures (e.g. Egypt, Kuwait, Saudi Arabia, Qatar), Confucian Asia (e.g. China, Japan, South Korea, Vietnam), Eastern Europe (e.g. Bulgaria, Hungary, Poland, Russia), Germanic Europe (e.g. Netherlands, Belgium, Austria, Germany), Latin America (e.g. Argentina, Brazil, Costa Rica, Mexico), Latin Europe (e.g. Italy, France, Spain, Portugal), Nordic Europe (e.g. Denmark, Finland, Sweden), Southern Asia (e.g. India, Indonesia, Thailand), and Sub-Saharan Africa (e.g. Nigeria, Zambia, South Africa). Countries in each cluster show strong cultural similarities, and differ distinctively from countries in other clusters.

As shown in the above-mentioned models, cultural differences can be presented in many different ways. These culture models focus on different aspects of social beliefs, norms, and values, helping us get a comprehensive understanding of culture. Meanwhile, they show some common themes, such as distribution of power and authority in society, centrality of individuals or groups as the basis of social relationships, people's relationship with their environment, use of time, and mechanisms of personal and social control.[24] These models allow international business practitioners to systematically examine and compare national cultures.

IV. Cultural Changes

It should be noted that culture is constantly changing over time. For example, America's attitudes toward women's roles have changed considerably since the 1960s, largely driven by the women's rights movement. The value systems of transitional economies have undergone a major culture shift after the collapse of communism in those countries. In Japan, workers used to have high organizational loyalty to their organizations, as displayed in their willingness to give up personal lives for company success. However, the new generation of Japanese workers have adopted the Western mentality. They show less loyalty to their organizations and are more likely to leave their jobs for better offers.

Economic development has facilitated urbanization and improved the quality of life and educational attainment while weakening traditional values. The trend of globalization also has significantly enhanced cultural exchange between countries and led to cultural changes. Increased global exchanges of goods, services, and knowledge, the development of transport and communication technology, and the expansion of MNCs have all contributed to the changing world culture. Especially, MNCs have become major cultural incubators. For instance, McDonald's fast food in China and Levi's jeans in India have played a major role in shaping local material culture, especially among young people. The value systems of local employees who work for MNCs have also changed. For instance, Romanians traditionally live largely without a regard for time, but those who work in American MNCs have gained a strong concept of time and a belief that time is money.[25]

Although globalization has pushed an increasingly homogeneous global culture, national cultural differences will persist due to differences in political economy, social structure, language, religion, and tradition. Cultural differences usually become barriers in communication and collaboration, leading to misunderstanding and even conflicts, thus increasing the costs and risks of international operations. To succeed in foreign markets, MNCs have to develop cross-culture literacy (i.e. in-depth understanding of cultural differences). Case 6.5 shows how Groupon stumbled in China due to lack of cultural understanding. Even within a country, there may be diverse cultures that require differential treatments. Meanwhile, cultural differences may also present unique opportunities. Case 6.4 shows how Islamic principles have generated new opportunities for banking services in the U.S. Certain cultural features of local workers may render a host country particularly attractive to foreign investors. MNCs may bring "culturally loaded" practices to the host country and use them as mechanisms for organizational control.[26] Many MNCs, Japanese MNCs in particular, influence their overseas subsidiaries through extensive socialization processes in which overseas employees learn behavior, values, beliefs, and social skills. Furthermore, exposure to different cultures may enable MNCs to develop new knowledge and capabilities, thus strengthening their competitive advantage in global markets.

Key Terms

Culture, value system, iceberg model, national cultural differences, Hofstede's dimensions, GLOBE, Hall's culture model, Schwartz's culture model, individualism, collectivism, masculinity, femininity, power distance, uncertainty avoidance, long-term orientation, indulgence, restraint, high-context culture, low-context culture, cultural change

Review Questions

1. How would you define national culture and what factors drive cultural changes?

2. What are the main aspects of national culture?
3. What are the main dimensions of Hofstede's culture model?
4. What are the main arguments of Hall's, Schwartz's, and the GLOBE culture models?
5. How can MNCs utilize these culture models?

Internet Exercises

1. Please visit the following website about cultural basics in different countries; http://guide.culturecrossing.net. Choose two to three countries of interest and read about their cultural features. Discuss their cultural similarities and differences.
2. Please visit https://aib.msu.edu/resources/exercisessimulations.asp to find a list of cultural simulations. Choose a simulation of international negotiation. Assign different roles to your group members and negotiate with each other. Discuss how cultural differences affect your negotiation process.

Notes

1 Kroeber, A. L. and Kluckhohn, C. (1952). Culture: A critical review of concepts and definitions. *Papers of the Peabody Museum*, (47), 643–656.
2 Hofstede, G. (1991). *Cultures and Organizations: Software of the Mind*. London, England: McGraw-Hill.
3 Eid, M. and Diener, E. (2001). Norms for experiencing emotions in different cultures: Inter- and intranational differences. *Journal of Personality and Social Psychology, 81*(5), 869–885.
4 Hofstede, G., Bond, M. H., and Luk, C. L. (1993). Individual perceptions of organizational cultures: A methodological treatise on levels of analysis. *Organization Studies, 14*, 483–503.
5 Peterson, B. (2004). *Cultural Intelligence: A Guide to Working with People from Other Cultures*. Yarmouth, ME: Intercultural Press.
6 BBC News. (2003). China's 'lucky' phone number. Retrieved from http://news.bbc.co.uk/2/hi/asia-pacific/3163951.stm
7 Autoblog.com. (2011, April 1). Ford reveals Europe's color preferences by country. Retrieved from www.autoblog.com/2011/04/01/ford-reveals-europes-color-preferences-by-country
8 Singh, S. (2006). Impact of color on marketing. *Management Decision, 44*(6), 783–789.
9 Cho, W. S. (2012). Riding the Korean Wave from 'Gangnam Style' to global recognition. *Global Asia, 7*(3), 35–39.
10 Abu-Nimer, M. (2001). Conflict resolution, culture, and religion: Toward a training model of interreligious peace building. *Journal of Peace Research, 38*(6), 685–704.
11 Korean Trade Association (2004). Product differentiation across countries (in Korean). Retrieved from www.kyobobook.co.kr/product/detailReviewKor.laf?mallGb=KOR&barcode=9788983930668&linkClass=13210104&ejkGb=KOR
12 Schwartz, S. H., Melech, G., Lehmann, A., Burgess, S., and Harris, M. (2001). Extending the cross-cultural validity of the theory of basic human values with a different method of measurement. *Journal of Cross-Cultural Psychology, 32*, 519–542.

13 Hofstede, G. (1980). *Culture's Consequences: International Differences in Work-Related Values*. Beverly Hills, CA: Sage Publications.

14 Furber, A., Smith, S. D., and Crapper, M. (2012). A case study of the impact of cultural differences during a construction project in Ghana. In S. D. Smith (Ed.), *Procs 28th Annual ARCOM Conference*, September 3–5, 2012. Edinburgh, UK: Association of Researchers in Construction Management, 553–562.

15 Hofstede, G. (2011). Dimensionalizing cultures: The Hofstede model in context. *Online Readings in Psychology and Culture*, 2(1). Retrieved from dx.doi.org/10.9707/2307-0919.1014

16 Hall, Edward T. (1976). *Beyond Culture*. New York: Anchor Books.

17 Korea Educational Broadcasting System (EBS). (2008). *East and West*, EBS Documentary, Yewon. Retrieved from www.kyobobook.co.kr/product/detail-ViewKor.laf?ejkGb=KOR&mallGb=KOR&barcode=9788952767318&orderCli ck=LAH&Kc=.

18 Schwartz S. H. (1992). Universals in the content and structure of values: Theoretical advances and empirical tests in 20 countries. *Advances in Experimental Social Psychology*, 25, 1–65.

19 Schwartz, S. H. (2012). An overview of the Schwartz theory of basic values. *Online Readings in Psychology and Culture*, 2(1), 11.

20 House, R., Javidan, M., and Dorfman, P. (2001). Project GLOBE: An introduction. *Applied Psychology*, 50(4), 489–505.

21 Brewer, P. and Venaik, S. (2011). Individualism–collectivism in Hofstede and GLOBE. *Journal of International Business Studies*, 42(3), 436–445.

22 Realo, A., Allik, J., and Greenfield, B. (2008). Radius of trust social capital in relation to familism and institutional collectivism. *Journal of Cross-Cultural Psychology*, 39(4), 447–462.

23 Lyness, K. S. and Judiesch, M. K. (2014). Gender egalitarianism and work–life balance for managers: Multisource perspectives in 36 countries. *Applied Psychology*, 63(1), 96–129.

24 Bhagat, R. S. and Steers, R. M. (2009). *Cambridge Handbook of Culture, Organizations, and Work*. Cambridge: Cambridge University Press.

25 Caprar, D. V. (2011). Foreign locals: A cautionary tale on the culture of MNC local employees. *Journal of International Business Studies*, 42(5), 608–628.

26 Ritzer, G. (1996). The McDonaldization thesis: Is expansion inevitable? *International Sociology*, 11(3), 291–308.

The Foreign Exchange Market and the International Monetary System

Learning Objectives

1. Understand the main functions of the foreign exchange market.
2. Describe how to ensure against foreign exchange risk.
3. Understand key factors that determine the exchange rates.
4. Explain how to manage foreign exchange exposure.
5. Understand international monetary systems and recognize the roles of the International Monetary Fund.

Cases

Case 7.1 Downfall of Brazilian Real in the Midst of Political Scandal and Soaring Inflation

The Brazilian real fell to its lowest level since its introduction in 1994 and its stocks plunged in response to concerns that President Dilma Rousseff would be unable to mend the country's budget and avoid further credit-rating drops. The currency plummeted to as low as 4.0665 real per dollar, the weakest intraday level since it was launched more than two decades ago.

Since Standard & Poor's downgraded the nation's currency to junk on September 9, 2015, the real has led emerging-market declines and concern is growing that the country may face further decline due to political instability and a corruption scandal, currently under investigation, involving the state-controlled oil company. Weeks before lawmakers determined her fate, Brazilian President Dilma Rousseff was desperately trying to demonstrate that she was still in charge of South America's most populous nation. It's a stunning turn of events for one of the world's most powerful women, but amid a crippling economic and political crunch, Brazilians have largely lost faith in the leader they gave a second four-year term. Ms. Rousseff was ultimately impeached and her unsuccessful second term ended in August 2016. Rousseff's proposals for tax increases and spending cuts did not receive much support. Lawmakers claimed that her proposals would afflict the middle class already suffering from a recession and inflation that was more than double the forecasted mid-point target by the country's central bank.

"The economy is in trouble, the economy needs to adjust, and we haven't yet seen that much progress," said Alberto Ramos, the chief Latin America economist for Goldman Sachs Group Inc. "The macro picture will get worse before it gets better, so we may see more damage going forward. Economists forecast the economy, even with the Olympics-funded boost, will shrink for the second straight year, the worst performance since 1930."[a]

Brazilian central bank analysts increased their 2015 median forecast for economic reduction from 2.55 percent to 2.7 percent. They were also pessimistic about 2016, expecting GDP to decrease 0.8 percent. Since August 2003, Petrobras, a semi-public Brazilian petroleum corporation, dropped to its lowest value. Its $2.5 billion USD in bonds due 2024 fell 5.06 cents, the most since the securities were issued in 2014, to a record low 71.07 cents on the dollar.

Brazil introduced the real in 1994 at parity with the dollar as part of an effort to end an economic crisis that included hyperinflation. The previous record low for the real was set in 2002, when the currency tumbled amid concern Luiz Inacio Lula da Silva would repudiate Brazil's debt if elected president. The currency ended its six-month plunge and rallied when Lula won and pledged to meet obligations to bondholders. "The real won't stop falling until we see a major shift in policy and government," Bianca Taylor, a sovereign analyst at Loomis Sayles in Boston, said in an interview. "Brazil needs structural reforms, and we don't see the minimum steps taking place right now for that to happen."[b]

Following a poor harvest, prices of staples such as corn and soy soared 61 percent, increasing pressure on Brazil's annual inflation rate that ended at 10.7 percent in 2015, the highest level since 2002. Brazil's central bank faced one of its toughest challenges yet as it struggled to return inflation to the 4.5 percent annual target as the country continued to spiral into a deeper recession, the worst in over a century.

While emerging markets are stumbling from economic stagnation in China, some economists warn that Brazil is also on the brink of "fiscal dominance," an economic scenario where a country's poor finances render monetary policy ineffective. Had Brazil's central bank hiked the country's standard Selic (overnight bank) rate beyond the current 14.25 percent, it would have increased the outstanding interest payments the government owes on its own debt. Theoretically, this may raise fears of a default that would result in currency depreciation and inflation making imports more expensive. Brazil's central bank is one of the few in the world that is not formally independent of the government. While the institution generally enjoys operational autonomy, concerns have grown about government interference since Rui Falcão, president of the ruling Workers' party, publicly called for an end to higher interest rates.[c]

It is a dismal scenario, predominantly for older Brazilians, who still vividly remember the consequences of hyperinflation in the 1980s and early 1990s; it completely destroyed savings and damaged livelihoods. In the first decade of this century, Brazil appeared to have moved past these troubled times and entered a new era of prosperity and stability centered on three key policies: fiscal responsibility, inflation targeting, and a floating currency. However, Ms. Rousseff's decision in 2011 to expand lending in the forthcoming years at the expense of the fiscal deficit, in combination with the end of the commodities super cycle, has laid the foundation for the current crisis.

Brazil's budget deficit is now operating at just under 10 percent with public debt close to 70 percent of GDP and rapidly growing. Although inflation remains far from reaching the same high levels of the 1990s, the economy's anticipated economic reduction to 2.5 percent in 2016 and 1.0 percent in 2017 rank as the deepest recession since records began in 1901 and the first consecutive years of contraction since the Great Depression of the 1930s. Mr. Tombini, the Governor of the Central Bank of Brazil, publicly stated that he upholds his position that the central bank can still play an integral role by controlling inflation. Most economists expect bank intervention and a hike of the Selic by 50 basis points to 14.75 percent, its highest since 2006. "The bank still has some ability to influence expectations," says Silvio Campos Neto, economist at the Brazilian consultancy Tendências. Other analysts believe that growing concerns about fiscal dominance are legitimate but premature.

Notes

a.   www.bloomberg.com/news/articles/2015-09-22/brazil-s-currency-tumbles-to-record-on-pessimism-over-budget
b.   Ibid.
c.   Ibid.

Sources

1.   Bloomberg News. (2015). Brazilian Real drops to record low against U.S. dollar. Retrieved from www.bloomberg.com/news/articles/2015-09-22/brazil-s-currency-tumbles-to-record-on-pessimism-over-budget
2.   Pearson, S. (2016, January 18). Surging inflation leaves Brazil's rate setters with headache. *Financial Times*. Retrieved from www.ft.com/intl/cms/s/0/8d67130c-bdfb-11e5-a8c6-deeeb63d6d4b.html#axzz3y6Hecj00

Questions for Case Discussion

1.   Why has the value of the Brazilian real sharply decreased against the U.S. dollar?
2.   Why has Brazil kept its interest rates high in the midst of political turmoil?
3.   What are the main lessons for other nations within BRICS to learn from the recent debacle of the Brazilian real?

Case 7.2 The Big Mac Index

The Big Mac index was introduced in 1986 as an informal guide to determine whether currencies were at their "correct" level based on the purchasing power parity (PPP) theory. PPP theory predicts that, in the long run, exchange rates should move toward the rate that would make the prices of identical basket of goods and services (in this case, a burger) the same in any two countries. Suppose that the average price of a McDonald's Big Mac in the U.S. in January 2016 was $4.93 USD while it was only $2.68 USD at market exchange rates in China. In this case, the "raw" Big Mac index indicates that the yuan was undervalued by 46 percent at that time.

As of January 2016, a Big Mac in the EU will cost you an average of $4.05 USD. This means that the euro is undervalued by 15.4 percent—a huge disparity from seven years ago when the euro was overvalued by some 50 percent compared to the U.S. dollar. Such a big change in the euro's purchasing power, more than 65 percent in favor of the U.S. dollar, is unparalleled. According to the Big Mac index, the Swiss franc is the single most overvalued currency, by 42.4 percent. This means a Big Mac would cost you $6.82 USD in Geneva—almost 70 percent more than in France, just across the border. Norway possesses the second most-overvalued currency in the world, by 17.9 percent, with a Big Mac costing $5.65 USD. Sweden and Denmark comprise the remainder of the only four overvalued Big Mac index countries whose currencies are 7 percent overvalued at $5.13 USD in Sweden and 6 percent overvalued at $5.08 USD in Denmark, respectively. Swiss and Scandinavian currencies have always been highly over-valued. However, the level of overvaluation plummeted in the past five years.

Conversely, you can purchase multiple McDonald's Happy Meals using your home currency in places such as India, Ukraine, and Venezuela. These three countries occupy the bottom of the barrel in regards to relative PPP. In India, a Big Mac will cost you just $1.83, a 61.7 percent undervaluation according to the index. Of course, it won't contain any beef, as cows are sacred in India. In the Ukraine, a Big Mac costs $1.55 USD, and in Venezuela you can buy a Big Mac for a mere 67 cents, which is an undervaluation of 86 percent. This undervaluation suggests that the country has sustained volatile politics and plummeting oil prices that have adversely affected the economy and depreciated its currency. Over the past few years, the principle argument has been the substantial appreciation of the U.S. dollar against all major curren-cies. However, we must remember that currency valuation is a relative game.

The Big Mac Purchasing Power Parity index is a useful yardstick for meas-uring the relative fair values of currencies. For two countries to possess equivalent purchasing power when exchanging goods, an adjustment to the exchange rate needs to be made. The theory of purchasing power parity accounts for these adjustments attributing these changes to market forces. Although exchange rates adjust between currencies, the purchasing power of one currency can still be qualitatively and even quantitatively over- or under-valued in comparison to another currency. Various factors are culpable for the undervaluation of most currencies relative to the U.S. dollar. However, the most significant factor is the implementation of expansive monetary policy by central banks, so-called quantitative easing. The Bank of Japan, the

People's Bank of China, and the European Central Bank have all moved from rate cuts to unconventional stimulus programs to revive economic growth, risking inflation. While these central banks have pursued quantitative easing policies, the Fed actually increased the short-term interest in December 2016 for the first time in almost a decade. As a result, a divergence in relative value of key currencies is developing. The monetary devaluation of the yuan has been highly monitored and criticized for its motives. Many experts believe that the yuan devaluation is manipulated to gain an unfair trade advantage in helping increase the value of China's exports.

Burgernomics was never intended as a precise assessment of currency misalignment, just a tool to make exchange-rate theory more comprehensible. Yet the Big Mac index has become a global benchmark, included in several economic textbooks and the subject of at least 20 academic research projects. For those individuals who take a more serious interest in fast food, *The Economist* has also created a gourmet version of the index. This adjusted index addresses the theory's main criticism that you would expect average burger prices to be less expensive in poor countries and more expensive in rich countries. It is because labor costs in poor countries are lower while the costs in rich ones are higher. PPP theory indicates the long-term overall trend of exchange rates as a country like China becomes wealthier, but it provides little information about today's equilibrium rate.

The relationship between prices and GDP per person may be a better guide to the current fair value of a currency. The adjusted index (refer to www.economist.com/content/big-mac-index) uses the "best fit line" between Big Mac prices and GDP per person for 48 countries (plus the euro zone). The difference between the price predicted by the red line for each country, given its income per person, and its actual price gives a supersized measure of currency under- and over-valuation.[a]

Notes

a.   The Big Mac index: Global exchange rates, to go. *Economist*. Retrieved from www.economist.com/content/big-mac-index/

Sources

1.   *Economist*. (2016, January 7). The Big Mac index: Global exchange rates, to go. Retrieved from www.economist.com/content/big-mac-index
2.   Dailyfx. (2015, August 14). Chinese yuan still undervalued according to purchasing power parity. Retrieved from www.dailyfx.com/forex/market_alert/2015/08/15/Chinese-Yuan-Still-Undervalued-According-to-Purchasing-Power-Parity.html.

Questions for Case Discussion

1.   What is the Big Mac index and why is it useful?
2.   Overall, why has the value of other currencies vis-à-vis the U.S. dollar recently been undervalued? In particular, what are the main reasons for undervaluation of the currencies of many developing countries such as China and Venezuela?

3.   What is a gourmet version of Burgernomics? Does it make more sense to you than the original version and if so, why?

Case 7.3 China's Yuan Depreciation and Alleged Foreign Exchange Manipulation

Policy advisers have been pressuring China's central bank, The People's Bank of China (PBOC), to let the yuan fall quickly and sharply, by as much as 10–15 percent, as its recent gradual softening is believed to be creating more harm than good. In the earlier months of 2015, the PBOC has spent billions of dollars buying the yuan to defend its exchange rate, but has failed to alleviate market and speculators' sentiments. The Chinese yuan progressively fell 2.6 percent against the U.S. dollar even after the PBOC abruptly devalued its currency by nearly 2 percent in August 2015.

The steady, managed depreciation of the yuan by the PBOC makes the Chinese currency a one-way bet for investors who see it continue to weaken even as the Chinese central bank intercedes to support it. Policy insiders are now advocating for a swift and severe yuan depreciation, supported by tighter capital controls to regulate speculation and capital flight. The yuan isn't allowed to trade freely inside China and the PBOC sets a daily price range. Outside China, the bank buys and sells the yuan as well as controls cross-border money flows to influence its price.

With many of China's companies ridden with heavy debt, letting the yuan fall sharply and quickly could help provide a cushion as the Chinese government pursues extensive structural reforms. The Chinese government is keenly aware of restructuring industries through "supply side" reform, specifically reducing industrial over capacity, but afraid that the corporate sector is too weak to handle it.

To restructure without triggering mass bankruptcies and redundancies, sources said the PBOC is being encouraged to let the yuan fall, keeping downward pressure on interest rates and mitigating some of the debt servicing burden on businesses. "If the economy slows sharply and we can't stabilize employment, how can you push reforms?" asked an influential government economist. "The yuan should depreciate at least 10 percent to have any impact on exports . . . but I don't think the authorities will take this step," said a researcher at the commerce ministry. "If China wants to rely on expanding exports to spur growth, other countries may follow suit." While a weaker yuan would make Chinese exports cheaper overseas, and foreign products more expensive in China, it would be unlikely to go down well among trade partners. For example, The United States, regularly accuses Beijing of manipulating its exchange rate. Exchange rate manipulation would allow China to dump underpriced goods on foreign markets.[a]

Many exporters into China face the prospect of further deteriorating revenue if their goods are too expensive for average households. Companies also face lower revenue after they convert their yuan sales into home currencies. Most vulnerable to this devaluation are European luxury good makers, U.K. auto and aerospace parts manufacturers, and European carmakers (BMW, Mercedes-Benz, Volkswagen, Porsche, Audi, and Skoda). Chinese consumers account for 30 percent of total spending in the global luxury goods sector, domestic and international spending. With the devaluation of the yuan, Chinese consumers could return to shopping in China rather than traveling abroad to purchase these goods.

Potential winners from the devaluation are manufacturers who source supplies in China, have factories in the country, or are liable for other manufacturing costs there. Lower buying costs over time should outweigh the negative short-term effect the weakened yuan will have on the company's performance.

The cost associated with PBOC's intervention has been high. China's foreign exchange reserves dropped by more than half a trillion dollars in 2015 as the central bank bought the yuan to support the exchange rate. In December 2015 alone, reserves fell by a record $107.9 billion USD. The yuan's continued plunge since August 2015 has also affected other Chinese financial markets. When the PBOC weakened its morning yuan guidance rate by 0.5 percent for the second time in one week, investors panicked and pushed the CSI300 index down 7 percent halting day trades. Policy advisers are concerned that the PBOC's gradualist approach risks initiating a self-fulfilling prophecy in which the bank will need to respond to a sharper fall in the offshore exchange rate, which is unregulated by the central bank.

> "Because of depreciation expectations, residents and firms want to convert their yuan into dollars. Those expectations are man-made," said another policy adviser, reflecting a common view. "Gradual depreciation sends a signal to the market (that) the yuan still has room to depreciate further. This helps form one-sided expectations."[b]

Investors are predicting that the yuan will fall and help spur capital outflows and potentially cause a credit crunch in which banks and investors will be unwilling to lend funds to corporations. Some companies that have borrowed heavily in global dollar debt markets are increasingly planning early repayments of their dollar-denominated loans and bonds as the Chinese yuan's weakness continues. Critics believe that the central bank is responsible for this dilemma by attaching the yuan's value to the dollar and using the dollar as the reference point to set its currency each day, making its direction easily predictable. They believe the best way for true market fluctuations is to allow the yuan to trade freely. The PBOC intends to decouple the yuan from the dollar and manage it against a basket of 13 currencies that include the dollar, euro, and yen.

Notes

a.   Yao, K. and Sweeney, P. (2016, January 7). Pressure on China central bank for bigger yuan depreciation. Reuters. Retrieved from www.reuters.com/article/us-china-markets-yuan-policymakers-idUSKBN0UL24020160107
b.   Ibid.

Sources

1. *Wall Street Journal.* (2015, August 11). Multinational firms reel in wake of China's yuan devaluation: Western manufacturers and exporters caught off guard by currency recalibration.
2. Wei, L. (2016, January 15). Confused by China's yuan? It's intentional. *Wall Street Journal.* Retrieved from https://www.wsj.com/articles/chinas-pboc-giving-mixed-signals-on-yuan-plans-1452773923
3. Yao, K. and Sweeney, P. (2016, January 7). Pressure on China central bank for bigger yuan depreciation. Reuters. Retrieved from www.reuters.com/article/us-china-markets-yuan-policymakers-idUSKBN0UL24020160107

Questions for Case Discussion

1. Why has the PBOC recently depreciated the Chinese yuan and why has the U.S. government accused this move of being a form of currency manipulation?
2. Which countries will benefit the most and lose the most due to the depreciation of the yuan? In particular, please evaluate the impacts of the depreciation on Chinese exporters, overseas markets, and foreign exporters to China.
3. China has been using the fixed exchange rate system that pegged its value to the U.S. dollar. Why do you think that the Chinese government has considered dropping its link to the U.S. dollar and allowing it to float freely?

Case 7.4 Abenomics and Toyota's Resistance to Tokyo's Reshoring Effort

Poor economic growth in Japan has caused mounting criticism of Abenomics. The Japanese prime minister, Shinzō Abe's deliberate economic policy has failed to raise wages or dramatically boost growth.

Abenomics consist of three "arrows" starting with fiscal spending and monetary easing. The result is a national debt headed to 250 percent of GDP by the end of the year. The Bank of Japan (BOJ) is buying bonds at $652 billion USD annual rate. Deflation continues because the banks haven't increased lending. The third arrow of Abenomics represents structural economic reform, which includes an effort to liberalize Japan's electric and gas industries, a more welcoming approach to immigrants, and Japan's participation in the TPP (Trans-Pacific Partnership) free trade agreement.[a]

The main idea behind Abenomics is that combined measures would end years of deflation and make Japan's economy sustainable. Japan's economy as a result of Abenomics has not resulted in the 2 percent inflation rate as promised and structural reforms have not yet materialized. Mr. Abe's economic program centered on weakening the yen to help the bottom lines of major exporters. However, Japan hasn't benefited much from the yen's 30 percent devaluation since 2012. Export growth has not responded as strongly to yen depreciation as expected. Although exporters have taken advantage of the cheaper yen to contribute to their reserves, the Japanese have seen a reduction in purchasing power due to the devaluation. Furthermore, companies continue to migrate production overseas, partly to compensate labor-market restrictions and to exploit proximity, closeness to fast-growing markets, as well as lower labor costs. The IMF has estimated Japan's exports by subsidiaries exceeded exports from Japan by more than 40 percent.

It should be no surprise that Toyota, flush with $18 billion USD in profits in 2015, has been a major beneficiary of Abenomics. But it's pretty shocking that Japanese employees will not share in Toyota's good fortune. Rather than reinvest in Japan, the leading Japanese auto company announced plans to spend $1.4 billion USD to build new factories in Mexico and China. The resurgence of one of Japan's most iconic companies is welcome news and Toyota's shareholders will certainly be satisfied with its CEO Akio Toyota's plans to shift production to emerging markets. Toyota is a rare example of a Japanese manufacturer that has figured out how to establish truly global operations.

Nonetheless, Toyota's move is a significant setback to the Japanese government's "reshoring" effort. Officials anticipated the yen's 29 percent fall since late 2012 would encourage manufacturers to bring back jobs they had moved abroad over the last decade. Analysts at the financial holding company Nomura argued that the yen would enhance the relative appeal of producing in Japan. Toyota obviously disagreed. The company decided that Japan's shrinking and aging population in addition to high labor costs inhibit growth potential in Japan. It may only be a matter of time until other Japanese companies decide to follow Toyota's lead.

From a broader perspective, the strategy behind Abenomics has been flawed. The Japanese government had been betting on a cash-for-paychecks deal between the Bank of Japan and companies. Executives, in exchange for a weak yen, would be expected to increase salaries, which would provide workers with additional disposable income to purchase goods and services and produce national economic growth. But executives have not expressed any interest in the quid pro quo. In March 2015, Toyota smacked the BOJ by giving its 63,000 union employees only a $33 USD per month pay increase.

Toyota is simply responding to the future growth potential by concentrating on foreign markets—for both sales and manufacturing. The company is intent on keeping up its strong position in North America, where economic growth is steady and wage gains, while mediocre, outpace those in Japan. Meanwhile, China is a longer-term project. In 2014, Toyota, for the first time, reached the one million mark for annual sales. Even if China expands less than the government's 7 percent target, rising income rates among its population (1.3 billion people) far outpace increases experienced by Japan's population (127 million people). The implementation of pro-growth policies is the only way Tokyo can lure production back to Japan. In the 1970s and 1980s, the weak-yen model was sufficient in Japan, but it is less relevant now that cheaper manufacturing hubs have entered the market creating new competition.

Japan should consider utilizing tax incentives as a means to attract producers home. A main pillar of Abenomics has been reducing Japan's 36 percent corporate tax rate. Slashing rates would greatly encourage executives to use their authority to create more domestic jobs. Additional incentives could be provided to companies who enter into profit sharing arrangements with employees. Tax penalties could be imposed on CEOs who stockpile excess cash that could be used to stimulate domestic demand. Unfortunately, there's little evidence that any of these steps are occurring. Rather, the public is closely watching the BOJ, which is expected to further devalue the yen in the near future.

Note

a. *Wall Street Journal*. (2015, November 17). Abenomics sputters in Japan. Eastern edition, A.18. Retrieved from www.fultonpostnews.com/opinion/abenomics-sputters-in-japan-h14944.html

Sources

1. CNN. (2015). Japan's economy contracted in the second quarter, a result that raises questions about the ambitious stimulus plan championed by Prime Minister Shinzo Abe. Retrieved from http://money.cnn.com/2015/08/16/news/economy/japan-gdp-abenomics/
2. Pesek, W. (2015). Toyota leaves Japan in the dust. Bloombergview. Retrieved from www.bloombergview.com/articles/2015-04-16/toyota-leaves-japan-in-the-dust
3. *Wall Street Journal*. (2015, November 17). Abenomics sputters in Japan. Eastern edition, p. A.18. Retrieved from www.fultonpostnews.com/opinion/abenomics-sputters-in-japan-h14944.html

Questions for Case Discussion

1. What is Abenomics and why has this economic policy failed to achieve its original goal?
2. How have major Japanese companies like Toyota responded to Abenomics? Why are they keeping manufacturing offshore instead of returning home?
3. What types of reshoring policy options are available for the Japanese government to lure Japanese companies back home?

Case 7.5 The IMF and Currency Swap

The Fed Swap Lines is a program that provides dollars to overseas markets at a cheaper rate. Essentially, the Fed lends dollars to foreign central banks in return for their local currency for a specific period. Since the Fed isn't directly lending to banks, the risk is effectively nonexistent. Furthermore, the Fed isn't exposed to changes in currency rates since the exchange rate is set for the duration of the swap.[a]

Liquidity swap arrangements have been used continuously throughout history to fund markets when tensions have arisen. They were used following the terrorist attacks of September 11, 2001, and were revived and used extensively during the global financial crisis in 2007, particularly when credit markets dried up after the collapse of Lehman Brothers. In February 2010, as market conditions improved, they were shut down but restored in May 2010 to combat the European sovereign debt crisis.

The IMF believes the sluggish demand in China threatened global growth and that the decreased Chinese imports and exports were weighing heavily on other emerging markets and commodity exporters. Global financial markets seem to be overreacting to a potential Chinese recession and falling oil prices. Oil prices place pressure on oil exporters. The IMF believes that continued market upheaval could further reduce growth if it results in major risk aversion and currency depreciation in emerging markets. Concerns over plunging oil and commodity prices and capital outflows from China have resulted in weak consumer demand in the U.S. and Japan in addition to weak emerging markets.

> Citing growing financial and growth strains in emerging markets, IMF Managing Director Christine Lagarde revived the idea that the IMF would provide emerging markets with short-term crisis credit lines. Emerging markets have pushed for the IMF to create a new emergency-financing tool similar to the dollar swap lines the U.S. FRB used during the global financial crisis to stem contamination.[b]

The idea focuses on the IMF providing dollars, euros, and other currencies to governments that are normally in decent financial shape but are under temporary financial stress and suffering from short-term liquidity problems. Previous proposals contain numerous technical issues, but the most difficult opposition to overcome is obtaining U.S. approval. The U.S. is the IMF's biggest shareholder and Washington opposes the proposal because FRB's swap lines provide the U.S. with political leverage. U.S. officials worry that the provision of such a lending tool could deregulate economic policy fostered by market downturns, fueling governmental moral hazard.

> Ms. Lagarde said that "given the risks facing emerging markets and their contribution to global GDP, it behooves the U.S. and other advanced economies to strengthen the global financial safety net. The existing system of swap lines between advanced economies creates a dangerous asymmetry in the global financial system since many emerging markets don't have access to them." "Rather than relying on a fragmented and incomplete system of regional and bilateral arrangements, we need a functioning international network of precautionary instruments that works for everyone," Ms. Lagarde said.[c]

Ms. Lagarde also said "the IMF's war chest may not be sufficient to manage the growing instability in emerging markets." In the past several years, the IMF has continuously strengthened its lending resources as the global financial crisis shook some of the world's largest economies. Currently, the IMF could have access to roughly $400 billion USD to bail out member countries in crises. But accumulating emerging-market liabilities to intermittent trillion-dollar capital flows substantiate a larger pool of reserves emerging markets could tap into. "Unless countries be tempted to accumulate even more reserves for self-insurance, we need to find ways to increase the resources that can be brought to bear in times of need," Ms. Lagarde said.[d]

While emerging-market turmoil may help solidify the need to bolster the international monetary system, it may be too early to expect another round of major overhauls. Meanwhile, in December 2015, the U.S. Senate as part of a budget bill, ratified reforms to improve the representation of emerging economies at the IMF. Passage of the bill will allow new industrial power-houses like China and India to have greater influence at the IMF. "Under the reform, all 188 members' quotas will increase as the Fund's quota resources will rise to about $477 billion special drawing rights, (the IMF currency worth about $659.67 billion) from about $238.5 billion," the Fund said in a statement.[e] The reforms are the biggest changes to IMF governance since its establishment after World War II. China's central bank embraced the move stating, "The reform will improve the representation and voice of emerging markets and developing countries in the IMF and is conducive to protecting the IMF's credibility, legitimacy and effectiveness."[f]

Notes

a. *Wall Street Journal.* (2011). What are Fed SWAP lines and what do they do? Retrieved from http://blogs.wsj.com/economics/2011/11/30/what-are-fed-swap-lines-and-what-do-they-do/
b. Talley, I. (2016, January 12). Emerging-market turmoil spurs IMF call for new crisis financing. *Wall Street Journal.* Retrieved from http://blogs.wsj.com/economics/2016/01/12/emerging-market-turmoil-spurs-imf-call-for-new-crisis-financing/
c. Ibid.
d. Ibid.
e. Chance, D. (2015, December 19). Senate passes IMF reform in budget bill. Reuters. Retrieved from www.reuters.com/article/us-usa-fiscal-imf-idUSK BN0U204J20151219
f. Ibid.

Sources

1. Lawder, D. (2015, January 19). IMF cuts global growth forecast as China slows. Reuters. Retrieved from www.reuters.com/article/us-imf-growth-idUSK CN0UX11Y
2. Talley, I. (2016, January 12). Emerging-market turmoil spurs IMF call for new crisis financing. *Wall Street Journal.* Retrieved from http://blogs.wsj.com/economics/2016/01/12/emerging-market-turmoil-spurs-imf-call-for-new-crisis-financing/
3. Chance, D. (2015, December 19). Senate passes IMF reform in budget bill. Reuters. www.reuters.com/article/us-usa-fiscal-imf-idUSKBN0U204J20151219

Questions for Case Discussion

1. What is a currency swap? Why does the IMF want to introduce currency swaps?
2. Why has the U.S. opposed the IMF's proposed introduction of currency swaps as a new emergency-financing tool to help emerging economies overcome short-term financial crises?
3. What action did the U.S. Senate take to increase the voice of emerging econo-mies at the IMF? What is the significance of this action?

The Foreign Exchange Market and the International Monetary System

I. The Foreign Exchange Market

In the previous chapters, we learned about international trade and foreign direct investment theories and practices. However, these transactions cannot occur without the payments and receipts of a certain currency. The term "foreign exchange market" refers to the market in which participants are able to buy, sell, exchange, and speculate on currencies. The foreign exchange market is considered to be the largest financial market in the world consisting of banks, commercial companies, investment management firms, retail foreign exchange brokers, etc. Since we don't have a global currency and each country uses its own currency, foreign exchange rates are instrumental in dealing with worldwide financial transactions. For example, Mexican pesos cannot be used to purchase goods or services in the U.S. To process such a transaction, the pesos must be changed into U.S. dollars applying the current foreign exchange rate. Because the currency markets are large and liquid, they are considered to be the most efficient financial markets. It is important to realize that foreign exchange markets in London, New York, Singapore, and Tokyo are closely integrated 24/7 through a global network of computers that connect participants from all over the world.

As we will explain in more detail below, the foreign exchange market serves different purposes for an individual and a company engaged in international business transactions.

II. Key Functions of the Foreign Exchange Market

I. Currency Conversion

Different countries adopt and use different currencies at home. An individual needs to change money when he or she is traveling outside his or her home country. For example, an American tourist needs to exchange U.S. dollars to euros when buying a museum ticket in Barcelona, Spain. Or Samsung, a Korean company, receiving payment in foreign currencies for its overseas sale of smart phones needs to convert these payments into their home currency, the Korean won. A U.S. company operating in Mexico needs to exchange the U.S. dollar to the Mexican peso to purchase land and necessary parts from local suppliers. An MNC may want to invest spare cash short term in a money market account. For example, GE can invest $100 million USD in a money market in France since investing in a French market account gives higher returns than in the U.S. market. However, the rate of return on this investment depends not only on the interest differential between the U.S. and France but also on the change in value of the euro against the U.S. dollar during the investment period. The impact of interest differential and inflation differential on exchange rate changes will be explained in greater detail later. An MNC can even speculate on the future value of a specific currency in the hope that purchasing the currency will increase its value while selling the currency will decrease its value. An accurate prediction of a change in the value of the two currencies will result in profits for a company.

The exchange rate is the rate at which one currency is converted into another currency in the market. In other words, foreign exchange rates denote the value of one country's currency relative to a different currency. Using the U.S. dollar and the Japanese yen as an example, exchange rates can be expressed in either U.S.$ (or U.S.$ equivalent) or per U.S.$ term relative to the Japanese yen. On February 1, 2016, the Japanese yen was worth 0.0083 dollars in terms of 1 U.S. $ or 1 U.S.$ was worth 121¥. The U.S. dollar value of the Japanese yen, i.e. 0.0083$/¥, equals the reciprocal of the value of Japanese yen per U.S. dollar, i.e. 121¥/$. Two different types of exchange rates exist. One is called spot exchange rate while the other is called forward exchange rate. The spot exchange rate is simply the current exchange rate as opposed to the forward exchange rate that will materialize at a specific date in the future.

2. Insuring against Foreign Exchange Risk

Providing insurance against foreign exchange risk is the other main role of the foreign exchange market. Anyone or any company holding foreign currency is exposed to risks that arise from changes in exchange rates between home currencies and foreign currencies. For example, due to weak foreign exchange rates and continued distress in Venezuela, Coca-Cola saw its profit take a 55 percent hit during its fourth quarter of 2015.[1] We only know the current exchange rate or spot exchange rate and do not know the future spot exchange rate, i.e. the exchange rate tomorrow. The value of the currency that one holds can either increase or decrease. *Appreciation* or *revaluation* means an increase in value while *depreciation* or *devaluation* refers to a decrease in value. In order to eliminate the risk exposed to fluctuations of future exchange rates, one can enter into contracting forward exchange transactions.

The forward exchange rate represents an exchange rate that is quoted and traded today but will be materialized and paid at a set future date. Sometimes, a business needs to handle a foreign exchange transaction, but at some time in the future. For example, a U.S. company sells its goods to a company in France but will not receive payment for at least three months. So how can this company set the price of its products without knowing what the foreign exchange rate will be between the U.S. dollar and the euro one year from now? The U.S. company can do so by signing a forward contract that allows it to lock in a specific three-month rate so that it can receive payment at an agreed-upon exchange rate after three months. The exchange rate applied to such future transactions are "forward exchange rates." If the forward exchange rate between the U.S. dollar and Japanese yen, expressed in U.S. $ terms, is higher than spot exchange rate, the Japanese yen sells at a *premium* in the foreign exchange market. This means that the value of the Japanese yen is expected to increase in the future. Conversely, if the forward exchange rate is lower than the spot exchange rate, the Japanese yen sells at *discount* since the value of the Japanese yen is expected to decrease in the future. As the forward exchange rate is considered an unbiased predictor of the future spot exchange rate, we can predict whether the value of the Japanese yen will go up or down by following the trend of forward exchange rates.

The following example will explain how entering into a forward contract will make a company hedge against future exchange rate fluctuations. Suppose a U.S. company has just contracted to import specially designed machines from Japan. When the shipment arrives in 60 days, the company must pay the Japanese supplier 360,000 yen for each machine. The dollar/yen spot exchange rate today is $1=¥120. The importer knows it can sell each machine for $4,500 on the day the shipment arrives. If the dollar depreciates against the yen over the next 90 days, for example to $1=¥100, how will this exchange rate change affect the income of the U.S. company?

In this example, the U.S. company may consider signing a 90-day forward contract that allows it to lock in the exchange rate, for example $1=¥110, to eliminate the exchange rate risk.

Currency swaps represent another popular method to deal with uncertainties involved in exchange rate fluctuations. A currency swap is a transaction in which two parties, typically financial institutions, agree to exchange both principal and interest, in two different currencies, at some agreed-upon time in the future to hedge exposure to exchange rate risk. Currency swap lines allow central banks to purchase and repurchase currencies from one another, which in turn makes it easier for banks in each relevant country to get hold of the underlying currencies. Currency swaps can also be arranged between MNCs from two different countries, which involve trading in their own local currencies, where both parties pay for import and export trade, at pre-determined exchange rates, without bringing in third country currency like the U.S. dollar. This type of transaction could be particularly beneficial for developing countries, such as India and China, who use soft currency which is not easily convertible in the foreign exchange market, as compared to hard currency, such as U.S. dollar and euro, which is more easily convertible.

III. Economic Theories of Exchange Rate Determination

1. Key Factors that Influence Change in Exchange Rates

In principle, the exchange rate is determined by demand for and supply of a certain currency relative to another currency. For example, if demand for the U.S. dollar is greater than the supply of the U.S. dollar, the price of the dollar will increase and vice versa. As Figure 7.1 illustrates, the exchange rates are influenced by many different factors, both political and economic, such as inflation rates, interest rates, current account balance, and political stability. Weak economies have adverse impacts on the country's currency. For example, if high inflation and an unstable government afflict a country's economy, the value of its currency will decline relative to that of other currencies. The recent economic situation in Brazil is a prime example. Comparing Brazil's inflation rate to the U.S. over the last five years, the United States' rates never went above 6 percent while Brazil's inflation rate over the same time period peaked at 10 percent. Therefore, as illustrated by Case 7.1, Brazil's

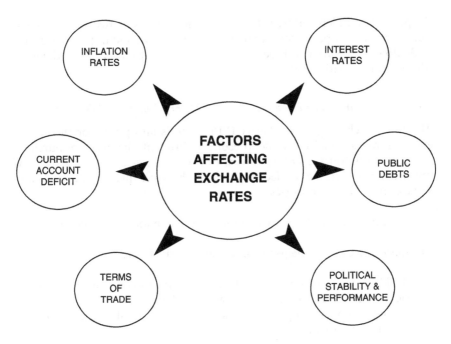

Figure 7.1 Key Factors that Determine Exchange Rates

currency, "real", dropped to its lowest level, approximately 4.1575 real per U.S. dollar since its introduction two decades ago.[2]

Political instability often brings about dumping domestic currency, usually accompanied by capital flight. Again, as case 7.1 illustrates, Brazil's recent political uncertainty and corruption have triggered undesirable fluctuations in the country's currency markets. Former president Dilma Rousseff of Brazil was under investigation for her involvement in a political scandal surrounding the alleged illegal financing of her 2014 election campaign. Many Brazilians lost trust in her as leader of the country and felt she created greater political risk. No one wants to hold a currency of a country whose political risk is high and unpredictable. A declining currency reduces the purchasing power of the affected country and its people. As for the impact of balance of payments on exchange rate movement, if a country continues to accumulate a trade deficit, the value of its currency is expected to weaken since it needs to sell more of its currency to pay for imported goods and services than its trading partners that need to buy its currency to pay for exported goods and services from that country. Here, we will focus on the impacts of two key economic variables, i.e. inflation rates, and interest rates, on the determination of exchange rates.

2. Purchasing Power Parity (PPP) Theory

As Case 7.2 indicates, the theory of purchasing power parity argues that in the long run exchange rates should move toward rates that would equalize the prices of an identical basket of goods and services in any two countries. Purchasing power parity focuses on the flow of export and import goods, i.e. trade flow. There are two types of purchasing power parity (PPP) theories: Absolute and Relative PPP.

(1) Absolute Purchasing Power Parity (PPP) Theory: The Law of One Price

Absolute Purchasing Power Parity (PPP) rate is an optimal or theoretical exchange rate at which consumers become indifferent wherever they purchase an identical product. In other words, PPP rate allows us to figure out how much currency will be needed to purchase the same quantity of goods and services in different countries.

PPP rate = P_h/P_f (Price at home vs. Price in foreign country)

The following example helps us understand the PPP rate.

If a jacket is selling for $100 USD in New York and one can buy the same jacket for ¥12,000 in Tokyo, what should the U.S. dollar against the Japanese yen exchange rate be according to the absolute purchasing power parity theory?

PPP rate = ¥12,000/ $100 U.S. = 120¥ /U.S.$

In this example, the price of the jacket is exactly the same at the PPP rate of 120¥/U.S.$ between the two countries. In competitive markets without barriers to trade and transportation costs, the Law of One Price should hold at PPP rate since identical products should sell for the same price in different countries. In other words, the same products sold in different countries must sell at an equal price when their price is quoted in terms of the same currency. Otherwise, arbitrage opportunities will arise to take advantage of price differences across countries. People will buy a product at a lower price in one country and sell at a higher price in another country. *The Economist* has been publishing the Big Mac index, which compares and contrasts the prices of the McDonald's Big Mac hamburger across countries since 1986.[3] The Big Mac PPP is the exchange rate that requires a burger in any country costs the same price across all countries. Although a hamburger might appear to be a simple product, this table helps us understand whether a certain currency is overvalued or undervalued.

Why is there a discrepancy between market or current exchange rate and PPP rate? Market exchange rates don't actually reflect different living costs because some goods are not easily traded. Thus, converting national GDP into dollars at market exchange rates is misleading. However, purchasing power parity (PPP) takes into account differences in living costs across countries. Accordingly, it makes more sense to use PPP rates, which account for price differences. For example, if you live in Sweden, it is irrelevant if a cheaper accommodation is available elsewhere in the world. What matters is how much your income is worth when you purchase a house in Sweden. If you have to pay double the price in Sweden than in China for relatively the

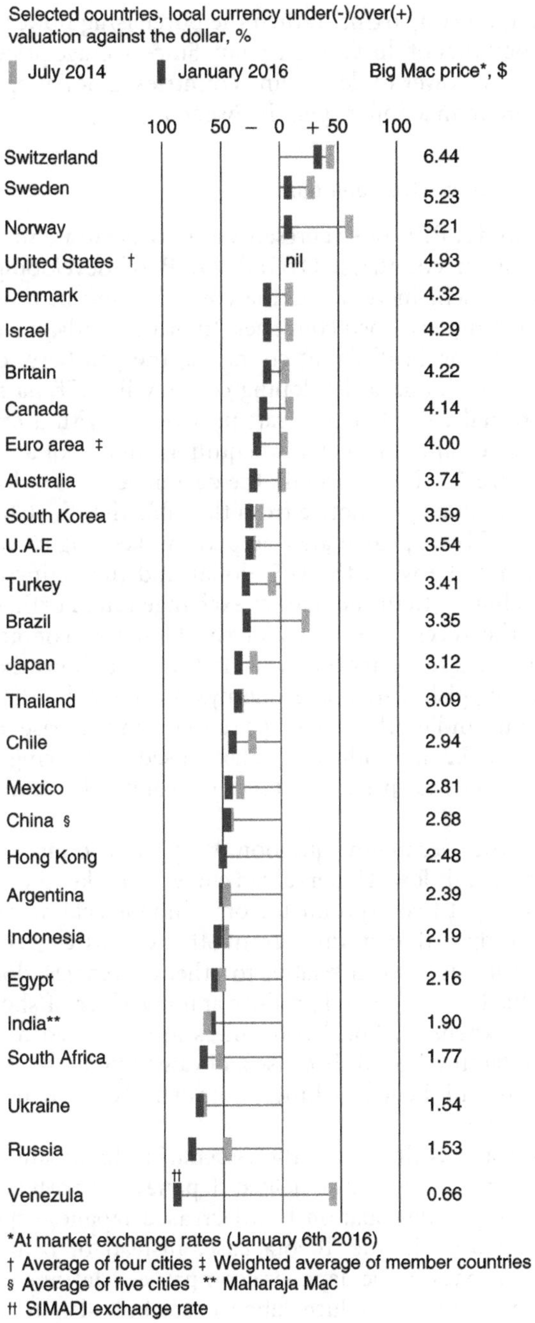

Selected countries, local currency under(-)/over(+)
valuation against the dollar, %

| July 2014 | January 2016 | Big Mac price*, $ |

	Big Mac price*, $
Switzerland	6.44
Sweden	5.23
Norway	5.21
United States †	4.93
Denmark	4.32
Israel	4.29
Britain	4.22
Canada	4.14
Euro area ‡	4.00
Australia	3.74
South Korea	3.59
U.A.E	3.54
Turkey	3.41
Brazil	3.35
Japan	3.12
Thailand	3.09
Chile	2.94
Mexico	2.81
China §	2.68
Hong Kong	2.48
Argentina	2.39
Indonesia	2.19
Egypt	2.16
India**	1.90
South Africa	1.77
Ukraine	1.54
Russia	1.53
Venezuela	0.66

*At market exchange rates (January 6th 2016)
† Average of four cities ‡ Weighted average of member countries
§ Average of five cities ** Maharaja Mac
†† SIMADI exchange rate

Figure 7.2 Big Mac Meal Value

Source: The Big Mac Index: After the Dips (2016, Jan 9), *Economist*. Retrieved from www.economist.com/
news/finance-and-economics/21685489-big-currency-devaluations-are-not-boosting-exports-much-
they-used-after

same size and quality apartment, then the purchasing power of the Swedish krona is only half that of the Chinese yuan. Since average prices of goods and services tend to be lower in developing countries, a dollar spent in China is worth a lot more than a dollar spent in Sweden.

(2) Undervaluation vs. Overvaluation

As explained above, PPP rate represents a more accurate measure of actual living standards in countries. Overall, GDP of developing countries in U.S. dollar terms will increase, as the cost of living in those countries is much lower than in developed countries. In other words, if we adjust for the relative cost of living in different countries, the gap between a developed country like the U.S. and a developing country like China becomes much smaller. Accordingly, absolute PPP rate provides us with useful information as to whether a certain currency is at equilibrium or not at a specific point in time. As Figure 7.2 shows, overall, the currencies of developing countries have been undervalued. We notice from the table that the Chinese yuan has been undervalued by approximately 50 percent, keeping its value artificially low since PPP rate between the U.S. dollar and the Chinese yuan in U.S. dollar terms is higher than the market exchange rate. Furthermore, as Case 7.3 indicates, the recent slowdown of the Chinese economy has led the Chinese government to depreciate the yuan further to boost exports and thus stimulate the sluggish Chinese economy. As a result, the discrepancies between PPP rate and market exchange rate continue to rise. However, as we learned from Case 7.2, if an adjusted index is used by drawing the "line of the best fit" between Big Mac prices and GDP per capita, the yuan is only slightly undervalued.[4]

This leads to the overarching question: Why has a country like China kept its currency artificially low? Undervalued currency makes the price of Chinese exports more competitive so products from China sell at lower prices to global consumers as compared to products from other countries. When the value of your local currency is cheaper relative to other currencies, domestic companies are more likely to invest and produce at home since offshore outsourcing becomes more expensive. Local consumers are expected to buy primarily domestic manufactured goods because a devalued yuan increases the cost of importing goods. This benefits Chinese output and employment as more jobs are created at home.

However, as Case 7.4 illustrates, these scenarios do not always materialize. Although the cheaper yen has helped Japanese exporters expand their cash reserve, the yen devaluation has decreased Japanese spending power. Furthermore, as seen in the Toyota case, instead of bringing manufacturing operations back home, Japanese companies continue to shift production abroad, not only to reduce labor costs but also to penetrate into fast-growing overseas markets. Rather than reaping the expected benefits, undervaluation of a country's currency often leads to an accusation of currency manipulation from its trading partner as the U.S. has long criticized China's exchange rate policy.[5] Undervalued currencies may cause inflation as it makes the prices of imports more expensive. It also increases a country's debt service burden because a certain number of yuan buys fewer dollars than before.

(3) Relative Purchasing Power Parity Theory

The absolute version of PPP is rarely used because it is often difficult to get baskets of identical goods across countries. While absolute PPP theory represents a cross-sectional analysis to compare the prices of identical products and services at a particular time, relative PPP theory takes inflation differentials across countries into account. The PPP rate is assumed to be the exchange rate adjusted from the base year to reflect inflation differential over time in both home and foreign countries. In a nutshell, relative PPP theory predicts that exchange rates will change due to changes in relative prices between two countries. A country with low inflation should expect its currency to appreciate against the currency of a country with a high inflation rate.

$$\frac{e_t}{e_0} = \frac{1+i_{h,t}}{1+i_{f,t}}$$

(e$_t$: PPP rate, e$_0$: equilibrium exchange rate at time 0, home currency/ foreign currency, $i_{h,t}$: rate of inflation between time 0 and time t in home country, $i_{f,t}$: rate of inflation between time 0 and time t in foreign country)

The following questions illustrate how the PPP rate is calculated using the above formula and how much a currency is either overvalued or under- valued.

Average prices of a basket of goods in the U.S., as measured by the consumer prices index, were 8 percent higher in 2015 than in 2010. Meanwhile, prices of the same basket of goods in Japan, as measured by their consumer price index, increased by 4 percent over the same time period. The market exchange rate between the two currencies was 91 ¥/U.S.$ and 120 ¥/US$ in 2010, respectively. To what value should the yen have risen in 2015 in order to keep purchasing power parity level if the two currencies were in parity in 2010? According to the PPP rate, is the Japanese yen overvalued or undervalued and how much, if so?

(4) Fisher Effect (FE) and International Fisher Effect

While PPP theory focuses on the trade flow, i.e. flow of goods and services, the Fisher effect concentrates on capital flow. It contends that real interest rates should be equal across countries. Real interest rates are defined as nominal interests adjusted for inflation rates. Simply put, if one country's inflation rate is higher than another country's, its nominal interest rate is also higher so that real interest rates in both countries should be the same.

$$\frac{1+r_{h,t}}{1+r_{f,t}} = \frac{1+i_{h,t}}{1+i_{f,t}}$$

($r_{h,t}$: nominal interest rate in home country between time 0 and time t, $r_{f,t}$: nominal interest rate in foreign country between time 0 and time t)

Relative PPP theory and Fisher effect can be combined to derive a relationship between interest differentials and changes in the spot exchange rate. PPP rate implies that exchange rates will move in the direction that reflects the inflation differentials between countries. For example, an increase in Mexico's inflation rate relative to that of the U.S. will be associated with a decrease in value of the Mexican peso. The Fisher effect predicts that this increase in the Mexican inflation rate will also correlate with an increase in Mexico's nominal interest rate relative to that of the U.S. so that expected real interest rates become equal across countries. In other words, higher nominal interest rates will be offset by higher inflation rates. This means that for any two countries, the future spot exchange rate should move in an equal proportion but in the opposite direction to the difference in nominal interest rates between the two countries. Otherwise, arbitrage will occur as people move capital from a country where return on investment is lower to a country where higher return is expected.

By combining formulas 1 and 2, the following formula can be derived:

$$\frac{e_t}{e_0} = \frac{1+r_{h,t}}{1+r_{f,t}}$$

The following question illustrates how exchange rate changes according to the international Fisher effect.

> While interest rates in the U.S. were 2 percent higher in February 2016 than in February 2008, interest rates in Brazil increased by 15 percent during the same period. The exchange rate between the two currencies was 1.7440/U.S.\$ and 3.9402/U.S.\$, respectively, in February 2008. What value should the Brazilian real have declined to according to the international Fisher effect? Is the Brazilian real overvalued or undervalued and how much, if so?

(5) Investor Psychology and Bandwagon Effects

We have so far examined the relationship between key economic variables such as inflation rates, interest rates, and exchange rates. However, empirical evidence suggests that either the PPP theory or international Fisher effect cannot accurately predict short-term exchange rate movements because of the time lag for which trade or capital flow needs to be adjusted. Furthermore, as previously stated, firms may not always behave as predicted by these theories and governments may restrict the flows of goods and capital, distorting market fundamentals. As a result, exchange rates may not necessarily change in the direction predicted by these theories but these short-term exchange rate movements may instead be influenced by a seemingly irrational and psychological phenomenon called "bandwagon effect." Suppose that George Soros, a well-known guru in currency speculation, is engaged in a tactic called short selling in which he borrows the British pound, immediately sells it as its value is expected to decline, then buys back the pound he sold at a much favorable exchange rate, and later repays the loan using these pounds. Other people tend to follow suit since they believe Mr. Soros can accurately predict the future value of the British pound. In this case, the initial depreciation of the British pound has very little to do with fundamental economic factors but more to do with the self-fulfilling prophecy of investors betting on the value of the pound to fall.

IV. MNCs' Strategies to Deal with Exchange Rate Fluctuation

So far, we learned how the foreign exchange market functions and what the major economic theories are for determining exchange rates. Then, how do MNCs manage foreign exchange exposure entailed by exchange rate fluctuation?

Financial managers should be able to measure and manage foreign exchange exposure caused by exchange rate fluctuations so as to maximize the profitability, market value, and net cash flow of the firm. Change in foreign exchange rates can have an impact on a firm's financial situation mainly in three ways: transaction exposure, economic exposure, and translation exposure.

First, transaction exposure assesses how currency fluctuations affect the income from individual transactions. Specifically, it measures gains or losses associated with the settlement of existing financial obligations involving a foreign currency in specified terms. Transaction exposure typically arises when a firm has a receivable or payable designated in a foreign currency. As explained above, many firms rely on hedging such as currency swaps and forward contracts in managing their currency exposures. While hedging can keep the owner of an asset from a loss, it also removes any gain from an increase in the value of the asset hedged. Instead of purchasing forward contracts or exercising currency swaps, firms can either lead or lag in payment terms. Lead strategy is used to collect receivables early when currency devaluation is anticipated and to pay early when the currency value is anticipated to appreciate. Meanwhile, lag strategy is adopted to delay receivable collection when anticipating currency appreciation and to delay payables when currency depreciation is expected. Accordingly, an accurate prediction of exchange rate fluctuation is required to effectively implement lead and lag strategies.

Second, economic (operating) exposure refers to the long-term outcome of fluctuations in exchange rates on future prices, costs, and sales. It is different from transaction exposure (explained above) that involves short-term business deals. As illustrated by Case 7.3, Japanese automakers have recently benefited from the continued depreciation of the yen since export prices for their cars have decreased in the U.S. dollar terms and made their products more attractive in comparison to their Korean or German competitors in the U.S. market. Suppose that Nissan produces a car that sells in Japan for three million yen. In February 2014, the exchange rate was 100 ¥: 1$. Consequently, Nissan set the U.S. sticker price at $30,000. By February 1, 2016, the exchange rate has dropped to 125 ¥: 1U.S. $. Nissan is very happy because it received $30,000 × 125¥/$ = ¥3, 750,000 per sale and kept the sticker price in dollar terms at the same level. The continued depreciation of the yen allowed Nissan to decrease the price all the way down to $24,000. Such an exchange rate change can affect Nissan's future sales and costs as well as future cash flow streams. To take advantage of the weak yen, Nissan can adjust its manufacturing strategies to increase domestic production by closing overseas factories.

Third, translation (accounting) exposure addresses the impact of currency exchange rates on consolidated results and balance sheets. This exposure measures accounting gains or losses resulting from exchange rate changes. Volatility in the foreign exchange market can substantially reduce the corporate earnings of an MNC's quarterly report. For example, profit at Kimberly-Clark Corp, manufacturer of Kleenex tissues and Huggies diapers, decreased by 25 percent as a result of currency effects in the third quarter of 2015. This occurred as a result of the depreciation of the euro, Brazilian real, and Canadian dollar against the U.S. dollar by 7.8 percent, 34 percent, and 16 percent, respectively, over the year. Companies in North America lost at least $19.3 billion USD due to the negative impact of foreign exchanges during that same period.[6] U.S. companies with accounting exposure could face total write-downs of more than $3 billion USD if they revalue their assets in Venezuela. Increased government regulations and lack of access to U.S. dollars at lower rates could force Goodyear, an American tire manufacturing company, to deconsolidate if they continue to lose control over their operations. Under the U.S. accounting rules, deconsolidation allows companies to treat a subsidiary in a volatile foreign market as an investment instead of an operating unit. Writing down the market value of that subsidiary protects the parent company from future negative impacts on its finances.[7] The recent significant depreciation of the Japanese yen also greatly reduced the dollar value of equity in a U.S. MNC's Japanese subsidiary which decreased the total dollar value of the firm's equity as reported on its consolidated balance sheet.

V. International Monetary System

I. Bretton Woods Agreement and Fixed Exchange Rate System

So far, we have discussed how the foreign exchange market functions and the major economic factors that affect changes in exchange rates. In principle, exchange rates will be automatically adjusted in the market based on the principle of demand and supply. However, what if exchange rates remain at disequilibrium potentially causing financial crises? Are there any global institutions that closely monitor exchange rate movements and capital flows across countries? The international monetary system consists of two major international financial institutions: the International Monetary Fund (IMF) and the World Bank. These two institutions were created by the 1944 Bretton Woods agreement that has adopted the fixed exchange rate system. Under the fixed exchange rate system, all countries agreed to link their currencies to the U.S. dollar, the only currency allowed to be converted to gold at $35/oz. The fixed exchange rate system has been working fine until the late 1960s when the U.S. suffered from high inflation mainly because it kept printing money to finance the Vietnam War and support President Lyndon Johnson's welfare programs. High inflation and continued accumulation of trade deficit led to speculation in the foreign exchange market that the value of the U.S. dollar would depreciate. In fact, speculators started purchasing German deutsche marks in response to this prediction and the Bundesbank, the German central bank, to maintain the dollar/deutsche mark exchange rate at its fixed exchange rate, continued to buy U.S. dollars. However, in the face of mounting pressure the Bundesbank had to give up fixed exchange rates and allow its currency to float for the deutsche mark to appreciate. By early 1970s, it became inevitable that the U.S. dollar had to be devalued. Under the Bretton Woods system, which designated the U.S. dollar as the key currency, devaluation of the U.S. dollar required the agreement of all member countries and the revaluation of their currencies against the dollar. Since many countries did not support this idea, President Nixon announced in August 1971 that the U.S. government would no longer allow the dollar to be converted into gold and imposed a new 10 percent tax on imports until its trading partners agreed to revalue their currencies against the U.S. dollar. The enactment of these measures made U.S. trading partners agree with an 8 percent devaluation of the U.S. dollar and in return the import tax was removed. Despite strenuous efforts to protect the value of the U.S. dollar, speculations on the U.S. dollar persisted and its value continued to fall. In March 1973, Japan and the majority of European countries let their currencies float against the U.S. dollar. Bretton Woods fixed exchange rate system collapsed when the U.S. dollar, the key currency, experienced ongoing speculative attack. Now, while many developing countries keep pegging their currencies to the U.S. dollar, most countries have adopted a managed-float system that allows a free movement of their currencies within a certain limit. In order to reduce the volatility associated with free float, central banks generally intervene in the currency markets to smooth fluctuations.

A case in point is the Chinese yuan. For decades, China pegged the yuan firmly to the dollar. In the 1980s, however, the Chinese government substantially devaluated its currency to make trade more favorable. The Chinese economy exploded, and eventually the yuan froze again.[8]

Facing international pressure a decade later, China let the currency appreciate in 2005. The value of the yuan has since risen by more than 20 percent. China takes several measures to control the value of the yuan. According to official guidelines, the yuan may trade only 2 percent above or below a midpoint set daily by the Central Bank, People's Bank of China (PBOC). In its letter of approval towards China's devaluation, the IMF encouraged China to aim to achieve an effectively floating exchange rate system within two to three years.[9]

What are the benefits and costs of a fixed or pegged versus a floating or flexible exchange rate system? Which system is better? Under a fixed exchange system, a specific currency is pegged to another currency (or basket of currencies) and the central bank promises to exchange this currency at a specified rate against the other currency. A fixed exchange rate system promotes international trade by providing stability in international prices and reducing trading costs. However, a fixed exchange rate system may restrict a country's ability to contract or expand its money supply because of its need to maintain exchange rate parity. On the other hand, a floating exchange rate system provides a country with monetary policy independence and trade balance self-adjustment. The government does not have to maintain exchange rate parity and trade balance is automatically adjusted based on demand for and supply of a country's currency. Since there is no need for market intervention, there is a very low requirement for international reserves. Under the Bretton Woods system, IMF approval was necessary for remedying permanent deficit in a country's balance of payments that could not be corrected by domestic policy alone. However, the argument over the merits of a fixed exchange rate system have recently been revived due to dissatisfaction with floating exchange rates that result in volatile currency fluctuations, potentially increasing the risk of international financial crises. A fixed exchange rate system imposes monetary discipline on a government and limits speculation.

Under the Bretton Woods Agreement, the IMF and the World Bank, i.e. International Bank for Reconstruction and Development (IBRD), were established to serve different purposes. Accordingly, the mandate of the IMF was different from that of the World Bank. The former was created mainly to help member countries get out of financial crises by extending short-term loans and credits while the latter was established to support the economic development of developing countries through the provision of long-term concessionary loans to support public-sector projects such as building social infrastructure, improving secondary education, controlling birth rates, etc. Although the original purpose of creating the World Bank was to help war-torn European economies, the Marshall Plan took over the initial purpose of creating the World Bank and shifted its focus to the economic development of developing countries.

2. Primary Responsibilities of the IMF

The IMF has the following as its main responsibilities. First, it closely monitors the exchange rate policies of the member countries to preempt potential international financial crises. For example, the IMF recently applauded a series of moves by the Chinese government to devalue the yuan, as it would allow market forces to play a bigger role in determining the exchange rate.[10] China is even considering unpegging the U.S. dollar as it did in the past. This would be an important step toward achieving monetary-policy autonomy for the Chinese government, but destabilizing capital outflows could restrict the Chinese central bank from implementing it.[11]

Second, the IMF provides short-term financial assistance (including credits and loans) to its member countries who are experiencing financial difficulties. As these countries struggle to find banks and other creditors that are willing to provide needed capital, the IMF's financial support sends a positive signal to the market, encouraging private financial institutions to follow suit. There are usually three types of financial crises: banking crises, debt crises, and currency crises. A banking crisis mainly occurs when banks cannot collect their non-performing loans and people start withdrawing their deposits as they lose confidence in the banking system. A foreign debt crisis results from a country's excessive borrowing from international banks or creditors and its inability to service debt. Currency speculation on the exchange value of a currency typically brings about currency crisis. Regardless of the type of crisis, a financial crisis is often caused by the following macro-economic risk factors: high price inflation rates, increased government fiscal deficit, widening current account deficit, excessive expansion of domestic borrowing, etc. Third, the IMF offers technical assistance for afflicted countries by providing them with expertise and strategic consulting in devising fiscal and monetary policy. Many economists and financial experts work for the IMF and they are mainly market fundamentalists.

A country can become a member of the IMF by paying a membership due called a "quota." Since the quota amount is determined by the size of a country's economy, developed countries contribute more than developing countries to the IMF's monetary pool. The world's top five economies account for about 60 percent of the IMF total quota. As Figure 7.3 illustrates, the size of the quota is important as it directly correlates to the number of votes that a member country can exercise. This is why some critics assert that the IMF is not an international but more of a de facto U.S. organization since the U.S. holds the largest voting power in proportion to its quota contribution. Against such criticism, "the U.S. Senate ratified reforms in December 2015 to strengthen the representation of emerging economies at the IMF as part of a budget bill that will allow them to increase their voice in the IMF. The bill included a measure that placed Brazil, Russia, India, and China (BRIC) among the IMF's top ten shareholders and gave emerging economies greater voting power within the IMF. China's vote within the IMF would increase from 3.8 percent to 6 percent making the country the third largest shareholder, previously sixth, under the changes."[12]

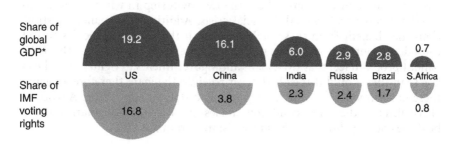

Figure 7.3 Shares of Global GDP and IMF Voting Rights 2014 (%)

Source: IMF.

3. IMF's Bailout Program

The IMF's prescription, a so-called bailout program typically includes measures such as currency devaluation, interest rate increase, and substantial
reduction in government spending, since it believes that financial crises are
attributed to hyperinflation, massive fiscal deficit, widening trade deficit, and
overvalued currency. In order to help countries eradicate the root causes of
financial crises, the IMF adopts the harsh austerity measures mentioned
above. Such a tough approach raises questions about the effectiveness of the
IMF bailout programs and whether they actually improve the affected country's economic and financial stability. The short-term focus of an austerity
package may adversely impact the economic development of bailed-out countries in the long term. In addition, frequent bailout actions can lead to moral
hazards as explained in greater detail below.

To summarize, the IMF's prescription has often been subject to the
following criticisms.

One-size fits all approach—The IMF follows an excessively rigid formula
when dealing with countries in financial distress. It applies more or less the
same approach to helping a country overcome financial suffering, although
the causes of a financial crisis may vary from one country to another. As a
result, the IMF is criticized for forcing recipient countries to adopt the same
policy reforms centered around austerity measures without considering
differences in economic status, business environment, and cultural norms
among the various countries. When the Asian financial crisis hit three countries in East Asia, i.e. Thailand, Indonesia, and South Korea, South Korea was
able to quickly recover from the financial downturn without following the
recommendations proposed by the IMF bailout program. In contrast,
Indonesia closely followed the IMF austerity measures but the country took
much longer than South Korea to recover from economic and financial
hardship.

Moral hazard issue—Moral hazard is a term used to describe reckless behavior
that people display when they know beforehand that such behavior will be
forgiven. In the context of the IMF, moral hazard refers to the imprudent
lending practices of international banks that assume that their loans are risk-
free since these institutions believe the IMF will step in when necessary to
avoid any large-scale global financial crisis. Additionally, financial institutions may benefit from these bailouts, even if they did lend recklessly and
caused or contributed to the problem. However, supporters of the IMF
bailout program feel that IMF loans allow governments to tighten their belts
less than they would if they had never received the loan, therefore allowing
these governments to avoid a complete shut down in spending. Advocates
also claim that the IMF's conditions are less punitive than the market would
be if the country didn't receive any assistance from the IMF.

Lack of accountability—Finally, the IMF has also been criticized for its
lack of accountability. As mentioned above, the IMF's austerity measures
often do not improve but exacerbate the already difficult economic and

financial situations of the country. Yet, there is no way to demand account-ability or responsibility from the IMF even when its bailout program does not work.

4. Evaluation of the IMF's Prescription

For the above reasons, there has been mounting resentment against the IMF. However, opposing views supporting the IMF prescriptions exist. We will analyze in detail the different views related to the effectiveness of the IMF's bailout program.

The IMF was created to promote global financial stability by helping member countries in trouble. However, some people question whether the IMF has effectively fulfilled its mission. Critics scrutinize the IMF's recent track record in handling the Asian financial crisis and declare its involvement as a failure. As mentioned above, economies of Indonesia and Thailand that have closely followed the IMF's prescriptions during the crisis have deteriorated while Malaysia and South Korea, countries that did not receive the IMF's support or strayed from IMF prescription, quickly recovered.

In evaluating these conflicting results, critics argue that the IMF's overall philosophy and models are outdated and only aggravate the economic situation of the countries it bails out.[13] When the IMF extends its short-term loans to a distressed country, it attaches conditions to the agreement. Critics believe that these economic policy requirements impose an extra burden on the people of the country. For example, the IMF typically demands that countries increase domestic interest rates, devalue currency, and reduce government spending, etc. In tackling the Greek debt crisis in the summer of 2015, the IMF required Greece to make public sector cuts, overhaul taxes, and change collective bargaining laws, if the country hoped to access the money to avoid financial collapse. In particular, the IMF insisted on deep reductions in pension spending as collateral for its involvement in the new rescue package, which elicited a strong resentment among the Greeks.[14]

These measures require further tightening of the belts of already cash-strapped countries and their people. In particular, emerging economies need to overcome severe difficulties in borrowing fresh capital during a downturn, and they often must tighten their belts or reduce spending when a more lax fiscal policy might otherwise be desirable. As Case 7.5 discusses, to meet this challenge, emerging economies have pushed for the IMF to create a new emergency financial device along the lines of the U.S. dollar swap that the FRB used during the recent global financial crisis. Unfortunately, the U.S., the IMF's largest shareholder, rejected this idea, contending that such a measure will make it more difficult to discipline emerging economies involved in currency swaps and create moral hazard issues.[15]

On the other hand, proponents of the IMF contend that the IMF prescrip-tion lessens austerity rather than aggravates it. To support this claim, first consider why the IMF becomes involved. The IMF rescues a country in financial trouble when no other institutions are willing to loan that country money. "Policymakers in distressed economies know that the IMF will intervene where no private creditor is willing to make loans at rates their countries could only dream of even in the best of times. In the short term, the IMF loans actually allow a distressed country to tighten its belt less than it would have to otherwise."[16] The economic policy conditions that the IMF imposes on a loan-recipient country are not as harsh as market forces would enforce without the IMF's intervention. Furthermore, making payments to the IMF is more manageable for the recipient country as the repayments to the Fund usually increase only after the financial crisis is over. The IMF also provides a key global economic forum for the exchange of ideas and best financial practices, and to assist nations in poverty along with the World Bank.

5. Future Prospect of the IMF

The IMF comes under greater scrutiny on what it does and could do better. Within the international community of stakeholders are valuable concerns and suggestions aimed at helping the IMF perform at maximum efficiency to better the global economy. The IMF should open communication among its members and increase transparency in relation to their prescriptions to increase implementation and identify areas of improvement. Greater input and involvement by the community in the IMF's decisions should produce greater performance by the Fund.

Furthermore, some crucial structural and political reforms are required within the IMF as a global financial institution to provide policy advice and finance countries when needed.

The IMF's governance needs to be fully modernized to reflect the increasing role of emerging economies. The Fund must revise its founding economic principles and expand its vision of the world's economic needs in order to provide meaningful and equitable growth. In this context, the launch of the New Development Bank or BRICS Bank, whose members include Brazil, Russia, India, China, and South Africa poses as a potential threat to the IMF and the World Bank. The organization aims to foster greater financial and development cooperation among emerging market economies. Additionally, the newly established Asian Infrastructure Investment Bank (AIIB), created through a Chinese initiative, may challenge the World Bank by offering global development funding. Greek response to the stringent terms of the IMF's bailout package implies that governments under pressure from their electorates might look elsewhere to borrow if alternatives are available. [17]

Key Terms

Foreign exchange market, spot exchange rate, forward exchange rate, currency swap, purchasing power parity, law of one price, undervaluation, overvaluation, Fisher effect, international Fisher effect, investor psychology, foreign exchange exposure, International Monetary Fund (IMF), Bretton Woods Agreement, moral hazard, fixed exchange rate, floating exchange rate

Review Questions

1. What are the main functions of the foreign exchange market?
2. How can an individual ensure against foreign exchange rate fluctuation? How does a company manage foreign exchange exposures?
3. What are the key economic variables that influence the determination of exchange rates? How is the absolute purchasing power parity theory different from the relative purchasing power parity theory?
4. How are the exchange rates determined in the short run?
5. What is the International Monetary Fund (IMF) and why has the IMF been subject to mounting criticism? What measures can be taken to improve the effectiveness of the IMF's prescription?

Internet Exercise

Please visit the following website: www.nytimes.com/interactive/2015/business/international/greece-debt-crisis-euro.html?_r=0 and discuss the main causes of the Greek debt crisis and its impacts on the global financial market. Why is Greece still in financial distress despite the rescue measures taken by the IMF and the European Central Bank?

Notes

1 McGrath, M. (2015). Currency swings take the air out of Coca-Cola fourth quarter profit. *Forbes*. Retrieved from www.forbes.com/sites/maggiemcgrath/2015/02/10/foreign-exchange-takes-the-air-out-of-coca-cola-fourth-quarter-profit/#46c55f3f10c7
2 Godoy, D., Orr, E., and Sambo, P. (2015). Brazilian real drops to record low against U.S. dollar. Bloomberg. Retrieved from www.bloomberg.com/news/articles/2015-09-22/brazil-s-currency-tumbles-to-record-on-pessimism-over-budget
3 *Economist*. (2015). The Big Mac index: Oily and easy. Retrieved from www.economist.com/news/finance-and-economics/21640370-some-currencies-lose-weight-diet-qe-and-cheap-oil-others-bulk-up-oily-and
4 D. H. and R. L. W. (2016). The Big Mac index: Global exchange rates, to go. *Economist*. Retrieved from www.economist.com/content/big-mac-index
5 Davis, O. (2015). Why is China devaluing its currency? U.S. lawmakers call it manipulation, others see China moving toward free markets. *International Business Times*. Retrieved from www.ibtimes.com/why-china-devaluing-its-currency-us-lawmakers-call-it-manipulation-others-see-china-2050418
6 Ngyuyen, L. (2016). Currency swings sap U.S. corporate profits most in 4 years. *Bloomberg Business*. Retrieved from www.bloomberg.com/news/articles/2016-01-13/currency-swings-sap-u-s-corporate-profits-by-most-in-four-years
7 McLaughlin, T. (2016). U.S. companies likely to take further big hits from Venezuela economic turmoil. *Business Insider*. Retrieved from www.businessinsider.com/r-us-companies-likely-to-take-further-big-hits-from-venezuela-economic-turmoil-2016-1
8 Davis, O. (2015). Why is China devaluing its currency? U.S. lawmakers call it manipulation, others see China moving toward free markets. *International Business Times*. Retrieved from www.ibtimes.com/why-china-devaluing-its-currency-us-lawmakers-call-it-manipulation-others-see-china-2050418

9   Ibid.
10 Ibid.
11 Wei, L. (2014). Why China is loosening the yuan's ties to the dollar. *Wall Street Journal*. Retrieved from www.wsj.com/articles/chinas-central-bank-defends-position-after-yuan-hits-four-year-low-1450068419
12 Chance, D. (2015). Reuters. Senate passes IMF reform in budget bill. Retrieved from http://www.reuters.com/article/us-usa-fiscal-imf-idUSKBN0U204J20151219
13 Stiglitz, J. (2001). Failure of the fund: Rethinking the IMF response. *Harvard International Review*. Columbia Business School. 14–18.
14 Resnikoff, N. (2015). Greece's new deal: From austerity to 'austerity squared.' Al Jazeera America. Retrieved from http://america.aljazeera.com/articles/2015/7/13/greeces-new-deal-from-austerity-to-austerity-squared.html
15 Talley, I. (2016). Emerging-market turmoil spurs IMF call for new crisis financing. *Wall Street Journal*. Retrieved from http://blogs.wsj.com/economics/2016/01/12/emerging-market-turmoil-spurs-imf-call-for-new-crisis-financing/
16 Rogoff, K. (2003). The IMF strikes back. *Foreign Policy, 134* (Jan.–Feb.), 38–46.
17 MacKenzie, K. (2015). Facing the future at the International Monetary Fund. BBC News. Retrieved from www.bbc.com/news/business-33652399

Part 3

Managing Global Business

Managing Entry and Exit Decisions

Learning Objectives

1. Know the key decisions a company should consider when entering a foreign market.
2. Learn to evaluate the benefits, costs, and risks of different location choices.
3. Understand major strategic directions and basic strategy types of international entry.
4. Compare and assess various entry modes a company may choose in a foreign market.
5. Recognize the importance of timing and entry scale as well as exit and relocation decisions.

Cases

Case 8.1 Disneyland Parks in East Asia

Disneyland Shanghai, the newest Disney theme park, opened in June 2016. It is the fourth Disneyland outside of the U.S. and the third in East Asia. Not far away from Shanghai, there is already one Disneyland in Tokyo and another in Hong Kong. Some industry observers doubt if the region can accommodate that many Disneyland parks and worry about possible self-cannibalization. But Disney seems to have high hopes and believes the three parks will attract different visitors.

Tokyo Disneyland in Japan was Disney's first theme park in Asia. Its construction began in 1980 and cost approximately 180 billion yen. The park officially opened in April 1983 and reached ten million visitors the following year. Tokyo Disney Resort is actually owned and operated by an independent Japanese corporation, Oriental Land Co., Ltd. (OLC). Disney has a licensing agreement with OLC and earns royalties on the revenue of

Tokyo Disney Resort. After continuous development, Tokyo Disney Resort currently has 494 acres of land, two theme parks (Tokyo Disneyland and Tokyo DisneySea), three Disney-branded hotels (with over 1,700 rooms in total), six independently operated hotels, as well as retail, dining, and entertainment facilities. In 2014, Tokyo Disneyland hosted 17.3 million visitors, making it the world's second most visited theme park behind Disney's Magic Kingdom in Florida. Also in that year, OLC announced a ten-year, 500-billion-yen investment plan for the resort. The plan included expanding Fantasyland at Disneyland, adding a Scandinavian-themed area at DisneySea featuring *Frozen*, a popular Disney movie, building the fourth Disney-branded hotel, and other improvements.

The second Disneyland in Asia is located in Hong Kong. Its construction began in January 2003 at a total cost of $1.8 billion USD. Hong Kong Disneyland officially opened in September 2005. It is owned and managed by Hong Kong International Theme Parks, a joint venture of Disney (47 percent equity) and the Hong Kong government (53 percent equity). In addition to return on equity, Disney also receives royalties and management fees based on the resort's operating performance. This resort has 310 acres of land and is located close to the Hong Kong International Airport. It includes one theme park and two resort hotels (about 1,000 rooms in total). The park consists of seven themed areas: Adventureland, Fantasyland, Grizzly Gulch, Main Street USA, Mystic Point, Tomorrowland, and Toy Story Land. A new themed area based on Marvel's *Iron Man* just opened in January 2017. A new hotel with 750 rooms is also under construction.

The newest development is Shanghai Disneyland, located in Pudong district, southeast of downtown Shanghai. Shanghai Disney Resort consists of one theme park, two theme hotels with a total of 1,220 rooms, a 46,000-square-meter retail, dining, and entertainment venue, outdoor recreational facilities, a lake, and associated parking and transport hubs. In particular, this Disneyland park has the largest theme park castle in the world. The resort is reportedly budgeted at a cost of 24.5 billion yuan (about $3.7 billion USD) for the theme park and an additional 4.5 billion yuan (about $700 million USD) for other facilities. It began the 963-acre first phase in April 2011 and eventually will be expanded to 1,730 acres. Shanghai Disney Resort is owned by Shanghai International Theme Park Company, a joint venture of which Shanghai Shendi Group has 57 percent and Disney owns 43 percent. Shanghai Shendi Group is a consortium formed by three state-owned companies. In addition, a management company, Shanghai International Theme Park and Resort Management Company, of which Disney owns 70 percent and Shendi 30 percent, has been created to design, construct and operate Shanghai Disney Resort on behalf of the owner. While the management company charges management fees based on the resort's operating performance, Disney collects royalties based on the revenue of the resort.

From negotiation to completion, this mega project took more than 15 years. Finally, tickets for Shanghai Disneyland are available for sale. The price of a one-day ticket is 370 yuan (about $56 USD) on weekdays and 499 yuan on weekends and holidays. There is a 25 percent discount for children, disabled people, and seniors (over 65 years old). A two-day ticket doubles the daily rate plus a 5 percent discount. All tickets are date-specific and cover all entertainment and attractions within the park. The two-tiered pricing and date-specific tickets were designed to spread visits throughout the year, according to a press release by the resort. In fact, Shanghai Disneyland has the lowest price among all Disneyland parks in the world. A one-day ticket at Hong Kong Disney is HK$539 (about $69 USD) while Tokyo Disneyland charges 6,900 yen (about $61 USD). Tickets in Florida, California, and Paris are priced even higher. The Shanghai resort estimates it will attract 16 million visitors in the first year, bringing in over 10 billion yuan in revenue. After all the construction is finished, it expects to handle 40 million visitors a year.

It is possible that this gigantic park will hurt the performance of the other two Disneyland parks in the region. Especially for Hong Kong Disneyland, 40 percent of its visitors are from mainland China, who may easily switch to the newer and bigger Shanghai Disneyland. Furthermore, amid a decline in Hong Kong tourism, Hong Kong Disney Resort had a HK$148 million ($19 million USD) loss for the fiscal year of 2015, a drop from a HK$332 million profit a year ago. Its revenue dropped 7.3 percent to HK$5.1 billion, and visitor numbers fell 9.3 percent to 6.8 million. Their executives have reportedly described the Shanghai park as a "devastating blow" to Hong Kong Disneyland.

However, Disney and the Shanghai government seem to have a different view. They believe that the two Disney theme parks in China do not necessarily compete with each other as they have different features and target different visitors. In a way, Shanghai Disneyland is different from all other Disney parks. It features an 11-acre greenbelt hub that is home to Enchanted Storybook Castle, the park's central icon. It has unique areas like Adventure Isle, Treasure Cove, Gardens of Imagination, and other one-of-a-kind attractions and experiences.

According to International Theme Park Services, there are more than 60 theme parks being planned in China.[a] Many foreign investors are eyeing China's dynamic economy, rising middle class, and huge population. For Disney, the world's largest theme park group, it is critical to quickly enter the huge market of mainland China. The new location provides not only a new venue to promote Disney's intellectual property but also a valuable intelligence gathering point to understand what will play best to Chinese audiences. For Shanghai, the Disney resort added a classic brand to its "international tourism zone" in Pudong district. "This project will help improve Shanghai's profile as a world-famous tourism destination and lend a big boost to the development of culture and leisure industries of Shanghai," said the mayor of Shanghai.[b]

Notes

a. He, A. (2016, January 14). Shanghai Disney to do well. Retrieved from http://usa.chinadaily.com.cn/business/2016-01/14/content_23093476.htm
b. BBC News. (2011, April 8). Shanghai Disneyland project breaks ground at last. Retrieved from www.bbc.com/news/world-asia-pacific-13009078

Sources

1. Barboza, D. and Barnes, B. (2011, April 7). Disney plans lavish park in Shanghai. *New York Times.* Retrieved from www.nytimes.com/2011/04/08/business/media/08disney.html?pagewanted=all
2. Disney Annual Reports. Retrieved from https://thewaltdisneycompany.com/investor-relations/#reports
3. MacDonald, B. (2016, March 30). Disney drives explosive theme park expansion in China. *Los Angeles Times.* Retrieved from www.latimes.com/travel/themeparks/la-trb-china-theme-park-expansion-20140903-story.html
4. Rapoza, K. (2012, March 21). Shanghai Disneyland driving foreign investment into city. *Forbes.* Retrieved from www.forbes.com/sites/kenrapoza/2012/03/21/shanghai-disneyland-driving-foreign-investment-into-city/
5. BBC News. (2011, April 8). Shanghai Disneyland project breaks ground at last. Retrieved from www.bbc.com/news/world-asia-pacific-13009078
6. Yang, J. (2016, February 4). Disneyland ticket prices announced. *Shanghai Daily.* Retrieved from www.shanghaidaily.com/metro/society/Disneyland-ticket-prices-announced/shdaily.shtml

Questions for Case Discussion

1. Is entering Shanghai the right move for Disneyland? Why?
2. Compare and evaluate the entry modes used by Disney in the three locations.
3. What are your thoughts on the future prospects of the three Disneyland parks in East Asia?

Case 8.2 Target's Departure from Canada

For many American retailers seeking international expansion, Canada seems like a natural destination just across the border. Wal-Mart and Sears have been in Canada for years. As one of the largest discount retailers in the U.S, Target has been looking for areas to expand. In 2011, Target ventured into the Canadian market by purchasing a part of Zellers, a Canadian retail chain, for about $1.8 billion USD. The deal allowed Target to take over the leases of about 220 of Zellers' 279 locations. It planned to spend $1 billion USD converting 150 Zellers stores to Target stores and sublet the rest.

According to the former CEO of Target, Gregg Steinhafel, the Canadian market has been something of interest to Target for a very long time.[a] It is geographically close to Target's headquarters in Minneapolis. Many Canadian consumers are familiar with the company and frequently shop at Target stores across the border. Furthermore, Canadian malls typically have much higher sales per square foot than American malls. Comparatively, the Canadian retail market is less competitive and less sensitive to economic recessions. Especially in 2011, with a strong Canadian dollar and a relatively robust economy, Canada looked very promising. Target's own research also showed that more than 10 percent of Canadians had shopped at Target stores in the U.S. during 2010. Naturally, Canada became the company's first international market.

In Canada, one major problem facing large retailers is the shortage of available space in prime locations. A small number of property companies controlled by pension and government funds largely dominate retail spaces. These companies are often unwilling to take risks on new retailers. Therefore, acquisition seemed like a good way for Target to gain an immediate presence in Canada without having to establish new stores from scratch. Similarly, when Wal-Mart arrived in Canada 17 years ago, it started with a base of 100 Woolco stores it had bought. Target's deal with Zellers allowed the company to select which locations it wanted to acquire. Most of the locations were located in dense urban areas, including Vancouver, Montreal, Ottawa, Edmonton, and Calgary. Target planned to open at least 125 Canadian stores in 2013 and largely copy the operations of American stores with only small changes. The company expected financial returns on the Canadian stores to be in line with new U.S. Target stores. "We've heard loud and clear from our guests that shop across the border that they want the true Target when it comes to Canada," said Lisa Gibson, a spokeswoman of Target.[b]

Nevertheless, in early 2015, right after the holiday shopping season, Target announced a plan to close its 133 stores in Canada just a few years after entry. This move would result in over $5.6 billion USD pre-tax losses due to the write-down of investment in Canada, exit costs, and operating losses. It also meant that about 17,000 people would lose their jobs. This hard decision seemed justified by numbers. The Canadian unit had a total loss of $122 million USD in 2011, $369 million USD in 2012, and $941 million USD in 2013. In the first nine months of 2014, while sales increased 90 percent to $1.32 billion USD, the loss already reached $627 million USD before interest and taxes. In total, the money-draining Canadian business had a net loss of $2 billion USD since 2011, severely hurting Target's overall profitability. Upon the store closing announcement, Target's stock price actually rose.

Indeed, cracking the Canadian retail market may be harder than it looks. First of all, business costs are generally higher in Canada. Since the Canadian retail market size is about one tenth of the U.S. market, it is harder to spread costs and gain economies of scale. Additional costs may be incurred due to costly regulations. Also, Canada has a bilingual requirement. All product packaging must be in both English and French. The province of Quebec requires large retailers to conduct business in French. However, retailers cannot simply increase prices to cover extra expenses related to the language issue. Since most Canadians live near the U.S. border, they can easily shop in the U.S. for lower prices. Furthermore, there is increasing competition. To fend off Target, other retailers stepped up their competitive efforts. Sears' Canadian unit refurbished its stores and changed merchandise. Wal-Mart adjusted prices to stress its low-price advantage. Other smaller or specialty retailers, such as Canadian Tire and Shoppers Drug Mart, upgraded stores, modified product offerings, or reinvented marketing campaigns.

After Target opened over 100 stores in the first year, problems cropped up quickly. Customers found prices at Target's Canadian stores were higher than expected. Many stores were poorly stocked with limited selections or even short of basic products. Shoppers complained that they could not find the brands they had seen and liked in American stores. Many Canadians said that even the old Zellers stores, which were mostly run-down, had offered better value and more products. Target also failed to differentiate itself from other retailers, whose offerings were similar to those of Target. Some Target executives believed that the company took on too much too fast from the beginning. Others noted that Target sent internal managers with little international experience to run the Canadian unit. Finally, a weak holiday season was the last straw.

Several other retailers have also failed in Canada. Sales slump forced Big Lots to close nearly 80 stores only three years after its acquisition of Liquidation World, a Canadian retail chain. The fashion company Mexx closed all of its 95 stores in Canada. The electronic giant Sony closed all 14 of its Canadian stores. Even Sam's Club, Wal-Mart's membership-only warehouse club, ceased operations in Canada. Certainly, there are also success stories. Wal-Mart entered Canada early in 1994 and has grown into the largest retailer in the country. Wal-Mart's Canadian unit carries only 20 percent of the products sold in its American stores, and offers a variety of products that are popular in Canada, such as wine gums and mini-pepperoni. Moving at a slow pace, Nordstrom opened its first Canadian store in 2014 and added two more in 2015. "You can't just say that we are close in proximity or we both speak English, so it should be the same," said Blake Nordstrom, president of the Seattle-based Nordstrom chain. "We recognize there are differences. That's probably why we've been slow in coming to Canada."[c] Many other retailers, including Costco, Home Depot, H&M, and Zara, are expanding businesses in Canada. Target's experience may have taught them a lesson.

Notes

a.   Target. (2012), Annual Report. Retrieved from https://corporate.target.com/_ media/TargetCorp/annualreports/content/download/pdf/Annual-Report. pdf?ext=.pdf
b.   Austen, I. and Clifford, S. (2012, September 14). American retailers face challenges in expanding to Canada. Retrieved from www.nytimes.com/2012/ 09/15/business/american-retailers-expanding-to-canada.html
c.   Ibid.

Sources

1.   Austen, I. and Tabuchi, H. (2015, January 15). Target's red ink runs out in Canada. *New York Times.* Retrieved from www.nytimes.com/2015/01/16/business/ target-to-close-stores-in-canada.html
2.   Kell, J. (2015, January 15). Target says it will pull out of Canada after failed expansion. *Fortune.* Retrieved from http://fortune.com/2015/01/15/target-to-exit-canada-market/
3.   Peterson, H. (2014, August 20). Target's Canadian expansion is still draining profits. *Business Insider.* Retrieved from www.businessinsider.com/targets-canadian-expansion-2014-8
4.   Tilak, J. (2011, January 13). Target to enter Canada with Zellers deal, own plans. Reuters. Retrieved from www.reuters.com/article/2015/01/15/us-target-canada-idUSKBN0KO1HR20150115

Questions for Case Discussion

1. What strategy did Target use to enter Canada?
2. Why did Target's strategy fail? Did the company do anything right?
3. If you were the CEO of Target, how would you enter international markets differently?

Case 8.3 Newcomers in European Automobile Markets

As one of the largest auto markets in the world, the European market always attracts much attention from automakers all around the world. It was dominated by European, American, and Japanese companies for decades until recently. Several newcomers or latecomers from Asia, notably Hyundai from Korea, Tata Motors from India, and Geely from China, have been making waves since 2007. These companies hope global expansion can bring them economies of scale, supply chain flexibility, and greater market access. Their presence has made the European auto market ever more crowded.

Founded in 1967, the Korea-based Hyundai Motor Company, has grown into a large multinational automaker. After its successful entry into the U.S. and China, Hyundai increased its efforts in Europe. In 1994, Hyundai set up its first European operation, an R&D center in Germany. The goal was to monitor car technologies in Europe and design new vehicles for European consumers. In 1997, Hyundai launched a manufacturing plant in Turkey to make cars for not only Europe but also Middle East and African markets. In 2007, the capacity of the Turkey plant was expanded 67 percent to 100,000 vehicles per year. Three models (Hyundai Accent, Hyundai Elantra, and Hyundai Santa Fe) were being produced there. However, Hyundai's operations in Europe were modest until the company built another plant in the Czech Republic. All models produced in the Czech plant (Hyundai i30, Hyundai i30 wagon, Hyundai i30 3-dr, Hyundai ix20, and Hyundai ix35) were specially designed for the European market. Using a three-shift schedule, the Czech plant reached its full capacity of 300,000 vehicles per year in 2012, and continued full-capacity production in 2013 and 2014. Moreover, a third plant was opened in Saint Petersburg, Russia. This plant has a capacity of 200,000 vehicles and is equipped with modern automation machineries including 185 robots. It produces affordable models like Hyundai Solaris mainly for the Russian market.

The R&D center and the three manufacturing plants are all part of Hyundai Motor Europe, a wholly owned subsidiary of the Korean parent company. Their expansion in Europe has generated many new employment opportunities. For instance, the Czech plant and its subcontractors have produced over 10,000 jobs, and over 96 percent of employees were hired locally. The Russia plant has created approximately 7,000 positions and reached 46 percent localization in 2015. Building plants in lower-cost areas to serve local markets has been a major strategy of Hyundai. The company has made its entry into the U.S. by selling quality cars at low prices. Hyundai is using the same approach in Europe by combining value, quality, and longer-than-average warranties.

According to the *European Vehicle Market Statistics Pocketbook 2013* issued by the International Council on Clean Transportation, new passenger car registrations in Europe have fallen from 15.6 million in 2007 to 12.0 million in 2013, a decline of 23 percent.[a] Despite the general downward trend, Hyundai's sales and market share both have gone up against most European mainstream competitors like Ford, Opel, Fiat, and Citroën since 2009. Hyundai's retail sales continuously increased from 405,040 vehicles in 2013 to 417,100 in 2014. Its market share also increased to 5.1 percent, ahead of Toyota, Mercedes-Benz, and Volvo. The company has become a serious challenger to Volkswagen, the market leader. At the Frankfurt show 2013, Hyundai announced plans to introduce 22 new models by 2017. "It's very important for Hyundai to be successful", said Allan Rushforth, Hyundai's chief operating officer in Europe, "Europe is a top priority because it affects how the company is perceived elsewhere."[b]

This comment was echoed by Tata Motors, the automobile company of Tata Group, a giant conglomerate based in India. Tata Motors was ranked 287th in the 2014 Fortune Global 500 ranking of the world's biggest corporations. In March 2008, Tata Motors acquired the Jaguar Land Rover (JLR) business from Ford for $2.3 billion USD in an all-cash transaction. Jaguar has manufactured cars for the British royal family and prime ministers. Land Rover is the second oldest four-wheel-drive car brand in the world (after Jeep). The purchase of JLR included intellectual properties, manufacturing plants, two advanced design centers in the U.K., and a worldwide network of sales companies.

Tata Motors also made a promise not to layoff workers after the acquisition. They kept the promise and there was not even an attempt to impose Indian managers. All key personnel retained their positions. Upon completion of the deal, Mr. Ratan Tata, Chairman of Tata Motors said:

> Jaguar Land Rover will retain their distinctive identities and continue to pursue their respective business plans as before. We recognize the significant improvement in the performance of the two brands and look forward to this trend continuing in the coming years. It is our intention to work closely to support the Jaguar Land Rover team in building the success and pre-eminence of the two brands.

In recent years, JLR has achieved strong performance. For fiscal year 2015, JLR recorded revenue of 21,866 million GBP, a 12.8 percent increase from 2014. Wholesale volumes in fiscal 2015 increased 9.5 percent to 470,523 units, and retail volumes increased 6.4 percent to 462,209 units. Since other units of Tata Motors have been losing money, JLR generates over 80 percent of consolidated revenue and almost 100 percent profit for the parent company. Acquisition of JLR has helped Tata Motors become a top global automaker and achieve financial success. With that, Tata Motors has started introducing its own line of Tata branded vehicles into Europe and the rest of the world. In 2010, Tata launched the electric version of Indica Vista by the name Indica Vista EV in Europe. At the International Geneva Motor Show in 2011, Tata Motors unveiled Pixel, a small city-car based on Indian-made Tata Nano, for European drivers.

Geely from China, a private automobile enterprise founded in 1986, has a similar global ambition. Geely's car models are known for unusual designs, unusual names, as well as incredibly low prices. Most of its cars are priced below 100,000 Chinese yuan (about $16,000 USD). Its vehicles are mostly sold in China, and the rest are exported to developing countries like Cuba, Algeria, and Iran. In 2010, Geely sold over 415,000 vehicles, about 2.6 percent market share in China. Also in 2010, the company completed the full acquisition of Volvo Cars Corporation from Ford for $1.8 billion USD.

Volvo, a Swedish premium automobile manufacturer, was founded in 1927 with headquarters in Gothenburg, Sweden. Volvo cars have gained a reputation for solidity and reliability. In 1999, Ford Motors acquired Volvo for $6 billion USD as part of its strategy to expand in the European luxury car market. However, in the mid-2000s, Volvo car sales faltered due to increasing competition, changing consumer preferences, and unfavorable exchange rates. Despite efforts of restructuring and cost cutting, Volvo continued to lose more money. Eventually, Ford decided to sell the Volvo unit to Geely.

Upon hearing the deal between Ford and Geely, Volvo was stirred up immediately. Both management and workers were worried that acquisition might lead to the relocation of production and the offshoring of jobs. Li Shufu, chairman and founder of Geely, assured Volvo that the automaker would keep its own management team, board of directors, headquarters in Sweden, and its Swedish heritage and cachet. Li said, "We will remain true to Volvo's core values of safety, quality, environmental care and modern Scandinavian design as it strengthens the existing European and North American markets and expands its presence in China and other emerging markets."* In Li's vision, Geely and Volvo, while managed separately, can help each other succeed in the global automotive industry.

In order to enter the global market, Geely needs technology and a global production and marketing platform. It hopes to become a maker of affordable high-tech cars rather than just another cheap, no-frills Chinese brand. The acquisition of Volvo, an established brand known for safety and quality, gave Geely a stepping stone. In 2015, Geely launched its new flagship vehicle called GC9, a mid-size sedan designed by Volvo designer Peter Horbury. The company is also set to release a new small crossover SUV, the first car to be built using a common platform jointly developed with Volvo. These cars are to be sold not only in China but also in Europe. The fruits of the acquisition are already evident.

Meanwhile, Geely has increased its investment in Volvo. In 2012, Geely announced an investment of $11 billion USD for a new engine factory, increased R&D, and technology upgrades in order to revive Volvo. Geely and Volvo opened a new R&D facility in Gothenburg in 2013. The first output of the investment program is the all-new XC90, launched in August 2014. Volvo also expanded manufacturing capacity from 200,000 cars a year to 300,000 at its plant in Torslanda, Sweden, adding over 1,300 new employees. Volvo returned to profit in 2013 and 2014. Driven by a complete renewal of its product line, the company is aiming to sell around 800,000 cars per year by 2020.

With Geely's support, China has become Volvo's largest market. Starting in 2013, Volvo has also expanded its manufacturing footprint in China. Some car models are made in two new plants in China to serve not only local needs but also international markets. According to the CEO of Volvo, Hakan Samuelsson, Volvo plans to start exporting some cars produced in China to the U.S. It would be the first time for a "Made-in-China" vehicle to be sold in America.

Notes

a. International Council on Clean Transportation. (2013). European Vehicle Market Statistics Pocketbook 2013. Retrieved from www.theicct.org/sites/default/files/publications/EU_vehiclemarket_pocketbook_2013_Web.pdf

b. Reiter, C. (2012, January 26). Having thrived in America, Hyundai takes on Europe. Retrieved from www.bloomberg.com/news/articles/2012-01-26/having-thrived-in-america-hyundai-takes-on-europe

c. Volvo Press Release. (2010, August 2). Zhejiang Geely completes acquisition of Volvo Car Corporation. Stefan Jacoby named President and CEO of Volvo Cars. Retrieved from www.media.volvocars.com/global/en-gb/media/pressreleases/34397

Sources

1. Bajaj, V. (2012, August 30). Tata Motors finds success in Jaguar Land Rover. *New York Times*. Retrieved from www.nytimes.com/2012/08/31/business/global/tata-motors-finds-success-in-jaguar-land-rover.html

2. Fidler, S. (2010, October 6). Geely wants to sell Chinese cars in Europe. *Wall Street Journal*. Retrieved from www.wsj.com/articles/SB10001424052748703735804575535944194891242

3. Hyundai Motor. Europe retail sales. Retrieved from http://worldwide.hyundai.com/WW/Corporate/InvestorRelations/IRActivities/SalesPerformance/EuropeRetailSales/index.html

4. Reiter, C. (2012, January 26). Having thrived in America, Hyundai takes on Europe. Bloomberg. Retrieved from www.bloomberg.com/bw/magazine/having-thrived-in-america-hyundai-takes-on-europe-01262012.html

5. Tata Group Company Profile. Retrieved from www.tata.com/investordesk

6. International Council on Clean Transportation. (2013). *European Vehicle Market Statistics Pocketbook 2013*. Retrieved from www.theicct.org/sites/default/files/publications/EU_vehiclemarket_pocketbook_2013_Web.pdf

7. *Economist*. (2014, September 5). The $11 billion gamble. Retrieved from www.economist.com/news/business-and-finance/21615677-volvo

8. Yang, J. (2015, March 27). With Volvo's help, Geely goes upscale. *Automotive News*. Retrieved from http://europe.autonews.com/article/20150327/BLOG15/150329873/with-volvos-help-geely-goes-upscale

Questions for Case Discussion

1. Why did Hyundai, Tata Motors, and Geely all invest in the crowded European market?
2. Compare and evaluate the strategic purposes of the three companies in Europe.
3. What entry modes did they use? Why did they use different entry modes?

Case 8.4 Starbucks' Journey in the Chinese Market

It was January 11, 1999, a chilly day in Beijing. The first Starbucks Coffee in China opened after a traditional lion dance. This marked the beginning of Starbucks' exciting journey into mainland China.

Established in 1987, the Seattle-based Starbucks has been expanding internationally. The first Starbucks store outside of North America was set up in Tokyo in 1996. The coffee chain entered the U.K. market in 1998 by acquiring Seattle Coffee Company and re-branding all its stores as Starbucks. Impressed by China's large urban population and fast-growing economy, Starbucks predicted the country's emerging middle class would become a great market for Western-style coffee experience. However, China is a complicated country with vast regional differences and a strong tea-drinking tradition. Starbucks decided to take a cautious approach to entering into this massive market by cooperating with local partners. Also at that time, it was required to form joint ventures due to government restrictions on ownership structure. Starbucks set the following criteria for partner selection:

- Share Starbucks' values, corporate citizenship, and long-term commitment
- Have multi-unit restaurant experience
- Possess financial resources to expand quickly to prevent imitations
- Own experience and knowledge in finding prime real estate locations
- Have knowledge of the retail market
- Keep people who are committed to Starbucks' projects.

Eventually, Starbucks identified three regional partners. Using their local resources and knowledge, these partners helped Starbucks break into the Chinese market.

In the north, Starbucks set up a joint venture called Beijing Meida coffee company with H&Q Asia Pacific, a leading private equity firm that has operations all over the Asia-Pacific region, and Beijing Sanyuan, a local food and beverage company. According to their contract, H&Q Asia Pacific had majority ownership, but Starbucks could buy more shares after five years in operation with price subject to negotiation. Starbucks authorized an exclusive license to Beijing Meida in Beijing and Taijin (a nearby port city).

Along the east coast line, Starbucks partnered with Uni-President Group and formed a joint venture called Shanghai Uni-President Starbucks Coffee. Uni-President Group was a large food conglomerate based in Taiwan and had significant market shares in China's dairy products, foods and snacks, and beverages markets. Starbucks and Uni-President Group already had another joint venture in Taiwan and opened Taiwan's first Starbucks store in 1998. The Shanghai joint venture was authorized to run Starbucks stores in Shanghai and neighboring Jiangsu and Zhejiang provinces. It opened Shanghai's first Starbucks store in 2000 and earned a net profit of 32 million Chinese yuan (about $4 million USD at that time) in less than two years.

In southern China, Starbucks set up Coffee Concepts (Southern China) Ltd., a joint venture with Hong Kong-based Maxim's Caterers. Starbucks granted Coffee Concepts an authorized licensee to operate Starbucks stores in Guangdong province. Maxim's Caterers was the largest food service company in Hong Kong, operating over 60 brands and 360 outlets including various restaurants, cake shops, and catering units. Starbucks also partnered with Maxim's Caterers in Hong Kong and Macau. They opened the first Starbucks store in Hong Kong in May 2000 and expanded to 30 stores within two years. In August 2003, they opened the first Starbucks store in Guangdong province.

Joint venturing seemed an effective way for Starbucks to quickly expand in China. In 2002, Starbucks has 88 licensed stores in China. The number increased to 116 in 2003 and 152 in 2004. Also, those shops turned profitable far more quickly than stores in any other overseas markets. It was forecast that China would soon become the firm's largest market outside of North America. Given China's strong growth, Starbucks felt it was time to adjust its strategy. The chairman and CEO of Starbucks, Howard Schultz said,

> The Starbucks growth model has been successful with many different types of ownership structures. From time to time we revise those owner-ship structures because of strategic opportunities. . . . In 1999, we didn't have the infrastructure that we have today in China. Now we are more prepared and more capable of doing things. That might mean, over time, some changes in equity.[a]

Meanwhile, after China joined the World Trade Organization in 2001, many government restrictions on foreign investment were removed, allowing Starbucks to change equity structures.

In 2003, Starbucks paid $21.3 million USD to raise its stake in Shanghai Uni-President Starbucks Coffee Ltd from 5 percent to 50 percent. Correspondingly, its partner Uni-President Group's share dropped from 95 percent to 50 percent. In June 2005, Starbucks increased its stake in Coffee Concepts to 51 percent from 5 percent for an undisclosed sum. In exchange for allowing Starbucks' equity increase, Maxim's Caterers received a ten-year contract extension in Hong Kong and was able to gain 30 percent equity in a new joint venture with Starbucks in Chengdu, a major city in southwestern China. In October 2006, Starbucks acquired shares of Beijing Meida from H&Q Asia Pacific, increasing its stake to 90 percent. Beijing Sanyuan continued holding 10 percent as a minority shareholder. Furthermore, to speed up market expansion, Starbucks opened nine wholly owned stores during 2005–6 in other Chinese cities, including Qingdao in eastern China's Shandong province, Dalian and Shenyang in northeastern China's Liaoning province. As of October 1, 2006, Starbucks had 190 stores in 19 Chinese cities. In 2008, Starbucks had more than 600 stores and expanded to 26 cities in China. It was estimated that Starbucks' sales growth averaged 30 percent annually from 2006 to 2011. According to Euromonitor, a London-based research firm, Starbucks dominated China's coffee shop market with a 66.3 percent share in 2010, trailed by Costa Coffee chain (8.9 percent) and McDonald's Corp (8 percent). While remaining mainly a tea-drinking nation, China's coffee sales witnessed strong growth and reached 6.25 billion Chinese yuan (about $995 million USD then) in 2011.

Today Starbucks is aiming to increase the number of wholly owned stores and to take full control of the stores in China. In June 2011, after purchasing the shares owned by Maxim's Caterers, Starbucks acquired full ownership of over 100 stores in southern China. "Full ownership of our stores in Central, South and Western China is part of our broader strategy to build China as our second home market outside the US," said John Culver, the head of Starbucks' international operation.[b] The only remaining exception is Shanghai and the nearby Jiangsu and Zhejiang provinces, where it still has a 50–50 joint venture with Taiwan's Uni-President. As of 2015, there were 1,811 Starbucks stores in more than 60 Chinese cities, among which 1,026 were Starbucks-operated and 785 licensed stores. The store average sales were above $700,000 USD per year. Their operating margin and sales growth were both greater than the stores in North America. The company had tremendous confidence in China and planned to build more stores to drive future growth.

Notes

a. Li, H. (2006, June 17). Starbucks still brewing up a storm. Retrieved from www.chinadaily.com.cn/bizchina/2006-06/13/content_616003_3.htm
b. Starbucks Press Release. (2011, June 1). Starbucks acquires full ownership of Starbucks stores in Central, South & Western China. Retrieved from https://news.starbucks.com/news/starbucks-acquires-full-ownership-of-starbucks-stores-in-central-south-west

Sources

1. Zhu, W. (2013, July 29). Starbucks sees big growth in China. CNN. Retrieved from http://money.cnn.com/2013/07/26/news/companies/starbucks-china-sales-surge/
2. Horovitz, B. (2013, September 16). China to become No. 2 market for Starbucks. *USA Today*. Retrieved from www.usatoday.com/story/money/business/2013/09/16/starbucks-china-flagship-stores/2820885/
3. Wong, V. (2013, November 1). Starbucks gets ready to go from tall to venti in China. *Business Week*. Retrieved from www.businessweek.com/articles/2013-11-01/starbucks-gets-ready-to-go-from-tall-to-venti-in-china
4. Sandholm, D. (2014, July 25). Finally, Starbucks has 'breakthrough' in China. CNBC. Retrieved from www.cnbc.com/id/101867508#
5. Knowledge at Wharton. (2012, April 3). Starbucks moves to the express(o) lane in China. University of Pennsylvania. Retrieved from http://knowledge.wharton.upenn.edu/article/starbucks-moves-to-the-expresso-lane-in-china/

Questions for Case Discussion

1. Why did Starbucks use joint ventures to enter China initially?
2. Why did Starbucks shift its focus to wholly owned stores later?
3. What can we learn from the evolution of Starbucks' ownership structure in China?

Case 8.5 KFC's Bold Entry into Myanmar

KFC is a large fast food chain with more than 18,000 restaurants in over a hundred countries. In 2015, KFC opened its first restaurant in Yangon,

Myanmar (Burma). It was also the first American fast food chain that entered the country. The chain's parent company, Yum! Brands, selected a Singaporean company, Yoma Strategic, to be the franchise partner for KFC in Myanmar. Yoma Strategic is a leading regional company in agriculture, automotive, tourism, and real estate. It made its first foray into Myanmar by acquiring a local beverage and alcohol distributor. In 2013, Yoma Strategic opened Myanmar's first international department store. Bringing KFC to Myanmar was an important step for Yoma Strategic to become a key player in the country's food and beverage sector.

Both KFC and Yoma Strategic were optimistic about future business growth in Myanmar. It is the second largest country in Southeast Asia with over 50 million people, bordering India, Bangladesh, China, Laos, and Thailand. Yangon is the country's largest city and capital. Myanmar was under military rule for nearly five decades until it transitioned to a civilian government in 2011. The new government has started political reforms and economic overhauls. In response, the U.S. and other governments lifted many economic sanctions on this huge, untapped market. A considerable amount of foreign investment has flowed into Myanmar to take advantage of its abundant natural resources, young labor force, and proximity to Asia's dynamic economies. Pledged foreign direct investment grew from $1.4 billion USD in 2012 to $4.1 billion USD in 2013. The country also witnessed significant economic growth. It scored an 8.3 percent annual GDP growth in 2013, and a 7.7 percent growth in 2014. GDP per capita increased from $4,400 USD in 2013 to $4,700 USD in 2014.

"Myanmar offers significant potential for an international quick service franchise, with a growing consumer class that is forecast to grow from 2.5 million today to 19 million in 2030," Yoma Strategic stated in its announcement of the KFC deal.[a] An increasing number of Western-style restaurants had rushed in to catch business opportunities. In Yangon, now there are Freshness Burger from Japan, Manhattan Fish Market from Singapore, Lotteria from South Korea, and Marrybrown from Malaysia. However, none of them has the cachet of a global brand like KFC.

Despite Myanmar's recent progress, foreign investors face many challenges, such as endemic corruption, poor infrastructure, rampant intellectual property violations, and the lack of skilled workforce. There are also serious concerns about political uncertainties and ethnic conflicts. "Crony companies", the businesses tied to the military regime, are still a big part of the local economy. Moreover, Myanmar remains one of the poorest countries in Asia. Nearly one-third of the country's population lives in poverty. The average salary of blue-collar workers in Yangon is about $180 USD per month. Most local people spend less than 1,500 kyats (about $1.24 USD) for a meal, while a meal in a Western fast food restaurant typically costs more than 5,000 kyats (about $4.13 USD).

Nonetheless, these challenges did not stop KFC and Yoma Strategic from moving quickly into the new market. In October 2014, KFC executives visited Yangon to evaluate locations. In June 2015, the two-story flagship store located in the heart of Myanmar's commercial hub opened for business. In addition to initial market entry in Yangon, they also planned for possible expansion to second and third-tier cities within the country. "The announcement of the first KFC coming to Myanmar reflects our ongoing strategy of global expansion in emerging markets," the CEO of KFC, Micky Pant, said in a statement.[b] The fast food chain believes that fast economic expansion in emerging markets helps accelerate its business growth.

Indeed, although it is always challenging to navigate the thicket of new countries with fundamental political and cultural differences, moving first has brought tremendous success for KFC. For example, early in 1987, KFC opened China's first Western fast food restaurant in Beijing. At that time, forming a joint venture was the only viable entry mode for foreign investors. KFC selected two local partners with government connections. Although pricier than most local food services, the KFC restaurant became an instant hit. Many Chinese customers rode bicycles, which were the main means of transportation then, to KFC for special occasions. One of KFC's main competitors, McDonald's was more cautious about entering China. In October 1990, McDonald's opened its first restaurant in Shenzhen, China. Similar to KFC's approach, McDonald's set up a joint venture with a local firm. When McDonald's opened in Beijing in 1992, KFC already had 9 stores in China. By September 2008, KFC had around 2,200 stores in China's 465 cities. While KFC was expanding at a rate of one store a day, McDonald's planned to have 1,000 stores in China by the end of 2008. By 2015, KFC had about 5,000 units in China and McDonald's had about 2,000. With KFC as its flagship chain, Yum! has become China's largest restaurant company, with more than 250,000 employees and about 40 percent market share of the fast food restaurant business. Its revenue in China has surpassed that in the U.S.

Similarly, KFC entered Vietnam in 1997 and was the country's first quick-service restaurant brand. As of 2015, KFC had about 130 franchise restaurants located in over 20 cities throughout the country. It has been continuously growing and reinforcing its first position in the Vietnamese fast food industry. McDonald's just opened the first store in Vietnam in Feb 2014. In Indonesia, KFC is also the top U.S. fast food chain. Its first store opened early in 1979 while McDonald's waited until 1991. By December 2013, KFC had 466 outlets and about 32 percent market share. Meanwhile, McDonald's had about 130 stores in Indonesia in 2013. In Malaysia, KFC's first restaurant was opened in 1973. As of 2014, the number of KFC Restaurants reached over 500. On the other hand, McDonald's opened its first store in 1982 and had about 250 stores in 2014.

Certainly, being a first mover is not always rewarding. KFC's race with McDonald's in India turned out to be rather intense. KFC opened its first store in India in 1995 and McDonald's followed suit quickly in 1996. McDonald's changed most menu items for Indian consumers and localized supply chain. McDonald's had 14 stores in 1998, and the number reached over 28 in 2001. However, KFC had only three outlets in India for its first ten years. KFC fell behind until 2012 when it increased the number of outlets 41 percent within a year. It became the fastest-growing restaurant chain in India. As of 2015, there were 372 KFC outlets in India while McDonald's had more than 250 stores.

Notes

a. Manjur, R. (2014, October 15). Yum Brands brings KFC to Myanmar. Retrieved from www.marketing-interactive.com/yum-brands-singaporean-company-pair-make-move-myanmar/

b. Kean, T. (2014, October 13). First KFC to open in 2015. Retrieved from www.mmtimes.com/index.php/national-news/11952-first-kfc-to-open-in-2015.html

Sources

1. Bell, D. and Shelman, M. L. (2011, November). KFC's radical approach to China. *Harvard Business Review*. Retrieved from https://hbr.org/2011/11/kfcs-radical-approach-to-china

2. MacLeod, C. (2013, May 19). From cars to cola, U.S. firms cross into Burma. *USA Today*. Retrieved from www.usatoday.com/story/money/business/2013/05/19/burma-business/2323845/

3. Reuters. (2014, October 13). Myanmar's first KFC restaurant to open in 2015. Retrieved from www.reuters.com/article/2014/10/13/yum-brands-yoma-myanmar-idUSL3N0S828S20141013

4. Nguyen, L. A. (2014, April 30). At the front of Vietnam's food queue. *Forbes*. Retrieved from www.forbes.com/sites/lananhnguyen/2014/04/30/at-the-front-of-vietnams-food-queue/

5. Yoma Strategic. (n.d.). Financial Reports, various years. Retrieved from www.yomastrategic.com/html/ir_report.php

6. Yum! Brand. (n.d.). Restaurant Count & Definitions, various years. Retrieved from www.yum.com/investors/financial-information/financial-reports/

Questions for Case Discussion

1. How would you rate the attractiveness of Myanmar to a global fast food chain like KFC?
2. How was the timing of KFC's entry? Was it too early?
3. What are the benefits and drawbacks of KFC's early entry strategy?

Managing Entry and Exit Decisions

If a company intends to explore international markets, it needs to carefully plan its entry. There are hundreds of countries out there; the company may conduct any of its value chain activities abroad; and it can control its overseas activities in various forms. This chapter will address the key decisions a company needs to consider for international entry. The first is the *where* question (i.e. which country/market the company will enter). Different locations present different opportunities and risks, requiring the company to organize business activities accordingly. Also, the company should address the *what* question (i.e. what specific business activities are to be performed in the chosen country/market). The answers to these questions are dependent on the company's general strategic direction. Furthermore, there is the *how* question—which particular mode of trade or FDI the company will use, how big or small the scale of entry will be, when the best time of entry will be, etc. Very importantly, all these decisions are interconnected with one another and thus should be considered simultaneously. For instance, the choice of entry mode may be prescribed in a certain location; the best location may be contingent on which entry mode is used.

I. Location Selection

Why did Disney build a new theme park in Shanghai while already having one in not-so-far-away Hong Kong? Why did KFC adventure into Myanmar, a newly opened economy? Why did Target, a large U.S. retailer, abandon the neighboring Canadian market? All these questions concern the location selection of international business. Among many possible locations, why would a company choose a specific country or city to enter? To assess a location choice, we need to examine potential market opportunities as well as costs and risks associated with doing business in that location.

I. Market Opportunities

The potential opportunities of making profits in a location largely depend on its market conditions, such as market size, purchasing power, future growth, and local competition. When pursuing sales expansion in a market, a company should examine not only market size by the number of buyers but also the purchasing power of those buyers. Some countries may have a large number of consumers, but their low living standards and disposable incomes can limit actual demand. In addition to the present status of a market, future growth is also a critical factor to consider for long-run monetary gains. Fast economic growth in some emerging markets has generated increasing demands for foreign products and services. An early entry into such markets may lead to brand loyalty and substantial payback.

Furthermore, in some situations, foreign firms may enjoy favoritism in public perception and government regulation.[1] Often times, when companies from developed economies invest in developing countries, they carry a "halo" effect[2]. Foreign products are not only perceived to be of superior quality but also associated with desirable social status in developing countries.[3] Due to consumers' limited knowledge of global brands and the inferior image of local brands, even less well-known foreign brands can be favorably perceived by simply being foreign. In addition, foreign companies are expected to have better technology and management. To encourage positive knowledge spillover, foreign firms are likely to receive favorable government treatments in developing countries.[4] For instance, there are trade policies that offer favorable duties on certain imported products, and FDI policies that provide preferential treatments like easy registration, tax breaks, infrastructure access, and financing assistance.

2. Cost Factors

When entering a foreign market, there are many costs to consider. The ease of doing business index created by the World Bank indicates various factors that directly affect business costs, such as starting a business, dealing with construction permits, getting electricity, registering property, getting credit, protecting investors, paying taxes, trading across borders, enforcing contracts, and resolving insolvency.[5] Companies have to cover those expenses, unless they can be lowered by government incentives.

Meanwhile, companies need to consider the supply of production factors in a foreign location. Especially for those who seek key resources, such as labor, raw materials, and technology, not only the costs but also the quantity and quality of resources should be carefully evaluated. Ideally, there should be an abundant supply of quality items at competitive prices. However, reality can be complicated. For instance, in China, western inland provinces offer low-cost labor but the skillset and productivity of their workers are not strong; eastern coastal provinces have capable workforce but local wage rate has been quickly increasing. Also, the costs of utilities and transportation should be added. One major concern of foreign investors in India is the underdeveloped infrastructure (e.g. lack of power, clean water, highways, airports, etc.). To deal with power outages, many companies have to obtain and maintain backup power systems. Moreover, to control total costs, companies need easy access to their related and supporting industries. One main reason that many electronic firms have invested in China is to access local supply chains, which are now capable of making almost all kinds of parts and components. If there are no adequate local supplies, extra logistical costs will be incurred to secure supplies from other countries.

In addition, foreign companies face extra costs because they are "foreign." Such costs arise from the need for cross-border coordination and the effort of overcoming spatial distance in business transactions.[6] For instance, when foreign companies send employees for overseas assignments, they often pay extra for those employees' salaries and expenses. The transfer of goods, services, and money incurs extra expenses like tariffs, government fees, and foreign exchange fees. The transfer of technology and knowledge requires coordination and collaboration between people from different time zones and cultural backgrounds.

3. Risk Factors

Business risks may arise from the political, economic, and legal systems of a foreign country. Political risks refer to the possible adverse impacts on business operations resulting from political changes and instability in a country. For instance, changes in political leadership, civil disorders, wars, and conflicts can cause drastic changes in government attitudes and policies toward businesses (see also Chapter 5). Economic risks arise from the uncertainty of macroeconomic conditions in a country. For example, significant inflation, financial crisis, or economic recession can greatly hurt business performance. Legal risks include the risks of loss caused by defective transactions or property rights violations. For instance, without strong contract enforcement, a business partner may opportunistically break a contract; without strong property rights protection, government agencies may expropriate private properties. Corruption and the lack of intellectual property protection are also common legal risks in international markets. In some cases, these risks are interconnected. Political changes may lead to new economic policies or new legislatures. Economic mismanagement may result in social unrest and expropriation of private property.

Furthermore, competitive risks arise from local competition. The intensity of local competition directly affects a firm's market position and profitability.[7] Competition may come from local firms as well as other foreign companies in the same market. Companies generally favor markets with low or moderate competition unless their technologies and brands allow them to gain competitive advantages over rivals. Compared to local firms, foreign companies may encounter more risks because they are unfamiliar with the location or face discrimination against foreign firms.[8] Cultural and social factors play an important role in shaping local business practices and attitudes toward foreign companies (see also Chapter 6). Embedded in local information networks, local firms usually have a better understanding of local markets than foreign counterparts. In order to overcome this disadvantage, foreign firms may collaborate with and learn from local firms,[9] or outperform local competitors with their proprietary resources.[10]

Table 8.1 summarizes the main determinants of location selection. Positive market opportunities, low costs, and low risks enhance the attractiveness of a location. To choose a promising foreign market, companies need to carefully weigh possible returns against costs and risks. They need to consider not only factors that affect all businesses but also items that specifically apply to foreign firms. To collect data on those factors, companies may seek information from various government agencies, trade associations, and international organizations. They can also hire professional consulting services, such as accounting and market research firms, to help with location selection.

II. Strategic Direction

Along with location selection, companies need to clearly define the main purposes of their entry into a foreign market. To increase profits, firms seek cost reduction and sales expansion. Accordingly, companies that compete in international markets typically face two imperatives: the need to reduce costs

Table 8.1 Major Determinants of Location Selection

Market Opportunities	Size of market Buyers' purchasing power Future market growth Positive perception of foreign firms Government incentives (e.g. tax breaks, financing assistance)
Cost Factors	Costs of regulation compliance (e.g. registration, taxation) Costs of production factors (e.g. labor, raw materials) Costs of support activities (e.g. transportation, supply chain) Costs of cross-border activities (e.g. communication, traveling)
Risk Factors	Political risks (e.g. change of government, social instability) Economic risks (e.g. inflation, economic crisis) Legal risks (e.g. contract enforcement failure, property rights violation) Local competition Liability of foreignness (e.g. unfamiliarity, discrimination)

and the need to respond to local demands.[11] The balance of these two imperatives results in different strategies that characterize the responsibilities and roles of a company's overseas operations.

1. Cost Reduction

With increasing global competition, companies often face pressures for cost reduction. The liberalization of international trade and foreign direct investment has allowed more and more companies to compete internationally. Meanwhile, converging consumer trends have enabled companies to provide standard or similar products for multiple markets. In commodity-like industries, it is difficult to create meaningful differentiation and thus price becomes the main weapon of competition. Furthermore, there has been a strong rise of low-cost productions and low-cost services in emerging markets like China and India. Those low-cost alternatives have significantly increased cost pressures for international businesses.

In response to such cost pressures, companies are seeking to improve the efficiency of their business processes. Here are some common approaches:

- Seeking economies of scale. By concentrating operations in a few select locations, companies can utilize mass production to achieve economies of scale.
- Standardizing products or services. Standard products and processes simplify operations and allow companies to realize learning effects in multiple markets.
- Relocating to low-cost locations. By relocating a value creation activity to an optimal location in the world, companies can obtain location-specific cost advantages (i.e. location economies). For instance, many multinational electronic companies have set up manufacturing in Vietnam to take advantage of low-cost labor and government incentives.

- Sourcing globally. Firms may source raw materials, components, labor, and services from low-cost foreign suppliers. For example, a number of U.S. companies have outsourced informational technology support and call center services from Indian companies.

These approaches generally require global integration, that is the coordination of value chain activities across countries. The purpose of global integration is to build a network of highly efficient operations and enhance internal synergies through resource sharing and knowledge transfer across locations. In order to coordinate worldwide activities, the headquarter office of a company needs to maintain strong control over its domestic and overseas operations. Without adequate control, its branches and subsidiaries may pursue different agendas and fail to work with one another.

2. Local Responsiveness

Although globalization has brought a convergence of consumer preferences, differences still exist across countries and cultures. To enhance sales in a foreign country, companies may need to respond to the specific needs of customers in that market. Pressures for local responsiveness arise from country differences. Such pressures are particularly strong in the industries that face significant national differences, such as food and beverage, consumer products, and clothing.

First, countries may differ in customer tastes and preferences. Lacking local roots, foreign products usually are not readily accepted by local customers. Foreign companies often need to customize their products and marketing campaigns to appeal to local tastes and preferences. For instance, KFC, an American fast food chain, has made drastic changes to its traditional menu and added location-specific items in foreign markets. Second, distribution channels may vary considerably from country to country. The retailing sector is rather fragmented in some countries, but dominated by a few large companies in others (e.g. the U.S.). Some countries allow direct access to final customers, others require layers of wholesalers and distributors. To effectively utilize local distribution channels, foreign companies may need to change their product offering and sales strategy. Third, host country rules and regulations may require local responsiveness. Companies need to adapt their operations and products to local technology standards. For example, each generation of the iPhone has multiple models that cater to different network technologies and frequencies used around the world. Also, foreign companies are subject to host government demands, such as technology transfer to locals, hiring local employees, sourcing from local suppliers, and restriction on pricing. Their business practices have to be changed to meet local requirements.

In order to increase local responsiveness, companies usually delegate considerable autonomy to the managers of their overseas operations. Through directly dealing with customers and distributors, those managers learn about specific demands of local markets. If equipped with sufficient autonomy, they can make and implement decisions according to local requirements in a timely manner. Otherwise, those managers may not be able to quickly respond to changes in foreign markets.

3. Basic Strategy Types

Firms seeking international expansion have varied degrees of need for cost reduction and local responsiveness. The combinations of these two imperatives can be characterized as four distinct strategies (see Figure 8.1).[12]

One strategy is global standardization (also called global strategy). This strategy emphasizes cost reduction whereas the need for local responsiveness is relatively weak. With this strategy, company headquarters control and coordinate worldwide operations in an effort to maximize efficiency, synergy, and integration. Business activities are usually standardized across locations. Management tends to view the world as one global platform and all operations as part of an integrated network. This strategy enables a company to effectively utilize its worldwide resources and capabilities, and to quickly disseminate innovations and knowledge across borders. It also helps maintain consistent product quality and brand reputation around the world. However, the global standardization strategy restricts a company's responsiveness to specific needs of individual markets. Local managers may be demotivated due to the lack of autonomy and flexibility.

Another strategy is multidomestic (also called localization strategy). This strategy focuses on local responsiveness whereas the need for cost reduction is weak. With this strategy, a lot of decision-making power is delegated to

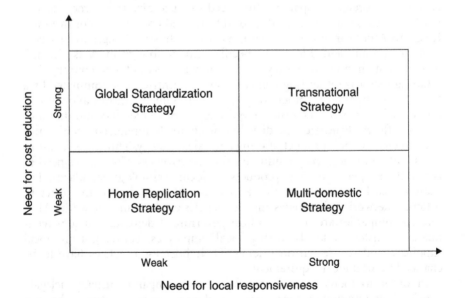

Figure 8.1 Basic Strategy Types

Source: Adapted from Bartlett, C. A. and Ghoshal, S. (1999). Managing across borders: The transnational solution (Vol. 2). Boston, MA: Harvard Business School Press.

business units in each country, allowing them to operate independently. This strategy recognizes national differences and enables country managers to customize value creation activities and products. While helping increase sales in individual markets, multidomestic strategy offers few incentives for business units to share knowledge. It also tends to create small-scale operations, duplication of activities, and diverse product offerings, thus reducing the total efficiency of a company. As international competition intensifies, multidomestic companies will have to reduce their costs.

Transnational strategy (also called hybrid strategy) is a strategy that combines cost reduction and local responsiveness. With this strategy, a company strives to be responsive to local needs while retaining enough central control to attain efficiency. The company may standardize or customize certain operations, depending on which approach is more appropriate. This strategy leads to diverse levels of integration between different functions. For example, an automobile company can centralize sourcing for its plants around the world, use flexible manufacturing to make customized cars for different markets on the same platform, and tailor sales and services to each country. While minimizing the disadvantages of global standardization and multidomestic strategies, transnational strategy is probably the most difficult to implement. It requires a delicate balance between central control and local responsiveness. Business units have varied roles and responsibilities, and the management system tends to be complicated.

The last strategy is home replication (also called export or international strategy). With this strategy, products are mainly designed for domestic customers, and foreign markets are viewed as an opportunity to generate incremental sales. Thus, products are exported with little consideration of achieving cost reduction or local responsiveness overseas. This strategy can be used when the company has a proprietary product or service that faces limited competition abroad. It allows the company to increase revenue by replicating home country success. Historically, many MNCs used a home replication strategy at the early stage of internationalization. As time went on, they faced increasing international competition and had to take measures to reduce costs. Also, in the long run, in order to fully exploit international markets, companies need to pursue some degree of localization because national differences are likely to persist.

III. Entry Mode Choice

Entry mode choice is an important "how" question a firm has to consider carefully before entering a foreign market. There are a variety of entry modes, and each mode has its advantages and disadvantages. International businesses need to determine which entry mode is most appropriate in a given situation and whether to switch to a different mode if the situation changes.

There are mainly two categories of entry modes: non-equity and equity-based modes. Non-equity modes are those based on transactions of goods, services, or intellectual properties, such as exporting, licensing, and franchising. Equity-based modes involve equity investment, such as joint ventures and wholly owned subsidiaries.

I. Exporting

Most companies start their international expansion by selling goods or services overseas. Exporting is a natural extension of a firm's domestic business. Utilizing production facilities at home, the firm gains additional sources of revenue and new knowledge about international markets. A firm can either export directly to foreign buyers or use intermediary services like export management companies.

If exporting directly, the firm first needs to identify potential foreign customers. It may use advertisements, trade shows, references, online platforms and other venues to attract buyers. Then the firm should "separate the wheat from the chaff," that is to pick real buyers who are willing and capable of paying. Especially in unfamiliar foreign markets, it is critical to examine buyers' credit history and avoid frauds and scams. Then the firm negotiates with the buyer on sale price and terms. Not only the actual costs of production but also the demand and competition of the foreign market should be factored into pricing (see also Chapter 12). Sometimes, it is possible to hike up the price in certain foreign markets. Moreover, transportation, insurance, custom clearance, and tariff should be addressed in negotiation. A set of standard terms of sale have been developed by the International Chamber of Commerce to define the rights and responsibilities between exporter and importer.[13] These terms, also known as Incoterms, are widely used in commercial transactions. Here are some commonly used terms:

- EXW—Ex Works. The seller delivers the goods to the buyer at its own premises (e.g. factory, warehouse); ownership and responsibilities are transferred once the buyer collects the goods.
- FOB—Free on Board. The seller delivers the goods on board the vessel designated by the buyer at the port of shipment; once the shipment is on board, the buyer takes ownership and bears all costs and risks from then on.
- CFR—Cost and Freight. The seller is responsible for the transportation to the destination port; but the risk of loss or damage is transferred to the buyer when the goods are on board the vessel, so the buyer bears the cost of insurance.
- CIF—Cost, Insurance and Freight. This term is similar to CFR except that the seller must contract for insurance coverage against the buyer's risk of loss or damage to the goods in transit.
- DDP—Delivered Duty Paid. The seller delivers the good to the named destination and bears all the costs and risks up to the delivery point, including all customs clearance for both export and import and paying duties and taxes.

In addition, to ensuring the collection of earnings, payment methods and foreign exchange risks should be considered (see Chapter 10 for details).

Given the complexity of exporting, many firms seek assistance from exporting management companies. Exporting management companies can help handle transportation, insurance, documentation, and customs clearance. Some even offer distribution, marketing, and financial services to exporters. Their services are especially useful to small and medium-sized firms, who typically lack resources and expertise to handle exporting transactions.

A lot of companies, big or small, have benefited from exporting. It provides a relatively quick and easy way to access international markets without substantial resource commitment. Also, it extends the life cycle of existing products and increases the scale of home country production, thus creating economies of scale and learning benefits. Its low marginal cost makes exporting a good entry mode choice when the firm perceives considerable uncertainty and lacks international experience.

Meanwhile, exporting faces certain limitations. First, it is restricted by transportation costs and trade barriers, which may make cross-border transactions uneconomical. To avoid high transportation costs and restrictive trade policies, the company may move close or into the target market. Also, exporting may be challenged by competition from lower-cost locations. In this case, the company can relocate production elsewhere to gain location economies. Moreover, when an exporter relies on foreign distributors, it has limited control over its overseas marketing, sales, and services.

2. Licensing and Franchising

Licensing is an arrangement in which the owner of a property (licensor) grants another party (licensee) the right to use the property within a specified territory for a specified length of time. In return, the licensor receives royalty payments from the licensee. Companies typically use licensing to obtain income from intellectual property, such as patents, trademarks, and copyrights. For instance, Google and Samsung have a broad, long-term deal to cross-license each other's patents in mobile technologies. Disney licenses its cartoon characters to merchandise manufacturers who produce items like toys, clothes, and souvenirs.

Licensing is generally considered a low-cost, low-risk entry mode.[14] In a typical international licensing transaction, while the licensor contributes existing intellectual property, the licensee bears most of the capital required for overseas operation. For the licensor, this is a fast and easy way to leverage its intellectual property to make extra income. Therefore, licensing is particularly viable for firms that lack capital for international expansion. Also, if a company is unwilling to make a substantial investment in a new country, it can use licensing to minimize risk exposure.

As discussed in Chapter 3, licensing has a few disadvantages in comparison with direct investment. First, licensing may incur considerable transaction costs. The licensor and the licensee need to negotiate detailed terms to define each other's rights and responsibilities. The transfer of technology and know-how may require lengthy training and constant interactions. Second, licensing does not provide the licensor much influence on overseas operations, which are usually owned and controlled by the licensee. Thus, the licensor is unable to fully exploit its home country experiences or location economies in the foreign market. The earnings the licensor can get are also limited. Third, by licensing proprietary assets, the licensor may lose its competitive advantage.

After gaining enough knowledge and experience, the licensee may become a strong competitor to the licensor in international markets.

Franchising is a special form of licensing in which a party (franchiser) not only grants specified property rights (e.g. trademarks and business models) to another party (franchisee) but also requires the franchisee to follow specified rules in business operations (e.g. specified processes and product/service standards). The franchiser often provides training and support, and receives some percentage of the franchisee's revenue as royalty payment. Franchising is commonly used in service sectors, such as hotels, restaurants, business, and personal services. For instance, among the hundreds of Hilton hotels around the world, only about 20 percent are owned by Hilton, and the rest are all franchises using the Hilton brand.

The advantages and disadvantages of franchising are similar to those of licensing. Since the franchisee assumes most of the investment, the franchisor is able to quickly expand its business in a new market with relatively low costs and risks. For service companies seeking to build a global presence, franchising is an efficient approach. By setting strict rules, the franchisor gains a certain degree of control over the franchisee's operations. However, without equity ownership, such control is still limited. When the franchisee fails to abide by the rules, product or service quality will be affected and the franchisor's brand reputation will be damaged.

3. Joint Venture

A joint venture is an entity jointly owned by two or more parent firms. An international joint venture has parent firms from different countries. To establish a joint venture, a company may either set up a new entity with another party or acquire some portion of equity in an existing firm. The parent firms combine their equity investments, exercise control over the joint venture, and consequently share assets, revenues, expenses and, risks. Joint venturing is a popular mode of international entry. Especially in developing countries, many MNCs partner with indigenous firms to gain access to local knowledge and networks.[15] In some cases, MNCs have to form joint ventures with local firms because of government restrictions on equity structure. For example, foreign companies are not allowed to hold more than 50 percent equity shares of a vehicle manufacturing enterprise in China. Thus, GM, Ford, Volkswagen, Toyota, Honda, and Hyundai have all set up joint ventures with local automobile companies to manufacture cars in China. The joint ventures not only comply with government requirements but also help those MNCs overcome cultural differences and political barriers.[16]

Joint venturing offers many advantages. First of all, it allows a firm to pool complementary resources from its partner(s). Because of their stakes in the joint venture, parent firms have incentives to contribute resources to the joint venture. Synergies and innovations may be generated by putting production factors together and having different teams collaborate. For instance, the foreign parent may contribute capital, technology, and access to global markets, while the local parent may offer facilities, labor, and local know-how. Specifically, the local parent's deep roots may help the foreign parent obtain institutional legitimacy and government support, mitigating the liability of foreignness. Moreover, by cooperating with its partner(s), a firm does not need to bear all the risks and costs associated with opening up a new market. Establishing a joint venture may require greater commitment than exporting and licensing, but it is less demanding than building a wholly owned overseas operation.

Nonetheless, these advantages come with potential drawbacks. One important challenge to joint venturing is the conflict of interest between parent firms.[17] When the individual interests of a parent firm are not aligned with its partner's interests or mutual interests, the parent firm may engage in opportunistic behavior. It may appropriate assets, hide earnings, or even steal technologies from its partner. In other words, one firm may lose its key assets to its joint venture partner, which may well become a future competitor. Another drawback is shared control. Each parent firm's equity contribution gives it a certain degree of control over the joint venture.[18] A parent firm's strategic direction and operational command are not necessarily accepted by its partner or readily followed by the joint venture management team. This will make it difficult for an MNC to integrate its joint venture with its worldwide network. Furthermore, conflicts often arise from shared control. Due to goal incongruence and distrust for each other, parent firms have a tendency to battle for control.[19] National differences in culture and managerial practices also increase the possibility of conflict. [20]

MNCs may take certain measures to minimize the drawbacks of joint venturing. First, they need to find the right partner that is capable of providing complementary resources and trustworthy enough to refrain from engaging in opportunistic behavior.[21] However, without in-depth knowledge about the target country, it is not easy to find a capable and trustworthy local partner. Second, MNCs may develop safeguard mechanisms to wall their key assets off from joint venture partners. For instance, many global automobile companies keep the manufacturing of the most sophisticated components at home, and their overseas joint ventures mainly work on assembling parts without access to advanced technology. However, such safeguards restrict the exploitation of proprietary assets and location economies, reducing the benefits of joint venturing. The third measure is to develop detailed contracts and control systems to regulate partners' activities. Such mechanisms define inter-partner relations and protect mutual interests. They are essential to joint venture success. Nonetheless, it can be costly to enforce contracts and exercise control, and too much control may introduce conflicts.[22] Fourth, the parent firms should work on building trust with each other. Strong trust can significantly reduce opportunism and conflicts, thus increasing the effectiveness of inter-partner collaborations. Yet, as the saying goes, trust takes years to build, seconds to destroy, and forever to repair. Lastly, to avoid the problems of joint ownership, MNCs may choose to set up wholly owned subsidiaries instead.[23]

4. Wholly Owned Subsidiary

As the name implies, a wholly owned subsidiary is an entity 100 percent owned by the investing firm. It usually requires significant equity investment and resource commitment. The firm may either set up a new entity (i.e. greenfield investment) or acquire an existing local enterprise. For instance, when entering the European market, Hyundai, from Korea, built new manufacturing capacity, whereas Geely, a Chinese automaker, acquired all the equity of the Volvo Car Corporation.

This entry mode gives an MNC full ownership and consequently all earnings generated by the subsidiary. Compared to other entry modes, it offers the highest degree of control, allowing the MNC to make and implement decisions on its own. Thus, the operations of a wholly owned subsidiary can be integrated with its parent firm's global network, improving cross-country resource allocation and collaboration. Also, full ownership reduces the risk of losing key assets. The MNC does not need to share its technology and know-how with another party.

Nevertheless, this entry mode requires the MNC to bear all the costs and risks of establishing an overseas operation. Both greenfield investment and acquisition can be costly, complex, and lengthy. To acquire a foreign enterprise, the MNC often needs to jump through regulatory hoops, conduct thorough due diligence, and outbid competing offers. After acquisition, it needs time and resources to assimilate the culture and system of the acquired enterprise. To conduct a greenfield project, the MNC needs to build everything from scratch. Compared to acquisition, it may need an even longer time to construct new facilities, accumulate local knowledge, and develop new customers. If the subsidiary fails, the MNC may suffer significant financial loss. Finally, without a local partner's support, the wholly owned subsidiary is more vulnerable to government scrutiny and discrimination against foreign firms. To combat this problem, the MNC may increase localization by hiring local managers and sourcing from local suppliers.

5. Choosing an Entry Mode

Table 8.2 summarizes the main advantages and drawbacks of each entry mode discussed above. Generally, a greater resource commitment is associated with greater control and return as well as higher costs and risks. When choosing an entry mode, a company faces tradeoffs between the advantages and the drawbacks. To make the right choice, the company needs to consider the target

Table 8.2 A Comparison of Entry Modes

Entry Mode	Main Advantages	Main Drawbacks
Exporting	Low resource commitment Increased domestic production	Transportation costs Trade barriers
Licensing/Franchising	Low setup costs Low risks	Low control Limited earnings
Joint venture	Complementary resources Shared costs and risks	Interest conflicts Shared control and return
Wholly owned subsidiary	Full ownership and return High control	High costs and risks Lack of local support

country's business environment, the company's own resource condition, and strategic intent.[24] A foreign entrant may encounter various risks derived from government regulation, cultural distance, industry structure, and competition. When the country presents significant risks, the company tends to favor low-risk modes, such as licensing or joint venturing with a local partner, over a wholly owned subsidiary. If the company lacks resources, it cannot afford an entry mode that requires considerable commitment. If the company has little international experience, it may prefer low-cost, low-risk entry modes like exporting and licensing. If the company's core competence is its proprietary technology, it is likely to favor an entry mode that provides tight control and protection. Finally, the strategic objective of the company influences entry mode selection. If the company stresses global integration of its business operations, it needs to choose high-control entry modes. If the company aims for long-term development in a country, it may favor high-commitment, high-return entry modes like a wholly owned subsidiary or a joint venture with majority ownership.

It should be noted that entry mode choice is a dynamic process. After a company selects its initial entry mode, it may switch to a different mode as time passes. For instance, many MNCs start with exporting to international markets; as international sales grow, they set up joint ventures in foreign countries to expand production and lower costs; after accumulating enough international experience, they buy out equity shares from foreign partners and convert joint ventures to wholly owned subsidiaries. Also, it is possible for a company to use multiple entry modes at the same time. While exporting finished goods, some manufacturing companies also use licensing to increase the installation base of their technology overseas. Some service companies first set up a partially or wholly owned master franchisor in a foreign country and then use franchising for local expansion.

In addition to the four major entry modes discussed above, there are several special entry modes. Countertrade refers to the exchange of goods or services with no or partial money payment. Countertrade can be made directly between two parties (e.g. barter) or through a third-party trading house (e.g. switch trading). It is used when trading countries lack hard currencies. A turnkey project is an arrangement in which a foreign investor builds an entire operation, including training staff, and then hands it over to a client. It is a way to export process technology and construction services. It is often used for large-scale projects such as airports, power plants, oil refineries, and metal mills. A holding company is an investment firm that is set up to own and control other companies. An MNC may set up a foreign holding company to manage its overseas investments and properties. This arrangement not only helps the MNC limit financial and legal liability but also may enhance coordination among overseas subsidiaries.

IV. Other Considerations: Timing, Scale, and Exit

1. Timing of Entry

When is the right time to enter a foreign market? This is also an important question firms have to consider. The timing of entry affects the relative market position of a company, and thus has significant performance implications.

When a pioneering company enters a foreign market before others, it may gain first mover advantages. First of all, facing limited competition, early movers are likely to attract a sizable group of customers, gain brand reputation, and thus create switching costs that make customers loyal to their products. Second, early movers are able to build sales volume faster than later entrants, leading to cost advantages based on economies of scale and learning benefits. Third, early movers often get priority access to local resources, such as scarce materials, distribution channels, infrastructure, and government support. Fourth, with their market power, early entrants can shape industry structure and preempt rivals. To obtain these first mover advantages, some MNCs have actively pursued early entry into international markets. For example, KFC entered China soon after the country opened up to international businesses. It gained much publicity and government support because it built the first American fast food restaurant in China. It quickly developed a strong presence and had a market share much bigger than that in its home country.

However, not all first movers are successful. There are also disadvantages associated with early entry into a foreign market. One disadvantage is environmental uncertainty. When entering a newly opened country, early movers often suffer from embryonic market structure, poor infrastructure, and underdeveloped regulation. A second disadvantage is the pioneering costs that early movers must bear but late entrants can evade. Due to unfamiliarity with the foreign market, early movers typically spend considerable resources and effort on learning and adaptation. When introducing a product or service that is new to the market, extra costs are needed to educate customers. The pioneering costs also include the costs of mistakes and failures early entrants tend to make. A third disadvantage is that later entrants can learn from the experience of early movers.[25] They may copy early movers' winning strategies, avoid their mistakes, or tap into the market established by early movers.

In comparison, later movers can avoid the risks and costs of being a first mover. However, they may miss the opportunity to occupy market and preempt competition. Thus, the timing decision involves a tradeoff.

2. Scale of Entry

As discussed earlier in this chapter, different entry modes require different levels of resource commitment. Even when using the same entry mode, international businesses vary in the scale of operation. How much investment a company can make depends on its own resource condition. While firms with limited resources cannot afford large-scale expansion, those with abundant resources can choose the scale of entry.

Large-scale entry implies a foreign company's strong commitment to its target market. It is likely to get support from suppliers, distributors, and governments because they believe the company will transfer plentiful resources and stay for a long time. Also, it enables the company to quickly expand its business operation, achieve economies of scale, and grab a significant market share. Such rapid expansion is likely to deter other companies from entering the country. For instance, when Volkswagen entered China, it invested much more than other global automakers. The German brand soon became the market leader in the Chinese automobile industry.

However, large-scale entry also means greater risk. If the entry fails, the company will suffer significant setbacks. And the long-term impact is difficult to reverse. On the other hand, small-scale entry has lower risks and greater flexibility. If its venture succeeds, the company can gradually accumulate experience and build up its operational scale. Otherwise, it can withdraw from the market without much loss. Therefore, risk-averse firms tend to favor small-scale entry. But they may miss the benefits of quick expansion in a foreign market.

3. Exit Plan

A company may choose to exit when it is no longer beneficial to operate in a given country. Traditionally, exiting is viewed as a result of business failure. However, as international markets become more and more competitive and integrated, many companies nowadays view exiting as a viable strategy to restructure their worldwide assets and control potential risks. Since some entry arrangements like joint venturing have an expiration date, it may be necessary to consider exiting even at the time of entry. Furthermore, because a number of countries have restrictions on capital and profit repatriation, exiting from such countries should be planned ahead accordingly. Specifically, here are a few exit options: (1) Relocating operations to another country. Because of changing economic conditions, another location may offer better location economies. (2) Selling the business to another party. The business remains in the country but the foreign company gives up ownership and control. In a joint venture, the foreign firm can also transfer shares to its local partner. Spin-off and management buyout are also possible options. (3) Liquidation. This is to sell the business in pieces, which often incurs financial loss; and the business ceases to exist.

Key Terms

Location choice, need for cost reduction, need for local responsiveness, global standardization, multidomestic strategy, transnational strategy, home replication, entry mode, exporting, Incoterms, licensing, franchising, joint venture, interest conflict, wholly owned subsidiary, timing of entry, first mover advantages, pioneering costs, scale of entry, exit plan

Review Questions

1. How can a company evaluate the attractiveness of a foreign market? What factors should be considered?
2. Describe the main strategic purposes of international expansion. What are the implications of these purposes for entry decisions?
3. Describe the basic strategy types of international expansion. How do they affect international business activities?

4. What are the main entry modes a company can use to enter international markets? How are they different from one another?
5. How should a company choose an appropriate entry mode for a given country?
6. What tradeoffs should be considered when deciding on the timing and scale of entry?

Internet Exercises

1. Visit the following website: www.doingbusiness.org/rankings. Compare the high-ranked countries with those low-ranked ones, and evaluate their market attractiveness to foreign companies.
2. Choose a global fast food chain (e.g. McDonald's, KFC, Burger King) or a global hotel chain (e.g. Marriot, Hilton, Intercontinental). Go to the company's website to find out their newest international locations. Try to explain why and how the company entered those locations.

Notes

1 Mudambi, R. and Navarra, P. (2002). Institutions and international business: A theoretical view. *International Business Review, 11*(6), 635–646.
2 Han, C. M. (1989). Country image: Halo or summary construct? *Journal of Marketing Research, 26*(2), 222–229.
3 Verlegh, P. W. J. (2007) Home country bias in product evaluation: The complementary roles of economic and socio-psychological motives. *Journal of International Business Studies, 38*(3), 361–373.
4 Borensztein, E., De Gregorio, J., and Lee, J. W. (1998). How does foreign direct investment affect economic growth? *Journal of International Economics, 45*(1), 115–135.
5 World Bank. 2014. *Doing Business 2015: Going Beyond Efficiency.* Washington, DC: World Bank. DOI: 10.1596/978-1-4648-0351-2.
6 Zaheer, S. (1995). Overcoming the liability of foreignness. *Academy of Management Journal, 38*(2), 341–360.
7 Porter, M. E. (1986) *Competition in Global Industries.* Boston, MA: Harvard Business School Press.
8 Zaheer, S. (1995). Overcoming the liability of foreignness. *Academy of Management Journal, 38*(2), 341–360.
9 Kostova, T. and Zaheer, S. (1999) Organizational legitimacy under conditions of complexity: The case of the multinational enterprise. *Academy of Management Review, 24*, 64-81.
10 Eden, L. and Molot, M. A. (2002). Insiders outsiders and host country bargains. *Journal of International Management, 8*, 359–388.
11 Ghemawat, P. (2007). *Redefining Global Strategy.* Boston, MA: Harvard Business School Publishing.
12 Bartlett, C. A. and Ghoshal, S. (1999). *Managing Across Borders: The Transnational Solution* (Vol. 2). Boston, MA: Harvard Business School Press.
13 International Chamber of Commerce. (2010). The Incoterm Rules. Retrieved from www.iccwbo.org/products-and-services/trade-facilitation/incoterms-2010/
14 Hill, C. W., Hwang, P., and Kim, W. C. (1990). An eclectic theory of the choice of international entry mode. *Strategic Management Journal, 11*(2), 117–128.

15 Beamish, P. (2013). *Multinational Joint Ventures in Developing Countries (RLE International Business)*. New York: Routledge.

16 Lee, J. W., Abosag, I., and Kwak, J. (2012). The role of networking and commitment in foreign market entry process: Multinational corporations in the Chinese automobile industry. *International Business Review, 21*(1), 27–39.

17 Luo, Y. (2002). Contract, cooperation, and performance in international joint ventures. *Strategic Management Journal, 23*(10), 903–919.

18 Chen, D., Park, S. H., and Newburry, W. (2009). Parent contribution and organizational control in international joint ventures. *Strategic Management Journal, 30*(11), 1133–1156.

19 Beamish, P. W. and Lupton, N. C. (2009). Managing joint ventures. *Academy of Management Perspectives, 23*(2), 75–94.

20 Shenkar, O. (2012). Cultural distance revisited: Towards a more rigorous conceptualization and measurement of cultural differences. *Journal of International Business Studies, 43*(1), 1–11.

21 Das, T. K. and Teng, B. S. (1998). Between trust and control: Developing confidence in partner cooperation in alliances. *Academy of Management Review, 23*(3), 491–512.

22 Mjoen, H. and Tallman, S. (1997). Control and performance in international joint ventures. *Organization Science, 8*(3), 257–274.

23 Chang, S. J., Chung, J., and Moon, J. J. (2013). When do wholly owned subsidiaries perform better than joint ventures? *Strategic Management Journal, 34*(3), 317–337.

24 Brouthers, K. D. (2013). A retrospective on: Institutional, cultural and transaction cost influences on entry mode choice and performance. *Journal of International Business Studies, 44*(1), 14–22.

25 Shaver, J. M., Mitchell, W., and Yeung, B. (1997). The effect of own-firm and other-firm experience on foreign direct investment survival in the United States, 1987–1992. *Strategic Management Journal, 18*, 811–824.

Managing People
Global Talent Management

Learning Objectives

1. Recognize the increasing importance and key components of global talent management.
2. Comprehend the benefits and costs of different staffing policies.
3. Understand the different types of training and development programs.
4. Describe appropriate compensation and performance appraisal schemes to retain talent.
5. Identify the key issues and concerns involving repatriation.

Cases

Case 9.1 How to Groom Future Global Managers?
Case 9.2 Expatriates Still Holding Top Positions in Asia
Case 9.3 "Sea Turtles" Return to China
Case 9.4 What Do Expatriates Want?
Case 9.5 Why Is It So Difficult to Return Home?

Case 9.1 How to Groom Future Global Managers?

Among the vast majority of business schools, "globalization" has become a buzzword. For instance, to enhance their international profiles, Duke University's Fuqua School of Business and the University of Chicago's Booth School of Business recently opened international campuses. Many schools not only offer programs in foreign countries but also include a global component in their curricula to prepare students for overseas assignments. The Haas School of Business at University of California, Berkeley, offers an international development class, in which students participate in mini-consulting projects for multinational companies. The aim is to conduct research and create a business plan on how to enter or expand in a foreign market. "This type of experience changes the way students think about the world," said Kristi Raube, executive director of the international business development program at Haas. Similarly, a study trip abroad would be a requirement at Harvard Business School.

To facilitate student and faculty exchanges with foreign counterparts, American business schools have set up various consortia and partnership agreements with schools around the world. Many have learned that collaboration with foreign schools is a cost-effective way to expand global reach. For example, Babson College has been actively developing an international consortium and recently added Bangkok University. Massachusetts Institute of Technology (MIT) has alliances with half a dozen schools, and their new partnership with Sabanci School of Management in Turkey would allow MIT students to access the Turkish business community.

However, some experts doubt if such efforts are adequate in preparing students for overseas work. "To become sophisticated enough to work and live in another country, you have to be there for at least six months to a year," said Warren Bennis, a professor at the University of Southern California's Marshall School of Business. A report by the Association to Advance Collegiate Schools of Business stated that many schools are still experimenting with various partnership models. The report questioned the legitimacy of some partnerships and identified weaknesses in their effectiveness.

Companies are also concerned that there may be a gap between business schools' efforts and specific skills required for global positions. "Many business schools provide students with opportunities to go abroad, but I don't know if that's sufficient in its own right," said Russ Hagey, the worldwide chief talent officer of consulting firm Bain & Co. Applicants for Bain's global positions need to demonstrate proficiency in a foreign language like Mandarin and French. Those having prior experience with international companies are at an advantage over other candidates. According to David Smith, a managing director at Accenture who works with clients to recruit global talent, "a broad global outlook, including understanding nuances in other cultures and a willingness to relocate, is key for landing top positions." Applicants should not only know how international markets are different but also demonstrate that they are able to manage team members in foreign countries.

Realizing the difficulty in finding candidates who meet all the requirements to manage their global businesses, some MNCs are increasing their efforts to directly groom local talent. For instance, together with China's Ministry of Education, IBM recently launched a major initiative to provide financial and technical support for Chinese students to learn skills in the fast-growing Big Data and Analytics (BD&A) area. The initiative, dubbed IBM U-100, aims to set up BD&A technology centers in 100 universities and launch undergraduate and graduate BD&A programs in 30 universities. IBM will provide BD&A software (worth about $100 million USD) and expertise to help train 40,000 students per year in big data skills like information management, data mining, and social media analytics. "IBM is privileged to extend its collaboration with the Ministry of Education and universities in China," said D. C. Chien, the CEO of IBM Greater China Group, "Together we will be able to accelerate the nurturing of skills in Big Data and Analytics and help prepare future business leaders to apply BD&A technologies to tackle complex societal issues, from health care to transportation and public services."[a]

In addition to working with governments and universities, IBM also announced a cooperative agreement with kaikeba.com, a Chinese online education portal, to establish an "IBM Zone of Big Data and Analytics." This agreement aims to provide Massive Open Online Courses (MOOCs) on interpreting and utilizing big data to its future workforce. Indeed, great demand for big data skills is expected in the decades to come. According to CCID Consulting, China's big data technology and services market would have grown from $2.3 billion USD in 2014 to $8.7 billion USD in 2016. While many businesses have realized the importance of big data for future innovation and competitiveness, there is a shortage of skilled professionals in this technology area. "Big data is big business, but its rapid growth has outpaced colleges' and universities' ability to develop and implement new curriculums," said Li Shu Chong, President of CCID Consulting, "IBM's extensive initiative is poised to help develop new talent in China that will be needed to realize the full potential of big data."[b]

Notes

a. PR Newswire. (2014, July 8). IBM commits U.S.$100 million to support China to nurture big data and analytics talent. PR Newswire. Retrieved from www.prnewswire.com/news-releases/ibm-commits-us100-million-to-support-china-to-nurture-big-data-and-analytics-talent-266202841.html
b. Ibid.

Sources

1. Middleton, D. (2011, April 7). Business education: Schools set global track, for students and programs. *Wall Street Journal*: B.7. Retrieved from www.wsj.com/articles/SB10001424052748703806304576244980620638072
2. PR Newswire. (2014, July 8). IBM commits U.S.$100 million to support China to nurture big data and analytics talent. PR Newswire. Retrieved from www.prnewswire.com/news-releases/ibm-commits-us100-million-to-support-china-to-nurture-big-data-and-analytics-talent-266202841.html

Questions for Case Discussion

1. How do U.S. universities and colleges educate students to prepare them for global management positions?
2. Do you think U.S. university programs are doing enough to meet the expectations of the MNCs that will hire these students after graduation? What are the strengths and weaknesses of these programs?
3. Why do you think IBM launched U-100? Do you think that IBM will bridge the gap between technology and business to deliver higher client value?

Case 9.2 Expatriates Still Holding Top Positions in Asia

While Western multinationals have been operating in Asia for decades, their top-ranked positions are largely held by expatriates rather than locals. Although the number of Asian employees has increased significantly, the majority of them still occupy lower-level positions. The top roles of Asian subsidiaries are often occupied by Westerners. A 2013 *Wall Street Journal* article reported:

40% more Westerners are placed in CEO-type roles in the region compared with other roles, according to Spencer Stuart, the recruiting firm. At the top ten banks globally, only three out of ten have Asian-Pacific CEOs who are Asian or of Asian descent (and two are co-CEOs); meanwhile, at the top 20 asset-management firms globally, only two CEOs are of Asian descent in the Asia-Pacific region, according to the recruiting firm Heidrick & Struggles.

Historically, when Western multinationals first enter Asia, they often send home country managers to train and manage overseas employees. It is partly because expatriates know how the business runs at home, and partly because headquarter executives tend to choose individuals from places with which they have a strong cultural affinity. However, this pattern persists even decades later. According to executive search firms, individuals who share similar image and culture with their bosses are more likely to be promoted, thus creating generations of white, male bosses in the Asian subsidiaries of many MNCs. Louisa Wong, founder of executive search firm Bo Le Associates, noted that "there is also a desire to save the coveted Asian-Pacific positions for ambitious executives from elsewhere in the company as experience in these markets is vital preparation for future top leadership." Therefore, those MNCs have failed to see and get the benefits that local candidates might bring.

"Expat executives may lack some of the skills needed on the ground," said Nicklas Jonow, a partner at Pacific Consulting Group, "For example, understanding consumer needs, trends, purchasing power, brand positioning—not just for luxury brands, and not just in Tier 1 cities—is becoming increasingly important. To fill those needs, multinationals have to shift their hiring practices to local talent who really understand these markets."

According to Kenneth Yu, President of 3M China, expatriates are needed to launch new subsidiaries, and local managers are preferred once they rise to the level to take control. However, many multinationals think local talent in Asia is still relatively young and has not reached that level. A study by Community Business, a nonprofit organization, found that Asian senior managers are five years younger than the world average (38 versus 43 years old), have four years less work experience (16 versus 22 years), and have two years less tenure with current employers (eight versus ten years). Also, Asian managers are mostly assigned to local positions. They have limited opportunities to move around in global postings and get exposure to different regions. Due to the complexity of running overseas subsidiaries, extra experience may make a difference. For instance, in the finance industry, "those in charge of regional operations aren't just charged with boosting sales but are expected to turn Asian-Pacific operations into multibillion-dollar businesses and deal with complex regulatory issues," said Steven McCrindle, a partner at Heidrick & Struggles.

Although many MNCs claim that they would be glad to hire locally, few are making adequate efforts to groom and cultivate local talent. "MNCs in Asia often fall into the trap of over-depending on expatriates and headhunters as an 'easy' fix to quickly fill vacancies," stated a 2011 study by CEB Inc., an advisory service firm. Meanwhile, business education systems in developing Asia have not produced enough managerial talent. "We lack the international talent to manage these (multinational) companies," said George Xue, Associate Dean of China's Fudan University's School of Management. In addition, the scarcity of Asian top managers can be attributed to their cultural differences with Western peers. For instance, many Asian cultures emphasize respect toward elders, seniority-based hierarchy, and the value of consensus. In business meetings, Asian managers often are not willing to speak up because they believe it is their job to sit on the sidelines listening and nodding until it is their turn to lead. However, these cultural traits are uncommon and usually not appreciated in Western communication and leadership styles.

Despite these challenges, some MNCs have realized the need to cultivate local talent in Asia. For example, Wal-Mart established its first Global Leadership Institute in June 2011 to help Asia-based managers develop skills to get senior leadership positions. It requires a new mindset to promote locals, who are traditionally hired for executing plans and tactics, to upper strategic roles. Meanwhile, due to the high costs associated with expatriate managers, a number of companies have restricted their use of expats. Foreign executives often earn higher salaries than locals. Even when they receive the same salary, expats require extra housing and educational allowances. "If I could find a top Chinese, Hong Kong-born, or Asian female executive, my clients would be over the moon," said Nick Marsh of executive search firm Harvey Nash.

Sources

1. Sanchanta, M. and Gold, R. (2013, August 14). In Asia, locals rise only so far at Western firms: Multinationals still rely on expatriates to fill top jobs decades after expanding into region. *Wall Street Journal*: B.6.
2. Hill, A. (2013, April 30). The only fix for China's managerial shortage. *Financial Times*, p. 12.

Questions for Case Discussion

1. Why do you think Western companies continue to rely on expats instead of hiring local talent for top management positions?
2. What are the main arguments that justify the increased use of local talent instead of expatriates?
3. What personalities or characteristics embody the ideal profile of local talent and why?

Case 9.3 "Sea Turtles" Return to China

Although China has seen record growth in the number of college graduates, the country is still in need of high-level talent for economic development. In recent years, the Chinese government has launched systematic efforts to recruit overseas Chinese technological and managerial professionals to return home. It aims to reverse the brain drain that occurred in earlier years and amass enough talent to build a knowledge-based economy. Governments, universities, research institutes as well as state-owned and private companies are all trying to hire those returnees, who are called "sea turtles" or "haigui" in Mandarin.

Mr. Wayne Chen is an example of the so-called "sea turtles." After working for Western MNCs for 20 years, Mr. Chen accepted the chief human resources officer position at Vanke Co., the world's largest residential-property developer by revenue based in Shenzhen, China. A Shanghai native, Mr. Chen moved to the U.S. many years ago. He did not plan to leave his former employer, a U.S. consulting firm. But Vanke successfully persuaded him with the prospect of housing for China's aging population and global expansion into cities like New York, San Francisco, and Singapore. When Mr. Chen started working for Vanke, he became one of a dozen "sea turtles" that joined the company within the past five years.

"Sea turtles" are those Chinese natives who have returned home after studying and/or working in Western countries for a period of time. They are highly sought by employers because of their understanding of both Chinese and Western practices. They can be especially instrumental to Chinese companies that intend to expand overseas. They can become "hybrid managers" that perfectly integrate global and local experiences. While being naturally comfortable with the nuances of Chinese culture, "sea turtles" are familiar with the operations of global companies. They are not only proficient in Mandarin but also capable of communicating in English or other foreign languages. Rooted in the Chinese market, they have knowledge about local business activities as well as international market trends. Over the past several years, the number of "sea turtles" has been increasing. According to China's Ministry of Education, some 350,000 "sea turtles" returned to China in 2015, about a 30 percent rise over the previous year. Similarly, the number of Chinese "seagulls," those traveling back and forth between China and the West, is also increasing. "Brain circulation" is a term that refers to such growing mobility of human talent.

Both MNCs' subsidiaries and Chinese companies are actively seeking these China-born, Western-educated managers. Traditionally, MNCs offset the shortage of local managers by bringing in Taiwanese and Hong Kong executives. However, "executives from Taiwan and Hong Kong don't possess a natural instinct for the local market as their China-born counterparts," said Xin Kai Hong, co-founder of Capvision, an expert network platform. When hiring those returnees, Western companies used to have an advantage because their pay was better than the level of wages of local firms. But this advantage is quickly disappearing. In some cases, local firms can even offer compensations as much as 50 percent higher than those at Western companies. Nowadays, many multinationals are concerned about a talent war, in which they compete directly with local firms for those internationally educated, experienced returnees.

The returnees are attracted by not only Chinese companies' compensation packages but also their global ambitions. "Chinese companies are looking to skill up so they can go international in the next 10 years, and want to get these executives into their business," said Max Price, a partner at Antal International, a global executive recruiter. Compared to Western firms, Chinese companies also offer the returnees higher positions with greater autonomy and job scope. After reaching career ceilings at Western multinationals, many Chinese natives return home to seek more powerful roles and make a greater impact. For instance, Joan Ren was once a top manager at GM, and she left the company in 2012 to become a partner at a Shanghai-based private equity firm. Guo Xin joined Beijing-based recruiting firm Career International as CEO after leaving a U.S. consulting firm, and he commented that "you're making global decisions rather than having these decisions made for you by Western headquarters." To attract job applicants, one Chinese state-owned enterprise reportedly claimed, "come join us because we don't have a glass ceiling." Certainly, the returnees are not guaranteed to succeed in China. After joining local companies, many "sea turtles" who have had years of working experiences at Western companies may face reverse culture shock. "The success rate is less than 50%," said Kitty Zheng, a Beijing-based recruiter for executive search firm Spencer Stuart.

Sources

1.   Chu, K. & Lublin, J. S. (2014, September 3). Brain circulation: The Chinese 'sea turtles' return in bids for power and better pay. *Wall Street Journal*: B.9. Retrieved from www.wsj.com/articles/chinese-firms-lure-native-executives-home-1409671081
2.   Hill, A. (2013, April 30). The only fix for China's managerial shortage. *Financial Times*, p. 12.
3.   Simon, D. F. and Fluid, L. M. (2010, August 23). WSJ executive adviser (a special report): Global business—prepare to be surprised in China. *Wall Street Journal*: R.5.

Questions for Case Discussion

1.   Why do Chinese managers who have previously worked for Western MNCs want to return home?
2.   What are the challenges these managers often face when they move from Western MNCs to local Chinese companies?
3.   Why are both MNCs and local Chinese companies interested in these Chinese natives?

Case 9.4   What Do Expatriates Want?

With the development of international business, the globally mobile workforce has seen significant growth. Despite the efforts MNCs have made to support overseas assignments, expatriates face challenges such as family stress, cultural differences, and increased workloads. In order to understand the needs of expatriates, Cigna, a global health service provider, and the National Foreign Trade Council (NFTC) conducted a worldwide survey in 2013.

"This survey allows us to examine disconnects between employees and employers—and sheds light on how to better support the globally mobile workforce, and in turn, the companies who appreciate their valued assets around the world," said Sheldon Kenton, Senior Vice President at Cigna, "An enhanced understanding of how expats feel about their experiences should cause companies to give greater consideration to the many factors that influence the success of global assignments when designing packages."

The survey results show that, when compared to a similar study by Cigna and NFTC in 2001, today's expats are older, on shorter assignments, and more likely to leave family back home. The age group of survey respondents between 25 and 34 decreased from 35 percent to 17 percent in 2013. Among those having a spouse or partner, about 92 percent moved together with their spouses or partners in 2001, but the percentage dropped to 73 percent in 2013. Similarly, 82 percent of expats with children brought their children along on overseas assignments in 2013, and the percentage decreased to 66 percent in 2013. In regard to the regional distribution of survey respondents, expats from Asia rose from five to 13 percent, those from North America dropped from 63 to 49 percent, expats from Europe also dropped from 43 to 22 percent, and those in Middle East/North Africa/Greater Arabia rose from 6 to 23 percent.

The 2013 survey revealed that most companies are able to provide critical support to expats. 80 percent of the respondents received general relocation services, 63 percent got settling in services, 65 percent had medical preparedness. However, there are also unsatisfactory areas. For instance, 59 percent of respondents were unaware of repatriation assistance (i.e. whether there is any company support after expats finish overseas assignments and return home). This low awareness may lead to job dissatisfaction if expats think their long-term career development is neglected by employers. The respondents under age 34 had very limited knowledge about their health plans. Compared to other age groups, they were considerably less informed about where to seek health care while traveling and how to handle claims.

According to the 2013 survey, 78 percent of the respondents accessed medical care while on assignment. Having a family significantly affected an expat's healthcare needs. While 64 percent of single expats and 67 percent of expats without children accessed healthcare, 91 percent of expats with spouses or partners had access to healthcare while only 64 percent of single expats and 69 percent of expats without children had access. Also, expats who left family members back home were more likely to get routine care in their home countries than their assigned locations. While 83 percent of expats having family with them accessed care locally, only 41 percent of expats without family did so.

Generally, large emerging markets such as Brazil, China, and India are considered relatively difficult countries for expat assignments. While confirming the challenges in those regions, findings from the Cigna-NFTC survey also revealed that developed countries like the U.S. can be challenging for foreign managers as well.

"Greater recognition of the challenges of being on assignment in the U.S. is vital. Navigating a complex health system, as well as developing an understanding of the financial and tax consequences of working in the

U.S., all present considerable challenges to U.S.-bound expats. My personal experience as an expat has further driven home the crucial need for better preparation, guidance and support," Kenton said.

Given that expats' discontent may threaten the successful completion of overseas assignments, it is imperative for MNCs to understand and fulfill the needs of their globally mobile workforce. "Survey results suggest many employers may be providing expatriates with services that adequately address the wider population, but not those on assignment in lesser developed countries," said Bill Sheridan, Vice President International Human Resources at NFTC, "Enhanced understanding, awareness, and flexibility are necessary when considering the complexity of global assignments. Customization is key, as a one-size-fits-all approach to developing packages for expatriates simply cannot provide a pathway to success in every geography."

Expats often mentioned human resource-related issues when answering open-ended questions about their experiences.

"Given the integral role human resource professionals play in designing programs for expatriates, an enhanced awareness of the typical challenges and potential barriers to success for expatriates while they're on assignment is critical. The survey results indicate companies could benefit from elevating this group's understanding of the unique needs and concerns of this population, either through consultancy or hiring HR professionals with actual expatriate assignment experience," Sheridan said.

Source

1. Business Wire. (2013, December 13). Cigna-NFTC survey: Expatriates want more from their employers, professional services close-up. Retrieved from www.businesswire.com/news/home/20131202005055/en/Cigna-NFTC-Survey-Expatriates-Employers

Questions for Case Discussion

1. What are the key findings of the recent survey on expatriates?
2. What are the key areas of concern on the part of the expatriates?
3. How do you think MNCs can better support expatriates?

Case 9.5 Why Is It So Difficult to Return Home?

Overseas assignments often help ambitious employees move to upper management positions. A 2012 survey by Mercer, a human-resource consultancy, found the majority of companies responding to the survey planned to increase long-term overseas assignments. However, not all companies are equipped to welcome those veteran expatriates when they return home. If a company fails to provide an appropriate position that rewards an expatriate manager's experience and skills accumulated abroad, he or she may feel frustrated, encounter career stumbles, or even leave the company. A 2013 *Wall*

Street Journal article, titled "After stints abroad, re-Entry can be hard," reported three such cases:

Lisa Lord was a former employee of SAP, a German software company. After working in the U.S. subsidiary of SAP for two years, Ms. Lord moved to Heidelberg, Germany, in 2006 to head a new talent-management team. However, due to department reorganization, she came back a year later. But there was no position waiting for her in the U.S. Although she was offered some project work, Ms. Lord believed that was not enough for her. Eventually, she received a prenegotiated severance package. SAP said in a statement that the company had retained 90 percent of overseas assignees but wouldn't comment on Ms. Lord's case. Ms. Lord later became a vice president for talent management at Shire PLC, a global biopharmaceutical company. Her experience in Germany had greatly benefited both her personal and professional life. "I was way more valuable to my next employer as a result of that experience," said Ms. Lord.

Brian Walker, while working for retail giant Wal-Mart, finished five overseas assignments in Indonesia and China and in both operation and human-resource functions. However, when he returned to the company's headquarters in Bentonville, Arkansas, he felt "nobody really cares about your experience." Mr. Walker also lost the authority and responsibility that he had while abroad. Tired of not being able to attend key meetings and influence main decisions, he asked for another overseas job in Hong Kong. During his last international assignment for the company, in Hong Kong, family issues made him return to the U.S. at the age of 46 but Wal-Mart didn't have a comparable job available for him "that would really excite me," he says. Eventually, Mr. Walker found a new position as the vice president of human resources at the international division of Kimberly-Clark, a U.S.-based consumer goods company.

Even top executives may experience a rough re-entry. After living in Asia for many years, John McCarvel joined the Singapore unit of footwear company Crocs. In 2010, he became the CEO for the company and moved to its headquarters near Boulder, Colorado. Mr. McCarvel admitted, "I still sometimes feel like a 'foreigner' at the office, puzzled by office politics and gossip." He also felt there was a lack of collaboration in comparison to what he had observed abroad. Knowing the hardship of re-entry, Mr. McCarvel kept track of newly returned expatriates at Crocs. He also thought longer international assignments could help. "Workers might feel more ready to come home after three to five years," he said, "whereas those on two-year assignments often spend their second year worrying about what comes next."

Many executive recruiters have also noted the challenges facing repatriates (i.e., returned expatriates). Their employers were criticized for not providing opportunities for repatriates to utilize their new capabilities learned overseas. "Companies send out company men and women, [and] these same people return as entrepreneurs," says John Touey, a principal at executive search firm Salveson Stetson Group, "Yet once they return, all of a sudden the pace of decision-making is slowed down. They have to get 10 signatures to get a project off the ground." Once a repatriate leaves, it becomes a real waste in investment. According to Ed Hannibal, a partner at human-resource consultancy Mercer, "it usually costs a company nearly twice an executive's $300,000 annual salary to send him from the U.S. to Shanghai for a year." It was estimated that between 8 percent and 25 percent of American managers leave their employers after returning from overseas assignments.

Some companies have taken steps to retain returning employees by offering support like career planning and opportunities to connect with top leaders. For instance, Kimberly-Clark Corp. sends employees on three-month assignments to expose them to new cultures without forcing them to leave current roles. At Xerox Corp., each expatriate is assigned a sponsor who ensures the assignment is a good fit and eases the manager's transition back to the U.S. Meanwhile, expatriates are advised to maintain their relationships with home country colleagues by making regular visits and communications. Newly returned managers should actively seek projects to leverage their skills and share their knowledge with co-workers.

Source

1.   Feintzeig, R. (2013, September 18). Careers: After stints abroad, re-entry can be hard. *Wall Street Journal*: B.6. Retrieved from www.wsj.com/articles /SB10001424127887323342404579081382781895274

Questions for Case Discussion

1.   Why are repatriates struggling after they return home?
2.   How do you think repatriates can alleviate the problems that they anticipate upon their return?
3.   What can companies do to improve repatriates' situations?

Managing People
Global Talent Management

I. Global Talent Management

The opening cases illustrate the various challenges involved in managing people within MNCs and offer examples of how individual managers who want to pursue borderless careers cope with changing environments. Managers need to continuously update their knowledge and skills to make themselves readily employable and marketable since, unlike previous generations, they are not expected to work for the same organization throughout their career. For MNCs, this means that these organizations need to continue looking for globally talented people and keeping them happy so that these individuals don't leave the organization and potentially work for competitors. MNCs increasingly recognize the effective management of human resources to win the talent war, i.e., global talent management, as a major determinant of success in the global market. As more knowledgeable workers are entering the global job market and businesses are moving across borders, innovative and adaptive HR practices are the only means to implement global talent management.[1]

As Figure 9.1 illustrates, global talent management refers to a company's comprehensive and deliberate efforts to identify, recruit, develop, and retain capable managers across borders.[2] Global talent management is vital as it helps enhance business performances and facilitates the alignment of a company's strategy with its vision, values, and the way it develops and manages its people.[3] The ultimate goal of global talent management is to possess a large number of cosmopolitan managers who can perform a requested job anywhere, anytime, in any manner. As an MNC expands its business in the global market, it creates a growing demand for managers who are capable of leading different groups within a global workforce who possess a global mindset as well as global skills. A global mindset is "the ability to influence individuals, groups, organizations, and systems that have different intellectual, social, and psychological knowledge or intelligence from your own."[4] It requires one to "think and act both globally and locally." Case 9.3 illustrates how Chinese companies are struggling to find talented groups of individuals to fill a growing number of key positions that require increasingly complicated skills and knowledge. To mitigate the shortage of capable managers, the Chinese government and companies together aggressively approach Chinese natives living abroad with lucrative offers to persuade them to return home. This chapter will examine how companies are dealing with the challenges involved in global talent management. First, we will look at the key issues related to recruiting and staffing.

II. Recruiting and Staffing

The very first challenge companies are facing is how and where to find a talented workforce. Many MNCs are struggling to identify a qualified person for open

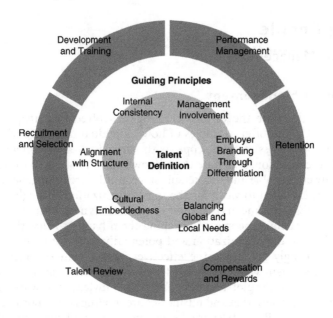

Figure 9.1 Talent Management Practices

Source: Determinants and Challenges of Global Talent Management. Retrieved from www.linkedin.com/pulse/determinants-challenges-global-talent-management-nermeen-ragab

positions at different levels of the organizational hierarchy. It is very costly and time consuming to find the right person for a vacancy. Therefore, MNCs need to develop deliberate strategies aimed at attracting people who are entrepreneurial, quick thinking, and able to solve problems convincingly. Case 9.1 illustrates how MNCs effectively meet this challenge; for example, IBM provides financial as well as technical support to local Chinese universities to teach skills the company wants from its future employees. Most business schools have integrated some type of global experiential learning ingredient into their curriculum to help their students prepare for careers in the global economy.

The following are suggested criteria to attract a talented workforce.[5] Companies need to build a global reputation and should be able to effectively communicate their employer value proposition to potential employees. The most popular companies have established strong brand awareness and a reputation for excellence. Talented prospective employees want to work for organizations that make a difference. It is critical for organizations to engage with their talented workforce and to display what it is like to work for the company. Promoting the company's values is also important so that employees can see a strong alignment between their personal values and corporate values. Promising employees want to know how their achievements will be recognized and rewarded. They are also interested in learning about career development opportunities that will help them advance their career and expand their skills. In fact, these criteria incorporate all the key dimensions of global talent management such as training and development, compensation, and performance appraisal. Once an MNC successfully recruits talented workers, it needs to figure out how to deploy them. Typically, the company can draw from three different pools of talented people: home country nationals, host country nationals, and third country nationals.

I. Three Staffing Policies

(1) Ethnocentric Orientation

Ethnocentric organizations believe that a parent company's way of conducting business is superior to a host country's and thus typically sends home-country managers, i.e., expatriates, to manage foreign operations. This type of staffing policy makes most sense when MNCs need to tightly control their global business operation by integrating and coordinating the activities of overseas subsidiaries in congruence with the overarching goal of headquarters. The main benefits of ethnocentric orientation include prompt and effective implementation of business decisions as the MNC's headquarters centralizes its communication channel with overseas subsidiaries by sending expatriates who are already familiar with corporate values and policies (see Case 9.2). Expatriates are expected to behave in accordance with a company's goals and objectives, without seeking opportunistic behaviors. The predictability of expatriates' actions will help alleviate information asymmetry between the parent firm and its overseas subsidiary.[6] Using an agency theory framework, they may be considered as agents who faithfully follow the corporate goals and business interests of the headquarters, i.e. principal. Expatriates can also facilitate the transfer of intangible firm-specific knowledge, which is often embedded in their technical competence and/or experiences.[7]

Expatriates are sent to teach local managers about business practices and processes that they can learn mainly through mentoring and coaching. This is why top management positions in Asia are still largely filled with expatriates (as Case 9.2 illustrates). MNCs can create an organization where important business policies and practices are standardized by instilling corporate culture and strategy through expatriates. As a result, ethnocentric orientation is likely to produce cultural convergence centering around the norms and values of an expatriate's home country.

However, there are downsides to using expatriates. Compared to host country managers, expatriates may not understand consumer needs, purchasing power, and brand positioning of the products and services that they are dealing with. These concerns are making many MNCs replace expatriates with local talent in Asia (see Case 9.2). In an extreme case, MNCs may try to impose headquarters' rules and business practices on the local market, as they believe their way of doing business is superior to the host country's. Western MNCs might feel that cross-cultural differences might be too great to hire local managers who may not understand cultural norms and values of Western countries and companies. The existing literature also recognizes the difficulty expatriates often experience in cross-cultural adjustment to a host country.[8] Another drawback stems from higher costs involved in using expatriates. Companies often need to offer expatriates double or triple compensation plus fringe benefits and incur other costs such as relocation.

(2) Polycentric Orientation

In contrast to ethnocentric orientation, polycentric orientation allows a substantial degree of autonomy and discretion to local subsidiary managers and thus makes the most sense when MNCs are faced with a higher need for local responsiveness. Accordingly, polycentric orientation promotes cultural divergence as it emphasizes in-depth understanding of the norms and values of the host country. This approach is based on the assumption that each market is substantially different from the other in terms of its political, economic, and sociocultural environments. Therefore, in order to effectively meet these different circumstances, MNCs need to use host country nationals who are more familiar with the institutional profile of the host country. A polycentric orientation includes the following benefits: First, MNCs can avoid the pitfalls of falling into cultural myopia, as host country managers are very well aware of the cultural values and norms of the local business environments. Second, polycentric orientation provides a good opportunity for host country managers to build their careers and understand the corporate and business strategies of the parent company. Third, companies can save costs involved in sending expatriates since it is much cheaper to hire locals rather than expatriates. Finally, employing host country nationals can build good relationships with and receive better treatment from host country governments by promoting a local corporate image. Demonstrating confidence in host country managers as well as a commitment to developing local talent can positively influence the perceptions about the MNC and, thus, increase local legitimacy.[9]

However, a polycentric approach has some drawbacks. First, host country managers might prioritize the business interests of local subsidiaries over those of headquarters. Using the agency theory paradigm, agents, i.e. host country managers, may behave against the interest of the principal, parent company. Also, a polycentric orientation makes it difficult for MNCs to build an organization where managers can see the role of subsidiaries from a global perspective since host country managers are often preoccupied with local issues at the expense of more important strategic issues from headquarters' perspective.

(3) Geocentric Orientation

Given the pros and cons of the ethnocentric and polycentric orientation we discussed, the best solution may be to combine the benefits of these two orientations. It would be ideal if MNCs could find managers who have not only a broad understanding of headquarters' global competitive strategies but also in-depth insights into a particular local market. The returning Chinese turtle case perfectly illustrates such a pool of managers who meet this requirement. A geocentric orientation seeks the most qualified person who best fits the managerial position regardless of nationality, ethnicity, age, gender, etc. The only relevant selection criterion is whether a candidate possesses the skills and knowledge to perform the job. Thus, geocentric orientation is more likely to take advantage of the benefits from a diverse group of managers consisting of those who are from the home country, a host country, and even a third country. Global learning can be obtained in this type of organization as the culturally diverse workforce contributes to developing new ideas and unbiased perspectives about issues at stake. Managers may feel more secure and comfortable as a geocentric orientation promotes an organizational culture that is not limited to values and norms of a specific home or host country. Therefore, it will breed cultural crossvergence, as a new organizational culture is likely to be shaped through the mutual influence of different cultural norms and values that a diverse workforce brings to the organization. A diverse workforce is more productive, innovative, and solution oriented than a homogeneous one, which can be potentially limited by groupthink. Geocentric orientation can balance the demands of local customers, employees, and government officials with those of headquarter managers.[10] Table 9.1 summarizes the relationship between each staffing policy and its pool of talented group.

Although a geocentric approach is most ideal and desirable, choosing the optimal staffing policy ultimately depends upon such underlying factors as an MNC's international business strategy and experiences, the availability of expatriates versus host country talent, the expatriates' cultural adaptability, and the expatriates' assignment cost. When MNC's understanding of local market insight and business experiences is critical, host country nationals would be preferred to expatriates. Conversely, when MNCs' business strategies require a great deal of control from headquarters, expatriates would be more suitable than host country nationals. As an MNC accumulates international business experience, expatriates are often replaced by host country nationals who have learned the required skills and knowledge from their expatriate predecessors. The types of staffing policies companies adopt will determine the candidates who possess the right traits to become leaders who can manage global workforces. The following selection criteria have been identified from the previous literature. These standards are particularly pertinent to expatriates. Yet, surprisingly, according to the recent survey conducted by Brookfield, 78 percent of respondents don't utilize any type of candidate assessment, formal or informal, for selecting candidates to take on an international assignment.[11]

Table 9.1 Staffing Policy and Talented Pool

Ethnocentric	Expatriates	
Polycentric	Host Country Nationals (HCNs)	
Geocentric	Expatriates & HCNs	Third Country National (TCNs)

Selection criteria of overseas assignees:

1. Technical ability: Candidates need to possess the adequate skills and knowledge to perform the job.
2. Managerial skills: Adequate communication and good leadership skills are expected of the candidates to effectively manage the host country's workforce.
3. Cultural empathy: Candidates are capable of understanding and approaching a crucial issue from another person's frame of reference or perspective.
4. Adaptability and flexibility: Refers to open mindedness in analyzing and solving problems.
5. Diplomatic skills: Candidates should have an ability to make good friends with key political and business figures of the host country and to articulate the company's contribution to the local economy.
6. Language aptitude: A good command of local language is useful to reduce miscommunication with the host country's workforce.
7. Personal motives: A "mission impossible" attitude is critical to overcome any anxiety associated with uncertainty and unpredictability. Candidates should not be solely motivated by financial remuneration but a drive not only to enjoy a new adventure abroad but also to broaden their perspective about different countries. In addition, candidates should be excited about acquiring new skills and knowledge that enable them to manage global workforces.
8. Emotional stability and maturity is important to overcome stressful situations caused by unfamiliar living and working environments. Accordingly, managers need to be independent and self-reliant.
9. Adaptability of Family: In the past, expatriate literature found expatriates failures within host countries could be directly attributed to expatriates' families' inability to adapt to the cultural environment.

As Case 9.3 illustrates, a new staffing policies targets China-born professionals who have accumulated extensive work experience at Western MNCs. The Chinese government as well as its companies are attempting to bring these managers back home. These managers understand not only the nuances of Chinese culture but also have a global business perspective from working in Western MNCs. We believe that such a phenomenon will spread to other developing countries like India which continue to suffer from brain drain.

Case 9.4 emphasizes that each host country poses distinctive challenges to expatriates and MNCs should adopt customized approaches to develop the right packages for expatriates to successfully perform jobs to the best of their ability. According to the Cigna-NFTC 2013 survey, the following areas were identified as the main concerns of expatriates:[12]

*   Lack of understanding—HR personnel may not understand the professional and personal challenges expatriates face.
*   Relocation—There is a lack of communication regarding this process.
*   Real estate market differences—Such differences are not commonly recognized by HR.

- Responsiveness—Responses from headquarters are often delayed.
- Process time—Some processes are slow or unclear, such as obtaining work permits.
- Policy limitations—There are restrictions on mobility and relocation.
- Travel costs.

III. Training and Development

Once an MNC completes the staffing process, the next step is to provide effective training to newly hired managers to help them perform the job to their highest potential. Effective training is essential for managers to demonstrate high performance. Although training needs vary depending upon who and why they were hired, one of the key goals of training should focus on globally aligning the company's values and norms among different groups of employees to create one unified and coherent corporate culture across borders. Employees' identification with the company will not only increase loyalty but also improve communication among different units of the MNC. Different staffing policies and practices will determine the types of training required of newly hired managers.

I. Expatriate Training

Expatriates are already equipped with technical competence and familiar with the corporate culture and the roles they are expected to play to fulfill the company's oversea objectives. Consequently, expatriates mainly receive cross-cultural training, language training, and practical training rather than task-oriented training. Short-term training is provided before and after the assignment. Pre-departure training usually covers a host country's culture, history, politics, economy, religion, and social and business practices. However, it mainly focuses on cross-cultural training and languages training while post-departure on-site training is geared toward helping candidates manage day-to-day living through practical training.

Cross-cultural training is designed to help expatriates learn about cultural values and norms in their assigned country so that they can effectively manage the host country workforce. Expatriates may have predeveloped or preconceived notions about people in the host country. Effective training will correct any bias being held against them and will help expatriates understand behaviors and attitudes of the host country workforce by helping them properly interpret various verbal and nonverbal cues. One of the most useful concepts related to cross-cultural training is cultural intelligence (CQ), which tests a candidate's ability to function effectively in a variety of national, ethnic, and organizational settings.[13] The notion of cultural intelligence is similar to cross-cultural competence but goes beyond this and actually examines intercultural capabilities as a form of intelligence that can be measured and developed. As Table 9.2 shows, cultural intelligence represents a four-dimensional model consisting of CQ drive, CQ knowledge, CQ strategy, and CQ action.[14] First, CQ drive refers to a person's interest and confidence in performing effectively in culturally diverse settings. How motivated is a person to undertake culturally diverse experiences and benefit from them? Does a candidate have a desire to effectively handle culturally diverse situations? If a candidate has no interest in or curiosity about new adventures, there is no use spending so much money and time on cross-cultural training. Second, CQ knowledge represents the cognitive dimension of the model, focusing on cultural systems and cultural values and norms. How much does a candidate know about cultural similarities and differences between his/her home country and a host country? Most pre-departure training for expatriates tends to focus on teaching the cultural norms and values of their assigned country. Third, CQ strategy concerns how a person makes sense of cross-cultural experiences. It consists of awareness, planning, and checking and becomes critical when people make judgments about their own thought processes and those of others. A candidate not only needs to be conscious about his/her existing cultural knowledge but also be able to strategize to reduce mistakes, check assumptions, and adjust mental maps when actual experiences are different from expectations. Candidates can practice CQ strategy using potential scenarios likely to happen in an assigned country. Finally, CQ action is a person's ability to adapt verbal and non-verbal behaviors to conform to various cultures.[15] It refers to how flexibly a person can engage in acceptable verbal and nonverbal behaviors in different cultural contexts. It is very difficult for a candidate to achieve a high level of CQ in all four dimensions prior to his/her departure. Expatriate candidates can only improve the use of CQ strategy and CQ action through accumulated experiences during their overseas assignment.

Cross-cultural training can be more effective when it is combined with language training. Understanding the host country's language will definitely help managers reduce the risk of miscommunication and misconduct arising from language barriers. In contrast to the pre-departure training program emphasizing cross-cultural and language training, on-site training after departure usually focuses on practical training. Living in a foreign country presents many different challenges and a company needs to help expatriates learn how to manage living in the assigned country.

2. Local Workforce Training

Host country nationals are required to receive a different type of training. As they are already familiar with the local business environments, their training

Table 9.2 The Four-Dimensional Model of Cultural Intelligence (CQ)

CQ Drive: Motivational CQ	CQ Knowledge: Cognitive CQ	CQ Strategy: Metacognitive CQ	CQ Action: Behavioral CQ
Intrinsic	Cultural Systems	Awareness	Verbal
Extrinsic	Cultural Norms &	Planning	Nonverbal
Self-Efficacy	Values	Checking	Speech Arts

Source: Livermore, D. (2010). Leading with cultural intelligence: The new secret to success. New York: AMACOM.

typically focuses on developing technical and managerial competence. The training contents vary depending upon the level of organizational hierarchy. While upper management needs leadership training or business-level strategy training to better understand the corporate goal of the parent company, managers at the middle and supervisory level should receive the basic management training or technical training to become effective supervisors.[16] Host country nationals also need to receive training about the parent company for which they are working. They should learn core values as well as best management practices of the parent company to identify them as an important member of the company.

In many cases, host country nationals don't have in-depth knowledge about the products and/or technologies they are dealing with and thus need to be educated. Promising local managers, called inpatriates, are often brought in to headquarters to imbue host country nationals with knowledge that is too difficult to learn locally and teach them how to bridge the gap between home and abroad. The case of IBM in China illustrates the proactive move of an MNC to recruit new employees who have already completed the basic technical training during their college years.

3. Global Leadership Development

While a short-term training program is useful to assure high performance of managers, an increasing number of companies are putting more emphasis on systematically nurturing and developing globally competent managers in the long run. Development of an effective global leadership program is an integral part of global talent management. A growing trend is to use international assignments as a tool to develop leaders with a global mindset.[17] As discussed above, companies should first hire candidates who are not only capable of performing the required task but also capable of playing a leadership role within the organization. As international work experience is required to change the way people think about conducting business globally, MNCs need to groom and organize a team of managers who have acquired both technical and cross-cultural competencies. It takes much more time than simply learning the assigned tasks to improve understanding of diverse cultures and develop a global mindset. The ability to work with people whose values and norms are different from your own is an acquired skill. A global mindset enables managers to have an open mind toward diverse cultures and an ability to detect common patterns across markets.[18]

For example, the Global Expert Program created by Samsung, a Korean conglomerate, illustrates efforts to develop global managers at the three different levels of organizational hierarchy. First, the company has a CEO development program that trains top managers to evaluate business opportunities and threats in a specific country. Second, the company has plans to handle issues related to competitive strategy and human resource management.[19] As previously explained, expatriate training is provided to help middle-level managers develop the abilities to effectively manage the host country's workforce (HCW) in an assigned country. Finally, Samsung also established the Overseas Regional Specialist Program in 1990. Unlike the two previous programs targeting upper and middle level management, this particular

Table 9.3 Samsung Global HRM Program

Global Expert Program	Internationalization of Managers	Acculturation of HCW to Samsung
CEO Development	Samsung MBA	Recruiting and Developing HCW
Expatriate Training Overseas Regional Specialists	Foreign Language Training	

Source: Rowly, C. and Paik, Y. (2009). *The Changing Face of Korean Management*. London and New York: Routledge, p. 173.

program is designed to help young lower-level managers develop cross-cultural leadership at the early stage of their career. Participants in the program are required to spend a year in a country of their choice to gain cross-cultural competence and hands-on experience by learning a local language, culture, and other important information about the country. Upon completing the program, they become reserves for future expatriates. It was these accomplished managers who filled the initial positions when Samsung opened a new subsidiary in Beijing, China.[20] Table 9.3 summarizes Samsung's Global HRM program.

Samsung's example is a good showcase to demonstrate how a leading global company deliberately develops a global leadership program that appears to be seamlessly integrated with the career development of their high performing managers. It is imperative that MNCs identify employees with high potential as early as possible and support their career goals through well-established leadership development programs supporting global talent management.

IV. Compensation

1. Retention and Global Employee Engagement

Once the process of training and developing global managers is completed, the next step is to ensure these promising managers are happy and stay with the company until they achieve their professional goals. It would be a waste of an investment, time, and money if well-trained employees leave the company. Talented individuals who are inappropriately matched and recruited into organizations are turning into entrepreneurial offerings within the market and establishing their own paths outside of the traditional work world causing a greater skills shortage within the traditional workplace.[21] This group of people, called expat-preneurs, are trying to build their own businesses based upon the significant level of technical or functional knowledge they acquired during their tenure with the previous company. Therefore, an MNC needs to keep track of the effectiveness of its HR policies and practices so as not to lose its talented workforce to its competitors.

The key to retaining these employees is to provide appropriate incentives to keep them engaged with the company. A talented workforce needs to be passionate about what they see and what they experience within their organization. A company that tries to make itself an exciting workplace creates a strong organizational culture and retains top-performing managers for longer. Engaged employees not only enjoy their work but also aspire to help their companies succeed. According to Towers Watson 2012 Global Work Study, only one-third of the global workforce are considered engaged employees who are willing to give their discretionary efforts to help their company achieve success.[22] To achieve this goal, MNCs need to establish the two most critical HR policies: fair and effective compensation as well as a performance appraisal system. Managers will lose their motivation for and interest in their job if their work is not properly recognized and rewarded. Depending upon the nature of the employment relationships,[23] the following three approaches can be used to determine a global worker's compensation package.

Headquarters-based approach: This approach maintains a standardized compensation scheme for expatriates anchored on headquarters' compensation structure. Since every expatriate will be paid an equal amount, it is relatively easy to manage but may cause problems in attracting and retaining expatriates from high-income countries. In contrast, expatriates from low-income countries may enjoy the increase in compensation but they may find it difficult to accept the significant drop in compensation upon their return home.[24]

Home-based balance sheet approach: This approach is probably the most common compensation method used for expatriates in a long-term contract with a large company. The main goal of this approach is to make sure that expatriates are not penalized in terms of quality of living simply because they have relocated to a new place and accepted an overseas assigned position.[25] It might be possible that expatriates have reluctantly accepted the offer due to the scarcity of capable managers for the open position. Therefore, a company should do everything possible to assure its expatriates enjoy the same living standard abroad as they do at home. In other words, this approach attempts to equalize purchasing power across countries by providing financial incentives to offset qualitative differences between assignment locations. To achieve this goal, typical compensation packages include such items as housing allowances, children's international school support, travel allowances, tax differentials, suitable holiday entitlements, and high salaries that may reach two or three times the amount allotted at home. It is these packages that entice so many expatriates to accept a job offer. For example, American companies need to consider their expatriates' tax burden. U.S. citizens living overseas are required to file not only tax returns but also FBAR (Foreign Bank Account Report) in order to comply with the Foreign Account Tax Compliance Act (FATCA).[26] Figure 9.2 illustrates a typical balance sheet approach.

Host country based model: Expatriates are paid in accordance with the living costs of the assigned country. Expatriates from a lower income country would benefit most from this approach as their compensation increases with their

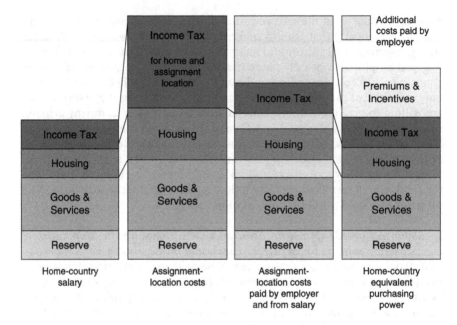

Figure 9.2 The Balance Sheet

Source: Expatriate Compensation Services. Figure was created based on the information retrieved from www.imercer.com/content/global-mobility-expat-compensation.aspx

overseas assignment. However, those from a higher income country may be unwilling to accept this approach unless they value nonfinancial benefits from overseas assignment, such as the exciting international experience itself, more than financial remuneration to balance or offset the decrease in compensation. Expatriates are more likely to agree to this type of compensation model when they are assigned to a rather permanent job and expect to stay there for a relatively long period of time.[27]

The 2015 Brookfield Global Relocation Trends survey showed that 78 percent of the respondents adopted the home-based balance sheet approach to determine expatriate compensation while 9 percent applied the host country approach and 3 percent used the headquarters-based approach.[28]

Typically, host country nationals are usually paid the equivalent to other local employees' pay scale. They generally understand that expatriates are paid a much higher compensation compared to local managers. However, it is crucial that local managers do not feel that they are not being recognized and are being substantially underpaid as compared to expatriates. The discovery of conspicuous compensation gaps negatively influences organizational commitment of the HCW, resulting in a lower level of employee engagement.[29] Unengaged employees won't be fully involved in or enthusiastic about their work. They do not care about the future of the company and are unwilling to invest any discretionary effort to see that their company succeeds.

Whatever compensation approach is adopted, a managers' compensation should be tied to their ability to manage the host country's workforce. How you retain local employees' engagement depends on managers' leadership skills as well as whether they are expatriates, host country nationals, or third country nationals. More often than not, it is more challenging for expatriates to keep the host country workforce engaged than a home country workforce due to cross-cultural differences in their values and norms. This does not necessarily mean that host country employees always prefer local managers to expatriates as their supervisors. For example, Mexican employees were found to prefer to work for American supervisors than their local Mexican counterparts who tend to care less about their career development.[30] The quality of the supervisor-subordinate relationship is more important than their belongingness to the same ethnic group in influencing the level of employee engagement. Employee engagement drivers vary from one country to another and only those managers who possess the cultural savvy to lead host country workforces will be able to leverage them.

V. Performance

Performance management directly affects compensation as companies pay for performance. An accurate and fair evaluation of the performance of expatriates as well as host country nationals present another challenge for MNCs as the outcome of the performance evaluation determines the level of compensation. Managers will be demotivated and dejected if they feel that they are not receiving adequate performance evaluations and compensation commensurate with their contributions. A well-established global performance system is vital for the following three reasons.[31] First, the performance management process constitutes a key mechanism to assure the alignment of company objectives and individual accomplishments. It is designed to build a mutual understanding about the role of specific employee behavior in realizing organizational outcomes. Second, it provides input to all functional HR processes, from recruiting and staffing to development and compensation. Through rigorous performance evaluation systems, the company can identify the weak areas where existing employees lack skills and competencies. This will help the company determine who to recruit and how to train newly hired employees. Finally, effective performance management helps employees focus on their tasks, recognizes and rewards them for completion of set tasks, and makes clear consequences for poor performance and behavior. Giving useful feedback and getting valuable input should be an integral part of a performance appraisal system. In order to realize the benefits of performance management, companies need to pay attention to the following underlying factors in designing effective performance appraisal systems.

I. Optimal Tradeoff between Standardization and Localization

In devising the most effective performance appraisal systems, an optimal balance should be sought to reconcile pressure on integration and standardization with pressure on differentiation and localization. In order to monitor the effective implementation of a parent company's strategic goals, the performance evaluation system should be consistent and congruent across borders so that employees clearly understand what is expected of them. Transparent and coherent performance assessments will enable managers to deal with cross-border transfers confidently and keep standards as required. This will encourage uniform desirable practices. For example, if an MNC sets a high priority on knowledge management and learning organization as its strategic goal, managers should make requirements clear, post what they have learned from the projects they have completed, and share acquired knowledge with their colleagues. Both the quality and quantity of contribution to the company's knowledge management should be reflected in the performance evaluation process.

At the same time, performance management should be flexible enough to accommodate local conditions and cross-cultural differences. For example, performance appraisal systems should vary depending upon the strategic mandate of a subsidiary whether it serves as a profit- or cost-center. It also needs to account for the local economic and sociopolitical environment where a subsidiary operates. For example, the existence of strong unionized workers may negatively affect the performance of expatriates compared to those working in a country where unions do not exist or tend to be cooperative. Expatriates assigned to a country where political and financial instability is high, might have their performance unfairly underestimated due to external conditions that are beyond their control. Distinctive cultural values and norms of a host country should also be incorporated into the design of appropriate performance appraisal schemes. For example, Japan is a collective society where group achievement is more valued than individual merit. Expatriates who have successfully adjusted to the host country culture are expected to demonstrate high performance.

2. Strategic Orientation

A company's staffing policy will influence the adoption of specific types and features of performance management.[32] Consistent with its philosophy, an ethnocentric orientation is more likely to use home country standards and instruments to measure the performance of subsidiary managers, often expatriates. In contrast, polycentric orientation will allow more autonomy and independence to decentralize or localize performance appraisal schemes suitable for local conditions with which the host country workforce is very familiar. Finally, considering the diversity of its workforce composition, geocentric orientation needs to create a new performance management system that is applicable and agreeable to managers from any cultural, racial, and/or ethnic background.

3. Transparency and Fairness

As mentioned above, employees should have a clear understanding about what constitutes a desired performance. The performance evaluation process should be transparent and explicit. The performance criteria should be as quantifiable as possible to objectively measure the employee's performance. Employees should be able to give their input in this process and supervisors are expected to give timely and useful feedback to improve their performance. Establishment of an effective communication channel is critical to assure the implementation of performance management. Whatever performance appraisal system is adopted, employees should have confidence that their efforts will lead to a strong performance evaluation, and in turn, will be rewarded with greater compensation. Employees should agree on job performance goals. If a manager is assigned to a task that will take more time than anticipated, a timeline should be specified to allow enough time to attain it.

4. Financial Performance and ROI on Expatriation

In a broad context, expatriates' performance evaluation schemes should be viewed as a return on investment or part of their assignment. How can a company measure the success of an expatriate's assignment? It would be ideal if the company can clearly evaluate the gains against the costs of the assignment.[33] However, about 95 percent of companies don't assess the ROI (return on investment) of their international assignments.[34]

While it is relatively easier to track expatriation costs including administrative costs and allowances, calculating the intrinsic value of the assignment may not be easy to quantify. Strong performance of expatriates will be reflected in the financial performance of the subsidiary. However, non-financial values of the overseas assignment, although indiscernible, will have a long-term impact as these investments in human capital help the company develop capable global managers for the future.

VI. Repatriation

Once expatriates complete their overseas assignment and return home, they often expect a hero's welcome. However, the reality is often the opposite of this positive scenario. Case 9.5 illustrates how difficult it can be for managers to readjust to their home country. First, the most common complaint from returning expatriates involves the parent company's inability to provide assistance in transitioning from the overseas assignment and host country back to the home country. As Case 9.5 demonstrates, unfortunately, repatriates often find that their newly acquired skills and knowledge are neither appreciated nor utilized after they return. "Reverse culture" shock is much more severe than the initial culture shock encountered at their departure. Managers usually take for granted the conscious effort needed to return home and readjust to the lifestyle of their home country. Contrary to this expectation, existing research has found that returning managers face many different challenges. First, they must readjust themselves to the work environment. This often poses a great challenge to returning expatriates since they may have been forgotten due to the "out of sight, out of mind" syndrome. They may expect a position that matches the newly acquired skills or knowledge through promotion. However, the reality could be quite different from their expectation since companies rarely prepare a position.[35] Typically, returning expatriates learn that colleagues at headquarters are uninterested in listening to stories pertaining to the assignment. Second, repatriates need to readjust themselves to general living environments at home. More often than not, they have to think of their home country as another foreign country, "Another new place to discover."[36] The more adapted their lifestyle is to an assigned country, the more difficult it is for them to readjust to the home country. Family issues could exacerbate this situation. The family's reverse cultural shock can interfere with the returning expatriate's ability to resume his/her responsibilities in the domestic office.[37]

Children might struggle at school having to deal with a new curriculum or having to catch up with subjects. Spouses might also complain about having to cope with changes in lifestyles that may not provide returning expatriates with enough free time to spend with their families. Finally, repatriates often find themselves financially strained as the hefty compensation they used to enjoy abroad has now been substantially reduced.

How can a company help repatriates and their families easily transition? First, they can appoint mentors who can facilitate the interests of expats during their overseas assignment. If they are repeatedly informed about proceedings at headquarters while abroad, there will be little surprise when they return home. Second, an effective cross-cultural preparation is required before they return home from the assignment and a repatriation program can immensely influence the success or failure of the assignment. The company needs to devise a proactive strategy that provides an effective support system to reduce concerns about career issues. One key transitional activity is to communicate clearly about the expectations the home office has for expatriates when they get close to returning.[38] A company's ability to relieve any difficulties concerning family issues is rather limited since most of these matters should be handled privately. The discrepancy between expatriates and HR managers in terms of their main concerns about reintegration makes the repatriation process all the more difficult. Typically, while expatriates prioritize re-assimilating the home country culture, HR managers place greater value on the corporate culture.[39] In order to preempt these issues involving repatriation, it is essential that companies perceive expatriate management as continuous from sending off to return, not a separate process. When an MNC sends expatriates abroad, they need to envision how the expatriates' skills and knowledge will be utilized upon their return. Maybe the root cause for discrepancies originates from conflicting interpretations regarding the purpose of the overseas assignment. Employees may accept the assignment for one reason while companies may be sending them on the assignment for different reasons. Expatriates usually accept assignments for career advancement, compensation, and adventure while the company sends expatriates to transfer the home corporate culture, meet project objectives, and expand business into various global markets.

We have so far discussed the key elements of global talent management, ranging from recruiting, staffing, training and development, to retention through compensation and performance evaluation. Global talent management begins with finding high performing employees who meet the increasingly demanding job specifications required by MNCs. Next, these employees' talent needs to be nurtured and fully developed through effective training and development programs. Companies might lose these talented employees after investing heavily in their development unless the organization can keep these employees engaged with their job and the organization. Throughout the process, managers should maintain balance between global integration and local responsiveness. Global managers must feel comfortable with the local business culture and familiarize themselves with the best practices at global companies. They should be able to communicate easily with both top executives at headquarters and local employees. And they must be capable of handling challenges embedded in local markets as well as issues in the global context.

Key Terms

Global talent management, staffing, expatriates, host country nationals, third country nationals, training, development, compensation, retention, engagement, performance appraisal, ethnocentric, polycentric, geocentric, cultural intelligence, global mindset

Review Questions

1. What is global talent management and why is it important for an MNC to effectively conduct businesses across borders?
2. Explain the three key staffing policies introduced in this chapter and then compare and contrast the pros and cons of each policy.
3. What are the main selection criteria that MNCs use in choosing the right candidate for an opening position at an overseas subsidiary? What are the primary concerns that expatriates typically raise in managing their assignments as well as living abroad?
4. How can an MNC keep talented employees and managers engaged with the organization and them? What types of compensation and performance appraisal schemes are available for MNCs to use to achieve this goal?
5. What are the key challenges that expatriates face when they return home? How can a company improve its repatriation policies and practices to help returning managers ease their transition?

Internet Exercise

Please visit the following website (www.towerswatson.com/Insights/IC-Types/Survey-Research-Results/2012/07/2012-Towers-Watson-Global-Workforce-Study) and discuss the current status regarding global workforce engagement. How do you think MNCs can improve employee engagement?

Notes

1   2015 Global Mobility Trends Survey. (2015). Booksfield Global Relocation Services. Retrieved from www.moving-on.co/brookfields-2015-global-mobility-trends-report-calls-for-mindful-mobility/

2   Tarique, I. and Schuler, R. (2010). Global talent management: Literature review, integrative framework, and suggestions for further research, *Journal of World Business*, 45(2), 122–133.

3   Vance, C. and Paik, Y. (2015). *Managing a Global Workforce: Challenges and Opportunities in International Human Resource Management*. New York: Routledge.

4   Cohen, S. (2010). Effective global leadership requires global mindset. *Industrial and Commercial Training*, 42(1), 3–10.

5   MichaelPage.com. How to attract top performers. Retrieved from www. michaelpage.com/employer-center/attraction-and-recruitment-advice/how-to-attract-top-performers

6   Tan, D. and Mahoney, J. T. (2006). Why a multinational firm chooses expatriates: Integrating resource-based, agency and transaction costs perspectives. *Journal of Management Studies*, 43(3), 457–484.

7   Ando, N. and Paik, Y. (2013). Institutional distance, host country and international business experience, and the use of parent country nationals. *Human Resource Management Journal*, 23(1), 52–71.

8   Yamazaki, Y. and Kayes, D. C. (2004). An experiential approach to cross-cultural learning: A review and integration of competencies for successful expatriate adaptation. *Academy of Management Learning & Education*, 3, 362–379.

9   Hyun, H., Oh, C., and Paik, Y. (2015). Impact of nationality composition in foreign subsidiary on its performance: A case of Korean companies. *International Journal of Human Resource Management*, 26(6), 806–830.

10   Roth, K. and Nigh, D. (1992). The effectiveness of headquarters-subsidiary relationships: The role of coordination, control, and conflict. *Journal of Business Research*, 25, 277–301.

11   Brookfield Global Relocation Service (2015).The 2015 Global Mobility Trends Survey.

12   Cigna-NFTC. (2013). Survey: Expatriates want more from their employers, professional services close-up. Retrieved from www.businesswire.com/news/home/20131202005055/en/Cigna-NFTC-Survey-Expatriates-Employers

13   Livermore, D. (2010). *Leading with Cultural Intelligence: The New Secret to Success.* New York: AMACOM.

14   Ibid.

15   Livermore, D. and Van Dyne, L. (2015). *Cultural Intelligence: The Essential Intelligence for the 21st Century.* Alexandria, VA: SHRM Foundation.

16   Vance, C. and Paik, Y. (2015). *Managing a Global Workforce: Challenges and Opportunities in International Human Resource Management.* New York: Routledge.

17   Brookfield Global Relocation Service (2015). The 2015 Global Mobility Trends Survey.

18   Levy, O., Beechler, S., Taylor, S., and Boyacigiller, N. A. (2007). What we talk about when we talk about 'global mindset': Managerial cognition in multinational corporations, *Journal of International Business Studies*, 38, 231–258.

19   Rowly, C. and Paik, Y. (2009). *The Changing Face of Korean Management.* London and New York: Routledge, 173.

20   Ibid.

21   Smit, T. (2014, August 20). Key considerations when choosing top talent for your organization. Retrieved from http://theosmit.co.za/key-considerations-when-choosing-top-talent-for-your-organisation/

22   Towers Watson. (2012). *Global Workforce Study: Engagement at Risk: Driving Strong Performance in a Volatile Global Environment.* New York: Towers Watson.

23 *Expat's Manual.* Retrieved from www.expatinfodesk.com/expat-guide/
negotiating-your-contract/things-to-take-into-consideration-when-negotiating-
your-expat-contract/
24 Vance, C. & Paik, Y. (2015). *Managing a Global Workforce: Challenges and
Opportunities in International Human Resource Management.* New York:
Routledge.
25 Reynolds, C. (2000). *Guide to Global Compensation and Benefits.* New York:
Harcourt Inc.
26 *Wall Street Journal.* (2014, December 15). Why does Uncle Sam hate American
expats? Foreign banks close U.S. citizens' accounts rather than deal with the
mess that Congress created. Retrieved from https://www.wsj.com/articles/neil-
gandal-why-does-uncle-sam-hate-american-expats-1418687615
27 Sims, R. H. and Schraeder, M. (2005). Expatriate compensation: An exploratory
review of salient contextual factors and common practices. *Career Development
International,* 10(2), 98–108.
28 Brookfield Global Relocation Service (2015). The 2015 Global Mobility Trends
Survey.
29 Tung, R., Paik, Y., and Bae, Y. (2013). Korean human resource management in
the global context. *International Journal of Human Resource Management,* 24(5),
905–921.
30 Paik, Y. and Teagarden, M. (1995). Strategic international human resource
management approaches in maquiladora industry: A comparison of Japanese,
Korean and U.S. firms. *International Journal of Human Resource Management,*
6(3), 568–587.
31 Vance, C. & Paik, Y. (2015). *Managing a Global Workforce: Challenges and
Opportunities in International Human Resource Management.* New York:
Routledge.
32 Perlmutter, H. (1969). The tortuous evolution of the multinational corporations. *Journal of World Business,* 4, 9–18.
33 Solomon, C. M. (1999). Measuring return on investment: Do you know what
your international assignments are worth? *Global Workforce,* March, 24–26.
34 Brookfield Global Relocation Service (2015). The 2015 Global Mobility Trends
Survey.
35 Stroh, L., Gregersen, H., and Black, S. (1998). Closing the gap: Expectations
versus reality among repatriates. *Journal of World Business,* 33(2), 111–124.
36 *Wall Street Journal.* (2014, December 22). Where is home for an expat? Retrieved
from http://blogs.wsj.com/expat/2014/12/22/where-is-home-for-an-expat/
37 Brett, J. A. I. and Stroh, L. (1992). Job transfer. In C. L. Cooper and L. T.
Robinson (Eds.), *International Review of Industrial and Organizational
Psychology* (pp. 323–362). Chichester, UK: John Wiley & Sons.
38 Hammer, M., Hart, W., and Rogan, R. (1998). Can you go home again? An
analysis of the repatriation of corporate managers and spouses. *Management
International Review,* 38(1), 67–86.
39 Paik, Y., Segaud, B., and Malinowski, C. (2002). How to improve repatriation
management: Are motivations and expectations congruent between the
company and expatriates? *International Journal of Manpower,* 23(7), 635–648.

Managing Money
Finance, Accounting, and Taxation

Learning Objectives

1. Understand the role and function of international trade finance.
2. Comprehend how companies finance international expansion.
3. Recognize important accounting issues in international business.
4. Identify key tax issues related to international business.

Cases

Case 10.1 The Financing of Alibaba
Case 10.2 Canada's Adoption of IFRS
Case 10.3 The Accounting Big Four in China
Case 10.4 The Merger of Burger King and Tim Hortons
Case 10.5 Apple's Tax Avoidance

Case 10.1 The Financing of Alibaba

On September 19, 2014, Alibaba, a Chinese e-commerce company, had its initial public offering (IPO) on the New York Stock Exchange and raised $21.8 billion USD. The IPO was the biggest ever in the U.S., outpacing Visa's $19.7 billion USD initial stock sale in 2008, and GM's $18.1 billion USD IPO in 2010. Alibaba's stock price on that day gave the company a market capitalization of $231 billion USD, greater than that of e-commerce giants like Amazon and eBay.

How did Alibaba get there? The company actually had a very humble start. It was created by 18 founders, led by Jack Ma, a former English teacher, in Ma's apartment in March 1999 with $60,000 USD. Its Alibaba.com website was an online business-to-business (B2B) marketplace. Alibaba soon encountered a money shortage, a common problem for start-ups. Ma met with various investors in order to finance the company's growth. In October 1999, Alibaba obtained a first-round investment of $5 million USD from a consortium led by Goldman Sachs. In 2000, at the height of the dot-com bubble burst, Alibaba, like many other dot-com companies, struggled to survive. Masayoshi Son, the Chairman of SoftBank, a Japanese telecom and Internet giant, encouraged Jack Ma to hang on and invested $20 million for 37% stake in Alibaba.

In May 2003, Alibaba launched Taobao, a consumer-to-consumer (C2C) retail website, and Alipay, an online payment platform. Taobao brought huge success and fame to Alibaba. In February 2004, Alibaba raised $82 million USD in venture capital from a group of investors led by SoftBank, the largest investment in the Chinese Internet sector at that time.

Alibaba also attracted strategic investment from Yahoo Inc. Yahoo first entered China in late 2003 by purchasing a keyword search firm for $120 million USD. After seeing success in Japan, Yahoo had high hopes for China. In order to position itself to compete with Google and other tech firms, Yahoo needed to tap into China's fast-growing Internet sector. However, Yahoo could not build a strong presence in China. Its e-commerce venture was defeated by Taobao, one of Alibaba's sites. "If you cannot beat them, join them," said Yahoo co-founder Jerry Yang.[a] Meanwhile, Alibaba was facing intense competition from both foreign and local e-commerce companies, including another American giant, eBay. Jack Ma needed more resources to face upcoming challenges and further develop his company.

In August 2005, Alibaba and Yahoo reached an exclusive partnership. Under their agreement, Yahoo invested $1 billion USD in cash to acquire 40 percent of Alibaba's equity; in return, Alibaba took over the running of Yahoo! China. This was the largest foreign investment in the Chinese Internet sector, making Yahoo the largest strategic investor in Alibaba.

Eventually, Alibaba's Taobao decisively outperformed eBay and other e-commerce competitors, snagging millions of Chinese consumers to its online marketplace. The victory boosted investors' confidence and furthered the expansion of Alibaba. In November 2007, the company listed its B2B business, Alibaba.com, on the Hong Kong Stock Exchange. On its first day of trading, Alibaba's opening price reached HK$30 per share, more than double the HK$13.50 issuing price. However, during the 2008 global financial crisis, Alibaba's stocks fell almost 40 percent below its 2007 peak.

Despite its sluggish stock price, Alibaba kept growing. To complement its C2C marketplace, Alibaba started Tmall (or Taobao Mall), a business-to-consumer trade website, in April 2008. In September 2009, Alibaba established Alibaba Cloud Computing. Also in that year, Alibaba received a $75 million USD investment from General Atlantic, a global growth equity firm, at a valuation of roughly $5 USD per share. However, what Alibaba needed was not capital but guidance to navigate its incredible growth. "We don't need capital," Jack Ma reportedly said.[b] General Atlantic offered strategic advice as Alibaba contemplated acquisition and expansion into new markets like India.

In 2011, Yahoo's relationship with Alibaba turned sour when Alibaba moved its crucial Alipay unit (a major online payment platform) from Alibaba to a separate entity controlled by Ma. Yahoo was shocked and planned to take action. However, having had multiple CEOs within a few years, the company was going through a lot of leadership changes. During this turbulent period, Yahoo management struggled with what to do with its stake in Alibaba.

After on-again, off-again negotiations, Yahoo and Alibaba reached an agreement in May 2012. Yahoo agreed to sell half of its stake, 20 percent of Alibaba's fully diluted shares, to Alibaba. Alibaba agreed to pay Yahoo $7.1

billion USD, including at least $6.3 billion USD cash and up to $800 million USD in newly issued Alibaba preferred stock. In September 2012, Alibaba closed the deal by paying US$7.1 billion USD in cash and stocks for half of Yahoo's stake in Alibaba. Another $550 million USD was paid to Yahoo under a revised technology and patent licensing agreement.

Also in 2012, Alibaba delisted its B2B business from the Hong Kong Stock Market through a buyout at HK$13.50 a share, the same as the original issue price but a 46 percent premium to the last closing price before the buyout announcement. Alibaba explained that it intended to be free from stock market pressures and acknowledged that its depressed share price had adversely affected employee morale. The B2B business buyout cost Alibaba approximately $2.5 billion USD.

Two years later, Alibaba went public again on the New York Stock Exchange. This time, most of its businesses, except financial and logistic services, were listed. Many believed China's local financial markets were not yet ready for such a high caliber company. The company initially considered the Hong Kong Stock Exchange. However, the Hong Kong Stock Exchange does not allow a dual-class share structure, in which pre-IPO owners have shares with superior voting rights. Alibaba preferred such a structure because it allows insiders to retain control after the firm goes public. Since the dual-class share structure is quite common in the U.S., the company eventually decided to launch its IPO in the New York Stock Exchange.

The IPO in New York was very successful. China's fast-growing market and Alibaba's strong position attracted many investors. China's online commerce market was expected to reach $395 billion USD in 2015, tripling its 2011 level. Alibaba handled about 80 percent of all online shopping in China in 2013, making large profits from transaction fees and online marketing.

The IPO also generated impressive returns for investors. Based on an agreement with Alibaba, Yahoo sold more shares and received around $8 billion USD. General Atlantic's initial $75 million USD stake was valued around $1.3 billion USD, 18 times the original investment. SoftBank's $20 million USD early investment in 2000 was worth more than $60 billion USD, making Masayoshi Son one of the richest men in Japan. Jack Ma, Alibaba's president and biggest individual shareholder, retained a 7.7 percent stake, valued at approximately $20 billion USD at Alibaba's IPO.

Notes

a.   Rao, L. (2015, September 26). The most expensive sake that Alibaba's Jack Ma ever had. Retrieved from http://fortune.com/2015/09/25/yahoo-alibaba-investment-jack-ma/
b.   Privcap. (2014, September 24). General Atlantic: Why we backed Alibaba. Retrieved from www.privcap.com/alibaba-private-equity-general-atlantic-ipo/

Sources

1.   Alibaba Group. (n.d.). History and milestones. Retrieved from www.alibaba-group.com/en/about/history

2. Barreto, E. (2014, September 22). Alibaba IPO ranks as world's biggest after additional shares sold. Reuters. Retrieved from www.reuters.com/article/2014/09/22/us-alibaba-ipo-value-idUSKCN0HH0A620140922

3. Egan, M. (2014, September 19). Boom: Alibaba surges 38% in huge IPO debut. CNN Money. Retrieved from http://money.cnn.com/2014/09/19/investing/alibaba-ipo-debut-nyse/

4. Picker, L. and Chen L. Y. (2014). Alibaba's banks boost IPO size to record of $25 billion. Bloomberg. Retrieved from www.bloomberg.com/news/2014-09-22/alibaba-s-banks-said-to-increase-ipo-size-to-record-25-billion.html

5. *Economist.* (2012, February 25). So long, for now: Why the Chinese web portal is giving up its stockmarket listing. Retrieved from www.economist.com/node/21548253

6. Strauss, G. and Shell, A. (2014, September 20). Alibaba's IPO debut roars, shares soar 38%. *USA Today.* Retrieved from www.usatoday.com/story/money/business/2014/09/19/alibaba-surges-in-first-day-trading/15828389/

Questions for Case Discussion

1. How did Alibaba finance its start-up and continuous growth? Please identify its main sources of financing.
2. What kind of roles did various financing sources play in Alibaba's growth? What were the benefits and drawbacks of those sources?
3. How do you evaluate the relationship between Yahoo and Alibaba? If you were a Yahoo executive, how would you handle the stake in Alibaba?

Case 10.2 Canada's Adoption of IFRS

International Financial Reporting Standards (IFRS) refer to the global accounting standards developed by the International Accounting Standards Board (IASB). Over a hundred countries have adopted or converted to IFRS. The Accounting Standards Board (AcSB) of Canada has also made its conversion from Canadian GAAP (Generally Accepted Accounting Principles) to IFRS. As the authority of standards governing financial accounting and reporting, AcSB's decision has significantly changed accounting practices in Canada. As of 2013, most business and nonprofit entities have adopted IFRS.

Before the adoption of IFRS, the development of Canadian GAAP had been greatly influenced by U.S. GAAP. This was largely due to close business ties between the two countries. For instance, the U.S. buys the majority of Canada's exports and provides the majority of Canada's imports. Therefore, Canadian regulators initially considered adopting or harmonizing with U.S. GAAP.

However, AcSB eventually chose IFRS. Compared to U.S. GAAP, IFRS is less rule-bound, easier and cheaper for companies to adopt. Since 2007, the U.S. Securities and Exchange Commission has stopped requiring the foreign companies that use IFRS to translate their financial statements into U.S. GAAP before they can operate and be listed in the U.S. Thus, Canadian firms do not have to convert to U.S. GAAP for activities in the U.S. An assessment by AcSB also noted that a majority of Canadian publicly traded companies had not conformed to U.S. GAAP. To benefit from an increasingly globalized world, Canada decided to switch to IFRS, which would provide access to broader international capital markets and make cross-border investments easier.

In order to facilitate the conversion to IFRS, AcSB established different timelines of implementation for different types of organizations, ranging from three to five years. AcSB also introduced long planning and phase-in periods. Typically, companies were asked to make plans first, then report in both Canadian GAAP and IFRS, publish expected differences, and finally convert to IFRS.

To meet deadlines, Canadian companies made tremendous efforts. They allocated manpower and resources to implement conversions. Accounting policies and information systems were modified. Documentations and controls were updated. Debt covenants, tax planning, employee incentive programs (e.g. profit sharing), business combinations, and investments were also affected. The conversion process required a retrospective application of IFRS standards and reconciliations from the "old" Canadian GAAP to IFRS. However, extracting historic information could be extremely difficult. Divergent calculations and definitions between the two standards might generate significant differences. For instance, assets were usually carried at historical value under Canadian GAAP, but could be revalued to fair market value under IFRS.

The conversion to IFRS was a highly complex process that went well beyond accounting and finance functions. Various other functions such as human resources, investor relations, business development, and information technology were involved. A considerable amount of training was provided to increase awareness and preparedness. Furthermore, the reporting and compliance requirements of IFRS not only changed business processes like budgets, forecasts, performance measures, and reward schemes, but also impacted the corporate decision-making process. Executives were required to understand the impact of IFRS and explain the "new" numbers.

In 2013, Financial Executives International Canada, a professional organization, published their findings on the costs borne by Canadian companies in their transition from Canadian GAAP to IFRS based on a survey of financial executives. According to their report, for smaller-sized companies (revenue less than $99 million Canadian dollars (CAD)), the average total cost was $154,800 CAD; for medium-sized companies (revenue from $100 million CAD to $999 million CAD), the average total cost was $512,800 CAD; for larger-sized companies (revenue more than $1 billion CAD), the average total cost was $4,041,177 CAD. Staff time was the largest item among all transition expenses. Costs for larger-sized companies were mostly consumed by internal staff while smaller-sized and medium-sized companies spent a higher proportion on external IFRS experts.

The move to IFRS has fundamentally changed the way Canadian companies report their business results to analysts, investors, and other stakeholders. Certain sectors, such as finance, real estate, retail, and transportation, experienced a more significant impact than others. Now that all Canadian publicly traded companies have converted to IFRS, people are looking forward to seeing the long-term benefits of the global accounting standard. To international investors, Canada's adoption of IFRS provides obvious informational benefits. It has significantly improved the international comparability of Canadian financial statements. As IFRS becomes widely adopted, Canadian regulators are confident that soon the long-term benefits will exceed the short-term costs.

Sources

1. CIBC Mellon. (2011). IFRS: A changing landscape for Canada. Retrieved from www.cibcmellon.com/Contents/en_CA/English/KnowledgeLeadership/KL201 104_IFRS.html
2. Cormier, D. and Magnan, M. (2014). Does IFRS adoption in Canada reduce the information gap between managers and investors? *CPA Magazine*. April 2014.
3. FEI Canada. (2013). The cost of IFRS transition in Canada. Retrieved from www.feicanada.org/
4. Guidi, J. (2007). The end of Canadian GAAP. *CGA Magazine*, Jul.–Aug. issue.
5. PwC. (2011). Putting IFRS in motion. Retrieved from www.pwc.com/ca/en/ ifrs/publications/ifrs-mcp-0209-en.pdf

Questions for Case Discussion

1. What motivated Canada's adoption of IFRS?
2. What are the implications of adopting IFRS for international businesses?
3. Should countries that have not converted to IFRS (e.g. the U.S.) follow Canada's step?

Case 10.3 The Accounting Big Four in China

As one of the largest economies in the world, China presents tremendous opportunities for multinational corporations (MNCs). To succeed in China, MNCs need to comply with local accounting and tax rules. For instance, in China, every enterprise is required to keep a set of financial statements presented in RMB (i.e. Chinese yuan) for statutory purposes. Foreign-invested enterprises are required to engage domestic registered accounting firms (including approved Sino-foreign cooperative accounting firms) to audit their statutory financial statements. Companies are required to file their annual income tax returns and audited statutory financial statements with local tax authorities within five months after the end of a tax year. China's tax system is complex and tax policies are changing rapidly along with economic development. Tax administration can be rigorous as tax authorities improve their resources, technology, and organizational systems.

In order to comply with local regulations, MNCs often need professional accounting and tax guidance. Large accounting firms, like the "Big Four" (i.e. PwC, Deloitte, EY, and KPMG), have grabbed the opportunity to expand professional services in China. After the country opened up to foreign investment in the late 1970s, the Big Four followed their clients' steps to establish business presence in China. Initially, what they could do was limited. Similar to many other countries, only local licensed accounting firms were allowed to perform auditing and other statutory tasks in China. Therefore, the Big Four mainly worked on helping MNCs understand local business practices and fulfill requirements from headquarters and shareholders overseas.

In 1992, in order to develop the accounting profession and gain access to international practices, the Chinese government approved foreign firms to perform audits, provided that they form a joint venture with a local firm. The Big Four set up joint ventures with local accounting firms. They recruited both expatriate partners from other offices and local partners. Since few expatriate partners had Chinese CPA (certified public accountant) licenses, local partners were usually designated to sign statutory auditing reports. Expatriate partners routinely signed reports used outside of China, which were typically reports sent to headquarter offices.

Therefore, the Big Four were able to offer a range of accounting services in China:

- Statutory reporting services (preparing financial statements required by laws).
- Accounting support services (such as conversion of financial reports according to different accounting standards, preparing financial reports for taxation purposes, bookkeeping, and producing financial reports).
- Auditing services (financial statement audits, advice, and training on financial reporting).
- Tax services (such as preparation of tax return, tax planning, tax strategies in cross-border transactions, and transfer pricing).

Very soon, the Big Four and their joint ventures secured the lion's share of audits related to foreign direct investment and international listings. They became major players in China's professional service market.

Meanwhile, the Big Four expanded their services to Chinese companies. Especially after China's accession into the World Trade Organization, Chinese companies started tapping into international financial markets. For instance, in 2009, seven of the ten largest global initial public offerings were from China. Accordingly, the Big Four offered services for initial public offerings, merger and acquisition activities, restructuring, and cross-border transactions.

Due to China's increasing connections with international markets, both foreign and local regulations have helped the Big Four develop accounting compliance and reporting services. For instance, after China decided to adopt IFRS (International Financial Reporting Standards), the Big Four were able to leverage their international practices to help companies in China with the conversion. Thanks to the Sarbanes–Oxley Act in the U.S., a legislation aiming to eliminate accounting errors and fraudulent practices, the Big Four advised U.S.-listed companies and helped implement new regulatory compliance initiatives for their operations in China. The Big Four aim to help companies not only meet local financial reporting requirements but also provide reliable financial information to worldwide capital markets and tax authorities.

After decades of doing business in China, the Big Four have developed in-depth knowledge about China and strong local connections. In recent years, they have been actively pursuing diversification by offering services beyond accounting, auditing, and tax preparation. For example, their risk management teams advise clients on improving systems and processes to create an appropriate balance between performance, quality, risk, and control. Their consulting teams educate, facilitate, and support MNCs in entering and penetrating Chinese markets. The Big Four also offer strategy formulation, investment execution, due diligence, expansion and exit, internal controls, human resources and talent management, finance and treasury, and supply-chain strategies. They even provide legal services that complement existing services, such as immigration (which fits nicely with expatriate tax work), labor (which goes together with human-resource consulting), and commercial contracts.

Sources

1. Accounting Verse. (n.d.). Big 4 Accounting Firms. Retrieved from www. accountingverse.com/articles/big-4-accounting-firms.html
2. Big Four Firms Network. (2006, November 6). PricewaterhouseCoopers goes for growth in China. Retrieved from www.big4.com/pricewaterhousecoopers/ pricewaterhousecoopers-goes-for-growth-in-china-233/.
3. Deloitte China. (n.d.). Services. Retrieved from www2.deloitte.com/cn/en. html.
4. Global Accounting Alliance. (2010, June 16). The balance of power with the Big 4 accounting firms in China. Retrieved from 5.www.gaaaccounting.com/the-balance-of-power-with-the-big-4-accounting-firms-in-china/
5. KPMG. (n.d.). Global China Practice. Retrieved from https://home.kpmg.com/ cn/en/home/services/global-china-practice.html

Questions for Case Discussion

1. What factors drove the expansion of the Big Four's China businesses in China?
2. What accounting challenges do MNCs face in international markets?
3. How can professional service firms like the Big Four help international businesses?

Case 10.4 The Merger of Burger King and Tim Hortons

Burger King is one of the largest global hamburger restaurant chains. At the end of fiscal year 2013, Burger King reported it had over 13,000 outlets in 79 countries, with 66 percent of the outlets in the U.S. Tim Hortons, founded in 1964, is Canada's largest fast food service operator. As of September 2014, it had 3,665 restaurants in Canada, 869 in the U.S., and 56 in the Persian Gulf region. It is well known in Canada for its coffee and doughnuts. On August 26, 2014, Burger King and Tim Hortons announced the merger of the two companies. The deal was valued at $12.5 billion CAD (about $11 billion USD) and created the world's third largest fast food restaurant company. The newly merged company has over 18,000 restaurants in around 100 countries, with combined sales of $23 billion CAD (about $20 billion USD). While the two brands retain separate operations, the new company's headquarters is located in Oakville, Ontario.

Investors and industry experts are excited about the merger. Tim Hortons' coffee products can help Burger King develop in the quick-serve breakfast market. Burger King can help Tim Hortons expand into the U.S. and abroad. Moreover, this deal could bring in tremendous tax savings. Canada's corporate tax rate in Ontario is 26.5 percent (the federal rate of 15 percent plus Ontario's provincial corporate tax rate of 11.5 percent), much lower than the 35 percent U.S. corporate tax rate. Because of the significant tax reduction, the merger of Burger King and Tim Hortons was viewed as a tax inversion by some observers.

The U.S. corporate income tax rate, 35 percent, is relatively high in the world. Among the OECD (Organization for Economic Cooperation and Development) countries, only five (Belgium, Germany, Greece, Italy, and Luxembourg) have a higher rate than that of the U.S., three countries (Mexico, Netherlands, and Spain) have the same 35 percent rate, and the remaining seventeen countries impose a lower tax rate. When U.S. companies bring foreign incomes home, they are subject to U.S. income tax. (They can defer tax payment if profits are retained overseas.) Many other nations, including the U.K. and Canada, tax only domestic profits. Therefore, an independent U.S. company may end up paying more taxes than an identical U.S. company owned by a foreign parent. By creating or buying a foreign parent, a company may escape U.S. taxes on worldwide income.

Before the merger, as a U.S. company, Burger King was required to pay tax on the profits repatriated from offshore operations, even though they had already been taxed in the countries where the profits were generated. Now that the new company is a Canadian company, Burger King can access its offshore profits without paying double taxes. According to Americans for Tax Fairness, an advocacy group for tax reform, Burger King could save $400 million USD to $1.2 billion USD between 2015 and 2018 by shielding its foreign profits from U.S. income tax. The merger and consequent change of headquarters location are likely to create substantial tax reduction.

Burger King has repeatedly asserted that the merger was not motivated by tax reduction, and claimed that the data from Americans for Tax Fairness were flawed. According to the company's statements, Burger King's effective tax rate was 27.5 percent in 2013, and Tim Hortons' rate was 26.8 percent. For the newly merged company, about 80 percent of its outlets are located in Canada and about two-thirds of its expected revenue comes from Canada. Since only a small portion of the revenue comes from the U.S. and other overseas locations, the new company's tax rate is not expected to change materially. As Burger King's Chief Executive Officer Daniel Schwartz put it, the merger is about growth rather than taxes.[a]

In fact, Burger King is not the only company that has been criticized for tax inversion, the practice of relocating legal domicile to a lower-tax country. In the pharmaceutical industry, where overseas sales generate significant income, there have been multiple mergers or acquisitions that led to the change of a company's legal domicile. For instance, in July 2014, Chicago-based AbbVie agreed to a $54.7 billion USD merger with Britain's Shire, slashing AbbVie's effective tax rate from 26 percent to about 13 percent.

Also in July 2014, Mylan NV announced its acquisition of Abbott Laboratories' European generic-drug business and subsequent move of its headquarters to the Netherlands, which could result in considerable tax reduction. Similarly, after acquiring Covidien, an Irish company, for $42.9 billion USD in cash and stock, Medtronic, a medical device company, moved its headquarters to low-tax Ireland and freed almost $14 billion USD it held overseas.

Nevertheless, such tax inversion deals are attracting increasing criticism in the U.S. Some politicians, believing the relocations will erode the U.S. corporate tax base, have called the deals "unpatriotic" and made several proposals to crack down on them. The Treasury Department is also working on regulations that will restrict companies from using tax inversion techniques.

Note

a. Jargon, J. (2014, August 26). Burger King defends plan to buy Tim Hortons. Retrieved from www.wsj.com/articles/burger-king-to-buy-tim-hortons-1409053466

Sources

1. BBC News. (2014, August 26). Burger King and Tim Hortons agree merger details. Retrieved from www.bbc.com/news/business-28939538
2. Ferdman, R. A. (2014, December 11). We finally have an idea of how much money Burger King will save by moving to Canada. *The Washington Post*. Retrieved from www.washingtonpost.com/news/wonkblog/wp/2014/12/11/burger-king-could-save-a-whopping-amount-of-money-by-moving-to-canada/
3. Hartley, J. (2014, August 25). Burger King's tax inversion and Canada's favorable corporate tax rates. *Forbes*. Retrieved from www.forbes.com/sites/jonhartley/2014/08/25/burger-kings-tax-inversion-and-canadas-favorable-corporate-tax-rates/2/
4. Hwang, I. and Patton, L. (2014, October 23). Burger King bears surge amid Tim Hortons deal anxiety. *Bloomberg Business*. Retrieved from www.bloomberg.com/news/2014-10-23/burger-king-bears-surge-amid-tim-hortons-deal-anxiety.html
5. Rockoff, J. D., Mattoli, D., and Cimilluca, D. (2015, October 29). Pfizer and Allergan begin merger talks. *Wall Street Journal*. Retrieved from www.wsj.com/articles/pfizer-allergan-considering-combining-1446079506

Questions for Case Discussion

1. What are your thoughts on the merger of Burger King and Tim Hortons?
2. In your opinion, why did the new company set up its headquarters in Canada?
3. Do you agree that tax inversion should be restricted? Why?

Case 10.5 Apple's Tax Avoidance

In May 2013, the U.S. Senate Permanent Subcommittee on Investigations (PSI) issued a 142-page report claiming that Apple, the U.S. consumer electronics titan, had been running a scheme to avoid paying taxes on $74 billion

USD overseas revenue. A hearing was held to examine how Apple used a variety of offshore entities and cross-border transactions to shift billions of dollars in profits away from the U.S. This incident obviously cast a shadow on Apple's public image. During the hearing, Apple stated that the company had fully complied with U.S. tax laws and what it did was no different from what other multinational companies had been doing.

There may be some truth in Apple's statement. The U.S. has a relatively higher statutory income tax rate than many other countries, although levies on overseas earnings are deferred until the earnings are repatriated to the U.S. Meanwhile, there are tax haven countries that charge little or no tax on overseas income. In international markets, U.S. MNCs have to compete with foreign firms that are subject to much lower tax payments. Thus, there are plenty of incentives for U.S. multinationals to direct as much income as possible to low-tax countries. Also, they may allocate as many costs as possible to high-tax jurisdictions like the U.S., where deductions are especially valuable. To a U.S. company that is subject to 35 percent income tax, one-dollar deduction is worth 35 cents; but its value is only one-third as much in Ireland where the tax rate is 12.5. percent. According to a report issued by the U.S. Public Interest Research Group, over 72 percent of Fortune 500 companies have subsidiaries in low-tax jurisdictions as of 2014.[a] Many of those subsidiaries were shell companies created for tax avoidance, which had few or no employees and hardly conducted any real business activities.

The U.S. Senate PSI report indicated that Apple had used overseas entities for tax avoidance. First, Apple deferred tax payment on foreign incomes. Since U.S. companies do not need to pay taxes on foreign earnings before repatriation, many never bring the money home. In 2013, Apple decided to spend $30 billion USD on dividends and stock buybacks. Rather than bringing back some of its $144.7 billion USD cash in offshore accounts, the company raised $17 billion USD by issuing bonds. In other words, they preferred paying interests on bonds to paying income tax on repatriated cash. According to Apple's annual report in 2015, about 70 percent of its profits were from foreign countries, where tax rates are often lower than that of the U.S.; the company had $186.9 billion USD of cash, cash equivalents, and marketable securities outside of the U.S.

The second approach was transfer pricing. Transfer pricing means setting prices for goods and services sold between entities controlled by the same parent firm. Firms are supposed to price these internal transactions at market value. However, certain assets, such as intellectual property, are difficult to price. For a company like Apple, technology patents and other intellectual properties make significant contributions to its revenue. By charging a pittance to an overseas subsidiary for the use of intellectual properties, the company can lower its revenue in the U.S. and retain more profit in the subsidiary.

Specifically, Apple set up a cost-sharing agreement between its corporation in the U.S. and two subsidiaries in Ireland. One subsidiary, Apple Sales International (ASI), contracted with third-party manufacturers to make Apple products, such as iPhones and iPads, and then sold them to overseas distributors. The other subsidiary, Apple Operations Europe (AOE), had about 400 employees and manufactured a line of specialty computers for sale in Europe. While making small royalty payments to the U.S. headquarters for intellectual properties, ASI and AOE collected vast sales revenues. In this way, Apple was able to funnel its pretax worldwide incomes to these two entities and benefit from the low tax rate in Ireland. Of its $34 billion USD total pretax income in 2011, $22 billion USD was allocated to these two entities. Similarly, in 2012 and 2013, a majority of Apple's revenues from international operations passed through these two entities.

In addition, Apple designed a corporate structure to exploit loopholes between different tax jurisdictions. Apple Operations International (AOI) was Apple's primary offshore holding company that directly or indirectly held shares in multiple subsidiaries, including ASI, AOE, Apple Distribution International, and Apple Singapore. AOI was also registered in Ireland. It served as a cash consolidator for most of Apple's offshore affiliates. It received and managed dividends from those affiliates and made contributions as needed. Under Irish law, a company's tax residence is where the company is managed and controlled. AOI did not meet the fact-specific residency requirements because it had no employees in Ireland and almost all directors were located in California. Since AOI was managed in U.S., it was not viewed as a tax resident in Ireland and thus freed from Irish taxation. On the other hand, under U.S. law, a company's tax residency is where the company is incorporated and paperwork is filed. AOI was incorporated in Ireland, therefore not a tax resident in the U.S. From 2009 to 2012, AOI had a net income of $30 billion USD, about 30 percent of Apple's total world profits, but paid no corporate income taxes to any national governments.

Such tactics remarkably reduced tax burdens for quite a few technology companies. From 2010 to 2012, the 71 technology companies in the S&P 500 index, including Apple, Google, Yahoo, and Dell, reportedly paid worldwide taxes at a rate that was a third less than other S&P companies. In comparison, Wal-Mart paid worldwide taxes of $5.9 billion USD on its booked profits of $24.4 billion USD in 2012. The effective rate was 24 percent, about the average for non-tech companies.

Various national governments and international organizations have strengthened investigations and restrictions on tax avoidance. For example, the European Commission has investigated Apple's tax payment in Ireland and issued a record penalty. The U.S. government has announced restrictions on tax inversion (i.e. using an overseas address to avoid paying U.S. taxes). The Organization for Economic Co-operation and Development (OECD) has also proposed measures to hinder corporate tax avoidance. In addition, some non-profit organizations have been actively monitoring companies' tax avoidance. For instance, the Bureau of Investigative Journalism, a U.K.-based nonprofit group, reported that Microsoft, Google, and Cisco had not paid taxes on interest income earned from the billions of U.S. Treasuries they held overseas.

Notes

a.   U.S. PIRG. (2015, October 6). Study: 72% of Fortune 500 companies used tax havens in 2014. Retrieved from www.uspirg.org/news/usp/study-72-fortune-500-companies-used-tax-havens-2014-0

Sources

1. Apple.com. (2013). Apple Testimony to PSI. Retrieved from www.apple.com/pr/pdf/Apple_Testimony_to_PSI.pdf
2. Doward, J. (2014, October 5). How Apple's Cork HQ became the centre of a bitter global war over corporate tax avoidance. *The Guardian*. Retrieved from www.theguardian.com/technology/2014/oct/05/apple-tax-investigations-europe-united-states-cork-ireland
3. Drucker, J. (2014, September 30). Crackdown on Apple in Ireland opens front on tax avoidance war. *Bloomberg Business*. Retrieved from www.bloomberg.com/news/2014-09-30/crackdown-on-apple-in-ireland-opens-front-on-tax-avoidance-war.html
4. Gleckman, H. (2013, May 21). The real story on Apple's tax avoidance: How ordinary it is. *Forbes*. Retrieved from www.forbes.com/sites/leesheppard/2013/05/28/how-does-apple-avoid-taxes/
5. Hickey, W. (2013, May 21). Apple avoids paying $17 million in taxes every day through a ballsy but genius tax avoidance scheme. *Business Insider*. Retrieved from www.businessinsider.com/how-apple-reduces-what-it-pays-in-taxes-2013-5#ixzz3POsAejdh

Questions for Case Discussion

1. How did Apple reduce it total tax payment?
2. What are your thoughts on Apple's tax avoidance practices? Were they "good"?
3. Should governments take actions to deter tax avoidance?

Managing Money

Finance, Accounting, and Taxation

Like human resources, financial resources are critical to international business success. A company needs to acquire, allocate, measure, record, and manage its financial resources. This chapter covers how a company finances its international trade and foreign direct investment. Key accounting and taxation issues in international business are also discussed in this chapter.

I. International Trade Finance

To support international trade, a variety of financing tools have been developed over the years. Some are designed to facilitate payment and collection, while others are used to acquire financial resources for exporting or importing.

1. Facilitating Payment and Collection

The exchange of products and payments requires basic trust between buyers and sellers. In international trade, exporters and importers are located in different countries and follow different laws. It can be difficult to obtain credible information and track down a foreign buyer or seller. Therefore, there is an inherent lack of trust between exporters and importers. Exporters are worried about not receiving payment after shipping their products to importers. Conversely, importers are concerned about receiving defective products or even no shipments after making payments to exporters.

To protect their own interests in international trade, exporters prefer cash in advance, i.e. receiving payment before shipment or delivery of goods. Especially when facing an unfamiliar buyer or a buyer with shaky credit, cash in advance can avoid potential default risk. Also, if a seller needs significant investment to fulfill an order, it may demand certain prepayment from the buyers. On the other hand, importers tend to favor methods that allow payment after shipment. An open account is an arrangement in which the exporter ships goods first and bills the importer later. Consignment is a variant of an open account in which the exporter gets paid after its foreign distributor has sold goods to the end buyer. Sales on an open account offers flexible payment dates and credit terms to the buyer. Usually only customers with a long positive relationship with the exporter or a strong credit history can get such treatments.

The above-mentioned payment arrangements favor one side but may not be accepted by the other side. A more widely accepted payment method in international trade transactions is letter of credit (or L/C). The letter of credit is a promise made by a bank on behalf of the buyer that the bank will honor the payment obligation if the seller presents the documents specified in the L/C. An L/C involves one or more banks as an intermediary, thus mitigating the lack-of-trust problem between importers and exporters.

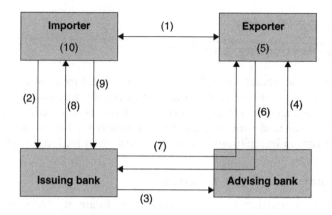

Figure 10.1 The Steps of Using Letter of Credit

Basically, the L/C process includes the following steps (see Figure 10.1):

(1) The importer and the exporter reach a sales agreement and agree to use an L/C
(2) The importer applies for an L/C with the issuing bank
(3) The issuing bank issues an L/C and forwards it to the exporter's advising bank
(4) The advising bank notifies the exporter about the L/C
(5) The exporter ships goods and prepares documents according to the L/C
(6) The exporter sends required documents through the advising bank
(7) The issuing bank makes payment to the exporter through the advising bank
(8) The issuing bank release documents to the importer
(9) The importer pays the issuing bank
(10) The importer claims goods from the shipping company

Using an L/C reduces the risk of payment delay or default for the exporter. The issuing bank actually lends credit to the importer by assuming the payment commitment. Therefore, it needs to verify the creditworthiness and paying ability of the importer. Meanwhile, the L/C serves as a contract between the issuing bank and the exporter. The exporter is guaranteed payment under conditions set forth in the L/C.

The L/C also provides benefits for the importer. It requires the exporter to conform to specific requirements, such as the quantity and quality of products and the timeliness of shipment. Payment is made only after presented documents meet the requirements. The banks are responsible for checking the documents. If there is any oversight, the importer can refuse to pay. The issuing bank charges the importer a fee for the L/C. The major drawback is that the fee, although negotiable, is relatively expensive compared to other payment methods.

The L/C process usually involves a variety of documents, such as draft, invoice, certificate of inspection, packing list, bill of lading, custom form, and others. Two key documents for payment collection are the bill of lading and draft. A bill of lading (or B/L) is a legal document issued by a carrier that indicates the ownership and specifics of a shipment. It is a receipt that details the type, quantity, and destination of shipped products. It also serves as the document of title in that the party who possesses it is entitled to receive the shipment. The exporter obtains the bill of lading from the shipping company and then forwards it to the issuing bank and the importer for payment.

A draft, also known as the bill of exchange, is a written order by one party (the drawer or maker) to another party (the drawee) to make a certain amount of payment to the exporter or designated beneficiary. It can be payable upon presentation (a sight draft) or on a specified future date (a time draft) for payment of goods or services received. The drawee accepts a draft by signing it, thus converting it into a binding contract and negotiable instrument. After shipping the products, the exporter sends the draft along with other documents to request a payment. When an L/C is not used, the drawee is the importer. When an L/C is used, the drawee is the issuing bank of the L/C. The exporter's bank, working as a collection agency, manages document transfers and the payment process. It holds the bill of lading until the importer or its agent (the issuing bank) pays the draft or accepts the payment obligation.

2. Financing Export Transactions

Financing is very important in many international trade transactions. Importers may need to obtain financing for their purchase, and exporters may need to acquire equipment and raw materials for production before receiving payment. They may seek financing from private sources and government agencies.

Importers often seek credit terms from exporters by pressing for longer payment periods. Exporters may attract potential buyers by extending credit. Such terms typically range from 30 to 180 days, and can be even longer for high-cost items. In some industries, credit terms are commonly expected. Those who are reluctant to extend credit may lose their sales to their competitors. Nonetheless, credit terms also bring additional costs and potential risks to exporters. Exporters need to carefully examine the payment ability of importers. Extra costs incurred during the process should be factored into pricing. To determine appropriate credit terms, exporters must weigh potential gains against costs and risks.

Commercial banks are an important external source of financing for export transactions. Exporters may obtain a line of credit from banks to support their business activities, such as capital investment, purchasing inputs, and extending credit. Another approach is to convert export receivables to cash at a discount. Banks may be willing to buy or lend against time drafts that a creditworthy foreign buyer has agreed to pay. Moreover, banks can make loans directly to foreign buyers of exported products so that exporters get paid immediately. Such third-party financing is usually used for the purchase of capital goods with a repayment period of one year or longer. All these services offered by commercial banks require interest and fee payment. Exporters should evaluate the financial liabilities of these options and identify the most feasible ones.

In addition, many countries have set up government agencies and programs to provide loans, guarantees, and insurance for export transactions. For example, the Export-Import Bank (or Ex-Im Bank) of the U.S. is a federal trade finance agency. Its primary purpose is to enable U.S. exporters to compete in international markets by offering necessary financial backing. Its direct lending operation offers fixed-rate financing up to 12 years in general to creditworthy foreign buyers in both private and public sectors, and finances U.S. exporters' local costs up to 30 percent.[1] Such direct loans allow U.S. exporters to secure competitive financing for their buyers that is not readily available from private sources. The Ex-Im Bank also provides government guarantee and credit insurance programs, which private financial institutions may use to facilitate export financing. When potential risks make private lenders reluctant to fund U.S. export transactions, the Ex-Im Bank's guarantee and insurance programs encourage them to do so. Under these programs, most risks are borne by the Ex-Im Bank, and the financing terms are on par with market terms. The Ex-Im Bank also sponsors the Foreign Credit Insurance Association (FCIA), a voluntary association formed by private insurance companies. The FCIA provides coverage against commercial risks (such as buyer insolvency and payment default) and political risks (such as war and foreign exchange control). Several other government agencies also offer financing assistance. The Small Business Administration (SBA) offers programs specifically for smaller exporters. The U.S. Department of Agriculture has credit programs to support agricultural exports. There are also government programs at the state and municipal levels. Similar export assistance programs can be found in many industrialized and developing countries.

II. Financing for Multinational Corporations

Finance, a key function in corporate structure, is responsible for acquiring and allocating financial resources for company's activities and projects. This function is more complex in a global environment because of monetary factors such as foreign exchange risk, currency flow restrictions, and differences in taxation.

I. Deciding Capital Structure

Before acquiring financial resources, an MNC must first decide on the capital structure of its foreign entity. Capital structure refers to the mix of equity capital and debts. Many companies start off with equity capital as an initial investment. With the growth of business, it becomes more important to develop an appropriate equity/debt mix, which significantly affects the cost of capital.[2]

Cost of capital is the major force driving the financing decision. It is calculated as the weighted average cost of all capital sources, also known as weighted average cost of capital (WACC). The formula for calculating WACC is:

$$WACC = (\text{Equity} / \text{Total market value}) \times R +$$
$$(\text{Debt} / \text{Total market value}) \times (1 - \text{Tax rate}) \times I$$
where R is cost of equity (or required rate of return of equity holders)
and I is cost of debts (or interest rate).

The degree to which a firm funds the growth of business by debt is known as leverage. Leveraging is often perceived as the most cost-effective route because interest paid on debt is a tax-deductible expense in most countries whereas dividend paid to equity owners is not. However, leveraging is not always the best approach. Excessive reliance on debt may increase financial risk, which causes investors and lenders to require a higher return or interest rate. Also, it can be difficult for foreign subsidiaries or newly established entities to obtain debt financing in many countries.

2. Acquiring Financial Resources

MNCs have a variety of sources for financing their overseas operations. They may obtain financial resources from internal sources like parent companies and sister subsidiaries as well as external equity and debt markets (see Table 10.1).[3]

Intercompany financing. An overseas subsidiary may be funded by its parent company or other subsidiaries in the form of equity, loans, or trade credit. Intercompany equity investment becomes part of the subsidiary's total equity that demands dividends. Intercompany loans are more flexible and require interest and principal payments. Due to money flow restrictions in some countries, loan payments are usually easier to be remitted than dividends. Also, interest expenses can often be deducted from the subsidiary's taxable income, thus reducing tax payment. Trade credit is given to the subsidiary by

Table 10.1 Main Ways of Acquiring Financial Resource

Intercompany Financing	Obtaining funding from the parent company or other subsidiaries in the form of equity, loans, or trade credit.
Debt Financing	Getting loans from financial institutions like banks, such as term loans, line of credit, revolving credit, or overdraft.
	Issuing bonds in domestic or international bond markets, including domestic bonds, foreign bonds and eurobonds.
Equity Financing	Issuing equity shares through private placements.
	Public offering in domestic or international stock markets.
Government Financing	Obtaining funding from domestic or foreign governments.

changing the terms of its transactions with the parent company and other subsidiaries, such as extension of accounts payable.

Intercompany financing is a common means of financing for overseas expansion. It allows the MNC to reallocate and better utilize its internal resources. For instance, one subsidiary may have surplus cash while another has a cash shortage; some subsidiaries may have complex intercompany transactions with big balances to settle among each other; one subsidiary may have a key project demanding currency that is different from the currency offered in the credit facility, etc. Intercompany financing may help resolve these issues. However, it should be noted that moving money across countries is subject to government regulations. Some countries have restrictions on remitting money out of the country while others are more lenient. As each country levies taxes based on their own tax laws, money transfer may affect total tax payments.[4]

Debt markets. Other than internal sources, MNCs may seek debt financing from domestic or home country markets as well as host country markets and international markets. Local banks in host countries may offer a variety of loans, such as term loans, line of credit, revolving credit, and overdraft, to MNCs' subsidiaries in local currency. Such financing at the subsidiary level provides MNCs direct access to host country financial resources and reduces the need to transfer and exchange foreign currencies. Hence, it may help lowering financial risks and the total cost of capital. International bank loans are often sourced in the Eurocurrency market. Eurocurrency or offshore currency refers to any currency banked outside its country of origin. A loan whose denominated currency is not the lending bank's national currency is called Eurocredit. The inclusion of the word "Euro" does not necessarily indicate the currency euro. For instance, banks in Europe may offer USD loans, and U.S. banks may offer loans in euro. Often times, lenders borrow foreign currency loans to finance their international trade or investment. The basic borrowing rate for Eurocredit has been traditionally tied to the London Interbank Offered Rate (LIBOR), which is a benchmark rate that major banks charge each other for short-term loans. Every day, the British Bankers' Association publishes LIBOR rates in major currencies with different maturities. Because of the large volume of transactions, Eurocurrency loans tend to have relatively lower interest rates than domestic loans. The increasing international trade and capital flows have led to a rapid growth of the Eurocurrency market.

Another important source of debt financing is the bond markets, in which MNCs can issue bonds to acquire capital for its business expansion. Bond markets can be broadly divided into three categories: domestic bonds, foreign bonds, and eurobonds. A domestic bond is issued by a domestic borrower and denominated in domestic currency. A foreign bond is issued by a foreign borrower in domestic currency. For example, when a German company issues a U.S. dollar-denominated corporate bond in the U.S., the bond is a foreign bond. A eurobond is a bond issued in a currency other than the currency of the market in which it is issued. For example, an Australian company may issue a eurobond in Japan that is denominated in USD. Compared to domestic bonds, foreign bonds and eurobonds offer greater flexibility and allow MNCs to choose a country and a currency with fewer regulatory constraints.

Equity markets. MNCs have several ways to obtain equity from external markets. First, they may gain access to capital through private placements with investors. For instance, there are angel investors, venture capital firms, and institutional investors who may be interested in financing MNCs' international growth.

Second, MNCs may raise capital through an initial public offering in a stock market (see Case 10.1). They can utilize stock markets in the parent firm's home country, the subsidiary's host country, or even a third country. MNCs may choose to either cross list shares abroad or sell new shares of equity. Cross listing shares means a company lists its stocks on both domestic and foreign stock exchanges. For example, IBM, a U.S.-based MNC, is cross-listed on the New York Stock Exchange and the London Stock Exchange. An alternative to cross listing the parent firm is selling shares of the local subsidiary. For instance, Yahoo! Japan, formed as a joint venture by the American Internet company Yahoo! and the Japanese Internet company SoftBank, is listed on the Tokyo Stock Exchange. International equity financing can be advantageous in attracting additional investments, improving liquidity of shares, lowering cost of capital, and enhancing visibility and acceptance in foreign markets. But this approach may also increase costs as the company now faces the reporting and compliance requirements of foreign stock exchange authorities.

Government financing. In addition to financial markets, MNCs may obtain financing from governments in certain situations. Government financing can be made in the form of loans or equity investment. Home country governments may provide financial assistance to MNCs' international expansion. Host country governments may offer financing incentives to local subsidiaries. During economic crises, governments may provide interim credit to help organizations survive and recover.

3. Allocating Financial Resources

After acquiring financial resources, MNCs need to decide how to use the money, i.e. how to allocate money among promising projects around the world. Capital budgeting is a technique to quantify the benefit, the cost, and the risk of an investment. It estimates the cash flows associated with the project over time. In most cases, cash flows are negative during initial investment and business ramping periods, and then turn positive afterwards as businesses grow and mature. Once cash flows are estimated, they need to be discounted to net present value using an appropriate discount rate. The most commonly used discount rate is either weighted average cost of capital (WACC) or required rate of return. This method provides an informative basis for management to compare projects and decide which ones to invest.

The capital budgeting process can be quite complicated for MNCs. The parent company needs to consider all subsidiaries and entities as a whole unit. Naturally, tax and currency issues are brought into consideration. For instance, how much will the project be taxed in the local country? How much cash flow can be remitted back to the parent company? In what currency should the investment be sent to the local country? In what currency would the project generate cash flow? How likely is a currency to devalue? Political and economic risks should also be considered as they have a significant impact on expected cash flows in foreign markets. For instance, how will a change in government affect regulatory requirements? How will economic growth (or decline) influence sales and costs?

4. Managing Financial Resources

In order to effectively manage financial resources, MNCs need to structure and position the bank accounts and cash balances of their subsidiaries. It is common that MNCs centralize certain cash management activities such as borrowing, global liquidity, international bank relations, and foreign exchange exposure. Meanwhile, subsidiaries usually handle local disbursement, collection, local banking relationships, and payroll, etc.[5]

Many MNCs prefer to hold a cash balance at a centralized depository account rather than having each subsidiary hold its own cash balance. Subsidiaries' bank accounts can be set up as Zero Balance Accounts, from which surplus cash would be transferred to a designated master account on a daily basis. Pooling cash centrally enables MNCs to accumulate a larger balance, which may receive a better interest from banks or allow management to pursue investment opportunities. Moreover, cash pooling reduces the need for financing. It is possible to use cash excesses from some subsidiaries to fund the cash needs of other subsidiaries. In addition, rather than maintaining precautionary cash balance at each subsidiary to cover unanticipated cash demand, MNCs can centralize precautionary cash balance, the required amount of which should be much lower than the sum of precautionary cash at subsidiaries.

Another important cash management approach is netting, a process to offset accounts payable and accounts receivable among the subsidiaries of the same parent firm. When there are many intercompany transactions (such as loan payments, sale of goods, licensing, etc.), rather than having each subsidiary transfer payments for each transaction, an MNC can coordinate cash inflows and outflows among subsidiaries through a central clearing account, and thus only net cash is transferred. This approach is particularly useful for cross-border transactions within an MNC. It reduces not only the number and amount of money transfers but also the costs of exchanging foreign currencies. In other words, by consolidating and offsetting payables against receivables on a global and multicurrency basis, netting reduces transaction costs for MNCs.

5. Protecting Financial Resources

While gaining access to various financing sources, MNCs are exposed to financial risks in international markets. Other than the usual factors to consider in financing decisions, such as interest rates, tax rates, and regulatory requirements, MNCs especially need to monitor and manage the risks that come with foreign currencies.

In Chapter 7, we discussed three types of risks caused by foreign exchange rate fluctuation—translation exposure, transaction exposure, and economic exposure. These risks are prominent in financing decisions. For instance, a creditor may offer several options regarding which currency an MNC can borrow. Not only aiming for a favorable interest rate, the MNC should also ensure the borrowed currency has stable liquidity. Suppose the MNC set up a subsidiary in Iceland and borrowed USD loans as the interest rate in USD was much lower than that in Iceland's local currency, króna. If the company earns most of its income in króna, then a depreciation of króna would put great pressure on the company.

To manage foreign exchange exposure, MNCs can use derivative financial contracts, such as forward contracts, option contracts, futures contracts, and swap contracts, as discussed in Chapter 7. Another approach is to match foreign currency inflows with foreign currency outflows in respect to the amount, timing, and currency. For instance, many MNCs incur debt in host country currencies to balance their exposed positions in assets and earnings. This tactic is especially useful in weak-currency countries, but interest rates in weak-currency countries are usually high. So there would be a tradeoff between the cost of debt and potential foreign exchange loss. Moreover, MNCs can adjust the timing of fund transfers to reduce risk exposure. They may lead (i.e. pay early) or lag (i.e. pay late). Typically, firms holding a weak currency would lead in paying debt and account payables denominated in a strong currency before the weak currency depreciates. Those holding a strong currency would lag in paying debt and accounts payables denominated in a weak currency. In addition, given the uncertainty in international financial markets, various financing sources and currencies may allow MNCs to diversify foreign exchange risks.

III. Accounting in International Business

Accounting is an important function in international business. It records and reports the business activities of an enterprise. The purpose of accounting is to provide useful and timely information to management and investors. For companies that operate in international markets, accounting can be quite complicated due to differences in accounting standards, tax codes, and currencies (see Case 10.3). It is critical to be aware of the key accounting issues in international business.

I. Following Different Accounting Standards

In many countries, accounting practices have been developed based on local business traditions and contexts, which in turn lead to different accounting requirements and standards around the world. Accounting requirements and standards are often referred to as Generally Accepted Accounting Principles (GAAP), which define how financial reporting should be conducted. Since countries usually have their own GAAP, financial statements, including balance sheets, income statements, and cash flow statements, may appear rather different in both form and content from country to country.

The accounting function of an MNC often needs to comply with different accounting standards. As a legal entity, each subsidiary of the MNC may be required to provide financial statements in accordance with its host country's GAAP. Thus, its financial reports are in compliance with legal requirements and can be used as the basis for local taxation. In addition, the subsidiary may be required to provide financial information based on the GAAP of the MNC's home country, and then the headquarter of the MNC can generate consolidated financial reports. If the MNC is a publicly held company, it is also required to file financial reports according to the GAAP of the capital market authority.

For example, a U.S.-based firm listed in London with one subsidiary in Hong Kong needs to comply with the GAAP of the U.S., the U.K., and Hong Kong. The subsidiary is required to prepare financial statements based on Hong Kong's GAAP. Since its information should be included in the parent firm's reports for legal and tax requirements in the U.S., the subsidiary also needs to provide its financial data based on U.S. GAAP. Furthermore, as the London Stock Exchange requires the financial statements to comply with the U.K.'s GAAP, the subsidiary has to prepare financial information accordingly in order to facilitate the parent company's financial reporting. In this situation, although the subsidiary conducts business activities in Hong Kong and has only one set of basic data, it needs to prepare three sets of reports following different standards.

When an MNC prepares financial information following varied accounting standards, it is likely to generate variations among different sets of reports. Therefore, it is not surprising that the same MNC may end up with totally different profit or loss numbers in its financial statements in different countries. To avoid confusion and misunderstanding, report readers should be aware of such discrepancies.

2. Recording Transactions in Foreign Currency

When setting up a new subsidiary in a foreign country, an accounting book is also set up in accordance with local accounting standards and tax requirements. During this process, three Cs—calendar, chart of account, and currency—need to be defined.

Calendar refers to the period used for calculating annual financial statements. Almost all countries require accounting and tax reports every 12 months. Some countries choose to set its fiscal year as same as the calendar year (i.e. January 1 to December 31). Others may choose different starting dates. For example, the fiscal year in Japan and U.K. runs from April 1 to March 31 of the following year, and the fiscal year in Australia and New Zealand runs from July 1 to June 30 of the following year.

Chart of account refers to a list of accounts that are used to record transactions. Countries may have specific requirements on account names and descriptions. Business transactions should be recorded in correct accounts based on local accounting standards.

Currency refers to the reporting currency that is used to record and present business transactions. For the purpose of taxation, most countries require business entities to use local currency as the reporting currency. Thus, an overseas subsidiary's reporting currency may be different from its parent company's reporting currency.

It should be noted that an overseas subsidiary's reporting currency is not necessarily its functional currency, i.e. the main currency actually used in business transactions.[6] For instance, a U.S.-based firm has a subsidiary in Brazil, which conducts most transactions in Brazilian real (BRL); thus BRL is not only the functional currency but also the reporting currency of this subsidiary. In a different case, a U.S.-based firm has set up a subsidiary in Singapore conducting importing and exporting transactions, most of which are settled in the U.S. dollar (USD); even though this subsidiary may set up Singapore dollar (SGD) as the reporting currency, its functional currency is the USD. Once determined, the functional currency does not change unless there is a change in the nature of underlying transactions, events, or conditions.

Due to the involvement of different currencies, it can be complicated for MNCs and their subsidiaries to record business transactions. Take that subsidiary in Brazil for example. When a transaction uses a currency other than BRL, it must be translated to and recorded in BRL so that this transaction can be aggregated with other domicile transactions for reporting.

Moreover, such a transaction creates receivables or payables in a foreign currency, thus subject to foreign exchange exposure. As demonstrated in the following two examples, accounting records should reflect the fluctuations of foreign exchange rates.

Example 1

The subsidiary in Brazil imported parts from a Mexican supplier for 100,000 Mexican pesos (MXN) and agreed to pay in MXN. The exchange rate was 1BRL=4.3MXN when the transaction happened. The transaction was recorded as

Debit: Purchases BRL23,255.81 (=MXN 100,000/4.3)
Credit: Accounts payable BRL23,255.81

If a payment is made immediately, the payment would be recorded as

Debit: Accounts payable BRL23,255.81 (=MXN 100,000/4.3)
Credit: Cash BRL23,255.81 (=MXN 100,000/4.3)

However, if the supplier offered 30-day credit and the exchange rate changed to 1BRL=4.4MXN 30 days later, the payment would be booked as

Debit: Accounts payable BRL23,255.81 (=MXN 100,000/4.3)
Credit: Cash BRL22,727.27 (=MXN 100,000/4.4)
Credit: Foreign exchange gain BRL 528.54

The difference means, due to the foreign exchange rate change, the subsidiary paid less than the amount it would have paid immediately. This gain on foreign exchange was recognized in the income statements.

Example 2

The subsidiary sold items to Europe for 5,000 euro and the customer agreed to pay in euros. The exchange rate was 1euro = 4.2BRL when the transaction happened. The transaction was recorded as

Debit: Accounts Receivable BRL 21,000(=euro 5,000×4.2)
Credit: Sales BRL 21,000(=euro 5,000×4.2)

When this customer asked for 60-day credit, the subsidiary agreed. The exchange rate became 1euro = 4.1BRL 60 days later. The subsidiary still received the same amount of euros, but the equivalent BRL number becomes smaller.

Debit: Cash BRL 20,500(=euro 5,000×4.1)
Debit: Foreign exchange loss BRL 500
Credit: Accounts receivable BRL 21,000(=euro 5,000×4.2)

In this case, the loss means the subsidiary received less cash than it would have collected immediately. The loss on foreign exchange decreased the profit of the subsidiary.

3. Translating Foreign Currency Financial Statements

To gather financial data on its global operations, an MNC may require its foreign subsidiaries to translate their financial statements into the MNC's reporting currency. As in a previous example, the U.S.-based MNC's subsidiary in Brazil, which uses BRL as its reporting currency, will need to submit financial information in USD to its headquarters for consolidation.

There are mainly two methods to translate financial statements.[7] One is the current rate method, used when the subsidiary's functional currency is different from the parent firm's reporting currency. This method stipulates all assets and liabilities on the balance sheet are translated using the exchange rate on the balance sheet date (with the exception that shareholder's equity is translated applying the historic rate when the corresponding shares were issued). All income statement items are translated with the average exchange rate of the period. When the subsidiary's operations occur in a different currency, this method can reflect the exchange rate risk the firm is exposed to at the reporting time, In the example of the U.S.-based MNC's subsidiary in Brazil, since the subsidiary does business in BRL, one should use current rate method to translate the subsidiary's financial reports into USD.

The other is the temporal method, used when the subsidiary's functional currency is not the local currency but the parent firm's reporting currency. This method requires that all nonmonetary assets and liabilities are translated with historical exchange rates (i.e. the exchange rate on the transaction date), but monetary assets and liabilities (such as cash, accounts payable and receivable, and debt) are translated using the current exchange rate (i.e. the exchange rate on the balance sheet date). In the example of the U.S.-based MNC's subsidiary in Singapore, the subsidiary conducts importing and exporting transactions in USD; its accounting records are maintained in SGD per local accounting and tax requirements; and thus the temporal method should be used to translate its financial statements.

Because of foreign exchange rate fluctuation, either method of translation may lead to gain or loss in net income and shareholder's equity. Readers of translated financial reports need to be aware of the impact of foreign exchange rates and interpret the performance data with caution.

In case a subsidiary is located in a highly inflationary economy, the requirement for translation will be different. A highly inflationary economy is an economy that has 100 percent or more cumulative inflation over a three-year period. High inflation makes the translated financial information less relevant. It will be difficult to determine whether a change in financial data is caused by a change in business or inflation. Translating financial statements prepared in the currency of a highly inflationary economy also introduces volatility unrelated to actual operating performance. Thus, the foreign entity's functional currency should be changed to its parent firm's reporting currency.

4. Consolidating and Analyzing Financial Statements

In order to have one set of financial statements in its own reporting currency, an MNC needs to consolidate the financial information of its headquarter and subsidiaries. Usually a foreign subsidiary is included in consolidation when the parent company owns a controlling interest in the subsidiary. The whole group is presented as one economic unit in its consolidated financial reports. Such reports allow the MNC's management and investors to understand its worldwide activities, while meeting the requirements of capital markets and tax authorities.

Consolidation is the process of combining translated financial statements into one set of reports after eliminating intra-group transactions. Because of the existence of internal transactions, one cannot simply add up all the entities' financials. For instance, a U.S.-based MNC's subsidiary in Brazil sold $20,000 USD of goods to its subsidiary in Singapore, then the Singapore subsidiary sold the goods to its clients for $30,000 USD. Simply adding up the numbers would give you $50,000 USD in sales, but the actual sale of the whole group was $30,000 USD. To avoid exaggeration of sales and income, the $20,000 USD sales of the Brazil subsidiary and the $20,000 USD COGS (cost of goods sold) of the Singapore subsidiary should be eliminated. Similarly, when a parent company invests in a subsidiary, the investment does not increase the total capital of the group. In the consolidation process, the investment account of the parent firm and the capital account of the subsidiary should be eliminated.

Consolidated statements provide a systematic and comprehensive view of the company's worldwide operations and performance. Financial statement analysis goes beyond the data on the surface to examine underlying relationships and trends. While the preparation of consolidated reports may demand advanced accounting knowledge, you do not need to be an accounting professional to read financial statements.

Key financial ratios are usually very helpful for managers and investors to understand and evaluate firm performance. For example, current ratio (= current assets / current liabilities) shows a company's ability to pay current liabilities; debt ratio (= liabilities / total assets) shows the liabilities and company's capital structure, etc.

Please bear in mind that, due to their differences in business operations, industries and companies may focus on different financial ratios. The retail industry may show better current ratio than the real estate industry. Service firms may have better inventory turnover than wholesalers. To get an accurate understanding of how a company is to perform in the future, one may examine the trends of financial ratios. Additionally, to reflect the big picture of the company, it is recommended to check multiple ratios in financial statement analyses.

5. Moving Toward IFRS

Given the differences in national accounting practices and standards, the demand for a common international accounting language has been growing. With the increasing number of MNCs and the expansion of global capital markets, the benefits of harmonizing different accounting practices are tremendous. A common accounting standard would result in comparable financial information and enhance the reliability of foreign financial statements. It would also reduce the costs of financial reporting, especially the costs of consolidation.

The International Accounting Standard Board (IASB) has been developing and promoting the International Financial Reporting Standards (IFRS) for years. As of 2015, the European Union and more than 100 countries (such as Australia, Brazil, Canada, India, Japan, Russia, and South Africa) have permitted or required IFRS for domestically listed companies (see Case 10.2).[8] This set of standards provides commonly accepted definitions, recognition criteria, and measurement concepts for assets, liabilities, income, and expenses.

One major criticism of IFRS is that the global standards have not been adopted in the U.S. yet. The IASB and the U.S. Financial Accounting Standards Board (FASB) have been working together to converge IFRS and the U.S. GAAP for years. But this turns out to be a complex and challenging process. In 2012, the U.S. Securities and Exchange Commission staff issued a report questioning the comprehensiveness, timeliness, global consistency, and appropriateness of IFRS. Nonetheless, quite a number of U.S. multinationals have started using IFRS as many of their subsidiaries are located in countries that have adopted IFRS.

Management must develop an accounting policy to ensure reliable financial reporting. When the accounting standards of an MNC's home country conform with IFRS, the MNC does not need to provide separate sets of financial statements. It is believed that the financial information conforms with IFRS as well as national standard. If national standards are different from IFRS, the MNC should include in its financial reports a reconciliation showing the differences between national accounting practices and the requirements of IFRS. Profit before taxation and shareholder's equity are usually reported twice by applying different accounting standards.

IV. Taxation in International Business

Among all the challenges MNCs face in foreign markets, taxation is always a top concern. Tax types and rates vary greatly based on location, ownership structure, and the nature of business. Tax payment affects not only MNCs' net income but also their relationship with local authorities. The tax implications of business activities should be carefully examined when making managerial and financial decisions.

I. Types of Taxes

There are many different types of taxes all over the world—income tax, sales tax, property tax, payroll tax, etc. Most MNCs are subject to two basic types: taxes on goods and services and taxes on corporate income and gains.

Taxes on goods and services. Such taxes are levied on transactions of goods and services. They may have different names and forms in different countries. For example, there are sales taxes in most states of the U.S., and value-added tax (VAT) is used in most European countries.[9] Sales tax is imposed on the retail sale and calculated as a percentage of the total purchase price. It is paid by the buyer, but sellers are required to collect it and pass it on to appropriate authorities. Resold items and raw materials are typically exempt from sales tax. Unlike sales tax, which is charged at the retail stage, VAT is imposed at every stage of the supply chain. It is calculated as a percentage of the increased value added to a product or service at each stage. VAT paid on business inputs is deductible at each stage. Eventually, VAT accumulated step-by-step is paid in full by the final buyers. While both taxation models have pros and cons, nowadays VAT is more widely used in the world than sales tax. Even the applications of a same taxation model in different countries may vary in scope, rate, jurisdiction, and compliance requirements. MNCs and their subsidiaries should check with local tax authorities to ensure compliance.

Taxes on income and gains. Typically, companies are subject to income tax, capital gains tax, and withholding tax. Income tax is levied on the income of an entity at the country (federal) and/or region (state, province, or municipal) levels. Capital gains are incomes derived from the sale of investments or capital assets, such as stocks, bonds, real estate, and equipment. Withholding tax is an indirect tax levied on passive income, such as dividends, royalties, and interest. The rate and application of taxes on income and gains vary from country to country.[10] MNCs are usually most concerned about income tax in different countries. The income tax rate can go up to 30, 40, or even 55 percent in some countries,[11] while those "tax haven" countries levy little or no income tax on foreign businesses. Among industrialized countries, the U.S. has the highest corporate income tax.[12] Furthermore, different approaches to determining taxable income can result in significant differences in tax burdens across countries. For example, the interest expense on an intercompany loan is tax deductible in some countries but not in others. Having entities in multiple countries, MNCs can take advantage of tax policy differences by arranging their investments and operations to lower total tax payment. Given the complexity of international taxation, MNCs may seek help from accounting and tax professionals.

2. Double Tax and Tax Treaty

As each country levies taxes based on their own tax codes, some cross-country transactions may be subject to double taxation. For example, MNCs may need to pay certain income taxes in both the home country and the host country. Dividends are a common method to transfer funds from a subsidiary to its parent company, but it is very likely to get double taxed. Only after the subsidiary pays income tax to local tax authorities, can the after-tax profit be used to distribute dividends. Those dividends are subject to income tax again when the parent company and shareholders receive them.

In comparison to dividends, royalties and fees have some tax advantage. When a parent firm franchises its business or provides technology, patents, or trade names to subsidiaries, it can charge royalties at a fixed monetary amount or a certain percentage of revenue. The parent firm may also charge subsidiaries for particular services (e.g. professional fees, management fees, service fees, technology support fees, etc.) Royalties and fees are usually counted as expenses for the subsidiaries and thus tax deductible in their host countries.

To avoid double taxation on international money transfer, some countries, like China and Iceland, have eliminated tax on foreign source income. Some countries offer tax credits to offset tax liabilities. For example, MNCs may get tax credits for income taxes paid to foreign governments. To ensure mutual tax enforcement, many countries have signed tax treaties with each other. The treaties regulate how much tax should be paid in each country regarding income transferred across borders; reciprocal tax reductions and exemptions for specific income items are offered to prevent double taxation; remedies and refunds are provided when double taxation occurs.

3. Transfer Pricing and Tax Havens

With operations in different countries, MNCs may seek to legally reduce their worldwide tax burden. Transfer pricing is a commonly used approach. Transfer prices refer to the prices of internal transactions of goods and services between a parent firm and its subsidiaries or between different subsidiaries of the same MNC. Unlike the prices of transactions between unrelated parties, which are determined by market forces and negotiations, transfer prices can be managed by MNCs. The high or low of transfer prices determines income distribution between buyers and sellers, who are subject to different tax liabilities in different countries.

MNCs may set transfer prices to reduce the total tax payment as a whole unit. Usually, higher transfer prices are set for goods and services supplied by a subsidiary with a lower local tax rate. Thus, a greater amount of income will be retained in the lower-tax country. Here is an example: An MNC's subsidiary in Ireland, which is subject to 12.5 percent income tax, exports $100,000 USD worth of goods to another subsidiary in India, which is subject to 34 percent income tax. If the price is changed to $110,000 USD, the subsidiary in Ireland pays $1,250 USD more tax (extra income $10,000 × 12.5 percent), while the subsidiary in India pays $3,400 USD less tax (income loss $10,000 × 34 percent). The tax saving for the MNC is $2,150 USD ($3,400 − $1,250 USD). Similarly, lower transfer prices are set for goods and services supplied by a subsidiary with a higher tax rate so that a smaller amount of income will be retained in the higher-tax location.

Transfer pricing also has the potential benefit of alleviating tariff burdens. Facing a fixed tariff rate, the exporting entity may reduce the invoice price, thus reducing tariff payment to the importing country. Moreover, transfer pricing can help manage foreign exchange risks. When the local currency of a subsidiary is expected to significantly devalue, MNCs can use transfer pricing to move funds out of that country to reduce risk exposure.

However, with the growth of MNCs, transfer pricing has attracted increasing scrutiny from tax authorities around the world. To ensure tax collection, many tax authorities require companies to follow the arm's length principle, under which the transfer price between two related parties should be the same as the price negotiated by two independent entities in an open market. Penalties will apply if transfer prices are manipulated to evade tax payment and regulation. Thus, MNCs are advised to research the method and range of transfer pricing allowed by tax authorities, and keep adequate documentation of transfer pricing in case of tax audits. In addition, transfer pricing causes the reallocation of profits and thus affects the performance of involved entities. MNCs should consider the influence of transfer pricing in their performance evaluation and reward policies.

Another common approach to reduce tax payments is to set up operations in low-tax locations. Especially in so-called "tax havens," the tax burden is significantly lower than that in other countries. Some well-known tax havens include Bermuda, the Cayman Islands, Dubai, Liechtenstein, Singapore, and Switzerland. In these countries, companies pay zero or minimum tax.

Many MNCs have set up subsidiaries in tax havens and shift income from high-tax countries to those locations (see Case 10.5). For instance, if a Chinese manufacturer sells products directly to the U.S. market, its profit is subject to 25 percent income tax in China; if the manufacturer sells products to its Bermuda subsidiary at cost and then sell to the U.S. at the regular price, the profit will be kept in Bermuda with no tax payment. Similarly, some MNCs have used holding companies in tax havens to lower tax payment. For instance, an MNC can transfer its assets to its holding company in Hong Kong, where all income from foreign sources is tax-exempt; then the holding company collects income generated from the assets, such as dividends, interest payment, and royalties.

To avoid high income tax in their original home countries, some MNCs even changed their incorporation location to low-tax countries. Such changes are known as tax inversions. For instance, Mylan, a U.S.-based pharmaceutical company, acquired Abbott Laboratories' European business and moved its headquarters to the Netherlands where it received a lower tax rate. The merger of Burger King and Tim Hortons was also viewed by some as tax inversion, as the newly merged company set up its headquarters in Canada (see Case 10.4).

Key Terms

Trade finance, letter of credit, draft, bill of lading, intercompany financing, international capital market, Eurocredit, cross listing, accounting standard, GAAP, IFRS, reporting currency, functional currency, value-added tax, double tax, transfer pricing, tax haven

Review Questions

1. What are the main payment methods used in international trade? Among these methods, why is letter of credit more widely used than others?
2. How can a company finance its international expansion? Please describe the major sources of funding?
3. What approaches can an MNC use to effectively manage and protect its financial resources around the world?
4. What challenges do different accounting standards and currencies impose on the accounting function of international business?
5. How do MNCs handle different tax rates and double taxation? How do they lower their worldwide tax payment?

Internet Exercises

1. BNY Mellon ADR Index comprises select non-U.S. companies listed in U.S. stock markets. Read the list of constituents of the Index: www.adrbnymellon.com/indices/adr-index/constituents. Choose a few companies and discuss how listing in the U.S. has affected their finance, accounting, and other business operations.
2. To facilitate cross listing, Euronext, the Pan-European financing center, has set up a fast path for companies already listed in the U.S. Please visit https://euronext.com/listings/international-listings/fast-path. Pick a cross-listed company and discuss how cross listing has affected its finance, accounting, and other business operations.

Notes

1   Export-Import Bank of the United States. Direct Loan. Retrieved from www. exim.gov/what-we-do/direct-loan

2 Fernandes, N. (2014). *Finance for Executives: A Practical Guide for Managers.* London: NPV Publishing.

3 Butler, K. C. (2012). *Multinational Finance: Evaluating Opportunities, Costs, and Risks of Operations.* Hoboken, NJ: John Wiley & Sons.

4 Chowdhry, B. and Coval, J. D. (1998). Internal financing of multinational subsidiaries: Debt vs. equity. *Journal of Corporate Finance, 4*(1), 87–106.

5 Eun, C. S. and Resnick, B. G. (2014). *International Financial Management.* Boston, MA: McGraw-Hill.

6 PwC. (2014). Foreign Currency. Retrieved from https://www.pwc.com/us/en/cfodirect/assets/pdf/accounting-guides/pwc-guide-foreign-currency-2014.pdf

7 Doupnik, T. S. and Perera, H. (2014). *International Accounting.* New York: McGraw-Hill Higher Education.

8 IFRS Foundation. (2016). IFRS application around the world. Retrieved from www.ifrs.org/Use-around-the-world/Pages/Jurisdiction-profiles.aspx

9 Ernst & Young. (2015). Worldwide VAT, GST and sales tax guide. Retrieved from www.ey.com/GL/en/Services/Tax/Worldwide-VAT-GST-Sales-Tax-Guide

10 Ernst & Young. (2015). Worldwide corporate tax guide. Retrieved from www.ey.com/GL/en/Services/Tax/Worldwide-Corporate-Tax-Guide

11 Tax Foundation. (2014). Corporate income tax rates around the world. Retrieved from http://taxfoundation.org/article/corporate-income-tax-rates-around-world-2014

12 OECD Tax Database. Table II.1 Corporate income tax rates: basic/non-targeted (last updated May 2015). Retrieved from www.oecd.org/tax/tax-policy/tax-database.htm

Managing Operations
R&D, Production, and Supply Chain

Learning Objectives

1. Describe the operations international firms typically perform.
2. Understand the rationales for offshoring and outsourcing in global operations.
3. Know the impact and location patterns of global R&D activities.
4. Learn how multinational companies locate and manage their global production.
5. Recognize the importance of global supply chain management.

Cases

Case 11.1 Zara's Production and Supply Chain

Zara, a famous Spanish fashion brand, has achieved remarkable global success. It mainly offers stylish women's clothing and accessories at reasonable prices. The first Zara store opened in 1975 by founder Amancio Ortega Gaona in Spain. In 1979, Inditex Group was established as a holding company for the sprawling network of Zara stores. After years of growth, Inditex became the world's largest fashion group in 2011. In the 2014 fiscal year, Inditex's annual sales reached 18.1 billion euros a year, with a net profit of 2.5 billion euros. Zara remains the flagship brand of Inditex, with over 2,100 stores located in 88 countries. Over 95 percent of Zara's products are sold in international markets.

Zara's path to success is rather unique in the fashion industry. It started in a region with neither fashion tradition nor cost advantage. While most companies outsource from developing countries like China, Zara has kept the majority of its production in Spain. Its approach to supply chain management, called "fast fashion," is very different from the traditional designer-led model of the industry, in which star designers create designs long before the season and subcontractors manufacture products months earlier. Unsure about consumer preferences, traditional fashion companies tend to market their products with heavy advertising. In contrast, Zara's "fast fashion" requires the company to understand what consumers like first and then design and produce accordingly. In other words, Zara tries to produce products that are proven to sell. To speed up the process, Zara has vertically integrated design, production, distribution, and retail sales.

Design. Zara has a large design team in its headquarters in Spain. While many fashion brands stress "big-name" designers, Zara's designers are basically anonymous. Zara believes in democratized fashion, which is largely driven by customers. Through direct interactions with customers, Zara's store staff and managers identify styles that sell well and those that do not. Customer information from stores all over the world is sent to the design team daily. Key store managers frequently visit the headquarters to share their street-level knowledge about fashion trends. Based on such information, the design team works on both initial collections and in-season responses.

Manufacturing. Zara owns 11 manufacturing facilities, mostly in Spain. Those facilities have advanced equipment for fabric dyeing, processing, cutting, and garment finishing. Owning plants and equipment allows Zara to directly control the manufacturing process. For example, Zara always tries to dye items at a later stage in production, thus maximizing color flexibility. It only buys fabric in four different colors and all contractors are located nearby to ensure on demand supply. Zara's own facilities mainly perform high-cost and high-skill tasks, such as cutting out garment pieces and putting on price tags. Some minor labor-intensive processes like garment stitching are outsourced from a network of contracted workshops in Spain and neighboring countries. By strategically using factories in close vicinity, either owned or contracted, Zara is able to produce the trendiest clothes within two to three weeks. Although the labor costs in Spain are definitely not low, the disadvantage is largely offset by greater flexibility and faster inventory turnover. Unlike trendy clothes, which account for the majority of the company's sales, Zara's basic T-shirts and sweaters are ordered about six months in advance from suppliers in low-labor-cost countries like China, Bangladesh, and Vietnam.

Distribution. Zara has a state-of-the-art distribution system. Its main distribution center in Spain is five million square feet and located next to the company's headquarters. All nearby factories are linked to the distribution center with tunnels and ceiling rails. Optical scanning devices sort and distribute more than 60,000 items of clothing an hour. Based on the needs of each individual store, garments are allotted piece by piece for shipments. About 150 million items pass through the distribution center annually. Twice a week, new styles are dispatched to stores. Trucks are used to distribute to European stores while air transportation is used for international stores. Europe can be supplied within 24 hours, U.S. and China in 48 hours, and Japan in 72 hours. Such an efficient system allows Zara to ship frequently in small batches and achieve quick in-season turnaround.

Sales. Zara has succeeded with little or no advertising. Instead of flashy campaigns, the company focuses on stores. Its main approach to attracting shoppers is opening stores in prominent locations, constantly updating store looks, and supplying stores with new designs. A new look comes out every 18 months. Several hundred stores are renovated every year. This has become a main item of Zara's capital expenditure, reaching over one billion euros per year. Meanwhile, every store receives a batch of merchandise tailored to the local market, twice a week. Over half of the items are designed and manufactured within three weeks before they hit the shop floor. Customers know that new items are arriving every few days in limited quantities, and popular items may disappear quickly. Even an incredibly popular item will never be exactly reproduced. So, customers are motivated to shop frequently at Zara—an average of 17 visits per year. Furthermore, Zara may offer surprisingly different arrays of items in different stores, even those in neighboring cities. Their product offerings are all dictated by respective shoppers.

Information Systems. In order to produce and ship the right items for customers, Zara has invested heavily in high technology. For instance, in 2014, Zara implemented a microprocessor-based tagging system, putting chips inside the plastic security tags that are attached to garments. The system allows items to be tracked from factory to the point of sale, until they are sold. Real-time information about what products are being purchased at different locations allows Zara factories to accommodate demand changes. In each country, one or more specialists are hired to monitor and analyze real-time sales data. The specialists use computer algorithms developed by the Massachusetts Institute of Technology to discover the right mix of styles and sizes for each store. Aided by this computer-generated information, store managers and regional directors make decisions according to local market conditions.

In addition, Zara has created a horizontal and flexible organizational structure that encourages employees to participate in identifying fashion trends and customer needs. Conversation and collaboration are stressed to facilitate bottom-up communication. Thus, when the latest information is received from customers, Zara can respond quickly—designers make quick changes, buyers adjust orders, and planners modify delivery batches, etc. Thus, customers, designers, factories, and stores are inextricably linked.

With speed and flexibility, the "fast fashion" approach has helped Zara lower costs and attract customers. It takes Zara about 15 days to turn a design into a product for sale, while the rest of the industry typically needs six to nine months to accomplish the same task. Inventory turnover in Zara's stores is approximately 12 times a year, while the industry average is three to four times. Zara has much fewer items for mark-down compared to competitors. While fashion retailers typically sell 30 to 40 percent of their items at discount, the number is 15 to 20 percent for Zara. Also, Zara is able to bring the quantity of unsold items to about 10 percent of stock while the industry average is 17 to 20 percent.

Sources

1. Inditex company website. www.inditex.com/
2. Berfield, S. and Baigorri, M. (2013, November 11). Zara's fast-fashion edge. *Business Week*. Retrieved from www.businessweek.com/articles/2013-11-14/2014-outlook-zaras-fashion-supply-chain-edge

3. Buck, T. (2014, June 18). Fashion: A better business model. *Financial Times*. Retrieved from www.ft.com/cms/s/2/a7008958-f2f3-11e3-a3f8-00144feabdc0. html#ide0
4. Butler, S. (2013, December 15). Inditex: Spain's fashion powerhouse you've probably never heard of. *The Guardian*. Retrieved from www.theguardian.com/ fashion/2013/dec/15/inditex-spain-global-fashion-powerhouse
5. Hansen, S. (2012, November 9). How Zara grew into the world's largest fashion retailer. *New York Times Magazine*. Retrieved from www.nytimes.com/2012/ 11/11/magazine/how-zara-grew-into-the-worlds-largest-fashion-retailer.html
6. Loeb, W. (2013, October 14). Zara's secret to success: The new science of retailing. *Forbes*. Retrieved from www.forbes.com/sites/walterloeb/2013/10/14/zaras-secret-to-success-the-new-science-of-retailing-a-must-read/

Questions for Case Discussion

1. Why did Zara concentrate its production in Spain?
2. How did Zara integrate its various operations around the world?
3. Given the trend of globalization, should Zara move more production to low-cost countries?

Case II.2 R&D Outsourcing in the Pharmaceutical Industry

The pharmaceutical industry is well known for its long R&D cycles and the continuous emergence of new technologies. To enhance speed to market and cost efficiency, many pharmaceutical companies have started outsourcing certain operations, such as screening and lead identification, preclinical studies, clinical trials, as well as marketing and manufacturing. Especially, the outsourcing of R&D has become a common practice in the industry. Activities such as animal toxicology testing and clinical operations used to be deemed essential but are rarely performed in-house nowadays. It is expected that large pharmaceutical companies will spend more than 40 percent of their R&D spending on outsourcing.

According to a report by Transparency Market Research, a market research firm, the outsourced research market is expected to reach $65.03 billion USD by 2018.[a] The market growth is likely to continue at an annual rate above 9 percent over the next ten to fifteen years. Consequently, there has been a fast growth of contract research organizations (CROs), which mainly provide research services to the pharmaceutical, biotechnology, and medical device industries on a contract basis. CROs range from large, international full-service companies to small, niche specialty firms, and provide a wide variety of research services such as biopharmaceutical development, commercialization, preclinical research, clinical research, and trial management.

Utilizing CROs allows pharmaceutical companies to avoid investments in capital equipment and specialist staff, thus reducing R&D expenses. Since the price for outsourced R&D work is usually predetermined, pharmaceutical companies can better control their costs. Moreover, CROs may have specialized knowledge and resources to work with different products and regulations. Their flexibility allows pharmaceutical companies to exploit various market opportunities. For instance, a company can expand into a new technological area that is not its traditional expertise by outsourcing from CROs. The company can shift its internal R&D effort to more strategic activities and core competencies, thus shortening the time needed to bring new products to market.

In recent years, many pharmaceutical companies have reduced R&D costs by cutting internal efforts and increasing outsourcing. Reportedly, the growth of R&D outsourcing has surpassed that of internal R&D investment. Technological advances have also strengthened the growth of outsourcing. CROs are able to provide increasingly specialized and resource-intensive services. Cloud-based systems and innovation by software vendors are making it easier for pharmaceutical companies to monitor outsourcing processes and manage risks.

Developing countries, especially China and India, have seen strong growth in R&D outsourcing services. By offering low-cost labor and facilities, they help pharmaceutical companies decrease payroll and capital expenditures. Despite recent wage increases in these countries, outsourcing still proves to be cost-effective. Meanwhile, the rapid expansion of domestic pharmaceutical markets also drives the development of local R&D. Large global pharmaceutical companies have spent billions in building local R&D centers and outsourcing to CROs in developing countries.

Plenty of companies have successfully used CROs to develop better drugs with lower costs. For instance, the pharmaceutical giant Pfizer has signed master service contracts with three international CROs—Parexel, Icon, and Pharmaceutical Product Development—for clinical trials. All three CROs have offices in dozens of countries and work with many subcontractors around the world. Covance, a U.S.-based CRO, has provided long-term drug development services to multinational pharmaceutical companies like Bayer, Sanofi-Aventis, and Eli Lilly. Its contract with Sanofi-Aventis is a ten-year deal worth up to $2.2 billion USD.

However, compared to routine business activities such as basic accounting and human resource practices, the outsourcing of R&D activities has additional challenges due to the inherent complexity and uncertainty of R&D. Particularly, in the pharmaceutical industry, companies are faced with growing R&D costs, pricing pressures, regulatory changes, merger and acquisition activities, patent expiration, and other difficulties. Managing outsourcing has become the number one challenge for many pharmaceutical R&D executives. According to Contract Pharma's eleventh annual outsourcing survey in 2015, despite growth in R&D outsourcing, both service buyers and providers noted significant problems in outsourcing relationships.[b] For pharmaceutical companies, the top issue was communication and culture (cited by 46 percent of respondents), followed by quality assistance (40 percent), vendor qualification and selection (37 percent), documentation (36 percent), and analytical method development (26 percent). From the service providers' perspective, the top challenge cited is insufficient information (63 percent), followed by unrealistic deadlines (62 percent) and infrequent communication (40 percent).

Pharmaceutical companies and CROs need to find the right outsourcing models to sustain their mutual growth. Strategic alliance seems to be an increasing popular approach that allows partner firms to share complementary expertise while ensuring flexibility. According to Parexel's President Mark Goldberg, there is a trend that the relationships between CROs and their clients are becoming more intimate and strategic.[c] More and more CROs are engaged to deliver technology and expertise through not just short-term transactions but long-term partnerships. Many pharmaceutical companies now regard collaboration as an important way to mitigate complexity, reduce transaction costs, and gain competitive advantage. For them, R&D outsourcing has changed from a tactical purchase of "off-the-shelf" services to various models of strategic partnerships. The 2015 Contract Pharma survey also revealed that pharmaceutical companies tend to take a more strategic rather than tactical, case-by-case approach to outsourcing. This trend is likely to continue as 82 percent of survey respondents planned on continuing to utilize the strategic approach. Certainly, R&D outsourcing alliances are not always successful. Partners need truly share risks and benefits to achieve commitment, value creation, and innovation.

Notes

a. Transparency Market Research. (2013, January 17). Healthcare Contract Research Outsourcing Market—Global Industry Analysis, Size, Share, Trends and Forecast 2012–2018. Retrieved from www.transparencymarketresearch. com/hcro-market.html

b. ContractPharma. (2015, May 13). 2015 Annual Outsourcing Survey. Retrieved from www.contractpharma.com/contents/view_outsourcing-survey/2015-05-13/2015-annual-outsourcing-survey

c. Outsourcing-pharma.com. (2014, February 10). 'Intimate partnerships': Parexel President shares CRO trends for 2014. Retrieved from www.outsourcing-pharma.com/Clinical-Development/Intimate-partnerships-Parexel-President-shares-CRO-trends-for-2014

Sources

1. Deloitte. (2015). 2015 Global Life Sciences Outlook. Retrieved from www2. deloitte.com/content/dam/Deloitte/global/Documents/Life-Sciences-Health-Care/gx-lshc-2015-life-sciences-report.pdf

2. Med-Tech Innovation. (2011, September 24). Benefits of using a contract research organisation. Retrieved from www.med-techinnovation.com/articles/articles/article/19/Benefits+of+Using+a+Contract+Research+Organisation

3. PR Newswire. (2015, April 10). Global pharmaceutical outsourcing market report 2015—new trends on the horizon. Retrieved from www.prnewswire. com/news-releases/global-pharmaceutical-outsourcing-market-report-2015---new-trends-on-the-horizon-300064158.html

4. Langer, E. S. (2012). Pharmaceutical outsourcing trends: The next decade. *BioPharm International*. Retrieved from http://bioplanassociates.com/publications/articles/2012/BioPharmIntl_PharmaOutsourcingTrends_Mar2012.pdf

5. KPMG. (2011). Outsourcing in the pharmaceutical industry: 2011 and beyond. Retrieved from www.kpmg.com/Ca/en/IssuesAndInsights/ArticlesPublications/Documents/Outsourcing-pharmaceutical-industry.pdf

6. Wright, Tim. (2015, May 13). 2015 annual outsourcing survey. Retrieved from www.contractpharma.com/contents/view_outsourcing-survey/2015-05-13/2015-annual-outsourcing-survey

Questions for Case Discussion

1. What factors drive the R&D outsourcing of pharmaceutical companies?
2. What locations are more likely to attract outsourced R&D services?
3. How can pharmaceutical companies effectively manage their outsourcing relationships?

Case 11.3 New Balance: Made in USA?

In the athletic footwear industry, it is a common practice to source production from low-cost countries. Indeed, almost all major athletic shoe brands sold in the U.S. market are manufactured in other countries. One outstanding exception is New Balance, a brand that takes pride in its tradition of "Made in USA."

New Balance was founded in 1906. It started from selling arch support accessories in Boston, Massachusetts and eventually grew into a major footwear company. Still headquartered in Boston, New Balance now sells athletic shoes, apparel and accessories for men, women, and kids across over 5,000 outlets worldwide under brands like New Balance, Brine, Aravon, Dunham, PF Flyers, and Warrior Sports. While most competitors have outsourced or offshored manufacturing, New Balance still operates five factories in the U.S. Also, it has a manufacturing facility in the U.K. to serve the European market.

Back in 1994, New Balance manufactured 70 percent of its shoes in the U.S. Nowadays, approximately 25 percent of the New Balance shoes sold in North America are "Made in USA." The remaining 75 percent are made in countries like China and Vietnam. While New Balance has moved some manufacturing offshore, its percentage of home country production is much higher than that of Nike or Adidas. The "Made in USA" claim has become a key component of New Balance's marketing campaigns. Flag stickers are put on shoe boxes. Heavy promotions are used to emphasize local roots. Select styles are decorated with the phrase "Made in USA."

So what does "Made in USA" really mean? New Balance once stated on its website that, "Where the domestic value is at least 70 percent, we label our shoes Made in USA." However, according to the Federal Trade Commission (FTC), the "Made in USA" mark is a country of origin label indicating the product is "all or virtually all" made in the U.S.; "all significant parts and processing that go into the product must be of U.S. origin"; and "the product should contain no or negligible foreign content."[a] To assess the percentage of domestic content, companies should examine the cost of goods sold including manufacturing materials, direct manufacturing labor, and manufacturing overhead.

It is not clear if New Balance shoes meet FTC guidelines. Back in September 1994, the FTC cited New Balance for misleading information in its advertising campaign featuring American-made shoes. The FTC believed that a substantial amount of New Balance footwear was not made in the U.S. Specifically, the soles of many New Balance shoes were manufactured in China. Instead of changing its practice as most companies would when being cited, New Balance argued that the FTC's standard was unreasonable as most U.S. manufacturers' products nowadays include some foreign content. After a two-year legal battle, New Balance agreed not to label any shoes made completely overseas as "Made in USA." But shoes made with both domestic and foreign content were not specifically addressed in the company's agreement with the FTC.

The "Made in USA" claim is a powerful marketing tool for American companies to increase sales both domestically and internationally. While some people think New Balance is taking advantage of the FTC's ambiguous standard, it is the only major footwear company that has maintained production in the U.S. The company claims that it makes more than four million pairs of athletic footwear per year in the U.S. Although the number accounts for only 25 percent of New Balance's total production, it is still quite remarkable in comparison to other footwear brands. For instance, Nike, also a leading U.S.-based athletic footwear maker, outsources manufacturing from more than 700 contract factories in over 40 countries, most of which are Asian countries like Indonesia, China, India, Thailand, Vietnam, and Pakistan. The Germany-based Adidas Group also outsources most of its production through working with more than 1,100 independent factories in over 60 countries.

While domestic production tends to result in higher costs, it also provides New Balance some benefits that cannot be easily achieved overseas: fast delivery and customization. Over the years, New Balance has reduced the time needed to make a pair of shoes from eight days to only three hours. Nowadays customers can order shoes online and receive them the next day. The company also provides more customization options than its competitors. The NB1 customization program allows buyers to change color schemes and looks online, and even have personalized messages embroidered on shoes. A number of models such as the classic 574, the performance-driven 990v3, and the 998 running shoes can be custom-made. New sneaker styles have been continuously added to the popular customization program.

Manufacturing in the U.S. also helps New Balance control quality. The company's American manufacturing workers have an average of 13 years' experience. They carefully inspect each pair of shoes before packaging. For customized shoes, the finished product has to match the original design. In addition, since New Balance directly manages its production, it is relatively easy to control the supply chain and protect intellectual property. For those companies that outsource from hundreds of contracts and subcontractors, it is hard to police global supply chains.

The "Made in USA" shoes usually retail for a price between $75 USD and almost $400 USD. Despite its high price tag, New Balance has achieved considerable success in the competitive athletic footwear industry. Its global sales reached $2.73 billion USD in 2013 and $3.3 billion USD in 2014. Also in 2014, it was ranked the fifth sportswear brands in terms of sales in the world.

Nevertheless, manufacturing in the U.S. has its limitations. New Balance once stated their biggest challenge was getting supplies domestically. As most athletic footwear companies went overseas, their suppliers followed suit. Moreover, the competitors have improved their supply chain management to achieve quality, speed, and customization. Nike has developed a sophisticated system to evaluate and monitor its sourcing and manufacturing contractors.

The system looks at built-in quality, just-in-time, operational stability as well as labor, health and safety, and environmental practices. Adidas has a Global Operations department that oversees the operations of its suppliers around the world. To seize short-term opportunities or satisfy niche requirements, Adidas sometimes sources from local suppliers in specific countries. All suppliers are required to meet specific standards set by the company.

Note

a. Federal Trade Commission. (n.d.). Complying with the Made in USA Standard. Retrieved from www.ftc.gov/tips-advice/business-center/guidance/complying-made-usa-standard

Sources

1. New Balance. (n.d.). Made in USA Sneakers. Retrieved from www.newbalance.com/made-in-us-and-uk/
2. Nike. (n.d.). Sustainable Business Report. Retrieved from http://about.nike.com/pages/sustainable-innovation
3. Adidas Group. (n.d.). Supply China Structure. Retrieved from www.adidas-group.com/en/sustainability/compliance/supply-chain-structure/
4. Federal Trade Commission. (1998). Complying with the MADE IN USA STANDARD. Retrieved from www.ftc.gov/system/files/documents/plain-language/bus03-complying-made-usa-standard.pdf
5. Aeppel, T. (2014, September 30). New Balance acknowledges shoe materials aren't all U.S. made. Wall Street Journal. Retrieved from www.wsj.com/articles/new-balance-shoe-materials-arent-all-u-s-made-1412109111
6. Schoen, J. W. (2010, April 16). New Balance sidesteps FTC ad rules. NBC News. Retrieved from www.nbcnews.com/id/36476797/ns/business-us_business/t/new-balance-sidesteps-ftc-ad-rules/

Questions for Case Discussion

1. Why has New Balance kept manufacturing in the U.S.?
2. Given the development of the global footwear industry, can New Balance sustain its current production model? And why?
3. How would you define "Made in USA"? Do you agree with the FTC standard?

Case 11.4 The Production of Boeing Dreamliner

On July 8, 2007, in its Everett, Washington assembly factory, Boeing revealed the first fully assembled Boeing 787 airplane, also known as the Dreamliner, to the world. This mid-size, long-haul airplane was Boeing's most advanced model. Its body was 50 percent composites and 20 percent aluminum. It was expected to be 20 percent more fuel efficient than similarly sized airplanes and emit 20 percent less pollutants. Boeing claimed that the Dreamliner would bring dramatic improvements, making air travel more affordable, comfortable, and convenient for passengers, more efficient and profitable for airlines, and more environmentally friendly for the earth. By then, Boeing had already received 677 orders for the Dreamliner with delivery scheduled for 2015, making it one of the fastest selling planes in aviation history. The first test flight was to take place in August or September 2007. The Dreamliner would enter commercial service in May 2008 once Japan's All Nippon Airways (ANA) received the first of the fifty 787 airplanes it had ordered back in 2004.

However, a number of delays occurred due to various problems with fasteners, software, engines, and other parts. A labor strike at Boeing's facilities also negatively affected the delivery schedule. In December 2009, more than two years behind schedule, the Dreamliner completed high-speed taxi tests and made its maiden flight. Afterward, Boeing encountered more problems with some suppliers of airplane parts. Finally, the first Dreamliner was delivered to ANA in September 2011, more than three years behind schedule. Tickets for the Dreamliner's first commercial flight from Narita to Hong Kong were sold in an online auction, and the highest bidder paid $34,000 USD for a seat. Despite people's enthusiasm, reports on the Dreamliner's incidents and flaws started to arrive. In February 2012, Boeing discovered a manufacturing error that required repairs in the fuselage section. In 2013, ANA and Japan Airlines reported fuel leaks and grounded the Dreamliner for four months because of overheating batteries. More technical or electrical issues like brake problems, cracked windshields, and electrical fires were subsequently discovered. Both American and Japanese governments announced investigations into the Dreamliner. Some analyst estimated that, given all the delays and repairs, the cost of building one Dreamliner airplane was about $232 million USD higher than the initial asking price of $120 million USD, suggesting a loss of over $100 million USD for each Dreamliner delivered.

What caused these problems? When launching the Dreamliner project back in 2004, Boeing decided to take a different approach to bringing this airplane to the marketplace by employing global design and supply chain resources. The Dreamliner was designed completely on computers without building a prototype or mock-up, engineering work was distributed globally, and a global supply chain was developed. Boeing functioned as the final assembler and integrator, performing about 40 percent of the design and production, outsourcing the remaining 60 percent. For instance, the Dreamliner's wings were sent from Nagoya, Japan to Everett, WA; fuselage Section 46 went from Grottagli, Italy to Charleston, SC, and then to Everett, WA. This approach made the Dreamliner the most outsourced product in Boeing's history. The company worked with about 5,400 factories around the world. About 50 of them (with 28 outside of the U.S.) were categorized as tier-one suppliers, which in turn sourced from lower-tier suppliers.

This outsourcing approach was supposed to make the production process faster and cheaper. Initially, it was applauded as visionary and brilliant because most of the costs of investments and inventories were shifted to upstream suppliers. For instance, Vought, a tier-one supplier, needed to invest in necessary technology and equipment to produce one-piece composite fuselages, thus reducing Boeing's risk exposure.

However, such decentralized, global sourcing generated certain problems. First, it required close collaboration, which turned out to be quite challenging. In the engineering process, multiple tiers of contractors were supposed to make their designs consistent so that all the parts fit together, but they did not. Many contractors did not have the experience and technology to collaborate with multiple firms to develop coordinated designs. Knowledge gaps among these contractors made it difficult for Boeing to develop parts and manage suppliers. Second, the complex supply chain added risks and costs. Boeing's fifty or so tier-one suppliers regularly subcontracted various modules to tier-two suppliers, who in turn outsourced certain components from tier-three suppliers. Cultural and language differences within this multi-tier supply chain led to more room for errors and less control for Boeing. When one part was unavailable, the next one could not be attached because it was dependent on the previous part. As a result, the global supply chain seized up. In 2009, Boeing spent $1 billion USD to acquire its suppliers and bring some work back in-house. In addition, this approach required significant managerial commitment from Boeing. The extensive supply chain demanded continuous communication and on-site involvement. However, as the prime contractor, Boeing did not provide instant quality control, supply management, and technical support. Instead, these responsibilities were delegated to subcontractors. Without adequate control over this complicated supply chain, Boeing exposed itself to huge managerial risks.

Given the requirement of airplane safety, there is little room for errors. Some industry observers argued that Boeing should have stayed away from a supply chain model with a high chance of producing errors. For Boeing, a supply chain that was short in time and distance might offer easier communication and more control.

Sources

1. Reuters. (2012, October 10). Boeing gets grip on 787 supply chain with upsized jumbos. Retrieved from www.reuters.com/article/2012/10/10/uk-boeing-dreamliner-production-correcte-idUSLNE89901Y20121010
2. *USA Today.* (2007, July 9). Boeing unveils 787 Dreamliner; Airbus sends congrats. Retrieved from http://usatoday30.usatoday.com/travel/flights/2007-07-09-boeing-787-debuts_N.htm
3. Chick, G. (2013, July 22). Supply chain innovation is a double-edged sword for sustainability. *The Guardian.* Retrieved from www.theguardian.com/sustainable-business/supply-chain-innovation-double-edged-sword
4. Denning, S. (2013, January 17). The Boeing debacle: Seven lessons every CEO must learn. *Forbes.* Retrieved from www.forbes.com/sites/stevedenning/2013/01/17/the-boeing-debacle-seven-lessons-every-ceo-must-learn/
5. Surowiecki, J. (2013, February 4). Requiem for a dreamliner? *New Yorker.* Retrieved from www.newyorker.com/magazine/2013/02/04/requiem-for-a-dreamliner

Questions for Case Discussion

1. What are the benefits and drawbacks of global sourcing?
2. Is it appropriate for a company like Boeing to use global sourcing?
3. How can the company improve the management of its global supply chain?

Case 11.5 The Reshoring of American Manufacturers

In recent years, General Motors (GM) has made several announcements to move certain operations from overseas locations back into the U.S. In 2012, GM launched a three-year initiative to bring offshored IT service jobs back home, aiming to have 90 percent of IT jobs in-house and the remaining 10 percent outsourced. In 2014, GM announced a plan to move the manufacturing of Cadillac SRX, its best-selling vehicle, from Mexico to Spring Hill, Tennessee. A year later, about 3,000 people were working in the 6.9 million square-foot Tennessee plant. Also in 2015, GM started a $119 million USD investment in tools and equipment for the production of vehicle components in Grand Rapids, Michigan. Several hundred employees were hired to work on three shifts making components for Chevrolet, Buick, GMC, and Cadillac.

GM is one of the many American companies that have reshored operations in recent years. Reshoring refers to the act of moving operations back to the home country from offshore locations. For instance, GE announced a plan in 2012 to bring manufacturing back from China. The company intended to spend $800 million USD to re-establish a manufacturing facility in Louisville, Kentucky and make cutting-edge, low-energy water heaters and high-tech French-door refrigerators domestically. Otis, an elevator manufacturer, also announced the relocation of production from Mexico to South Carolina. In 2013, Apple's Singapore-based contract manufacturer, Flextronics, started to build Mac Pro desktop computers in an advanced facility in Austin, Texas. In the same year, Whirlpool began to move production of commercial washing machines back to the U.S. from Mexico. After decades of offshoring, some business operations and jobs are slowly returning home.

As lowering cost is a key driver for offshoring, changes in relative costs contribute to the trend of reshoring. Some resources like natural gas cost much less in the U.S. than in Asia. Rising transportation costs have made long-distance shipping of low value-density goods, such as consumed goods, appliances, and furniture, less economical. More importantly, labor costs in some traditionally low-cost countries have been increasing fast. According to the International Labour Organization, real wages in Asia typically grew at least 7 percent per year between 2000 and 2008, while the annual pay raise in advanced economies was less than 1 percent.[a] Pay and benefits for the average Chinese factory worker rose by 10 percent a year between 2000 and 2005 and sped up to 19 percent a year between 2005 and 2010, according to Boston Consulting Group.[b] A recent study by Hay Group,[c] a consulting firm, showed that pay for senior managers in such emerging markets as China, Turkey and Brazil, now either matches or exceeds that in America and Europe.

Changes in customer demand also contribute to the trend of reshoring. Many companies have realized that cost cutting is no longer the only effective tool to gain a competitive advantage. There is an increasing demand for customer responsiveness. While factories could thrive on high-volume/low-mix production (i.e. making a large quantity of the same product) in the past, customers nowadays need more variety and customization. Moving production near customers enables a company to bring products to market faster and respond rapidly to customer orders. Comparatively, offshore production is usually less agile and customizable. Domestic manufacturing tends to improve quality and intellectual property protection. Therefore, U.S. companies may utilize domestic operations to better serve American customers' needs.

Meanwhile, technological advancement in manufacturing has made reshoring more feasible. Automation and flexible manufacturing enable companies to cost-efficiently perform low-volume/high-mix production. Industrial robots are gaining popularity and becoming more and more affordable. According to a study by McKinsey, a global consulting firm, the relative costs of automation fell about 45 percent from 1990 to 2012.[d] The economics of production is changing as the percentage of labor costs in total manufacturing costs decreases.

In addition, in order to attract manufacturing jobs, some states such as Tennessee and North Carolina offer generous incentives to companies. Labor unions have also made compromises on wages to keep and increase domestic jobs. For instance, United Auto Workers accepted a two-tier wage structure under which new workers are paid half as much as those long-serving ones. Consequently, the big three American automakers hired more new workers and brought some production back to the U.S. Ford reportedly reshored at least 3,000 jobs during 2012–15.

However, the road to reshoring can be bumpy. Decades of offshoring has led to a shortage of skilled workers in the U.S. The regulatory systems that govern American manufacturing are rather complicated. Also, it has been argued that reshoring does not necessarily bring back jobs. When reshoring, companies typically deploy advanced manufacturing that involves automation, which requires fewer and more educated workers.

Compared to the flood of offshoring, the reshoring flow is only a trickle. In most reshoring cases, companies are only bringing back a portion of their production destined for the U.S. market. Especially for large firms, the amount of work offshored largely outweighs the amount being brought back. Many manufacturing activities offshored over the past several decades still remain outside of the country. While the attractiveness of American manufacturing increases, other locations are also developing new advantages. For example, Caterpillar announced the opening of a new factory in Texas to make excavators, but also expanded its R&D activities in China. It seems that the trend toward reshoring is neither the straight reversal of offshoring, nor an indication of a decline in offshoring.

Notes

a.   International Labour Organization. (2010, December 15). Global Wage Report 2010/11: Wage policies in times of crisis. Retrieved from www.ilo.org/global/publications/ilo-bookstore/order-online/books/WCMS_145265/lang-en/index.htm

b.   Sirkin, H.L, Zinser, M., and Hohner, D. (2011). Made in America, again why manufacturing will return to the U.S. Retrieved from www.bcg.com/documents/file84471.pdf

c. *Economist.* (2013, January 19). Reshoring manufacturing: Coming home. Retrieved from www.economist.com/news/special-report/21569570-growing-number-american-companies-are-moving-their-manufacturing-back-united

d. McKinsey & Company. (2012). Manufacturing the future: The next era of global growth and innovation. Retrieved from www.mckinsey.com/business-functions/operations/our-insights/the-future-of-manufacturing

Sources

1. Bargent, James. (2012, August 20). What drove GM to kill offshoring contracts and bring work back to Detroit? Nearshore Americas. Retrieved from www.nearshoreamericas.com/caused-gm-shift-offshoring-onshoring/

2. Bunkely, N. (2015, February 15). Ford tops GM in U.S. factory jobs. *Automotive News*. Retrieved from www.autonews.com/article/20150215/OEM/302169970/ford-tops-gm-in-u.s.-factory-jobs

3. *Economist.* (2013, January 19). Coming home. Retrieved from www.economist.com/news/special-report/21569570-growing-number-american-companies-are-moving-their-manufacturing-back-united

4. Puri, R. (2012, December 17). Why outsourced jobs are returning stateside. *Forbes*. Retrieved from www.forbes.com/sites#/sites/bmoharrisbank/2012/12/17/why-outsourced-jobs-are-returning-stateside/#407b15b921fb

5. Semuels, A. (2015, October 26). 'Good' jobs aren't coming back. *The Atlantic*. Retrieved from www.theatlantic.com/business/archive/2015/10/onshoring-jobs/412201/

Questions for Case Discussion

1. What factors are driving the trend of reshoring?
2. What kind of companies are more likely to bring production back home?
3. Will the trend of reshoring become stronger in the future? Why?

Managing Operations

R&D, Production, and Supply Chain

I. An Overview of Global Operations

To deliver a product or service to customers, companies must perform a chain of activities, starting from initial conception to final delivery (see Figure 11.1).[1] To fulfill customer demands, companies need to first design the product and production process (R&D), then acquire necessary supplies (inbound logistics), make the product (production), and finally send the product to specific markets (outbound logistics). To generate customer demand, companies need to attract customers and fulfill orders (marketing and sales) and provide related services (service). Meanwhile, to support the above activities, companies need to create managerial infrastructure and manage human resources, financial resources, and information systems.

When entering a foreign market, international businesses need to first secure human and financial resources, and then set up functional operations to deliver products to their customers. Chapters 9 and 10 have discussed managing people and money, respectively. Chapter 12 will address the management of foreign customers. In this chapter, we focus on a few key functions that deal with products—research and development, production, and supply chain (including inbound and outbound logistics). Thanks to globalization, these functions can be sourced from one's own subsidiaries or independent suppliers in foreign countries.

I. Offshoring

Should a specific operation be conducted at home or overseas? This is a key question to consider when an MNC arranges its global operations. The term offshoring refers to a company's practice of relocating operations to foreign locations. For instance, after the installation of the North America Free Trade Agreement, many U.S. companies have offshored their manufacturing functions to Mexico. The primary reason for offshoring is to lower costs as foreign locations may provide low-cost labor, raw materials, and product components. However, offshoring may hurt market responsiveness and corporate image in

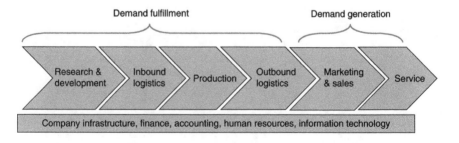

Figure 11.1 The Chain of Operations

the home country. When the drawbacks outweigh the cost saving of offshoring, MNCs may move back to their home countries, a practice known as reshoring or onshoring. For instance, GM brought the production of small gas engines from Mexico to Texas, and Ford brought the assembly of Ford Fusion from Mexico to Kentucky.

2. Outsourcing

Another related question is whether a company should conduct a specific operation by itself or outsource the operation to an independent contractor. When the company outsources from a foreign supplier, it is called offshore outsourcing. Almost all functional operations can be outsourced, including product design, manufacturing, logistics, as well as marketing, services, human resources, finance, and accounting. Outsourcing provides MNCs the flexibility to seek the most cost-efficient suppliers and switch suppliers when needed. For instance, Apple outsources the majority of its manufacturing and assembly to contractors in Asia. However, outsourcing offers an MNC limited control over its suppliers. The suppliers may be unwilling to make a specialized investment to conform to the MNC's requirements; the MNC risks losing proprietary knowledge, and lacks control over supply quality and scheduling. Especially when sourcing from foreign suppliers, MNCs are also subject to trade barriers, transportation costs, cultural and language barriers. For instance, after receiving multiple customer complaints about its technical support, Dell stopped outsourcing this service to call centers in India. In comparison, in-house operations enable stronger control and better coordination. An MNC can also use cross-border intrafirm trade between its own entities to lower tax payments (see Chapter 10). Therefore, MNCs must compare the pros and cons of outsourcing versus in-house operations and then decide how to best arrange global operations.

In addition, MNCs may use strategic alliances, a hybrid mode of market transactions and in-house operations. Strategic alliances are explicit partnership agreements between two or more firms. Partner firms may contribute equity to form a joint venture (see Chapter 8), or just establish a contractual agreement to share responsibilities and profits (such as R&D consortium, joint production, co-marketing, long-term supply, etc.). Strategic alliances provide more flexibility than in-house operations but greater stability and control than short-term contracts. They allow MNCs to share risks and costs with partners, obtain partners' resources and knowledge, and gain access to target markets through partners. Certainly, strategic alliances face their own challenges. Interest conflicts between partners may cause opportunistic behavior; shared control may lead to conflicts and alliance instability; some partners may acquire key knowledge through cooperation and become potential competitors. To achieve alliance success, MNCs need to select partners with congruent objectives and complementary resources, have detailed alliance agreements that govern various aspects of cooperation, establish well-structured control systems and develop strong trusting relationships.

Overall, MNCs can allocate their operations to multiple countries. They may set up their own operations abroad, outsource from independent foreign suppliers, or form strategic alliances with foreign partners.

II. Global Research and Development

Research and development (R&D) is a key business function that companies conduct to develop new products and procedures or improve existing products and procedures. Since innovation is regarded as a major competitive advantage, many firms have steadily increased R&D expenditures, especially in high-tech industries like aircraft, computer, pharmaceutical, and medical equipment.[2]

1. The Role of Global R&D

For MNCs, R&D is a key function to develop and sustain firm-specific advantages in international markets. Traditionally, R&D activities were concentrated in the headquarters of MNCs. In the last couple of decades, this function has become increasingly globalized. According to a 2015 study, 94 percent of the world's largest R&D spenders conduct some elements of their R&D overseas.[3] MNCs from developed countries have extended their R&D activities not only to other developed countries but also developing ones. For instance, technology companies like Microsoft set up R&D centers in Ireland and India; global pharmaceutical companies like Merck sourced basic clinical-trial tasks from India. At the same time, MNCs from newly industrialized and emerging markets have also substantially expanded R&D activities internationally. For example, Huawei, a large Chinese telecommunication equipment manufacturer built an R&D center in Silicon Valley to tap into local knowledge pools.

Depending on MNCs' strategic directions, foreign R&D units may play different roles. Some are mainly in charge of technology transfer and local adaptation. Their main function is to utilize existing knowledge from the parent company or other subsidiaries and make necessary modifications to adapt to the target country's market. They may even develop new products or services specifically for the target country. For instance, in 2014, IBM's China Research laboratory launched a ten-year research initiative, called "Green Horizon," to develop a renewable energy forecasting system to help energy grids manage alternative energy sources.[4] Another type of foreign R&D centers is part of an MNC's innovation network. Such centers focus on developing new technologies to serve the global marketplace. For instance, while Google's services are not available in mainland China, the company has kept a research office in Beijing where engineers develop core Google products for international markets.[5] MNCs may assign specific tasks to different units and coordinate their R&D activities. The advancement of communication technologies has significantly facilitated such long-distance, multilateral R&D collaborations. Certainly, as an MNC changes its strategy or status of international expansion, the role of its overseas R&D unit may change over time.

2. Benefits and Drawbacks

Global R&D has many potential benefits. First, it allows MNCs to access a wide range of scientific and technical resources, including knowledge and talent, in other countries. For instance, a multitude of software development tasks have been conducted in India due to an abundant supply of local software engineers. Other than setting up their own R&D centers, MNCs can cooperate with foreign partners via R&D alliances. Some governments also offer incentives like financing assistance and tax breaks for local R&D activities. Second, globalizing R&D enables MNCs to efficiently respond to international markets. In order to succeed in a foreign market, MNCs may need to customize their products or services to meet specific local requirements. Having local R&D in the target country increases proximity and speeds up responsiveness to local demand. In other words, decentralized R&D may accelerate adaptation and innovation for different markets. Third, MNCs can integrate and leverage their knowledge across a global network of R&D centers. While technology often flows from the parent firm to overseas entities, foreign R&D units have become critical sources of new knowledge. Cross-unit knowledge flows allow MNCs to exploit the strengths of each R&D center and produce synergy through multilateral collaboration. For instance, to pursue the "Green Horizon" initiative in China, IBM tapped into the company's network of 12 global research labs and created an innovation ecosystem that linked various government offices, academic institutions, and private enterprises around the world.

Meanwhile, global R&D presents some challenges for MNCs. First of all, given the resource requirements of R&D activities, MNCs cannot have an R&D unit in every country they operate. Also, if an MNC has multiple international R&D units, it may be difficult to develop a critical mass of talent at each unit. Such a critical mass is essential for generating new ideas through close interaction as well as achieving economies of scale in R&D activities. Furthermore, knowledge transfer and R&D collaboration may require a lot of control and coordination. It can be costly to organize and integrate the R&D activities of different units. National differences in technology, culture, and regulation may further increase the costs of managing foreign R&D units. The bigger, the more dispersed an R&D network is, the higher the costs of control and coordination tend to be.

3. Selecting R&D Locations

Given these considerations, MNCs need to select their R&D locations strategically. So, what is an ideal R&D location? First of all, this location's infrastructure and market condition should be conducive to technological innovation. The rate of new product development in a country depends on factors such as local technological capability, underlying demand, customer purchasing power, and the intensity of competition.[6] Competition pushes companies to seek innovation from basic and applied research, which in turn will be rewarded by market demand. When all these factors are strong, companies within the country tend to be more active in R&D activities. Meanwhile, government and cultural factors should be considered. Some host governments encourage R&D activities with various incentives, or even require local technological content in some cases. They may also directly fund or participate in research projects that will enhance innovation. Furthermore, because R&D largely relies on the creativity of human beings, the sociocultural setting

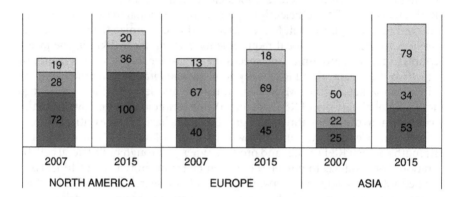

Figure 11.2 R&D Expenditures by Top Spenders in Different Regions (in billion USD)

Source: Strategy&. (2015) Global Innovation 1000. Retrieved from www.strategyand.pwc.com/innovation1000.

Data from the top 100 companies in terms of R&D spending across all industries, the top 50 companies in auto, healthcare, and computing and electronics, and the top 20 companies in the industrials and software and Internet sectors. The total number of companies was 207, reflecting overlap in the top 100 and the five selected industries. These 207 companies were headquartered in 23 countries and conduct R&D activities at 2,041 R&D sites in more than 60 countries.

of a country may affect local R&D productivity. It also impacts the recruitment of foreign talent as well as communication and collaboration with foreign R&D partners.

According to the Global Innovation 1000 Study by Strategy&, PwC's strategy consulting business, the majority of R&D activities by MNCs are located in Asia, North America, and Europe. While most R&D spending in a region usually comes from domestic firms, the amount of R&D spending from foreign-based companies has been increasing in recent years (see Figure 11.2).[7] Asia has become the top destination in terms of overseas R&D spending by large MNCs, followed by North America and Europe. Especially, China and India have attracted a large amount of R&D spending. In China, MNCs set up R&D units to be close to high-growth markets, key manufacturing sites, and capable suppliers. India is the largest global destination for software R&D; low labor costs and access to technical talent are often the main reasons that MNCs conduct R&D in India.

III. Global Production

Production is the process in which a company converts inputs into finished products. It is a common practice for MNCs to set up production activities in foreign countries.

I. The Reasons for Global Production

Traditionally, the primary purpose of overseas production is to access low-cost inputs, especially low-cost labor. For instance, many Western European companies have relocated their manufacturing and assembly to low-cost Eastern European countries. Developing countries with a combination of low labor costs, favorable regulations, and adequate infrastructure, such as China, India, and Mexico, have grown into major global manufacturing hubs. If a location's cost advantage disappears, MNCs may relocate to another low-cost location or move back home.

Moreover, foreign production allows MNCs to access qualified personnel. Some Eastern European and Asian countries offer big pools of educated engineers and managers. Tapping into those talent pools helps improve MNCs' overall productivity. In addition, local production helps MNCs access the target country's market. They are able to gain a better understanding of local customers and quickly respond to local market changes. For instance, utilizing its assembly plant in China, GM has modified its product offerings along with design features and brand image for Chinese car buyers.

As times goes by, some foreign production sites have also become centers for design and manufacturing excellence. After accumulating years of manufacturing experience, those production sites have developed enough capabilities to improve their cost structure and customize products for different markets. Also, economic development in some host countries has increased the supply of advanced factors of production, thus enabling certain manufacturing sites to expand their strategic role. For instance, Sony's largest TV production plant is located in Malaysia. It is not only a low-cost manufacturing site but also where the company handles product planning, design, and development.

2. Locating Global Production

For firms seeking global production, it is essential to select appropriate locations. Various country and industry factors may affect the benefits and costs of overseas production. Specifically, firms should consider the following factors:

- *Location advantages.* Does the foreign location offer an abundant supply of key production factors, such as labor, raw materials, technology, and supporting industries? If so, MNCs may select this location as their production site, which will help minimize costs and improve quality. For example, many cell phone manufacturers are located in China because the country has skilled low-cost labor forces and full-fledged suppliers of electronic components.
- *National differences.* Does the foreign location significantly differ from the home country, in terms of political economy, culture, and business practices? If so, national differences will hinder cross-country control and coordination, rendering the country an undesirable location for foreign production. To overcome those national differences, companies need to develop experience and capability, which may cost extra time and resources.

- *Need for customization.* Does the company's product serve universal needs? If yes, there is less need for foreign production as the company can serve a target market from its existing production facilities. If not, the company is more likely to set up new production facilities to make customized products for foreign markets. For example, industrial equipment and electronics manufacturers typically offer standard products from a few production sites, while consumer goods producers tend to have a more dispersed production network to make different products for different markets.
- *Flexible manufacturing.* Is flexible manufacturing available so that the company can efficiently make a wide variety of products? If yes, the company is able to customize production for different markets using its existing facilities, without incurring much setup and retooling costs. For instance, Toyota is able to manufacture multiple versions of Prius, a popular hybrid car, in its plant in Japan and export them all over the world. Without flexible manufacturing technology, new production facilities are needed to make customized products for international markets.
- *Fixed costs.* In order to achieve efficient production, companies may need to build large-scale plants and install state-of-the-art equipment. In some cases, the fixed costs of building a plant are so high that a company cannot afford many plants and has to serve the world market from a few locations. For instance, it costs several billions of U.S. dollars for Intel to set up a plant to make semiconductor chips; hence, this large MNC only has a handful of manufacturing sites. If the fixed costs are relatively low, the company may be able to build more factories to serve different markets.
- *Trade-related expenses.* If a company has concentrated production, it will need to ship its products from one or a few sites to many others countries, thus exposed to trade-related issues such as trade barriers, transportation costs, and foreign exchange risks. Therefore, when trade-related expenses are high, the company is less likely to concentrate its production to very few locations. Instead, it tends to disperse production to individual markets, serving local customers with local production. Conversely, low trade-related expenses can make it more economical to implement concentrated production.

Since these factors may point to different directions, it is often hard to find the perfect production location. Companies need to weigh and balance these factors together, and decide whether to keep production in a few key locations or disperse production into various regional or national markets.

In the last several decades, low-cost locations in Latin America, Eastern Europe, and most of Asia have attracted considerable production investment. Developed economies like the U.S., Japan, and Western Europe have been typically viewed as having high production costs. Nevertheless, after years of steady increase of wages and other cost factors, some traditional low-cost locations are losing their advantages. According to a study conducted by Boston Consulting Group, manufacturing costs in Brazil, China, the Czech Republic, Poland, and Russia have significantly increased between 2004 and 2014 (see Table 11.1).[8] These countries' competitiveness seems to be deteriorating. The study estimated that Brazil is now more expensive than many Western European countries, and China's manufacturing cost advantage over the U.S. is less than 5 percent. Meanwhile, due to low wage growth and productivity gains, countries like the U.S. and Mexico have gained a substantial competitive edge in manufacturing. Such changes in relative costs could change the landscape of global manufacturing.

As the relative disadvantages of high-cost countries shrink, a new trend of reshoring has emerged recently. For instance, GM and Ford have brought

Table 11.1 Comparing the Manufacturing Costs of the Top 25 Exporting Economies

Exporting Economy	2004 Manufacturing Cost Index (US = 100)		2014 Manufacturing Cost Index (US = 100)	
	Labor Costs	Total Costs	Labor Costs	Total Costs
China	4.5	86.5	10.2	95.6
Germany	34.6	117.4	35.2	121.1
United States	18.2	100	18.2	100
Japan	23	107.2	24.2	111
South Korea	16.3	98.7	15.5	102.4
France	32.8	114.6	39.1	124.3
Italy	28.1	112.4	35.8	122.7
Netherlands	30	112.7	27.3	111.5
Belgium	34.1	116.7	37.9	123.3
United Kingdom	25.6	107.4	23.4	108.7
Canada	22.4	104	33.9	115.5
Russia	7	87.1	17.8	99
Mexico	9.5	92.1	8.9	91.5
Taiwan	9.9	92.3	10.9	97.2
India	5.3	86.8	4.3	87.2
Switzerland	32.3	115.4	37.3	125.4
Australia	27.2	109	45.4	129.6
Spain	22.5	104.2	22.7	108.6
Brazil	14.2	96.7	36.2	123.7
Thailand	4.3	85.6	7.2	90.5
Indonesia	1.2	82.3	1.3	83.1
Poland	12.9	94.4	16.2	101.2
Sweden	25.6	108.5	30.4	116.4
Austria	24.8	108.1	25.6	110.7
Czech Republic	14.7	96.6	21.8	106.7

Data source: Boston Consulting Group. (2014). The Shifting Economics of Global Manufacturing.

some auto part manufacturing back home. Apple started domestically sourcing the production of Mac Pro desktop computers in the U.S. In 2015, to encourage its suppliers to reshore, Wal-Mart committed to increasing its U.S. purchases by $50 billion USD annually until January 2023. According to The Reshoring Initiative, a not-for-profit organization that helps manufacturers reshore, about 67,000 domestic manufacturing jobs were added in the U.S. in 2015.[9] However, despite this progress, it is not clear how long and how strong the trend of reshoring will be. A 2015 study by A. T. Kearney showed that offshoring is still a major force in manufacturing and has continuously outpaced reshoring in the U.S.[10]

3. Managing Global Production

In order to have successful global production, a company first needs to clearly define the main objective of its overseas production. Often times, the firm seeks to reduce costs and improve quality. In order to lower costs, it needs to strategically locate its production units to access low-cost production factors. In order to improve quality, the firm usually uses high-quality inputs and advanced technology. Traditionally, low costs and high quality are viewed as incompatible or even conflicting objectives. However, current understanding has redefined the relationship between quality and cost.[11] High-quality production processes can increase productivity, reduce defects, and eliminate waste, thus lowering total manufacturing costs. High-quality production may also lower warranty and service costs for the company.

Advanced production techniques have been applied to both enhance quality and lower costs. For instance, computer-integrated manufacturing uses computers and robots to secure productivity and quality. Total quality management implements specific steps and tools to eliminate defects and mistakes. Six sigma is a data-driven approach that requires the number of errors below 3.4 out of a million (i.e. six sigma or standard deviations in statistics).

Another important issue is how to effectively control overseas plants and coordinate them with other business functions. A common approach is to standardize the production process. Standardization helps ensure the consistency of business operations in different locations. It enables MNCs to leverage their best practices, guarantee quality, and improve efficiency. For instance, Intel has a "Copy Exactly" approach to managing its semiconductor chip factories. By duplicating everything from a model plant, such as process flow, equipment set, supply, plumbing, and training, "Copy Exactly" allows the company to quickly install and run volume manufacturing facilities. Some MNCs seek to have their manufacturing processes and products certified under international standards such as ISO 9000. Such universal standards can lower technical barriers and be applied worldwide. Standardization reduces setup costs and managerial complexity. Because each new plant is essentially a replication of an existing one, there is little need to develop new technologies or capabilities. Standardized systems also minimize the need for technical support and simplifies the management of production processes.

However, because the costs and quality of production factors vary considerably across countries, it may be hard to have standard production systems in all locations. An MNC may have a combination of factories differing in scale, equipment, technology, and management systems. Such differences will create additional challenges for the control and coordination of global production. International firms should consider if and to what extent their production processes should be standardized. To accommodate national differences, some companies may have a combination of capital-intense and labor-intense processes so as to achieve both quality and efficiency.

IV. Global Supply Chain

Due to the globalization of markets and production, international businesses move large quantities of raw materials, components, work in progress, and finished goods across national borders. The traditional view on logistics focuses on interface with immediate customers, suppliers, and intermediaries.[12] Nowadays, business practitioners look beyond inbound and outbound logistics to manage a supply chain that encompasses the flow of resources, goods, and information among layers of suppliers, different units within the company, and various distributors around the world.[13] The purpose of supply chain management is to optimize the steps it takes to get a product or service to its customers, thus serving customer needs and reducing costs for the company.

Since input costs typically account for a significant share of product value, an improvement in supply chain efficiency can have a substantial impact on profitability. Recent progresses in business operations have also made supply chain management increasingly important. For instance, the rise of global sourcing requires companies to effectively manage suppliers. The workloads, schedules, and relationships of suppliers need to be carefully arranged so as to achieve competitiveness in cost, quality, and speed. Another example is just-in-time (JIT) inventory system, by which a company receives goods only as they are needed in the production process. As a way to minimize inventory costs, the JIT system requires companies to not only identify suppliers that are capable and reliable but also coordinate their production and delivery processes.

The development of electronic systems has significantly enhanced supply chain management. For instance, electronic procurement systems allow prospective buyers and suppliers to exchange information instantly. Real-time global tracking systems allow companies to track goods location and status. Point-of-sale data collection enables companies to know what products are selling, when and where. Data mining and inventory management software helps companies forecast sales and make production plans accordingly. Enterprise resource planning (ERP) is a suite of integrated software applications that companies can use to plan, manage, and record business resources and activities. Electronic data interchange (EDI) provides technical standards for companies to exchange documents, such as purchase orders, invoices, and shipping documents. Internet and web-based applications have further simplified supply chain management.

While standardization reduces costs, some adaptations may be necessary when managing global supply chains. In comparison to standard products, customized products usually bring more challenges to packaging, warehousing, transportation, and distribution. To meet local customer preferences and government regulations, international companies may be required to change package material, size, language, label, etc. For instance, many European countries require recyclable packages; the U.S. requires all food products to be labeled with nutritional values. In addition, due to differences in infrastructure development, the ideal mode of transportation may vary in different countries.

Like other functions, supply chain management can be performed in-house or outsourced. When a company's competitive strengths lie within its supply chain, it tends to prefer direct control. For instance, to supply over 5,000 stores, Wal-Mart has set up a global network of sourcing offices and distribution centers. The company uses state-of-the-art technologies, such as satellite communication and advanced computer systems, to collect data on warehouse inventory and real-time sales. The data is also shared with suppliers to coordinate shipping schedules. When a company lacks the necessary capabilities to efficiently manage its supply chain, it may outsource from outside specialists. For example, FedEx, DHL, and UPS can help handle and track shipping within and across nations; Amazon.com has warehouse facilities and online portals that help vendors manage inventory and fulfill orders. Some logistics companies can offer a wide range of services including warehousing, distribution, shipping, custom clearance, and brokerage.

Key Terms

Offshoring, reshoring, outsourcing, in-house operation, strategic alliance, global R&D, technology transfer, R&D location, global production, low-cost location, foreign production site, flexible manufacturing, fixed costs, supply chain management, logistics, just-in-time production

Review Questions

1. What factors drive a company to allocate its business operations in foreign countries? Are there any potential drawbacks?
2. Under what conditions should international companies outsource their business operations? Have in-house operations? Or form strategic alliances?
3. What is the impact of global R&D on international firms? What factors drive the location of R&D activities?
4. What key factors should international firms consider when deciding the location and management of global production?
5. Why has global supply chain become increasingly important for international firms?

Internet Exercises

1. Some consulting firms periodically publish reports on manufacturing costs in different countries. A few examples are listed below. Review and

compare these reports. Select several countries to discuss their cost advantages and disadvantages.

- Deloitte's Global Competitiveness Index: www2.deloitte.com/us/en/pages/manufacturing/articles/global-manufacturing-competitiveness-index.html?
- Boston Consulting Group's Global Manufacturing Cost-Competitiveness Index: www.bcgperspectives.com/content/interactive/lean_manufacturing_globalization_bcg_global_manufacturing_cost_competitiveness_index/
- KMPG's Competitive Alternatives: www.competitivealternatives.com/

2. IBM is a company that provide outsourcing services to its clients. They have listed a few outsourcing case studies on their website. Please visit the following webpage: www-935.ibm.com/services/us/en/sourcing/see-it-in-action/index.html. Review the cases and discuss the implications of outsourcing in international business.

Notes

1 Porter, M. E. (1985). *Competitive Advantage: Creating and Sustaining Superior Performance*. New York: Simon and Schuster.
2 OCED Directorate for Science, Technology and Industry. (2011). *Technology Intensity Definition*. Retrieved from www.oecd.org/sti/ind/48350231.pdf
3 Jaruzelski, B., Schwartz, K., and Staack, V. (2015). The global innovation 1,000: Innovation's new world order. *Strategy+Business Magazine*, Winter 2015.
4 Meza, E. (2014). IBM Research launches Green Horizon in China. *PV Magazine*. Retrieved from www.pv-magazine.com/
5 Google. (n.d.). Google Beijing Office. Retrieved from www.google.cn/about/careers/locations/beijing/
6 Porter, M. E. (2011). *Competitive Advantage of Nations*. New York: The Free Press.
7 Strategy&. (2015) Global Innovation 1000. Retrieved from www.strategyand.pwc.com/innovation1000
8 Boston Consulting Group. (2014). The shifting economics of global manufacturing. Retrieved from www.bcgperspectives.com/content/articles/lean_manufacturing_globalization_shifting_economics_global_manufacturing/
9 The Reshoring Initiative. (2015). *2015 Reshoring Report*. Retrieved from www.reshorenow.org/
10 A. T. Kearney. (2015). U.S. Reshoring: Over before it began. Retrieved from www.atkearney.com/documents/10192/7070019/US+Reshoring.pdf/
11 Garvin, D. A. (1984). What does product quality really mean? *Sloan Management Review, 26* (Fall 1984).
12 Marien, E. J. (2003). SCM & logistics: What's the difference. *Inbound Logistics*. Retrieved from www.inboundlogistics.com/cms/article/scm-and-logistics-whats-the-difference/.
13 Cooper, M. C., Lambert, D. M., and Pagh, J. D. (1997). Supply chain management: More than a new name for logistics. *The International Journal of Logistics Management, 8*(1), 1–14.

Managing Customers
Marketing and Sales

Learning Objectives

1. Explain the pros and cons of standardization and adaptation in international marketing.
2. Discuss the main factors involved in deciding whether to pursue standardization or adaptation.
3. Describe product and promotion strategies as well as their combinations.
4. Explain how distribution channels differ from country to country.
5. Identify basic pricing policies and the factors that affect pricing decisions.

Cases

Case 12.1 Haier's Marketing Strategy in the U.S.
Case 12.2 Kellogg's Products in India
Case 12.3 Pricing of Luxury Automobiles in the U.S.
Case 12.4 Distributing Hyundai Automobiles in the Chinese Market
Case 12.5 Luxury Fashion Brands and Social Media

Case 12.1 Haier's Marketing Strategy in the U.S.

The China-based Haier Group is one of the world's largest manufacturers of consumer electronics and home appliances. The company produces various products such as air conditioners, computers, microwave ovens, mobile phones, refrigerators, televisions, and washing machines. Haier's headquarters is located in Qingdao (also known as Tsingtao), China. The company started as Qingdao Refrigerator Company in 1984. It became a leading refrigerator brand in China after forming a partnership with Liebherr, a German refrigerator manufacturer. Liebherr provided technology, equipment, and new management processes. The refrigerators they produced were branded as Qingdao-Liebherr. The name "Liebherr" was translated into "Li Bo Hai Er" in Chinese. After its success in the refrigerator business, the company adopted the name Haier and expanded into other business areas. Beginning as a small, struggling refrigerator manufacturer, Haier has successfully reinvented itself repeatedly and become a brand known for quality products and services.

When entering the U.S. market, Haier started with niche products like compact refrigerators. In the category of full-sized refrigerators, there existed strong established American brands like Frigidaire, GE, Maytag, and Whirlpool. Hence, Haier decided to start its entry with compact refrigerators, a low-margin section neglected by most competitors. Haier was able to tap into the demand of college students and small households who could not afford or accommodate larger-sized refrigerators. The company also offered other niche consumer appliances like wine cellars and small-size washing machines, which were seldom offered by others at that time. Later in 2000, Haier opened a production facility in North Carolina and started manufacturing large-size refrigerators for the U.S. market.

Haier also decided to focus on high quality rather than low price in the U.S. market. It believed that American consumers would care more about product quality than low price. In fact, Haier is regarded as a premium brand in its home country. It has implemented a "high quality-high price" policy in China. For instance, Haier typically sets the price for air conditioners about 20 percent higher than its main competitors. The company also has a strong tradition of quality control. The Chairman and CEO of Haier, Zhang Ruimin, once hammered a number of defective refrigerators in front of tearful employees. Haier intends to maintain the same brand image of quality in international markets. Another important factor in Haier's strategy is customer satisfaction. It tries to research and analyze local consumption habits and consumer opinions. The results and data are then used to create specific products tailored to consumers' wants and needs. Haier has named this system Dealer—Design—Haier Manufacturing System.

Many industry experts thought it would be difficult for Haier to gain a competitive advantage in the U.S. because many American consumers perceived Chinese products as being of low quality. To overcome this disadvantage, Haier adopted a localization strategy. It set up a design center in Los Angeles to design customized products for the American market, and opened a marketing center in New York to enhance consumer awareness about Haier brand and products. For promotion, Haier worked with various magazines like *Good Housekeeping, People,* and *Electronics Appliance Report.* The company also published its own *Haier* magazine. In addition, Haier utilized a variety of advertising strategies to generate brand awareness, including outdoor advertising, airport carts, and sponsorships. Especially, the company sponsored the Beijing Olympic Games and was the first international appliance brand to sign a global strategic cooperation agreement with the NBA.

Supply chain and distribution are also essential parts of Haier's business model. Other than large appliances, most Haier products sold in the U.S. were imported from manufacturing bases in Asia. In order to respond to emerging customer needs and control logistical costs, Haier signed a strategic cooperation agreement with COSCO, China's biggest international shipping company. This agreement allowed Haier to utilize COSCO's global networks to explore overseas business opportunities. In the U.S., Haier initially sold products through Wal-Mart and the Haier America website. Nowadays, it has gained access to many major chain stores, including Wal-Mart, Lowe's, Best Buy, Home Depot, Office Depot, Target, Bed Bath and Beyond, P.C. Richards, BJ's, Fry's, and others.

Haier is expecting further growth in the U.S. market. In January 2016, it acquired GE's appliance division for $5.4 billion USD. The two companies also issued a memorandum of understanding promising to cooperate globally on various growth projects such as industrial Internet, healthcare, and advanced manufacturing.

Sources

1.   Bai, C. (2005). *Haier Development*. Beijing, China: Tsinghua University Press.
2.   Chen, F. B. (2009). Haier's success. *Market Modernization*, Issue 20, page 46.
3.   Fischer, B. (2016, January 15). Haier and GE: Understand the magic behind the deal. *Forbes*. Retrieved from www.forbes.com/sites/billfischer/2016/01/15/haier-ge-understanding-the-magic-behind-the-deal/#7bb93a367927

Questions for Case Discussion

1.   What are the key elements of Haier's marketing strategy in the U.S.?
2.   What is unique about Haier's marketing strategy compared to its competitors?
3.   In your opinion, how should Haier increase its market share in the U.S.?

Case 12.2 Kellogg's Products in India

Kellogg Company is an American multinational food company that produces cereal and convenience foods. The company has many brands, including Froot Loops, Corn Flakes, Rice Krispies, Special K, Keebler, Pop-Tarts, Kashi, Cheez-It, and many more. In the late 1980s, Kellogg built a remarkable record by occupying 40 percent of the U.S. instant food market with cereal products. As the U.S. cereal market became more and more competitive and saturated, Kellogg's management team diverted the company's attention to international markets. India seemed a promising market as the country had a large population of over one billion. In 1994, Kellogg introduced its best-selling corn flakes as well as wheat and basmati rice flakes to the Indian market.

Despite their quality products and resource advantages, Kellogg's initial market performance in India was far from satisfactory. It was estimated that Kellogg had only gained a 2 percent market share in India. The company's sales even experienced a gradual drop in 1995. It turned out that Indian consumers disliked the taste of Kellogg's products. 98 percent of the products were bought by first-time buyers, and only 2 percent were sold to regular buyers. The company had trouble generating repeat purchases from experimenters. Kellogg realized that the quality and crispiness of its flakes were important to Indian consumers. However, unlike Americans, Indians boiled their milk and consumed it warm. Warm milk made the flakes soggy and diluted the taste. Thus, the flakes were not sweet and crispy enough for consumers. Kellogg asserted that its products offered healthy and convenient breakfast alternatives. It got into direct competition against the country's staple breakfast food. Replacing traditional breakfast with cereal was a completely new concept in India. Kellogg expected consumers to discover the benefits of cereal products. But those products failed because they did not align with Indian breakfast habits.

After the initial stumble, Kellogg launched two new products—Chocos (wheat scoops coated with chocolate) and Frosties (flakes coated with sugar frosting). The sale of these two products increased quickly as many Indians purchased and consumed them as snacks. The surprising success of Chocos and Frosties drove Kellogg to work on "Indianizing" its flavors. After a year of extensive research on consumer preferences, Kellogg introduced Mazza—a crunchy, almond-shaped corn cereal in three local flavors "Mango Elaichi," "Coconut Kesar," and "Rose." Mazza was branded as a tasty, nutritious breakfast cereal for families. Kellogg also introduced different sizes of retail packs. Thus, consumers with different consumption patterns and income levels could all find suitable packs.

The company held "The Kellogg Breakfast Week" to increase public awareness about the importance of breakfast. A series of nutrition workshops were conducted for both individuals and families in Chennai, Delhi, and Mumbai. The company also launched a nation-wide public-service initiative program together with the Indian Dietetic Association (IDA) to raise awareness about iron deficiency. This program included nutrition promotion initiatives like symposiums, educational programs, and research sponsorships. In those activities, Kellogg stressed their product modifications in response to consumers' nutritional needs, especially the addition of iron fortification in breakfast cereal.

In addition to breakfast cereal, Kellogg also introduced Chocos biscuits to India. It was viewed as a risky move as the Indian biscuit market was competitive and crowded. However, in order to grow its business, the company needed to develop more products specifically for Indian consumers. Kellogg's experience showed that product customization was necessary to succeed in India. Given India's long-standing food traditions, it might take a long period of time for Kellogg's new products to significantly influence the local palate.

Sources

1. Kellogg Company website: www.kelloggcompany.com
2. Haig, M. (2003). *Brand Failure: The Truth about the 100 Biggest Branding Mistakes of All Time*. Philadelphia, PA: Kogan Page Business Books.
3. ICMR India. Kellogg's Indian experience: A failed launch. Retrieved from www.icmrindia.org/free%20resources/casestudies/Marketing%20freecasestudyp1.htm

Questions for Case Discussion

1. What were the initial mistakes Kellogg made in introducing cereals to India?
2. How was Kellogg able to correct these mistakes? What were the main lessons that Kellogg learned from these mistakes?
3. Discuss what kinds of new products Kellogg may introduce to India.

Case 12.3 Pricing of Luxury Automobiles in the U.S.

Tesla Motors is an American company that manufactures electric cars and powertrain components. In 2006, Tesla earned its fame after launching the first all-electric sports car, Tesla Roadster, at a selling price of $109,000 USD.

Several years later, Tesla switched its focus to the Model S sedan and the Model X SUV targeting luxury auto markets. The company aims to offer electric cars at prices that are affordable to average consumers. Its next generation all-electric Model 3, scheduled to be launched in 2017, will be offered at the low price of $35,000 USD. Also, Tesla reportedly plans to introduce a certified pre-owned program that will cut the price of the Model S sedan in half. American consumers seem to be embracing Tesla's shift toward affordability.

German luxury brands, Audi, BMW, and Mercedes-Benz, have adopted similar strategies by offering lower-priced models. For example, the price of Mercedes-Benz's CLA-Class, a compact four-door luxury sedan, starts at $29,900 USD. The price for the BMW 2 Series is set at about $32,000 USD. Audi sells its A3 at around $29,000 USD. These luxury automakers are fighting for the orders of future mainstream consumers. Generation Y will be the primary car buyers for the next 20 years. If an automaker sets its price at $60,000 USD, the company may need to wait for ten years for these prospective consumers to become wealthy enough to afford this price. At that time, it is probably too late as they may have developed loyalty to other brands. To attract Generation Y, Mercedes-Benz once placed a TV commercial during the Super Bowl to highlight the low price of the CLA-Class. It soon sold more than 30,000 units and became one of the best-selling cars of Mercedes-Benz. The median age of the buyers was 47, and the majority of them were either Generation X or Generation Y. About 75 percent of the CLA-class buyers had never purchased a luxury brand before. In contrast, the average age of buyers for Mercedes' other models was 55. Many luxury car makers believe it is important to attract buyers when they are young to instill customer loyalty and assure repeat purchases.

Meanwhile, mainstream brands are also stepping up their efforts to retain loyal customers. They have added a number of used-to-be luxury features to their models, such as cruise control, leather interiors, heated seats, and rear-view cameras. Such deliberate efforts have enabled these value brands to raise average prices. For instance, the price of Ford Fusion increased from about $24,000 USD in 2011 to $26,000 USD. Honda Civic, known as an entry-level car, is gaining a new premium brand image. Customers buying Honda Accord are wealthier and expect greater luxury than the past buyers. By simultaneously adding luxury features and increasing prices, Ford and Honda are creating brand loyalty within current and future generations.

With luxury brands moving down and mainstream brands moving up, a new battleground has emerged. As mainstream volume brands keep adding more features, luxury brands are invading the mainstream territory. If buyers are willing to pay for a premium Ford or Honda, luxury brands expect them to buy an Audi or BMW at a similar price.

Even some of the highest-end automakers have changed their strategy by slashing their prices to attract new buyers. For instance, Aston Martin, a British manufacturer of luxury sports cars, decided to sell the Vantage GT at below $100,000 USD, only a third of the price of its Vanquish Volante. Maserati, an Italian premium car brand specializing in ultra-luxury vehicles, also added a lower-priced, mid-sized model to its lineup. This model, called Ghibli, has an Italian flair, a Ferrari engine, and a lower price tag (about

$35,000 USD less than other Maserati models). Some industry experts are worried that those price-cutting efforts made by luxury automakers to attract mainstream customers could cannibalize sales of other premium-priced models and dilute those brands' value.

Sources

1. Harwell, D. (2014, October 9). Tesla and luxury carmarkers' surprising strategy to hook new buyers: Lower prices. *Washington Post*.
2. Healey, J. R. (2012, November 25). Gap between luxury, mainstream cars shrinks. *USA Today*. Retrieved from www.usatoday.com/story/money/cars/2012/11/25/gap-between-luxe-mainstream-auto-market-shrinks/1725879/

Questions for Case Discussion

1. What are the key factors that you consider when you purchase a car? How much does the level of price influence your purchasing decision?
2. For luxury car makers, what are the benefits and drawbacks of lowering prices?
3. Do you agree that consumers would prefer an entry-level model of a premium brand to a higher-end model of a value brand if their prices are about the same?

Case 12.4 Distributing Hyundai Automobiles in the Chinese Market

Hyundai Motor Company, founded in 1967, is a large multinational automotive manufacturer based in South Korea. In 2002, Hyundai established a joint venture with Beijing Automotive Group, called Beijing Hyundai Motor Co., Ltd. The joint venture started manufacturing of select Hyundai-branded automobiles for the Chinese market. Hyundai's popular mid-size Sonata sedan was the first model Beijing Hyundai manufactured and sold in China. The company modified the appearance and specifications of the Sonata model to meet customer needs while maintaining its quality and brand image at a reasonable price.

In order to succeed in China, Hyundai had to carefully consider its distribution strategy. Chinese customers typically purchase cars at large-scale, specialized dealerships, and then receive after-sale services at 4S shops. The 4S shop is a "Four in One" automotive franchise business model, which includes Sale (vehicle sales), Sparepart (parts), Service (services), and Survey (information feedback). This model was introduced into China from Europe in 1998. In response to customer demand, many automobile manufacturers embraced the idea of "car service solution for life" and launched 4S shops. Meanwhile, the traditional sales agent system still exists.

Automobile makers have used distinctive distribution strategies in China. Should Hyundai choose multiple distribution channels like Volkswagen did? Or should the company only use authorized 4S shops as its distribution channel like Honda did? In other words, Hyundai needed to decide the composition of its distribution channels. If Hyundai chose both 4S shops and traditional dealers, it would achieve greater market coverage. However, there could be a loss of control over brand image and product pricing, and the distribution costs might be higher. If Hyundai chose 4S shops only, it would gain greater control over sales and distribution, but the market coverage might be limited.

Moreover, the company had to consider whether to combine or separate distribution channels for domestically produced models and imported ones. If Hyundai put both domestically made and imported models in the same distribution channel, like Nissan and Toyota did, it would benefit from a consistent corporate identity. Nonetheless, Hyundai had planned to position its imported models among the high class premium cars, while domestically made cars were more affordable and targeted at the middle-income class. If high-end models were exhibited side-by-side with domestically made models, it would be hard to create production differentiation, and might even result in self-cannibalization.

Hyundai's own market research suggested that a majority of customers would prefer convenient, trouble-free car service solutions. Also, complicated multilevel channel structures had caused many problems before. After several executive meetings, the company decided to only use 4S shops to sell cars, including both imported and domestically made models. To enhance market coverage and branding, Hyundai also devoted more resources to expand and upgrade its 4S shop distributional channel.

A subsequent decision Hyundai had to make was to select the locations of 4S shops. The company realized that it would be impossible to cover the whole Chinese market in a short period of time due to the country's sheer size and substantial regional differences. Therefore, Hyundai executives developed a sequential channel expansion strategy (see Figure 12.1).

Hyundai first divided the Chinese market into seven areas including North China, South China, East China, Northeast China, Central China, Southwest China, and the Northern area. Then these regional groups were classified into two clusters—"all city dispersion group" (including North China, South China, East China) and "key city dispersion group" (including Northeast

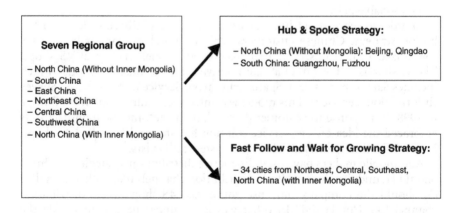

Figure 12.1 Hyundai's Regional Channel Expansion Strategy in China

Source: Lee, Rhee, and Park. (2008). A case study on channel strategy of Beijing-Hyundai Motor Company in Chinese market. *Management Education Review*, 11(2), 53–79

China, Central China, Southwest China, the Northern area). A "Hub and Spoke" strategy was implemented in the "all city dispersion group." After considering income, population, and competition in those areas, Hyundai picked seven main hub cities—Beijing and Qingdao in North China; Nanjing, Hangzhou, and Shanghai in East China; and Guangzhou and Fuzhou in South China. In the hub cities, Hyundai implemented area-specific promotion plans and established core distribution functions, which also supported distribution and sales in nearby spoke cities. Comparatively, the "key city dispersion group" had a lower level of economic development. For this group of areas, Hyundai used a "Fast Follow and Wait for Growth" strategy. It had small-scale entries into 24 key cities and provided them support from the hub cities. Those key cities were strategically selected so that the company could identify and monitor markets with growth potentials.

Sources

1. Lee, Rhee, and Park. (2008). A case study on channel strategy of Beijing-Hyundai Motor Company in Chinese market. *Management Education Review, 11*(2), 53–79
2. Lee, Rhee, Lee, and Kim. (2007). Marketing strategy of Beijing-Hyundai Motor Company in Chinese market—focused on 'Sonata' brand case. Proceedings of International Area Study.

Questions for Case Discussion

1. What factors should be considered when choosing distribution channels in a foreign market?
2. Did Hyundai have a right distribution strategy? were there any alternatives?

Case 12.5 Luxury Fashion Brands and Social Media

The fashion industry traditionally markets their products through magazines, flyers, paper catalogues, and one-way promotions via company web pages. These methods are limited in terms of time and location. They are relatively slow in providing consumers with information. Differently, social media networks, such as Facebook and Twitter, enable two-way and detailed information exchanges. Consumers are able to selectively absorb useful information and provide fast feedback. Some global fashion brands have embraced social media marketing, which is well suited for an industry with fast-changing trends and diverse consumer tastes. In terms of efficiency and costs, social media has advantages over traditional marketing methods (see Table 12.1).

Compared to other products, fashion is more fun and interesting to follow on social media. Pretty clothes, beautiful people, and high-quality photos can go a long way in attracting attention. However, many luxury fashion brands are skeptical about the impact of social media. They are concerned that being active on social media may make them seem "common" and hurt their luster of heritage and exclusivity. According to a 2015 study by Brandwatch, a social media research firm, luxury fashion brands made no more than two tweets per day while leading food and beverage brands tweeted

Table 12.1 A Comparison of Traditional Marketing and Social Media Marketing

	Traditional Marketing	Social Media
Communication method	One-way	Two-way
Accessibility	Passive	Active
Information transmission speed	Slow	Fast
Advertisement promotion costs	High	Low

Source: Rhee, S. and Kim, S. (2011). A case study on fashion brand marketing utilizing social network service. Journal of the Korean Society of Design Culture, 17(3).

about 27 times on average. Among the 32 brands Brandwatch studied, Chanel, Christian Dior, Calvin Klein, Louis Vuitton, Ralph Lauren, Tiffany & Co., Burberry, and Gucci were relatively active, but the others were quiet or paying little attention to social media.

For some fashion brands, social media has changed how they conduct businesses. Top modeling jobs are given to those with a massive following on social media sites like Instagram, Pinterest, Facebook, and Twitter. The number of online followers a model has can be more important than his or her qualification and experience. Even make-up artists, stylists, and photographers are sometimes selected based on their influence on social media. A photoshoot is not just going to a billboard or magazine. The whole team can lend and leverage their following to promote the product.

Fashion brands also collaborate with celebrities to promote their products on social media. When a celebrity mentions a fashion brand, it will be discussed and followed, which is likely to improve brand visibility and future sales. According to the Brandwatch study, the pop singer Justin Bieber was particularly influential. His name was mentioned in relation to the fashion brand Calvin Klein over 87,000 times on social media.[a] Brooklyn Beckham, the son of David and Victoria Beckham, was hired by Burberry to photograph an ad campaign. His behind-the-scenes pictures and videos on the company's social media feeds generated 15 million views within eight hours.

Another key feature of social media is that it is personal and responsive. It is important for fashion brands to pay attention to existing and prospective consumers online. Being responsive is essential to a successful social media campaign. It requires not only answering questions or comments but also actively conversing with followers and closely following industry trends. By being personal and conversational, fashion brands are likely to engage more fans, especially younger audiences. Nonetheless, in order to control brand image, their interactions with followers are typically highly curated.

It should be noted that people's social media activities vary across countries. Asian consumers tend to be more sensitive to celebrities' behaviors. They have a strong tendency to copy the preferences of their favorite celebrities. In contrast, European consumers have strong desires for independent consuming and are keen on purchasing products that appeal to their own tastes. Therefore, fashion brands may need to adapt their social media marketing strategies to different countries.

As smart phone and Internet penetration rates increase, social media is expected to continuously grow. Businesses and consumers are able to quickly exchange information and feedback regarding products and services through brief interactions. Social media makes it possible to plan effective promotion with minimal marketing costs. For instance, Burberry was the first big fashion brand to "live stream" its catwalk shows. It even revealed new collections on Snapchat before the official debut. Using creative contents, Burberry has attracted about 40 million followers across 20 different social media platforms, on some of which customers can click to buy items right on the screen.

Notes

a. Brandwatch. (2015, September 30). Brandwatch fashion & luxury report shows Calvin Klein, Christian Dior and Louis Vuitton lead in social. Retrieved from www.brandwatch.com/brandwatch-fashion-luxury-report-release/

Sources

1. Rhee, S. and Kim, S. (2011). A case study on fashion brand marketing utilizing social network service. *Journal of the Korean Society of Design Culture, 17*(3).
2. Hope, K. (2016, January 5). How social media is transforming the fashion industry. BBC News. Retrieved from www.bbc.com/news/business-35483480
3. Ilyashov, A. (2015, October 1). Here's how luxury brands are doing social media very wrong (& the few who break the mold). Refinery 29. Retrieved from www.refinery29.com/2015/10/95018/luxury-fashion-brands-social-media.

Questions for Case Discussion

1. What are the benefits and costs of social media marketing?
2. How can a company effectively use social media marketing in a foreign market?
3. Do you follow any international brands in social media? How does it affect your purchasing behavior?

Managing Customers

Marketing and Sales

Globalization has changed the way companies market products internationally. Some companies implement a strategy that uses similar promotional messages with the same product in different markets. Others realize that they must modify the physical attributes of their products as well as sales and marketing approaches in order to accommodate the tastes and preferences of foreign customers. This chapter focuses on the issue of standardization and adaptation in international marketing, i.e. if and to what extent international companies should customize their marketing practices for different countries.

I. Marketing Mix: Standardization vs. Adaptation

When a company decides to enter a foreign market, it needs to contemplate key marketing decisions.[1] Specifically, the company's marketing manager must consider four important issues: (1) What product should be brought to the market? (2) How to set a price for the product? (3) How to distribute the product to final customers? (4) How to promote the product to potential buyers? These issues are collectively known as the marketing mix, or the 4Ps of marketing—product, pricing, place (i.e. distribution), and promotion. As Case 12.1 (Haier's marketing strategy) shows, decisions about international marketing mix are more complex and complicated than domestic marketing mix in a number of ways.[2]

Before addressing individual components of the marketing mix, we need to first consider an overarching question of international marketing: Should a company standardize marketing practices across countries or adapt them to various local conditions?

On one hand, because of converging consumption trends in the global market, companies can market and sell many products in the same way across countries.[3] They are able to save production and marketing costs by standardizing product features and marketing strategies. For instance, red wine has become increasingly popular in Asian markets, even though it is not a traditional local drink. Many European and American wineries are able to export relatively standard products to Asian countries. On the other hand, standardization is not always effective as national differences in consumers tastes and preferences still exist. Sociocultural, political, legal, and economic environments tend to influence consumer behavior, determining what products are in demand and how they should be delivered. For example, cultural aesthetics may affect consumers' color preferences.[4] Many American consumers prefer electronics products in white, black, or silver, while red is more popular in Southern Europe. Companies may adapt to consumer demand by changing their product designs.

Specific advantages and disadvantages of standardization and adaptation in international marketing are listed in Table 12.2. Given the tradeoff between standardization and adaptation, MNCs must carefully consider which marketing operations they should standardize, and which they should modify, adapt, and to what extent. For instance, while red wine may be relatively

Table 12.2 Advantages and Disadvantages of Standardization vs. Adaptation in International Marketing

	Standardization	Adaptation
Advantages	1. Reduces marketing costs 2. Facilitates centralized control of marketing 3. Promotes efficiency in R&D 4. Results in economies of scale in production 5. Reflects the trend toward a single global marketplace	1. Reflects different conditions of product use 2. Acknowledges local legal differences 3. Accounts for differences in buyer behavior patterns 4. Promotes local marketing initiatives 5. Accounts for other differences in individual markets
Disadvantages	1. Ignores different conditions of product use 2. Ignores local legal differences 3. Ignores differences in buyer behavior patterns 4. Inhibits local marketing initiatives 5. Ignores other differences in individual markets	1. Increases marketing costs 2. Inhibits centralized control of marketing 3. Requires customized R&D 4. Requires customized production 5. Leads to inconsistent brand images

Source: Levitt, T. (1983). The globalization of markets. *Harvard Business Review* (May/June), 92–102.

standard, consumers differ in when, where, and how they drink wine. Therefore, wineries can standardize their products but customize their pricing, distribution, and promotion for different markets.

II. Product Strategy

A product has both tangible features, such as shape, package and physical characteristics, and intangible features, such as image, installation, and warranty.[5] A firm's ability to compete in international markets depends on whether the tangible and intangible features of its product can meet customers' needs in different countries. For example, the success of Toyota Motor Corporation in Europe, Asia, and America reflects the company's ability to successfully accommodate various customer needs by providing reliable products, strong brand reputation, and dependable warranties.

In order to decide between standardizing and adapting their products, MNCs usually need to consider the following factors:

1. Laws, Regulations, and Technical Standards

Many countries have specific laws and regulations regarding product safety and quality. There are also technical standards and traditions set by local governments, industries, and customers. International companies may need to modify their products to conform to the local rules of the target market. For instance, to sell food products in the U.S., companies are required to meet FDA health standards and follow specific labeling requirements. The brewer of Corona beer, Grupo Modelo, had to reduce the nitrosamine level of the beer in Germany, Austria, and Switzerland to meet those countries' health standards.[6] For each generation of iPhone, Apple had to create different versions because countries have chosen different mobile technology standards—GSM networks are dominant in Europe while the U.S. also has CDMA networks; the latest generation of data service has two competing standards, LTE and WiMax, and China even has its own TD-LTE standard.

Different standards and regulations add extra R&D and production costs for international firms. Although many efforts have been made to create international standards, there are still considerable national differences. For example, a "Chocolate War" took place when European Union members tried to standardize chocolate content regulations. One side known as the "cocoa purists," including Belgium, France, Germany, Spain, Italy, the Netherlands, Luxembourg, and Greece, argued that the chocolate industry should use only 100 percent cocoa butter. The other side or "non-purists," including the United Kingdom, Denmark, Portugal, Austria, Finland, and Sweden, favored adding vegetable fats. Before the end of the "Chocolate War," milk chocolate products from the "non-purists" were banned in the purist countries.

2. Cultural Differences

As Case 12.2 (Kellogg in India) shows, national cultural characteristics drive consumer tastes and preferences.[7] To succeed in foreign markets, companies need to adapt their products accordingly. For instance, to assimilate into Chinese culture, Adidas introduced a shoe line decorated in Western design with an ancient Chinese cloud pattern that represents luck.[8] Nike also introduced a new line called 1984, which commemorated the first year China participated in the Olympics. The company even offered city-specific editions of shoes in China. One design included a new kind of webbed mesh pattern material, supposedly designed for Shanghai's extreme humidity. A logo that combined Nike's "swoosh" and a historical shortened name for Shanghai were featured on all the Shanghai designs, along with the text "Luwan Never Gone 310103," a reference to the city's former Luwan District and the home of Shanghai street fashion and culture.

Mobile phone manufacturers have also been modifying the features of their products to accommodate local cultural characteristics. Targeting Middle Eastern markets, Samsung and LG's mobile phones included a compass feature. Muslims, as dictated by the Quran, must pray five times a day in the direction of Mecca. To fulfill this need, these companies developed a Mecca indicator in their phones. In India, Samsung also launched a mobile phone that contained five different languages that are used in India; LG introduced an application for its mobile phones that allowed consumers to follow India's favorite sport, cricket.

The influence of culture is even more noticeable in the fast food industry. KFC adopted multiple localized menus in China to meet Chinese consumers' tastes.[9] "Lao Beijing" burger is a China-specific item with Beijing roast duck flavor. Their local menus also include egg drop soup, rice congee, custard tarts, wood ear mushroom salad, and a variety of rice dishes (e.g. bacon mushroom chicken rice, curry pork chop rice). KFC even created drastically different flavors for different regions in China. People in Chengdu, the provincial capital of Sichuan, traditionally enjoy eating spicy food. So KFC chicken in Chengdu is seasoned with red pepper. In contrast, people in Shanghai and Wuxi, two cities in eastern China, traditionally like sweeter cuisine. So KFC chicken in those cities is seasoned with sweet sauce. In China, KFC offers an average of 50 different menu items per store and introduces two new items each month.

3. Economic Considerations

People's consumption activities are also subject to their purchasing power. Relative affordability is an important factor to consider in regard to product standardization or adaptation. Especially, in low-income countries, it is often challenging for highly priced products to find a sizable market. One possible solution is to make adjustments to product offerings, such as simplification and repackaging, so that the products become more affordable. For instance, Procter & Gamble sells shampoo and conditioner in small packets in India, thus local buyers do not have to buy big bottles. In fact, the profit margin of small packets is comparable to, if not higher than, that of big bottles. When Volkswagen started manufacturing and selling cars in China in the 1980s, it started with older, less expensive models rather than more advanced, pricier models. This approach was necessary to obtain a large sales volume and economies of scale.

Certainly, as a country's economic condition improves, local consumers' demand may change. In China, after decades of fast economic development, more and more consumers want quality cars with advanced technology; affordability has become a less important issue. Therefore, carmakers have introduced more premium models and models specifically designed for the Chinese market. In developed countries, consumers are often willing to pay higher prices for their preferred product attributes. For instance, when Hyundai initially entered the American automobile market decades ago, despite its highly competitive pricing, Hyundai sales struggled for years. One of the main problems the company faced was the perception of low quality. Most American consumers did not want to trade desired attributes and quality for a lower price.

4. Physical Conditions

The physical conditions of a country, such as natural climate and geographical features, may also become an obstacle for product standardization. Certain product modification may be necessary to fit local physical conditions. For instance, cars equipped with heat- and dust-resistant engines are popular in Saudi Arabia because of the country's high temperature and desert terrain. In India, due to frequent power outages, home appliances need to have extra protection mechanisms.

III. Pricing Strategy

Pricing is another critical component of the international marketing mix. It directly determines firms' profitability and overall success in foreign countries. For instance, Toys "R" Us became successful in Germany, Japan, and other countries mainly by selling toys at low prices in warehouse-like settings. The pricing strategy also affects a firm's competitiveness and product positioning as it influences the image of the product in consumer perception. Establishing a standard price across markets helps the company maintain a consistent position in the market. However, MNCs should also consider charging varied prices because of differences in transportation costs, demand conditions, price elasticity, competitive and substitute products, tariffs, and price regulations.

I. Environmental Factors in Pricing

The environmental factors mentioned in the previous section (i.e. legal, sociocultural, economic, and physical conditions) also affect the pricing strategy of international companies. For example, harsh natural conditions may add special requirements and extra sales expenses. Consumers in different countries may have distinct understandings of product value and bargain. Governments may impose taxes and duties, which should be incorporated into prices. Industrial policies and antitrust laws may allow governments to directly control or interfere with companies' pricing strategy.

The most important factor to consider is price elasticity of demand, a measure of how responsive the demand of a product is to a change in its price. When price elasticity of demand is high, increasing price will result in a significant loss of demand. Charging a low price may help a company substantially increase its sales volume. In contrast, when price elasticity of demand is low, market demand is less reactive to a price change. Since increasing the price does not significantly reduce sales, charging a relatively high price may help increase revenue. Typically, high-income countries tend to have lower price elasticity than low-income countries. In the pharmaceutical industry, MNCs usually focus on selling new drugs to high-income industrialized countries at high prices so that they can quickly recover R&D costs and maximize profits.[10] In addition to high incomes product necessity and customer loyalty also make consumers less sensitive to price increases. Upscale fashion brands hardly lower prices because their high prices actually enhance brand image and customer loyalty. MNCs need to take all these factors into account when deciding whether to use worldwide standard pricing or differential pricing.

2. Standard Pricing

Standard pricing is a strategy in which MNCs charge the same price for products and services regardless of geographic location. MNCs competing in globally integrated commodity markets often use this pricing strategy. For example, producers of crude oil such as Aramco, Kuwait Oil, and Pemex sell their products to all customers at prices determined by supply and demand in the world oil market. Companies selling products that can be easily shipped across borders also tend to adopt standard pricing. For example, if a manufacturer of DRAM memory chips charges different prices in different countries, some customers may resell their chips to other customers, a practice called arbitrage. Moreover, some MNCs attempt to charge standard prices for high-end luxury goods and sophisticated products. For instance, Tesla positions themselves as a premium brand and charges similar prices in developing and developed countries. GE has sold jet engines at a standard price in U.S. dollars in the global market. Without considering taxes, Apple's iPhones are priced roughly at the same levels in most countries.

3. Differential Pricing

Differential pricing, also known as price discrimination, is an approach to selling the same product or service to different customers at different prices. As shown in Case 12.3, the pricing strategy is often used by MNCs to maximize profits by charging optimal prices in different countries. Because of variance in market conditions, the optimal prices may differ substantially across countries. For instance, BMW and Porsche are known for charging much higher prices for their luxury SUVs in China than in the U.S. These companies face lower competition in China, and Chinese consumers who are able to afford luxury SUVs are less sensitive to price increases. Price discrimination can be used when countries have different levels of price elasticity of demand and different country markets are separated (i.e. cross-market arbitrage is restricted). To ensure market separation, Porsche and BMW prohibit their U.S. dealers to export new cars and require new car buyers to sign a non-export agreement. In addition, since distribution costs vary significantly country by country, MNCs may need to charge differential prices to absorb cost variances. For instance, in countries that lack efficient distribution systems, profit margins required by tiers of distribution channel members add to the final prices for consumers.[11]

IV. Distribution Strategy

Distribution is the process of getting a product from its producer to its final user. A company may distribute its products directly to customers or utilize tiers of distributors like wholesalers and retailers. Distribution decisions are often connected with other aspects of the marketing mix. Nonetheless, these decisions are typically long-term decisions, which are harder and costlier to change than pricing, product, and promotion strategies. Therefore, companies need to be very careful with their distribution decisions in international markets.

1. Standardized Distribution

If a company can copy its domestic distribution structure in a foreign market, it is relatively easy for the company to leverage previous experience and coordinate global distribution. For instance, Avon Corporation is a U.S.-based manufacturer and direct seller of beauty and personal care products. Avon has successfully expanded into more than 50 countries with its door-to-door direct selling approach. Despite some minor modifications due to country differences in attitude toward home visits and income level, Avon has applied a relatively standard distribution strategy both at home and in foreign markets. This distribution approach is an essential part of Avon's business model and a main source of its competitive advantage. Another standardized distribution strategy can be found at Romanson, a company that produces watches, handbags, wallets, and leather products. Romanson has used a "one distributor in one country" strategy. It carefully selected overseas distributors with preset criteria and provided active support to them. The company was able to maintain control over its distribution channels and avoid confusion among its channel members. It also set up coordination mechanisms, which allowed channel members to exchange information about design trends around the world. However, although MNCs generally prefer to standardize their international distribution, they face considerable constraints of location-specific distribution channels and environmental factors.

2. Localized Distribution

As shown in Case 12.4, Hyundai has created a localized distribution strategy to sell automobiles in China. Localizing distribution is often necessary due to cross-country differences in the availability and features of distribution channels.[12] These challenges make it difficult for MNCs to manage worldwide distribution channels. They often delegate distribution decisions to local subsidiaries when direct negotiations with local distributors are necessary.

One major difference between distribution systems is retail concentration, the degree to which a distribution system is concentrated in a small number of distributors. In a concentrated system, MNCs must rely on a few powerful distributors to make their products available to final buyers. While those distributors can help MNCs quickly increase market coverage, they tend to have strong bargaining power against MNCs. For example, in the U.S., large national discount retailers dominate the market; companies have to use these retailers to access the mass market. In a fragmented system, where there are many distributors and no one has a major market share, it would be harder for MNCs to establish a large market coverage. Retail systems in developing countries are typically fragmented.

Another major difference is channel length, which refers to the number of intermediaries between a producer and its final customer. The channel is long if the producer sells through a number of intermediary distributors. A short distribution channel allows MNCs to quickly reach their customers. This concept is related to retail concentration. Usually, large retailers in concentrated systems source directly from manufacturers, thus shortening channel length. In fragmented systems, it is often impractical or too costly for MNCs to directly deal with a large number of individual retailers, so they use layers of wholesalers. A longer distribution channel allows MNCs to penetrate the market but adds to distribution costs and consequently the final price for customers.

Furthermore, distribution channels may not be readily accessible for MNCs. For example, Japan's retail system is known for its exclusivity. Because Japanese retailers stress long-term relationships with their suppliers, it is difficult for newcomers to gain access to shelf space. Also, in some cases, there are simply no qualified local distributors. This is a common challenge for MNCs entering developing countries. For example, in several developing countries, Unilever realized that their ice cream products were often half-melted because many local distributors lacked freezers. The company had to rebuild distribution systems at great costs in these countries, including leasing numerous freezers to retailers.

In addition, environmental factors may push MNCs to adapt their distribution decisions. For instance, difficulties in transportation tend to require distribution outlets to carry a large inventory. Governments may have specific regulations on distribution channels. Consumer shopping patterns may shape the structure of distribution. For instance, when it comes to grocery shopping, most American consumers buy large quantities at large discount stores. In Japan, however, consumers often make multiple purchases in small quantities as Japanese households usually prefer fresh food and have limited storage space at home.

V. Promotion Strategy

One of the key challenges facing MNCs is to effectively deliver the right message about their products to customers around the world. Promotion is about communicating with prospective customers to raise product awareness, generate sales, and create brand loyalty. An MNC has to decide whether (and to what extent) its promotion strategy should be modified to meet local market demand, or whether the domestic advertising strategy can be extended into overseas markets. The standardization strategy is to use the same advertising in all international markets. In contrast, the localization strategy is to use modified advertising methods that cater to consumers' needs and preferences in different markets.

I. Standardized Advertising

Due to similarities in consumer tastes and preferences, it is possible to have standard advertising across countries. Instead of addressing specific needs of a particular market, MNCs may focus on universal needs in their advertising. Thus, successful advertising in one country can be immediately applied to another country with no or minimum adaptation.[13] Standardized advertising has several advantages. First, it helps save costs. If the same advertisement produced in a country can be distributed globally, MNCs would not create customized advertisements for each country. For example, British Airways created a themed advertisement, "Manhattan Landing," and displayed it in many countries. Coca-Cola's polar bear is another example of a standardized advertisement image.

Second, standardized advertising allows MNCs to keep a uniform and consistent brand image in different markets. Consumers typically assign a certain value to a product based on their knowledge about its brand image. Nowadays more and more consumers travel abroad and become familiar with global brands. Using standardized advertising across countries, MNCs can effectively communicate with consumers around the world and prevent unnecessary confusion.[14] Toyota's Lexus brand was originally translated into "Lin Zhi" by independent importers in China, loosely following the sound of "Lexus" and meaning "Flying Ambition." When Toyota officially started selling Lexus cars in China, it decided to have a globally consistent brand name and translated "Lexus" into "Lei Ke Sa Si", exactly mimicking the sound but having no actual meaning in Chinese.

2. Localized Advertising

Despite the potential benefits of standardized advertising, local adaptation may be necessary because of substantial differences in consumer needs. The trend of globalization is not likely to remove the impact of political, economic, and sociocultural differences on consumer behaviors. First of all, MNCs may need to modify their advertisements in countries that have different advertising regulations. For example, child modeling or acting in commercial advertisements is allowed in the U.S., but prohibited in France. As a result, Kellogg, which often has child actors in their U.S. advertisements, could not use child models to promote its cereals in France.[15]

Cultural differences are dominant barriers to standardized advertising. Due to cultural differences, the same advertisement may generate distinct implications in different countries. The objective of the advertisement will be lost if the underlying message cannot be accurately conveyed. For example, Pepsi's slogan "Come alive with Pepsi" was wrongly interpreted as "Come out of the grave with Pepsi" in Germany. Colgate's toothpaste named "Cue" was not well accepted by French consumers as it is also the name of a French pornographic magazine. A display ad from an American pen company conveyed the message "Avoid embarrassment" (from leaks and stains). However, in Mexico, "embarrassment" also means "to conceive." Many consumers who were not proficient in English thought the advertisement was for a counter-contraceptive product. These marketing mistakes illustrate some pitfalls of simple standardized advertising.

Effective advertising requires not only proper translation but also a deep understanding of local cultures. Especially, brand name translation should be conducted very carefully. For instance, Coca-Cola's low-calorie soft drink is called "Diet Coke" in weight conscious North America, but is known as "Coca-Cola Light" in some European markets.[16] The Chinese brand name of Coca-Cola means "just the right taste and pleasure in the mouth," which is well liked by Chinese consumers.[17] Without adequate cultural understanding, localized advertising may fail. For instance, Nike once made a TV commercial for the European markets featuring famous European soccer stars playing against devils. The company received many complaints because many viewers found the commercial too scary and violent. Nike's other TV commercial called "Chamber of Fear" set the background in China to attract Chinese consumers. However, the commercial was not well received because several cultural symbols, like Kung Fu master and dragon, were portrayed negatively.

In recent years, as more and more consumers demand individualized attention, MNCs are feeling an increasing need to connect to local consumers' core values.[18] For instance, in China, Coca-Cola is positioned as an innovative brand because locals are all about pursuing new products. In North America, Coca-Cola is more attuned to values of family and security. Indeed, a brand's ability to adapt to customers' core values in different countries directly affects its performance in those markets. This ability is much more than just creating customized products and advertisements. It is about creating a personality that resonates with prospective customers. For example, Colgate connects with its Russian consumers by stressing physical beauty and being attractive to the opposite sex, while in China the brand is all about being healthy, active, and strong.

In addition, a notable cultural trait is people's general impression toward foreign products. The country-of-origin effect means that the production site of a product may influence customers' perception and buying decision. For example, French wine, Italian clothes, and German cars enjoy favorable global reputations, whereas manufactured goods from developing countries are often associated with lower prices and shoddy quality. When the country-of-origin effect is positive, MNCs may stick to their original marketing concepts and minimize customization, thus preserving and highlighting their national origins. However, when the country-of-origin effect is negative or undesirable, MNCs may customize their advertising to enhance their brands' own reputations, tune down their national origins, or even link to another country. For instance, to expand in the U.S. market, two Chinese sportswear brands Peak Sports and Li-Ning spent considerable money to sponsor NBA players. Apple mainly promoted iPhones as "Designed in California" rather than "Assembled in China." The U.S.-based ice cream maker Häagen-Dazs intentionally chose its European sounding name.

3. Other Aspects of Promotion

In addition to advertising, MNCs may utilize other promotion approaches, such as personal selling, social media, and public relations. Unlike mass advertising, which "pulls" potential customers, personal selling "pushes" a product to buyers. MNCs may choose various combinations of advertising and personal selling depending on relative costs, product types, and media availability. Typically, makers of industrial products rely more on personal selling than mass advertising to promote their products. Large consumer goods companies are more likely to use advertising to reach the mass market. Certainly, this promotion decision may vary across countries. For instance, in some developing countries, personal selling can be quite effective for newly introduced and high-end consumer goods. Appropriate media channels are not necessarily available in certain countries, restricting the use of advertising.

A notable trend in promotion is the use of social media. An increasing number of firms now market their brands and products through social media networks domestically and internationally. Case 12.5 describes how companies in the fashion industry have turned their attention to communicating with the public through various social networking tools such as Facebook and Twitter. Obviously, how people follow social media varies from country to country. For instance, in China, while Facebook and Twitter services are not available, Weibo and WeChat are the most popular social network applications. Also, location-specific pop culture strongly influences what kind of individuals and entities are likely to attract attention in social media.

Public relations is the practice whereby a company applies various methods of communication to create positive publicity and maintain a good reputation in the public. Due to MNCs' increasing global presence, it has become imperative for them to manage their public perceptions in foreign markets. Especially when facing nationalism and anti-multinational sentiment in some countries, MNCs must campaign actively to minimize the negative feelings toward them. Some MNCs engage in philanthropy and charity work in their host countries. Others highlight their local roots and connections in their marketing campaigns. For instance, in the U.S., the Europe-based Airbus often stresses that the company sources from American suppliers in its advertisements. Foreign automakers, like Toyota, Honda, and BMW, also frequently proclaim their local production in the U.S.

VI. Managing the Marketing Mix

In order to succeed in international markets, MNCs need to effectively manage the combination of products, price, distribution, and promotion.[19] The four components can be combined in various ways to serve different purposes. In particular, there are five combinations of product and promotion as regard to standardization and localization (see Figure 12.2).

- *Product/Communication Extension*: Product and communication extension refers to a strategy that uses the same product and promotion campaign in both domestic and overseas markets. Many global companies enter foreign markets with this strategy because it offers an easy and quick way to expand. This strategy has been widely used in the soft drink industry. For example, Pepsi entered over 100 countries with similar products and advertising. Certainly, this strategy is not necessarily effective in every market. For example, Campbell Soup once sold the same tomato soup in both the British and U.S. markets. While succeeding in the U.S., it suffered a significant loss in the British market. The company later discovered that British people preferred their soup more bitter than most Americans would.
- *Product Extension/Communication Adaptation*: In this strategy, MNCs sell the same products in both domestic and overseas markets, but their advertisements are adapted to local circumstances. This is a useful approach when people use a same product to serve different purposes and functions. So, the product can be standardized but adjustments are made to advertising. For example, the main reason U.S. consumers buy bicycles is for leisure whereas consumers in developing countries use bicycles as a basic means of transportation. This strategy is relatively

Product

	Do Not Change Product	Adapt Product	Develop New Product
Do Not Change Promotion	Straight extension	Product adaptation	Product invention
Adapt Promotion	Communication adaptation	Dual adaptation	

(Promotion labels on left axis; Product invention spans the right column)

Figure 12.2 Five International Product and Promotion Strategies

Source: Keegan, Warren J. (1995). *Multinational Marketing Management,* 5th ed., Upper Saddle River, NJ: Prentice Hall, pp. 378–381.

inexpensive to implement. R&D, manufacturing, and inventory costs are not affected because there is no change in product attributes.

- *Product Adaptation/Communication Extension*: This strategy has the same advertising theme in both foreign and domestic markets but requires products to be adapted to local circumstances. Some products face significant differences in the conditions of product use, thus requiring modifications that cater to different markets. However, the same communication strategy could be replicated. For example, Exxon adjusted the composition of gas based on local climatic conditions, but had a global standard advertising theme, "Put a tiger in your tank."[20]
- *Product/Communication Adaptation*: This strategy requires adjusting both product and promotion, and thereby adapting to local circumstances. This strategy can be used when both the operating condition and the function of a product vary significantly across countries. For instance, people differ in their preferences for coffee taste and purposes of drinking coffee. In the U.S., coffee is mostly a kind of drink. In China, coffee represents the Western lifestyle and Chinese consumers like sweeter and milkier coffee. Because of these considerations, coffee companies must adapt their products and advertising concepts to appeal to local consumers.
- *Product Invention*: The four strategies discussed above will not be useful when neither existing nor modified products work for foreign customers. A new product needs to be created to meet international market demand. For example, to enter the global luxury car market, Toyota launched Lexus as a separate line of products. Consumers in developing countries, who account for three-quarters of the world's population, generally have limited purchasing power, so they may need entirely new products at low prices. For example, the development of a hand-operated washing machine might be necessary for households in some low-income countries.

Given the trend of globalization, many MNCs now aim to build global brands with strong market recognition and sales volume. A global brand image can become a valuable asset, which helps create brand loyalty, cut marketing expenses, and achieve economies of scale. For instance, McDonald's golden arch is recognized almost everywhere in the world. While offering local variants in its menus, McDonald's strives to maintain a consistent brand image.[21] Meanwhile, it is also important to connect to local consumers' core values. For instance, Nescafé speaks of enjoying life to the fullest, emphasizing being successful and well respected. Such values connect with consumers and have helped the company to perform well in many countries.

Overall, MNCs need to deliberately coordinate their product, pricing, distribution, and promotion. For instance, Heineken started its business in Amsterdam in the Netherlands and became a leading beer producer in the world. The company strictly controls product quality by placing a quality control department in all distribution centers to maintain the same flavor and freshness in each market worldwide. It also positions itself as an environmentally friendly beer producer by emphasizing freshness and promoting a green image. Meanwhile, the company uses localized advertisements in each country by considering local cultural characteristics associated with beer. In an advertisement for the French market, a famous middle-aged actor was holding a glass of Heineken beer toward lights as if the beer were fine wine.

Key Terms

Marketing mix, standardization, adaptation, product strategy, standard pricing, price discrimination, distribution channel, retail concentration, channel length, promotion strategy, standardized advertising, localized advertising, country-of-origin effect, global brand

Review Questions

1. What are the benefits and costs of standardization versus adaptation in international marketing?
2. What factors drive companies to customize their products for foreign markets?
3. What is differential pricing (or price discrimination)? Under what circumstances can companies use this pricing strategy in international markets?
4. How can MNCs structure their overseas distribution channels?
5. How do MNCs adapt their advertising to local circumstances?
6. What are the strategies MNCs can use to manage the marketing mix?

Internet Exercises

1. Interbrand ranks the top 100 global brands every year. Find their latest rankings here: http://interbrand.com/best-brands/ Review the list and find a brand that is foreign in your country. Research online and discuss how the company markets its products and services in your country.

2. Find the best-selling foreign automobile brands in your country. Research how they customize product, pricing, distribution, and promotion in your country. You may find a study on how automobile companies adapt to the Thai market on the following webpage: www.emeraldinsight.com/doi/full/10.1108/00251740810912019. Compare your own finding with this study. Do you see any differences between the automakers' marketing in your country and their practices in Thailand?

Notes

1   Papadopoulos, N. and Heslop, L. A. (1993). *Product-Country-Images-Impact and Role in International Marketing.* New York: International Business Press.
2   Cheng, B. (2009). Haier's success. *Market Modernization, 20,* 30.
3   Levitt, T. (1983). The globalization of markets. *Harvard Business Review,* May–June, 92–102.
4   Priluck Grossman, R. and Wisenblit, J. Z. (1999). What we know about consumers' color choices. *Journal of Marketing Practice: Applied Marketing Science, 5*(3), 78–88.
5   Lannon, J. (1991). Developing brand strategies across borders. *Marketing and Research Today, 19*(3), 160–168.
6   *Wall Street Journal.* (1993, January 19). Mexico's Corona brew wins back cachet lost during the late '80s, p. B.6.
7   Arora, R. and Sharma, R. (2012, July). Effective branding strategies of multinational corporations in international markets: The case of India. *PRIMA 3*(1), 4. Publishing India Group.
8   *Wall Street Journal.* (2008, March 29). Stylish sportwear with designs on China, p. B.1.
9   Zhou, L.Y. and Zhang, Q.(2012, June 20). Cultural adaptation pattern analysis of McDonald's and KFC in the Chinese market. DiVA [Online]. Retrieved from www.diva-portal.org/smash/get/diva2:534795/FULLTEXT01.pdf.
10 Danzon, P. M. and Towse, A. (2003). Differential pricing for pharmaceuticals: Reconciling access, R&D and patents. *International Journal of Health Care Finance and Economics, 3*(3), 183–205.
11 Sims, C., Phillips, A. and Richards, T. (1992). Developing a global pricing strategy. *Marketing and Research Today,* March, 3–14.
12 Kotabe, M. and Helsen, K. (1998). *Global Marketing Management.* New York: John Wiley & Sons.
13 Fastoso, F. and Whitelock, J. (2007). International advertising strategy: The standardization question in manager studies: Patterns in four decades of past research and directions for future knowledge advancement. *International Marketing Review, 24*(5), 591–605.
14 Szilagyi, T. and Chapman, S. (2004). Tobacco industry efforts to erode tobacco advertising controls in Hungary. *Central European Journal of Public Health, 12*(4), 190–196.
15 Calvert, S. L. (2008). Children as consumers: Advertising and marketing. *The Future of Children, 18*(1), 205–234.
16 Galloni, A. (2001, July 18). Coca-Cola tests the waters with localized ads in Europe. *Wall Street Journal.*
17 CNN Money. (2015). What's in a brand name? In China, everything. Retrieved from http://money.cnn.com/2015/09/07/news/foreign-firms-china-branding/

18   Shaw, H. (2011, May 20). 'Globalization' rules the world. *Financial Post*. Retrieved from http://business.financialpost.com/news/glocalization-rules-the-world

19   Keegan, W. J. (1995). *Multinational Marketing Management (5th edition)*. Prentice Hall.

20   Pandya, A. and Venkatesh, A. (1992). Symbolic communication among consumers in self-consumption and gift giving: A semiotic approach. *Advances in Consumer Research, 19*(1), 147–154.

21   Vignali, C. (2001). McDonald's: 'think global, act local'—the marketing mix. *British Food Journal, 103*(2), 97–111.

Managing Sustainability
Corporate Social Responsibility and Business Ethics

Learning Objectives

1. Explain the concept of sustainability at the global level and the company level.
2. Discuss the role of multinational companies in sustainable development.
3. Identify and examine the three key dimensions of corporate sustainability.
4. Describe the pyramid of global corporate social responsibility.
5. Discuss how to recognize and resolve cross-border ethical dilemmas.

Cases

Case 13.1 The Chilean Mining Accident, Rescue and Aftermath
Case 13.2 iPhone's Troubled Supply Chain in China
Case 13.3 The Environmental Impact of a Cell Phone
Case 13.4 Corporate Social Responsibility Activities in the Chinese Auto Industry: Examples from Toyota Motor Company and Hyundai Motor Company
Case 13.5 Indian Farmers and Monsanto

Case 13.1 The Chilean Mining Accident, Rescue and Aftermath

For about 70 days in 2010, Chile grabbed global media attention when a significant cave-in accident buried 33 miners deep beneath the surface. The collapse happened in the afternoon of August 5 at an over-100-year-old copper mine located in the Atacama Desert in northern Chile. A group of 33 men were trapped 2,300 feet underground and three miles from the entrance via spiraling ramps. However, the private owner of the mine, San Esteban Mining Company, had incurred significant debt and lacked the resources to mount a rescue.

The accident soon raised strong public concern in Chile, and people were deeply sympathetic toward the trapped miners and their grief-stricken families. Chilean President Piñera cut short an overseas trip to visit the mine. The national government took over the rescue operation and turned to Codelco, the country's state-owned mining company. Contributing a significant amount of resources, Codelco was able to drill multiple exploratory boreholes into the mine. Half a month after the accident, however, there were still no signs of life. Many believed that the miners had not survived the collapse.

On August 22, 2010, 17 days after the accident, rescuers pulled the drill bit out of the eighth borehole and they were surprised to find a note taped to it. The note was written in bold red letters and read "*Estamos bien en el refugio, los 33*" ("*We are well in the shelter, the 33 of us*"). It turned out that the trapped miners had found a shelter and managed to survive on a two-day supply of food. The country erupted with relief and hope.

To bring the miners safely from the depths, the Chilean government developed a comprehensive plan, deploying experts and employing technologies from around the world. The rescue was truly a global effort. Teams from South Africa, the U.S., and Canada were charged with drilling three man-sized escape holes concurrently, using equipment delivered by multiple international corporations, such as U.S.- and Canadian-made rigs, New Zealand sensors, Australian 3D mapping technology, and Japanese video technology. Meanwhile, Chile's navy constructed a capsule to lift the miners, relying on designs sent by NASA and other government agencies. NASA specialists also helped develop a sophisticated health agenda for the miners.

On October 9, 2010, the drill, operated by the U.S.-Chilean company Geotec Boyles Bros., broke through first, ahead of schedule. The rescue effort to save the miners started a couple of days later. On October 13, after 69 days trapped underground, all 33 miners were safely brought outside, almost all in good physical condition. After rescuing the last trapped miner, the rescue team held up a sign for the TV cameras reading "*Misión cumplida Chile*" ("*Mission accomplished Chile*"). It was estimated that over one billion people witnessed the moment live. The media glare made the 33 miners into international celebrities and attracted an outpouring of donations, gifts, and even a film deal. The high-profile rescue was hailed a great triumph for Chile and the global mining industry.

Despite its happy ending, the Chilean mining accident has highlighted the safety issue facing the industry. Chile is the world's largest producer of copper, a metal widely used in manufacturing and construction. The Chilean economy is highly dependent on copper mining, the top sector in terms of GDP contribution and exports. Surging demand for copper in global markets, especially demand from emerging markets, has led to near-record prices. Mining companies, both big and small, have amped up operations to meet demand. While large state mining firms and MNCs have above-average safety records, small firms like San Esteban generally have lower safety standards. During the 12 years before the collapse, geological instability and safety violations had caused a series of accidents and fines for the company, including eight deaths. San Esteban was fined 42 times for breaching safety regulations between 2004 and 2010. The mine was temporarily closed in 2007 when a miner was killed during a rock explosion, but then reopened in 2008 although it did not comply with regulations. Due to its poor safety record, wages at the mine were about 20 percent higher than wages at other Chilean mines.

After the mine collapse, Chilean President Piñera vowed that those responsible for the disaster would not escape punishment. He also fired top officials from the country's mining regulatory agency and promised to embark on a major revamp of the department. Eighteen mines were closed and a further 300 put under threat of possible shut down. Both the mine owners and government officials of the mining agency responsible for enforcing safety standards were under investigation. In July 2013, days before the third anniversary of the collapse, the investigation was closed with no charges filed. The prosecutor concluded that not enough evidence was found to determine the cause of the accident or to accuse the mine owners or government officials of criminal responsibility for the collapse. The decision reveals a reality of Chile's legal system: due to a lack of corresponding law codes, it's still difficult to impose criminal penalties on mine owners for accidents that result from safety infractions.

In response to the accident, President Piñera also established a special commission on work safety in 2010. The commission recommended 30 proposals including improvements in sanitation and better coordination between local regulatory authorities. This bill, along with several others designed to improve mining conditions, remained in gridlock in Chile's legislature. In December 2010, Chile's legislature failed to ratify Convention 176 of the International Labor Organization, a U.N. resolution that gives miners the right to refuse to work in any location that could reasonably pose a serious danger to safety or health. The government mining agency did make some adjustments by changing the mining code and performing more frequent inspections. Although the agency increased regulatory requirements for small mines, government data from 2012 and 2013 show that small operations still had greater accident fatality rates than large companies.

In addition to safety, the collapse also called the aging condition of Chile's mines into question. By 2025, Chilean ore is expected to fall from over one percent to about 0.7 percent. To adapt to poorer ore, the mining industry faces tremendous pressure for expansion. Some companies have started to extract ore that was once considered too low-grade to be worth mining. Moreover, decades of digging has made miners extract ore from deeper pits. The cost of mining has been increasing, which threatens the financial condition of mining companies, especially the small ones.

Other costs are increasing too. Mining needs a lot of water. The Chilean Water Code facilitated conversion of agricultural water to large-scale, water-intensive mining developments. The expansion of the mining industry has created great pressure on water supply in the Atacama Desert area, the hub of Chilean mining. Mining also has had a troubling impact on water resources and the environment of the area. Water shortage is threatening to dry out wetlands—the habitats and feeding grounds of Andean Flamingoes and many other species. The future of indigenous populations that have relied on traditional irrigation for thousands of years is being challenged. To relieve environmental concerns, BHP, a large multinational mining company, has switched to using desalted water pumped from a seaport, rather than emptying local water tables. Unfortunately, this adds to overall costs.

Energy is expensive and likely to get more expensive in Chile. Mining is one the most energy-intensive industries in the world. Chile has few local energy sources in addition to hydropower, and the dams are far away from the mines. Because of energy scarcity, companies are reportedly prepared to shut down non-essential machinery. Many mining companies have their own sources of backup power generation that can cover most but not all local power shortfalls. However, the use of backup generators adds significantly to costs.

Sources

1. Froetschel, S. (2010, October 18). Chilean rescue offers lesson in globalization. Yale Global. Retrieved from http://yaleglobal.yale.edu/content/chilean-rescue-offers-lesson-globalization
2. *Economist*. (2013, April 27). Copper solution. Retrieved from www.economist.com/news/business/21576714-mining-industry-has-enriched-chile-its-future-precarious-copper-solution
3. Sustainable Development Strategies Group. (2010). Report: Current issues in the Chilean mining sector. Retrieved from www.sdsg.org/wp-content/uploads/2010/02/10-10-08-CHILE-REPORT.pdf

Questions for Case Discussion

1. What are the ethical, legal, and economic responsibilities of San Esteban Mining Company, owner of the collapsed mine?
2. What do you think about the result of the criminal investigation? What are the implications for Chile's mining companies?
3. Given the future prospect of the industry, how should Chile's mining companies manage their relationship with their workers and communities?

Case 13.2 iPhone's Troubled Supply Chain in China

On the back of the iPhone, Apple's iconic mobile product, an embossed note states, "Designed by Apple in California. Assembled in China." This small note highlights the critical role China plays in Apple's supply chain. iPhones contain hundreds of parts from all around the world, such as advanced semiconductors from Germany, memory from Japan, display panels from Korea, circuitries from Taiwan, and various components and accessories from China. All the parts are put together by Apple's manufacturing contractors in China.

iPhone's success was partially attributed to its highly efficient and flexible supply chain in China. In 2007, just a few weeks before the iPhone's scheduled market launch, Steve Jobs, the legendary leader of Apple, demanded a total redesign of the screen. This last-minute change forced an assembly line overhaul. As new glass screens arrived at the plant near midnight, 8,000 workers were convened from nearby dormitories and immediately started on a 12-hour shift fitting glass screens into slanting frames. The plant began producing over 10,000 iPhones a day within four days. For that to happen in the U.S., it would take nine months. Mr. Jobs reportedly said that those manufacturing jobs "aren't coming back" to the U.S.[a] What drove Apple to China was not just low-cost labor, which accounted for only 2 percent of the iPhone's total cost, but the entire established supply chain.

With an abundant supply of engineers and workers, factories in China can scale up and down in a timely fashion. After decades of development of its manufacturing sectors, most electronic parts can be easily obtained within the country.

Despite its commercial success, Apple's supply chain has drawn criticism from labor advocates in recent years. At the center of this criticism is Foxconn Technology, a Taiwan-based contract manufacturer that operates dozens of gigantic plants throughout China. With about 1.2 million workers, the company manufactures approximately 40 percent of the world's consumer electronics. For years, nearly all of the world's iPhones were manufactured at Foxconn's plants in China. Each plant typically has tens of thousands to hundreds of thousands of employees, most of whom live in crowded on-site dormitories. Shifts run 24 hours a day and assembly lines almost never stop. Employees are subject to semi-military management and harsh ridicule. They often work too many overtime hours, in some instances seven days a week. It was reported that long working hours and repetitive daily routine had caused physical and mental stress to some employees.

The working conditions at Foxconn triggered public concern when a series of worker suicides occurred in 2010. In that year, an estimated 18 Foxconn employees attempted suicide by jumping off the building. At least 14 of them died. Although the suicide rate was lower than that of the nation, such a large number of continuous workplace suicides put Foxconn under a lot pressure. In response, the company installed suicide-prevention netting around buildings, brought in counselors and Buddhist monks to soothe shattered nerves, and eventually increased wages at select plants. Workers were asked to sign no-suicide pledges and legal documents that prevented them from suing the company if they were to attempt suicide.

There was a growing list of incidents at Apple's suppliers throughout China. In 2007, underage workers were discovered at a few factories. In 2010, 137 workers were injured after using a poisonous chemical to clean iPhone screens. The substance evaporates much faster than alcohol, supposedly improving efficiency. In 2011, two explosions at two plants killed four people and injured 77. Both explosions were attributed to combustible aluminum dust that could have been removed with proper ventilation. In 2012, a fight at worker dormitories escalated into a riot involving 2,000 people and had to be quelled by security. In 2013, Apple recruited another contractor, Pegatron, for iPhone production. Allegedly, the working conditions of Pegatron factories were even worse than those of Foxconn.

In recent years, Apple has made efforts to address these concerns. In 2005, Apple issued a code of conduct, demanding "that working conditions in Apple's supply chain are safe, that workers are treated with respect and dignity, and that manufacturing processes are environmentally responsible."[b] From 2006, the company started inspecting its suppliers and publishing an audit report every year. Apple continuously increased the number and the scope of its audits. In 2012, the company conducted 393 audits, including labor inspections, environmental audits, and safety assessments, at all levels of its supply chain covering facilities with over 1.5 million workers. Those inspections identified hundreds of violations of Apple's code of conduct. If a violation is detected, Apple requires suppliers to deal with the problem within 90 days and to adopt preventive measures.

Apple claims to have been making steady progress in reducing excessive working hours and improving working conditions. In 2012, Apple also requested the Fair Labor Association conduct an independent audit of its largest assembly supplier, Foxconn. The external audit indicated that Foxconn addressed several labor concerns: enforcing breaks, changing equipment to reduce repetitive stress injuries, and updating equipment maintenance policies.

The problems Apple faces in its supply chain are not uncommon. A number of MNCs have been accused of using Chinese factories that employ child labor and mistreat employees. According to some observers, conditions at Apple's suppliers are actually not that bad compared with many others. Foxconn typically pays a higher salary than its peer firms. Food and lodging are subsidized and extensive recreational facilities are provided. Despite a 30–40 percent annual turnover, a constant stream of young migrant workers replace those who quit. Many workers want to work overtime so that they can earn extra money. Local governments usually welcome such companies as they create a lot of jobs and contribute to the local economy.

Notes

a. Duhigg, C. and Bradsher, K. (2012). How the U.S. lost out on iPhone work. *New York Times*. Retrieved from www.nytimes.com/2012/01/22/business/apple-america-and-a-squeezed-middle-class.html?pagewanted=all
b. Duhigg, C. and Barboza, D. (2012, January 25). In China, human costs are built into an iPad. *New York Times*. Retrieved from www.nytimes.com/2012/01/26/business/ieconomy-apples-ipad-and-the-human-costs-for-workers-in-china.html?pagewanted=all

Sources

1. Greene, J. (2012, September 25). Riots, suicides, and other issues in Foxconn's iPhone factories. CNET. Retrieved from http://news.cnet.com/8301-13579_3-57515968-37/riots-suicides-and-other-issues-in-foxconns-iphone-factories/
2. Duhigg, C. and Barboza, D. (2012, January 25). In China, human costs are built into an iPad. *New York Times*. Retrieved from www.nytimes.com/2012/01/26/business/ieconomy-apples-ipad-and-the-human-costs-for-workers-in-china.html?pagewanted=all
3. Duhigg, C. and Bradsher, K. (2012). How the U.S. lost out on iPhone work. *New York Times*. Retrieved from www.nytimes.com/2012/01/22/business/apple-america-and-a-squeezed-middle-class.html?pagewanted=all

Questions for Case Discussion

1. What are the causes of the labor problems in Apple's supply chain?
2. What do you think of Apple's efforts to address the problems? Are they appropriate and adequate?
3. Will those problems drive Apple out of China? Why?
4. The Chinese public seems ambivalent toward these problems. How so?

Case 13.3 The Environmental Impact of a Cell Phone

Cell phones have become an indispensable product in modern societies. While drastically changing peoples' lives, cell phones have generated a noticeable impact on the natural environment throughout their life cycles. To manage their environmental performance, cell phone manufacturers need to control the quantity and types of materials, monitor energy efficiency and waste emission in manufacturing, and be mindful of product recyclability.

> According to Apple's Environmental Status Report, the life cycle of the iPhone5 involves energy efficiency, material productivity, climate change, and restricted substances. It is estimated that total Greenhouse gas emissions for iPhone5 are 75kg CO_2, with 76% from production, 18% from customer use, 4% from transportation, and 2% from recycling. To minimize these emissions, Apple sets strict design-related goals for energy and material efficiency. iPhone5 is equipped with power-efficient components and software that allows a smart management of power consumption. Its power adapter also outperforms the requirements of the ENERGY STAR® specification. The iPhone 5 consists of aluminum, stainless steel and other materials that recyclers highly desire. Its retail box is made mostly from bio-based materials and fiberboard containing 90% recycled content. The cell phone's ultra-compact design and packaging not only reduces its material footprint but also helps maximize shipping efficiency. Apple also restricts the use of hazardous substances in production and packaging. iPhone5 uses arsenic-free display glass and mercury-free LED-backlit display. It is also brominated flame retardant-free and PVC-free. In addition, Apple offers and participates in various product take-back and recycling programs in 95% of the region where Apple products are sold. All products are processed in the country or region in which they are collected.[a]

Despite such efforts, cell phone companies have drawn criticism for their environmental impact, some of which can be traced to raw materials like rare earth minerals. Rare earth minerals are crucial ingredients for making such parts as glass displays and magnets in speakers, headphones, and vibrating motors. To mine rare earth minerals, ores are dug out of the ground, pounded into pieces, and then mixed with water and chemicals. After taking out the rare earth concentrate, the remainder of the mix, which has no commercial value but contains radioactive thorium and uranium and other toxic chemicals, has to be disposed of. If leaking into groundwater occurs, the waste can cause environmental hazards.

China alone provides more than 90 percent of the world's supply of rare earth minerals. Baotou, the center of rare earth mining in China, has witnessed the ensuing environmental wreckage. Radioactive waste, collected in an artificial lake west of the city, has seeped into the ground. A study by local authorities in 2006 showed that the level of thorium in soil near the lake was 36 times higher than the rest of the city. It has been reported that agricultural plants cannot grow and animals get sick. Local residents have also complained about teeth falling out and hair turning prematurely white. For human beings, exposure to thorium may even cause lung and pancreatic cancer. In recent years, the Chinese government has increased efforts to reduce the environmental damage of rare earth mining. There are new laws focused on water pollution and treatment as well as plans to enforce them. The country has instituted quotas and restricted the export of minerals, though some suspect the move was also intended to drive up prices.

In the process of cell phone production, which uses a number of toxic metals and solvents, waste disposal has become a major environmental issue. For example, according to a 2011 report titled "The Other Side of Apple," an association of environmental organizations found problems of poisoning and pollution in Apple's supply chain in China. The report claimed that many suppliers failed to appropriately dispose of hazardous waste and at least 27 of them had environmental problems.[b] They were accused of discharging polluted waste and toxic metals into surrounding communities and threatening public health. Residents near a Foxconn factory, the main manufacturing contractor of iPhone, repeatedly filed complaints about the factory's irritant emissions resulting from metal surface processing. Meiko Electronics, a supplier of printed circuit boards, was cited more than ten times for pollution discharge exceeding authorized standards.

It is not uncommon in the cell phone industry that global sourcing and production creates pollution problems. Environmental organizations hope cell phone companies convert their sourcing power into a driving force for pollution control. Many cell phone companies have recognized this problem in their production process. In its environmental report, Apple promises to manage its supply chain in a more environmentally friendly manner.[c] Working with external environmental groups, the company has gone beyond direct suppliers to audit upstream material suppliers, where environmental problems are usually more severe. Apple has also allowed third-party verification to ensure results of its corrective actions and cleanup orders.

At the end of a cell phone's life, it becomes electronic waste. Much electronic waste has been sent to developing countries for recycling. However, most developing countries do not have or use modern methods to recycle the glass, circuits, metals, and plastics. When dead cell phones move through informal recycling chains, they often end up doing more damage to the environment than good. At Guiyu, a dumping site in China, villagers heat circuit boards over coal fires to recover lead. The ash from the burning of coal is dumped into local streams and poisons the water supply. The village reportedly has the highest level of cancer-causing dioxins in the world, elevated rates of miscarriages, and children with high levels of lead poisoning.

Cell phone companies like Apple have taken steps to prevent their products from winding up in places like Guiyu. They encourage consumers to send spent devices to local recyclers that safely process electronic waste. Nonetheless, plenty of used cell phones do not go through responsible channels and end up being inappropriately recycled in developing countries. In some developing countries, the environment, despite its increasing degradation, seems a second-tier concern for the public and government. For instance, several national polls in China in 2012 consistently showed that people put such economic and social issues as income inequality and corruption ahead of environmental issues. The enforcement of environmental laws have historically been lax in the country, especially at the local level.

Notes

a. Apple.com. iPhone6 environmental report. Retrieved from www.apple.com/euro/environment/pdf/a/generic/products/iphone/iPhone6_PER_Sept2014.pdf

b. He, H. and Yuan, D. (2011, January 25). Apple's darker side. Retrieved from www.chinadialogue.net/article/show/single/en/4072-Apple-s-darker-side

c. Apple, (2014). Environmental Responsibility Report: 2014 Progress Report, Covering FY2013. Retrieved from http://images.apple.com/environment/pdf/Apple_Environmental_Responsibility_Report_2014.pdf

Sources

1. Greene, J. (2012, September 26). Digging for rare earths: The mines where iPhones are born. CNET. Retrieved from http://news.cnet.com/8301-13579_3-57520121-37/digging-for-rare-earths-the-mines-where-iphones-are-born/

2. Greene, J. (2012, September 26). The environmental pitfalls at the end of an iPhone's life. CNET. Retrieved from http://news.cnet.com/8301-13579_3-57520123-37/the-environmental-pitfalls-at-the-end-of-an-iphones-life/

3. Institute of Public and Environmental Affairs. (2013). Apple opens up. Retrieved from www.ipe.org.cn/Upload/Report-IT-V-Apple-I-EN.pdf

4. *Economist*. (2013, August 8). The East is grey. Retrieved from www.economist.com/news/briefing/21583245-china-worlds-worst-polluter-largest-investor-green-energy-its-rise-will-have

Questions for Case Discussion

1. What are the environmental responsibilities of cell phone companies?
2. How would you evaluate China's response to its environmental problem of rare earth mining?
3. What do you think of Apple's response to the pollution problem in its supply chain?
4. Why is recycling not necessarily a good idea? How do we solve this predicament?

Case 13.4 Corporate Social Responsibility Activities in the Chinese Auto Industry: Examples from Toyota Motor Company and Hyundai Motor Company

Toyota represents one of the top three global automobile companies in terms of the number of vehicles produced and sold. In its 2012 sustainability report, the company clearly stated, "We pursue initiatives for social contributions that focus on 'the environment,' 'traffic safety,' and 'education.' Such activities centering on automobile manufacturing are designed to help people in the wider community and bring them happiness—this is Toyota's aspiration." In a nutshell, Toyota's business activities are based on the concept of ensuring sustainable growth by promoting the virtuous circle, "Producing always better cars. Enriching lives of communities. Establishing a stable base of business."[a]

Consistent with its sustainability principle, Toyota's CSR activities in China focus on the three areas of environmental protection, traffic safety, and human resource development. First, using the Toyota network throughout China, Toyota has introduced an integrated environmental management system in order to reduce environmental pollution caused by automobiles. Recognizing the environmental policy of the Chinese government and the increasing concern about environmental protection among the Chinese, the company has established the China Environmental Commission in order to bring environmental issues to the public's attention. Second, Toyota is vigorously engaged in environmental management at its production sites. Thirteen factories have obtained ISO 14001 certification, the international standard for environmental management systems, and the company provides an education program to make their employees more conscious of environmental issues. Third, Toyota has actively developed and promoted the sale of hybrid vehicles, and launched fuel-efficient motors such as WT-1 in order to reduce environmental pollution emissions and save energy. Fourth, in order to increase the awareness of environmental protection among the Chinese, in collaboration with the relevant Chinese government agencies, the Toyota Environmental Protection Award for China Youth has been given to groups or individuals who made an outstanding contribution to environmental protection. Finally, as part of the implementation of "The 21st Century Chinese Metropolitan Area Environment Greening Initiative," the drinking water project of Hebei Province for combating desertification has been in place since 2001, and by the end of 2009, approximately 3,000 hectares of green space had been created. The significance of this project is noted as it materialized via collaboration between the Chinese and Japanese governments.

As an automobile manufacturer, Toyota is aware of the increase in traffic accidents due to the fast-growing number of vehicles in China and is enthusiastically engaged in reducing the number of accidents by implementing various initiatives. To ensure the safety of its automobiles, Toyota closely monitors the whole process of product development and production, publicizes vehicle safety test results, and holds traffic safety experiment expos. In addition, they take initiatives that increase safety awareness of the entire Chinese society including traffic safety educational events for the general public in collaboration with the Chinese Ministry of Public Security.

Toyota scholarships offer assistance to low-income group students in western China who have shown excellent academic performance, and since 2000, the company has sponsored primary school construction and remodeling, mainly in Sichuan province and Tianjin. Second, the Toyota-Jean Bay Industrial Center was established to train a specialized labor force and technicians for automotive manufacturing in a rural community. The Toyota Technical Education Program (T-TEP) was introduced to develop a labor force trained for after sales service. Third, Toyota has established the Study Assistance Fund and research centers on industrial development and environmental protection in collaboration with the School of Public Policy & Management at Tsinghua University. Finally, Toyota has supported the establishment of vocational schools for auto operation, maintenance, and repair by providing its own educational program to the Chinese Ministry of Education.

Hyundai Motor Company, a South Korean automobile company which has recently risen to the sixth largest producer in the global auto market has also been engaged in various types of CSR or sustainability initiatives to demonstrate good corporate citizenship and thus enhance its corporate image. The following statement appears on the company's website. "As an active corporate citizen of the global society, Hyundai Motor Company has a clear and firm philosophy and conviction about its social responsibilities."[b] Hyundai's CSR slogan of "Moving the world together," symbolizes the company's feature of being an automobile company. It has four "Move" businesses that involve environmental protection (Green Move), community service (Happy Move), transportation safety expansion (Safe Move), and facilitation of convenient transport access for the disabled (Easy Move).

Due to its very nature as an automobile company, Hyundai's CSR activities focus on environmental management. The Green Zone China Project is its flagship program to achieve this goal in China. This project is being implemented in the Chakan Nore region, approximately 660 km north of Beijing, close to Kunsantak Desert in Inner Mongolia known as the origin of the yellow dust storm. The effective prevention of desertification and an ecological restoration campaign between 2008 and 2012 have turned 38 million square meters of the desert in the region into a green prairie. This successful transformation of desert land has drawn a lot of attention from the media and enhanced the company's image as it was a result of the collaborative efforts among Hyundai employees, global as well as Chinese student volunteers, the Chinese government, and the Inner Mongolian Autonomous government. Other green zone projects were also implemented in Beijing such as cultivating forests to support the Beijing Green Olympics. For this cause, Hyundai Motor participated in "Planting Activities of Multinationals for Beijing Green Olympics" organized by China's Ministry of Commerce. Donations were also made for green zone projects in Beijing Olympic Park.

Hyundai Motor has supported building schools and supplying vehicle-related learning equipment and materials throughout China. First, in April 2007, the company founded Hyundai Automobile Technical Training School in Rizhao, Shandong province to provide vocational and professional training for people who would like to pursue a career in auto engineering and mechanics. Second, in April 2009, Hyundai sponsored the "Economics Students Debate Competition" among the students attending universities in Beijing in which 15 excellent students from Beijing University, Tsinghua University, and other schools participated. Third, from April 2008, in Beijing, the film "Invisible Wings" was screened to more than 200 elementary and junior high school students. The film contains a public message aimed to help elementary and middle school students cultivate leadership and develop an ability to overcome any adversity that they might face at young ages. Fourth, Hyundai donated 7,000,000 RMB worth of computers and books, stationery and supplies, etc., to K–12 students in poor regions. In addition, dozens of vehicles and hundreds of engines were donated to major universities throughout China, including Tsinghua University and Peking University, for professors and students to enjoy a better learning environment with the latest educational tools.

Hyundai is also actively engaged in a variety of community service activities in those areas devastated by natural disasters. From late January to early February of 2008, Hyundai donated five Tucson vehicles in an area of heavy snowfall in southern China for disaster recovery and also donated one million RMB to the Chinese Red Cross. In May 2008, to support the restoration of earthquake-affected areas in Sichuan province, Hyundai contributed 16.22 million RMB in relief funds through the Chinese Red Cross.

Notes

a. Toyota Motor Corporation. Toyota Sustainability Report, 2012. Retrieved from www.toyota-global.com/sustainability/report/sr/12/pdf/sustainability_report12_me.pdf
b. Hyundai Corporate Social Responsibility. Retrieved from http://worldwide.hyundai.com/WW/Corporate/CorporateInformation/CSR/index.html

Sources

1. Toyota Motor Corporation. Toyota Sustainability Report, 2012. Retrieved from www.toyota-global.com/sustainability/report/sr/12/pdf/sustainability_report12_me.pdf
2. Hyundai Corporate Social Responsibility. Retrieved from http://worldwide.hyundai.com/WW/Corporate/CorporateInformation/CSR/index.html
3. Koo, M. (2013, June 21). Greening Inner Mongolia: Hyundai's CSR strategy to improve the environment. *Forbes*. Retrieved from www.forbes.com/sites/meehyoekoo/2013/06/21/hyundai-motor-group-greening-inner-mongolia-with-csr/
4. Min-Kyo Seo. (2011). A comparative case study on the CSR strategies of Toyota and Hyundai Motor in China. *International Commerce and Information Review* (in Korean), *13*(4):151–176.
5. Japanese Corporate News Network. (2008, April 8). Toyota environmental protection aid program for China's youth hands out awards. Retrieved from www.toyota-global.com/sustainability/social_contribution/environment/overseas/env_youth/

Questions for Case Discussion

1. What are the similarities and differences in CSR activities between Toyota Motor Company and Hyundai Motor Company in China?
2. Which company do you think has more successfully integrated its CSR activities into its business strategy and why?
3. What suggestions do you have to improve corporate sustainability for each company?

Case 13.5 Indian Farmers and Monsanto

In the year 2009, 17,638 farmers committed suicide in India, about one farmer every 30 minutes. According to a 2011 report by the Center for Human Rights and Global Justice (CHRGJ) at New York University, more than a quarter of a million Indian farmers have committed suicide in the last 16 years, the largest wave of recorded suicides in human history.[a] Many of those farmers are cash crop famers, and small cotton farmers in particular.

The CHRGJ report indicates that this tragedy is mainly attributable to market reforms, multinational agribusiness, and inadequate government policies. Years of economic reforms have opened Indian farmers to global competition and new biotechnology. MNCs have made deep inroads in rural India, a vast and alluring market, with new agricultural tools and products. To improve productivity, many farmers have turned away from traditional farming methods to high-cost seeds, fertilizers, and pesticides. Those promising but expensive tools and products have pushed Indian farmers to take on larger loans, often from moneylenders charging exorbitant interest rates, and exposing them to greater risks. Pest problems and unexpected weather conditions have become more perilous than they used to be. The Indian government has responded to the crisis by expanding rural credit and promising investment in rural infrastructure. But more action is needed to ensure businesses are not intruding upon the pleasures of human rights, according to the CHRGJ report.

The report highlights Monsanto, a biotechnology company based in St. Louis, Missouri, for its role in cotton farming. Monsanto invented Bt cotton, a genetically modified seed that is resistant to bollworm infection. In 2002, the Indian government allowed Monsanto to sell Bt cotton. Since then, the seed has spread through cotton farming in India. Costing nearly twice as much as ordinary varieties, the seed can reduce the use of pesticides by 25 percent. A U.S. Department of Agriculture study reveals that the adoption of hybrid cotton containing the Bt gene has increased India's cotton yields and exports. It is expected that yield growth will continue as the planted area increases and cultivation practices advance. However, cotton farming in non-irrigated fields is risky as the harvest consumes a lot of water. It takes only 500 liters of water to produce a kilogram of potatoes but it takes more than 25,000 liters to produce a kilogram of cotton. The crops of Bt cotton with irrigation are typically higher than those without irrigation. Many Indian farmers borrow money to purchase the Bt cottonseeds, but when the crop fails due to lack of water, they often become indebted, and some kill themselves.

As one the world's largest biotechnology companies, Monsanto is aware of its social responsibilities. In its 2012 Sustainability Report, the company states that its mission is to deliver agricultural production solutions to help meet the world's growing food, energy and fiber needs, conserve natural resources and protect the environment, and improve lives.

> Monsanto has promised to support farmers in doubling yields in core crops (corn, soy canola and cotton) by 2030 and also committed to produce each ton with one-third fewer resources (land, water and energy). Additionally, the company pledged to help farmers, including five million people in resource-poor farm families, improve their standard of living by 2020.[b]

According to the company's report, cotton farmers in India are ahead of the pace to achieve the goal of doubling yields. Through many partner-based initiatives, Monsanto has been developing and providing solutions for smallholder farmers in India. For instance, Monsanto introduced Project V-Care in India's Vidarbha region. Crops in Vidarbha, located in central India, need a lot of rain. When droughts frequently hit the region, crop yields and farmers' incomes decrease. Project V-Care was proposed to upgrade crop management practices, primarily through education and training in eight cotton districts. Three goals were set: implementing better crop management, providing customized recommendations on fertilization, and exhibiting the economic benefits of new farming practices. The Monsanto team brought together cottonseed dealers and agricultural scientists, and met with farmers regularly based on the crop's stage and conditions. They guided farmers on sowing spacing, application of pesticides, and drip irrigation. In its first year, Project V-Care produced a 42 percent growth in cotton production and a 15 percent rise in earnings per acre. Monsanto also identified 250 influential farmers and asked each to share knowledge with at least 50 more farmers.

Monsanto has invented the first biotech drought solution, a drought-tolerant genetic trait for agricultural crops. The trait is one of the first technologies developed as part of research collaboration between Monsanto and BASF, a chemicals giant based in Germany. The collaboration is pioneering a suite of "stress traits" that will improve crop yields under water stress and other tough environmental conditions. Unlike reversing market reforms, innovation in the field of sustainable agriculture is politically feasible and less likely to have adverse consequences. It is probably the only way to simultaneously raise yields, increase the efficiency with which inputs are used, and reduce the negative environmental effects of food production.[c]

Nevertheless, the controversy over genetically modified organisms (GMOs) continues. GMOs are now the only seeds available in some areas and farmers have to pay an annual royalty whenever they are replanted. The GMOs may need additional fertilizers, more pesticides, more water, and consequently more money from farmers. In addition to the hidden costs, people are becoming concerned about the health effects of GMOs, especially in developed countries. While some researchers confirm the safety of GMO crops, others claim that GMO foods can be toxic and allergenic. BASF recently announced that it planned to stop its production of GMO crops in Europe because the majority of consumers, farmers, and politicians do not accept them. In the U.S., many people would like see GMO labeling mandatory. This is a reality multinational agribusinesses have to face nowadays.

Notes

a.　The Center for Human Rights and Global Justice (CHRGJ) at New York University School of Law. (2012, May 11). Every thirty minutes: Farmer suicides,

human rights, and the agrarian crisis in India. Retrieved from http://chrgj.org/
wp-content/uploads/2012/10/Farmer-Suicides.pdf
b.   AgriMarketing. (2013, June 20). Monsanto releases its annual sustainability
report. Retrieved from www.agrimarketing.com/s/82698
c.   Pentland, W. (2011, May 18). Every 30 minutes an Indian farmer commits
suicide, biotech is not to blame. *Forbes.* Retrieved from www.forbes.com/sites/
williampentland/2011/05/18/every-30-minutes-an-indian-farmer-commits-
suicide-biotech-is-not-to-blame/

Sources

1.   Sengupta, S. (2008, September 19). On India's farms, a plague of suicide. *New
York Times.* Retrieved from www.nytimes.com/2006/09/19/world/asia/19india.
html.
2.   Monsanto. Monsanto 2015 sustainability report. Retrieved from www.monsanto.
com/whoweare/Pages/corporate-sustainability-report.aspx.
3.   Pentland, W. (2011, May 18). Every 30 minutes an Indian farmer commits suicide,
biotech is not to blame. *Forbes.* Retrieved from www.forbes.com/sites/william-
pentland/2011/05/18/every-30-minutes-an-indian-farmer-commits-suicide-
biotech-is-not-to-blame/
4.   Huffington Post. (2012, September 21). 'Bitter Seeds' film tells of suicide and
GMO effects on India's farmers. Retrieved from www.huffingtonpost.com/
zester-daily/bitter-seeds-film_b_1902221.html

Questions for Case Discussion

1.   Is Monsanto responsible for the suicide of Indian cotton farmers or not? Defend
your position.
2.   What are the social responsibilities of Monsanto in conducting business in a
developing country like India?
3.   How would you evaluate Monsanto's efforts to meet social responsibilities?
4.   What is the role of genetic engineering for crop improvement in achieving
economic, environmental, and social sustainability?

Managing Sustainability

Corporate Social Responsibility and Business Ethics

I. What is Sustainability?

As the impact of corporate business practices on society and the environment have become increasingly profound, people are more and more concerned with issues such as sustainable development, corporate sustainability (CS), corporate social responsibility (CSR), and business ethics. These terms, especially "sustainability," have become buzzwords for companies. What is sustainable development? How is corporate sustainability related to corporate social responsibility? More importantly, how should MNCs address these issues when they conduct business in global markets? The ever growing cross-border trade and investment have made these issues more significant for MNCs and brought complex and complicated implications to their stakeholders.

The term "sustainability" concerns the long-term survival of a society or an organization since it measures the ability to sustain or the capacity to endure. Sustainable development is defined as development that meets the needs of the present without compromising the ability of future generations to meet their own needs.[1] Similarly, corporate sustainability deals with meeting the needs of a company's stakeholders such as shareholders, employees, and suppliers without compromising its ability to meet the needs of future stakeholders.[2] On the other hand, corporate social responsibility is defined as "the continuing commitment by business to behave ethically and contribute to economic development while improving the quality of life of the work force and their families as well as the local community and society at large."[3] Firms are expected to practice ethical behaviors in order to fulfill corporate social responsibility. Both CS and CSR encompass how a company incorporates social and environmental concerns in business operations and interactions with stakeholders.[4] In recent years, these two terms have been converging and often used interchangeably.[5] Yet, distinction may still exist due to different academic traditions. CS usually pays more attention to environment while CSR tends to focus on the social aspects of business.

Figure 13.1 illustrates how these terms are related to one another. As sustainable development is the ultimate goal for the global community to achieve, companies contribute to this by fostering corporate sustainability, which is obtained through the practice of engaging corporate social responsibility with ethical behavior. Using this framework, we will first discuss sustainable development.

II. Sustainable Development

Sustainable development focuses on achieving balance between current economic growth and environmental preservation for future generations. It includes three interdependent but mutually reinforcing pillars, as depicted in Figure 13.2, of economic growth (profit), social development (people), and

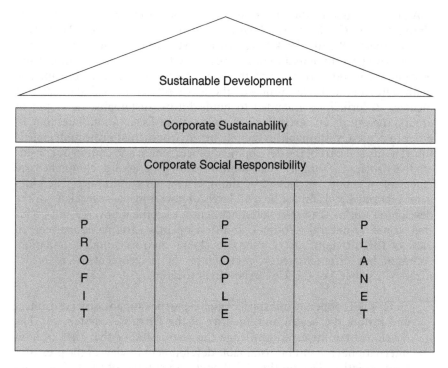

Figure 13.1 Relationship between Sustainable Development, Corporate Sustainability, and Corporate Social Responsibility

Source: Kaptein, M. & Wempe, J. (2002). *The Balanced Company: A Theory of Corporate Integrity.* New York: Oxford University Press.

environmental protection (planet).[6] The notion of sustainable development reminds us of environmental limitations that inhibit present and future needs. Leaders from developing countries claim that developed countries are at fault because their lavish food and energy consumption patterns produced massive amounts of waste and pollution. For instance, it was estimated that 70 percent of annual global industrial carbon dioxide emissions originate in developed countries where only about 20 percent of the world's population resides.[7] On the other hand, developed countries blame developing countries for their rapid but reckless industrialization without paying adequate attention to protecting the environment. The Chilean mining incident of Case 13.1 demonstrates typical social and environmental issues associated with economic growth in developing countries. Despite these conflicting views, it is generally accepted that unrestrained population growth combined with overconsumption has contributed to uninterrupted environmental degradation. In order to preserve irreplaceable natural resources and reduce pollution of the planet, governments need to redirect international and national policies for economic and social development.

A key milestone in the history of sustainable development was the 1992 United Nations Conference on Environment and Development (UNCED) in Rio de Janeiro, Brazil, also known as the Earth Summit. One hundred and seventy-two governments and thousands of NGOs attended the Summit and brought the world's attention to the issue of sustainable development. The main outcome of the Summit was the Rio Declaration, a document that includes 27 principles intended to guide future sustainable development around the world.[8] In particular, Principle 4 of the Declaration states that, in order to achieve sustainable development, environmental protection constitutes an integral part of the development process chain and cannot be considered in isolation from it.[9] The Summit also generated a comprehensive blueprint of action sanctioned by the international community. The blueprint presented a vision for how all levels of government—especially in the developing world—can take voluntary action to combat poverty and pollution, conserve natural resources, and develop in a sustainable manner. In view of the different contributions to global environmental degradation, common but differentiated responsibilities of governments were recognized.[10] Principle 7 of the Rio Declaration proclaims,

> States shall cooperate in a spirit of global partnership to conserve, protect and restore the health and integrity of the Earth's ecosystem. . . . The developed countries acknowledge the responsibility that they bear in international pursuit of sustainable development in view of the pressures their societies place on the global environment and of the technologies and financial resources they command.[11]

Today, efforts to ensure proper implementation of the Rio Summit principles and action plan continue. In 2012 the U.N. organized the Rio + 20 Conference on Sustainable Development in Rio de Janeiro to celebrate the 20th anniversary of the 1992 United Nations Conference on Environment and Development. At the conference, a document called "The Future We Want" was constructed to reaffirm all the principles of the Rio Declaration and commit to the action plan.

III. Corporate Sustainability

Corporate sustainability is the concept of business being accountable for how it manages the impact of its processes on stakeholders, and taking responsibility for producing a positive impact on society.[12] Consistent with the concept of sustainable development, the notion of corporate sustainability encompasses three dimensions: social, environmental, and economic. The three dimensions reflect the three Ps of the so-called "triple bottom line" illustrated before as the pillars in Figure 13.2: people, planet, and profit. Any entities participating in economic activities should do their best to find the right balance among these dimensions in making key decisions. They should operate in ways that secure long-term economic performance and avoid short-term behavior that is socially detrimental or environmentally wasteful.[13] They should be encouraged to identify new and innovative ways to create

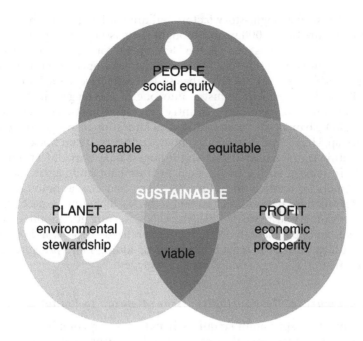

Figure 13.2 Corporate Sustainability

Source: Defining Sustainability: Triple Bottom Line, New Leaf Sustainability Consulting. Retrieved from http://newleaf-llc.com/2013/07/defining-sustainability-triple-bottom-line/

value and mitigate risk in the social, environmental, and economic dimensions of sustainability. Specifically, corporate sustainability can be explained based on three principles that we now will examine in more detail: social integrity, environmental responsibility, and economic prosperity.[14]

I. Social Integrity: Issues Related to People

Social integrity focuses on fulfilling the social responsibility of companies to various stakeholders with whom their business has a direct or indirect relationship. For example, companies are responsible for maintaining safe working conditions and providing wages above sustenance levels for their employees. To consumers, companies have an obligation to deliver safe and reliable products. Companies are also expected to ethically source raw materials or ingredients from their suppliers.

For MNCs, most commonly cited issues related to people include child workers, sweatshops, low wages, poor working conditions, etc. Due to the continuous expansion of the global supply chain both vertically and horizontally, MNCs find it increasingly challenging since they have to work with a number of suppliers to pursue social integrity worldwide. The controversies involving Apple's suppliers in China, described in Case 13. 2, exemplify some difficult social issues MNCs face in their outsourcing process.

The collapse of an eight-story factory building in Bangladesh in May 2013 that killed more than 1,000 people brought these issues once again to global attention. Bangladesh is one of the developing countries where workers receive the lowest wages in the world and factories operate with the worst health and safety conditions. Nonetheless, low costs have made Bangladesh's $20 billion USD garment industry into one of the biggest in the world, accounting for 80 percent of the country's annual exports. The country has about 4,500 garment factories that make clothes for many global retailers such as Gap, H&M, Wal-Mart, J.C. Penney, and Sears. It's on track to surpass China within the next several years as the largest apparel manufacturer in the world.[15] To prevent such a tragic incident from happening again, nearly 20 North American retailers including Wal-Mart and Gap announced a five-year safety plan for Bangladesh garment factories, including inspecting every factory within a year.[16] Meanwhile, the U.S. government announced that it would suspend Bangladesh from the Generalized System of Preferences (GSP), a favorable tariff-reduction program, adding more pressure for the improvement of working conditions in Bangladesh.[17]

2. Environmental Responsibility: Issues Related to Planet

Environmental responsibility requires firms to not only comply with the laws and regulations that govern the treatment of the environment but also actively adopt business practices that are conducive to environmental protection. Traditionally, environmental protection was considered to be "in the public interest" and thus governments have assumed principal responsibility for assuring environmental management.[18] Nowadays, companies are expected to make greater contributions to environmental protections, not simply following government regulations and directions. Their responsibilities include not only reducing the adverse effects of product use on the environment but also utilizing resources more efficiently through reusing and recycling. Companies are expected to be environmentally responsible throughout their business activities, from sourcing to production, distribution, and disposal. Case 13.3 describes the environmental impact of a cell phone in its life cycle and corresponding responsibilities of cell phone companies.

Air pollution and waste dumping are among the key environmental problems facing MNCs. For example, multinational oil companies are often charged for seriously threatening the livelihood of their neighboring communities due to the many forms of oil-generated environmental pollution. In some cases, farming and fishing have become impossible or extremely difficult in oil-affected areas, and even drinking water has become scarce.[19] These problems can be costly to the public and society. It has been estimated that the total damage costs associated with emissions of air pollutants in the U.S. are between $71 billion USD and $277 billion USD per year (0.7–2.8 percent of GDP).[20] In the case of China, the estimated health costs of air pollution are even higher, representing about 3.8 percent of that country's GDP, according to the World Bank.[21]

As governments and the general public become more conscious of and concerned about environmental issues, MNCs are facing increasing pressure and scrutiny. Some have taken the initiative in changing business practices. Starbucks, for instance, has developed a three-year climate change mitigation plan to reduce emissions by buying renewable energy and developing energy management measures.[22] Since 1990, McDonald's has utilized the McRecycling program in order to decrease the company's overall environmental impact. The purpose of this program is not only to lessen the amount of materials and resources used through efficient packaging and design but also to reduce as much waste as ecologically and economically viable and then recycle what is left. On average, each U.S. McDonald's restaurant recycles over 17 tons of corrugated cardboard and approximately 13,000 pounds of used cooking oil annually.[23]

While all firms are obligated to abide by local environmental regulations, not all MNCs strive for environmental responsibility. Some intentionally choose to locate their operations in places where environmental regulations are relatively lax and loose.

3. Economic Prosperity: Issues Related to Profit

Economic prosperity emphasizes that a company should use its resources in the most efficient and responsible manner so that the business maintains its profitability and stability in the long run. The fundamental basis of long-term, above-average financial performance is sustainable competitive advantage.[24] This dimension of corporate sustainability aims at creating competitive advantage for the company by discovering new ways of lowering costs and/or increasing value for their customers and society. The key is to identify product offerings and business operations that are economically profitable as well as socially and environmentally responsible.[25]

If a company's business is closely tied to a social issue, this will create new opportunities for the company to leverage its resources and capabilities, not only making profits but also benefiting society. For instance, Toyota's response to public concern about auto emissions gave rise to the hybrid-engine Prius, which has not only reduced pollutants but also given Toyota a technological advantage and handsome profits.[26] Toyota has continued to develop next-generation electric powered vehicles that use lightweight and energy-saving technologies. The company tries to conserve natural resources and reduce CO_2 emissions at all stages of new car development including design, manufacturing, and logistics.[27] This illustrates how the notion of sustainability is understood as a shared value between the company and society and is integrated into the company's competitive strategies.

IV. Corporate Social Responsibility

Corporate social responsibility typically encompasses the economic, legal, ethical, and discretionary expectations that society has of organizations at a given point in time.[28] The goal of CSR is to accept responsibility for the company's actions and encourage a positive impact through its activities on the environment, consumers, employees, shareholders, communities, and other stakeholders. As seen in Figure 13.1, CSR can be understood as an intermediary stage where the three aspects of CS are materialized. In other words, sustainability objectives can be embodied in specific social responsibilities companies need to fulfill. The key is to consider not only current but also future stakeholders.

As illustrated in Figure 13.3, the pyramid of global CSR suggests that companies need to fulfill four different types of responsibilities to global business stakeholders.[29] They consist of economic, legal, ethical, and philanthropic responsibility from the bottom to the top. *Economic responsibility* means that firms exist to make a profit. They need to fulfill their basic responsibility to their stakeholders such as paying wages to their employees and dividends to their investors. Companies that cannot fulfill this fundamental responsibility do not have a *raison d'être*. Certainly, this does not mean that companies can do anything to make a profit. *Legal responsibility* requires that firms do not violate the laws and regulations of the countries where they are conducting business. They are allowed to make a profit only within the legal boundary that prescribes acceptable behavior. Legal systems and requirements for firms may vary from country to country. However, meeting legal responsibility does not always result in fulfilling ethical responsibility. For example, although transfer pricing is a legally permitted business practice for MNCs to take advantage of through their globally integrated operations, it may not always be considered ethical as they could manipulate the prices of exports and imports charged for their internal transactions to maximize profit. *Ethical responsibility*, a higher level of commitment, requires companies to do the right thing, which may or may not be specified in laws and regulations. Companies should not make a profit out of human misery under any circumstances since human rights represent a universal core value. It should be noted, however, that the moral standards and criteria used to

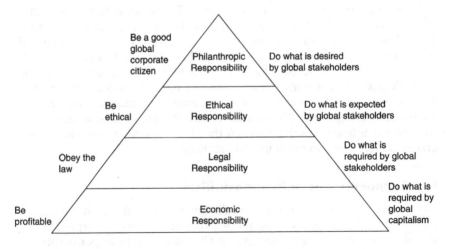

Figure 13.3 Pyramid of Global Corporate Social Responsibility

Source: Carroll, A. (2004). *Managing Ethically with Global Stakeholders: A Present and Future Challenge.* Academy of Management Executive.

determine ethical responsibility are not necessarily identical across countries. Therefore, many MNCs adopt their own corporate codes of ethics, surpassing most country standards, that serve as a global guideline for their employees' moral behavior. For example, as different countries may have various regulations to control CO_2 emissions, it is MNCs' own policies and practices that decide the self-controlled level of CO_2 emissions to fulfill their ethical responsibility. Finally, *philanthropic responsibility* comprises any kind of voluntary activities by a company that are neither required by law nor expected of businesses in an ethical sense. These activities are mainly targeted to help people live better and support the communities in which they live and work. They include monetary donations and aid given to local organizations and impoverished communities in developing countries. Case 13.4 illustrates how global auto companies such as Toyota and Hyundai are practicing philanthropic responsibility.

The Global Compact is the world's largest and most inclusive corporate citizenship program, covering ten principles in the areas of human rights, labor, environment, and anti-corruption (Refer to Table 13.1). The U.N. took an initiative to launch the Global Compact in 2000 to encourage businesses

Table 13.1 Ten Principles of the U.N. Global Compact

	PRINCIPLES
HUMAN RIGHTS	1. Businesses should support and respect the protection of internationally proclaimed human rights; and 2. make sure that they are not complicit in human rights abuses.
LABOR	3. Buinesses should uphold the freedom of association and the effective recognition of the right to collective bargaining; 4. the elimination of all forms of forced and compulsory labour; 5. the effective abolition of child labour; and 6. the elimination of discrimination in respect of employment and occupation.
ENVIORNMENT	7. Businesses should support a precautionary approach to environmental challenges; 8. undertake initiatives to promote greater environmental responsibility; and 9. encourage the development and diffusion of environmentally friendly technologies.
ANTI-CORRUPTION	10. Businesses should work against corruption in all its forms, including extortion and bribery.

Source: www. unglobalcompact.org/what-is-go/mission/principles

worldwide to adopt sustainable and socially responsible policies, and to report on their implementation.[30]

In response to mounting pressure from government organizations as well as NGOs who closely monitor business practices, MNCs have intensified their efforts to align their values and behaviors with the expectations of various stakeholders. Why do MNCs have to care about CSR and what are the anticipated benefits of upholding CSR? First, CSR helps to build and promote a positive company reputation by demonstrating good corporate citizenship. CSR initiatives reveal the values of a company and thus can attract and retain customers who share the same values. A company's reputation based on CSR can also be used to recruit a global capable workforce as employees often feel proud of their company's positive impact on society. Second, CSR can be integrated with the development of an MNC's competitive advantage. A thorough understanding of the social perspective and context in which a company's business operates can help develop a strategy that will mutually benefit the company and society.[31] If MNCs can leverage CSR to create a competitive advantage, they achieve better performance than their competitors who cannot. Despite these benefits, however, some companies are still hesitant to increase expenditures on CSR initiatives as they are not sure whether the additional costs incurred will eventually be reclaimed in terms of higher profit. They tend to view CSR as simply eroding shareholders' profit by requiring costly investments in socially responsible activities.[32]

V. Ethical Challenges to CS and CSR Issues

Although the importance of CS and CSR is generally recognized, people and business practitioners in particular in different countries may have diverse moral standards when deciding on their CS and CSR activities. How should MNCs deal with the health and safety of global workers, compensation for suppliers, air pollution, and depletion of scarce resources across borders? As business ethics (i.e. moral principles that guide the way a business behaves) differ from one country to another, so does the ethical responsibility expected of MNCs. Case 13. 5 presents an ethical challenge Monsanto, a multinational biotech company, has to face in rural India.

If business ethics between home and host country clash, which one should MNCs follow? Three different views are introduced here to help shed some light on this question.

Ethical Absolutism (Universalism): This is a view that the same ethical responsibility or moral standards should be applied to all companies conducting business across all borders. A few years ago, Mattel, the world's largest toy manufacturer, was accused of an incident that caused the deaths of children due to an allegedly lethal level of lead content in the toys produced by a Chinese factory that Mattel contracted. Critics argue that Mattel should have closely monitored the safety standards of the toys to assure the quality of their products, whether produced domestically or abroad. According to this view, firms are expected to fulfill the same level of ethical responsibility regardless of the business environment in which they operate. However, this view is often subject to criticism since it uniformly applies the same yardstick without considering unique business environments in different countries.

Ethical Relativism: This view takes the host country's values and norms into consideration when making moral judgment on companies' business practices. As a result, it contends that companies should adopt the ethics of the host country in which they operate since ethics are culturally determined. According to this view, the regulations on child labor or environmental protection vary across countries. It is generally perceived that developing countries assign their first priority to rapid economic growth rather than environmental protection. Furthermore, environmental regulations and enforcement in these countries are not as rigorous as those in industrialized countries. According to the view of ethical relativism, therefore, some flexibility should be allowed in determining what is ethical or not, in consideration of the values and norms of a specific country. This means that what is regarded as unethical behavior in a home country may be regarded as ethical behavior in a host country and vice versa. For example, in some developing countries, a higher level of CO_2 emissions is allowed as industrialization is desired as a more imminent goal to achieve than environmental protection.

Naïve Immoralists: This view suggests that companies simply watch and follow the practices of their competitors rather than apply an internally developed moral standard. Companies use others' activities, which may not even be considered ethical, as standards to measure the morality of their own employees' business activities. For example, if their competitors are bribing government officials to obtain business deals, the naïve immoralists would not mind doing the same thing. It is not the legal requirement or moral standard but business practices of their competitors that become the yardstick to judge whether a business practice is ethically acceptable or not.

VI. How to Resolve Ethical Dilemmas

An ethical dilemma refers to a situation in which guiding moral principles are in conflict for determining which course of action is right or wrong. Reflecting different perspectives toward moral standards, MNCs conducting businesses in the global market often find it difficult to reconcile these differences. How can they resolve the differences between home country ethics and host country ethics? Under what circumstances can they justify ethical absolutism versus ethical relativism? Two major approaches have been introduced to help managers resolve these issues.

I. Ethical Algorithm

Thomas Donalson, a professor in Ethics at the Wharton School, introduced this approach of developing and using an algorithm—an interpretive tool or mechanism—that managers can use in determining the ethical implications of their decisions. With this approach he classified the moral reasons involving a company's decision-making into two categories.[33] The first category specifies that the moral reason that a company's practice is permissible has to do with the relative level of economic development. The second category specifies that the moral reason that a company's practice is permissible has nothing to do with the relative level of economic development. If the disagreement between home and host country belongs to the first category, the company's practice is permissible if and only if the members of the home country would, under conditions of similar economic development, regard this particular practice permissible.[34] For example, an MNC can pay a lower wage to workers in a host country if the wage was acceptable in the home country when it was at relatively the same level of economic development with the host country. In other words, economic underdevelopment can justify why the company is not paying the same wage. In the case of the second category, corporate practice is permissible only if it is not a direct violation of basic human rights, or it is impossible to conduct business without undertaking that particular practice.[35] For example, many MNCs contend that it is impossible to conduct business in certain developing countries without paying bribes. However, if you can find any other company that is not involved in bribery, you are not justified in using bribery either. In addition, a company should not tolerate any kind of inhumane behavior since economic underdevelopment cannot be used as an excuse for violating basic human rights.

2. Contingency Model

Another useful framework for resolving ethical dilemmas was developed by Kohles and Buller, scholars in Ethics, and focuses on three dimensions: intensity, urgency, and influence.[36] Intensity refers to whether or not the particular practice under scrutiny relates to universal core values such as human life

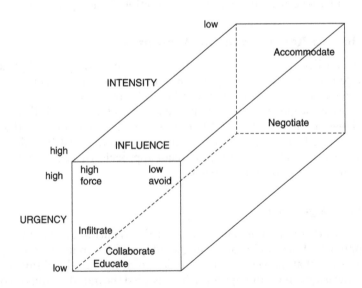

Figure 13.4 A Contingency Model of Cross-Cultural Ethical Conflict Strategies

Source: Kohles, J. and Buller, P. (1994). Resolving cross-cultural ethical conflict: Exploring alternative strategies. *Journal of Business Ethics.* 13(1): 31–38.

and freedom, and the consensus of society on the issue. Urgency looks at how quickly the practice needs to be corrected, such as requiring immediate action to stop a devastating effect on human beings or the environment. Influence measures how much power firms can exert in changing the situation or practice. Firms need to evaluate these three dimensions simultaneously in order to identify optimal strategies to effectively deal with ethical dilemmas across borders. They can adopt one of the following seven strategies depending upon the relative level of each of these dimensions: avoiding, forcing, education, infiltration, negotiation, accommodation, and collaboration.[37] Figure 13.4 illustrates a contingency model that suggests optimal strategies under different situations where firms are faced with ethical dilemmas across countries. For example, if an MNC with a strong reputation abuses workers in a host developing country by not providing a safe working environment, it needs to use the "forcing" strategy to correct such malpractice immediately since it meets all three conditions of intensity, urgency, and influence at the highest level.

Key Terms

Sustainability, sustainable development, corporate sustainability, corporate social responsibility (CSR), United Nations Conference on Environment and Development (UNCED), Earth Summit, social integrity, environmental responsibility, economic prosperity, Global Compact, pyramid of global CSR, ethical absolutism, ethical relativism, naïve immoralists, ethical dilemmas, ethical algorithm, contingency model

Review Questions

1. Who do you think should be more responsible for sustainable development between developed and developing countries? Defend your position and compare your answers with those of your classmates.
2. Evaluate the progress of the 1991 Rio Summit agreement documented in 27 Principles of the Rio Declaration. What have been the most significant achievements to date?
3. What are the main challenges that MNCs are going to face in practicing corporate sustainability when conducting business across borders, and how can they effectively meet them?
4. Discuss a specific ethical dilemma that falls into category 1 or category 2 respectively as introduced in the ethical algorithm model. How useful do you find this model in resolving ethical dilemmas?
5. Using the contingency model, identify and discuss an ethical dilemma that may justify an adoption of each of the seven different strategies introduced in the model.

Internet Exercise

The following website (www.corpwatch.org) provides news, analysis, and research tools to respond to corporate wrongdoings and exploitation around the globe. Using this website, please identify and discuss each of the most recent unethical issues concerning human rights, anti-corruption, environment, and labor.

Notes

1 World Commission on Environment and Development (WCED). (1987). *Our Common Future.* Oxford: Oxford University Press, 4.
2 Dyllick, T. and Hockerts, K. (2002). Beyond the business case for corporate sustainability. *Business Strategy & the Environment, 11*(2), 130–141.
3 World Business Council for Sustainable Development defines corporate social responsibility. World Business Council for Sustainable Development (WBCSD) http://old.wbcsd.org/work-program/business-role/previous-work/corporate-social-responsibility.aspx
4 Van Marrewijk, Marcel. (2003). Concepts and definitions of CSR and corporate sustainability: Between agency and communion. *Journal of Business Ethics, 44*(2/3), 95–105.
5 Montiel, Ivan. (2008). Corporate social responsibility and corporate sustainability: Separate pasts, common futures. *Organization & Environment, 21*(3), 245–269.
6 World Health Organization. (2005, September 15). 2005 World Summit Outcome Document.
7 Boden, T. A., Marland, G., and Andres, R. J. (2011). Global, regional, and national fossil-fuel CO_2 emissions. Carbon Dioxide Information Analysis Center, Oak Ridge National Laboratory, DOI: 10.3334/CDIAC/00001_V2011. 2009 and 2010 estimates also from CDIAC, by Tom Boden and T. J. Blasing.
8 United Nations Environment Program (UNEP). Rio Declaration on Environment and Development. Retrieved from www.unep.org/Documents.multilingual/Default.asp?DocumentID=78&ArticleID=1163
9 Ibid.
10 United Nations. (2012, June 20–22). *Report of the United Nations Conference on Sustainable Development.* Rio de Janeiro, Brazil.
11 Ibid.
12 Fontaine, Michael. (2013). Corporate social responsibility and sustainability: The new bottom line? *International Journal of Business and Social Science, 4*(4), 110–119.
13 Porter, Michael and Kramer, Mark. (2006). The link between competitive advantage and corporate social responsibility. *Harvard Business Review* (December), 78–92.
14 Bansal, Pratima. (2005). Evolving sustainably: A longitudinal study of corporate sustainable development, *Strategic Management Journal, 26*(3), 197–218.
15 Fox, E.J. (2013, May 1). Shoppers face tough choices over Bangladesh. CNN Money. Retrieved from http://money.cnn.com/2013/05/01/news/companies/bangladesh-garment-factory/
16 Huffington Post. (2013, July 10). Walmart, Gap Announce Bangladesh factory safety plan with other North American Retailers. Retrieved from www.huffingtonpost.com/2013/07/10/bangladesh-factory-safety-plan-walmart_n_3573209.html
17 *Washington Post.* (2013, June 28). U.S. suspends Bangladesh's trade privileges due to labor concerns.
18 Mazurkiewicz, Piotr. (2004). Corporate environmental responsibility: Is a common CSR framework possible? Working Paper. World Bank.

19 Essential Action and Global Exchange. (2000, January 25). Oil for nothing: Multinational corporations, environmental destruction, death and impunity in the Niger Delta. www.essentialaction.org/shell/report/

20 Muller, Nicolas Z. and Mendelsohn, Robert. (2007, July). Measuring the damages of air pollution in the United States. *Journal of Environmental Economics and Management, 54.*

21 The World Bank (2007). Costs of pollution in China: Economic estimates of physical damages, rural development, natural resources and environment management unit, East Asia and Pacific Region. Retrieved from http://documents.worldbank.org/curated/en/782171468027560055/pdf/392360 CHA0Cost1of1Pollution01PUBLIC1.pdf

22 CERES Report (2008). Corporate governance and climate change: Consumer and technology companies. Retrieved from www.ceres.org/resources/reports/corporate-governance-and-climate-change-2008

23 McDonald's 2009 Worldwide Corporate Responsibility Online Report: The Values We Bring to the Table. Retrieved from www.mcdonalds.at/file/1049/download?token=_N0FQy0O

24 Reinhardt, Forest L. (1999). Bringing the environment down to Earth. *Harvard Business Review,* July–August, 149–157.

25 Friedman, Milton. (1970, September 13). The social responsibility of business is to increase its profits. *New York Times Magazine,* 32–33, 122, 124, 126.

26 Porter, Michael and Kramer, Mark. (2006). The link between competitive advantage and corporate social responsibility. *Harvard Business Review,* December, 78–92.

27 Toyota Motor Corporation. (2012). Sustainability Report. Retrieved from www.toyota-global.com/sustainability/report/sr/12/pdf/sustainability_report12_me.pdf

28 Carroll, Archie. (1979). A three-dimensional model of corporate performance. *Academy of Management Review,* 4, 497–505.

29 Carroll, Archie. (2004). Managing ethically with global stakeholders: A present and future challenge. *Academy of Management Executive,* 18(2), 114–120.

30 The Ten Principles of the UN Global Compact. United Nations. Retrieved from www.unglobalcompact.org/what-is-gc/mission/principles

31 Porter, Michael and Kramer, Mark. (2006). The link between competitive advantage and corporate social responsibility. *Harvard Business Review,* December, 78–92.

32 Katrinli, Alev, Gunay, Gonca, and Biresselioglu, Mehmet Efe. (2011). The convergence of corporate social responsibility and corporate sustainability: Starbucks Corporation's practises. *The Business Review,* 17(1): 164–171. Izmir University of Economics, Izmir, Turkey.

33 Donalson, Thomas. (1985). Multinational decision-making: Reconciling international norms. *Journal of Business Ethics,* 4(4), 357–366.

34 Ibid.

35 Ibid.

36 Kohles, John and Buller, Paul. (1994). Resolving cross-cultural ethical conflict: Exploring alternative strategies. *Journal of Business Ethics,* 13(1), 31–38.

37 Ibid.

Index